CW01653234

30130 128177994

Collins

HAZEL SOAN'S

African Watercolours

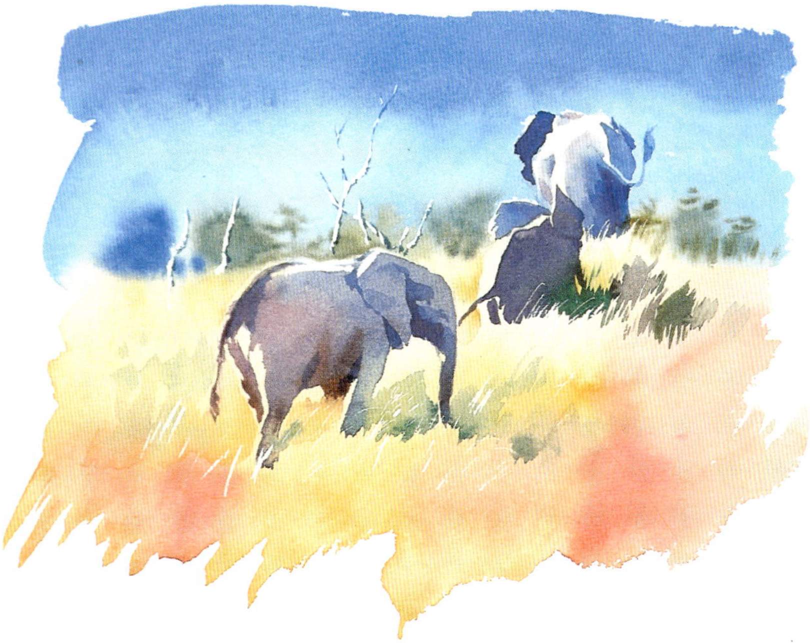

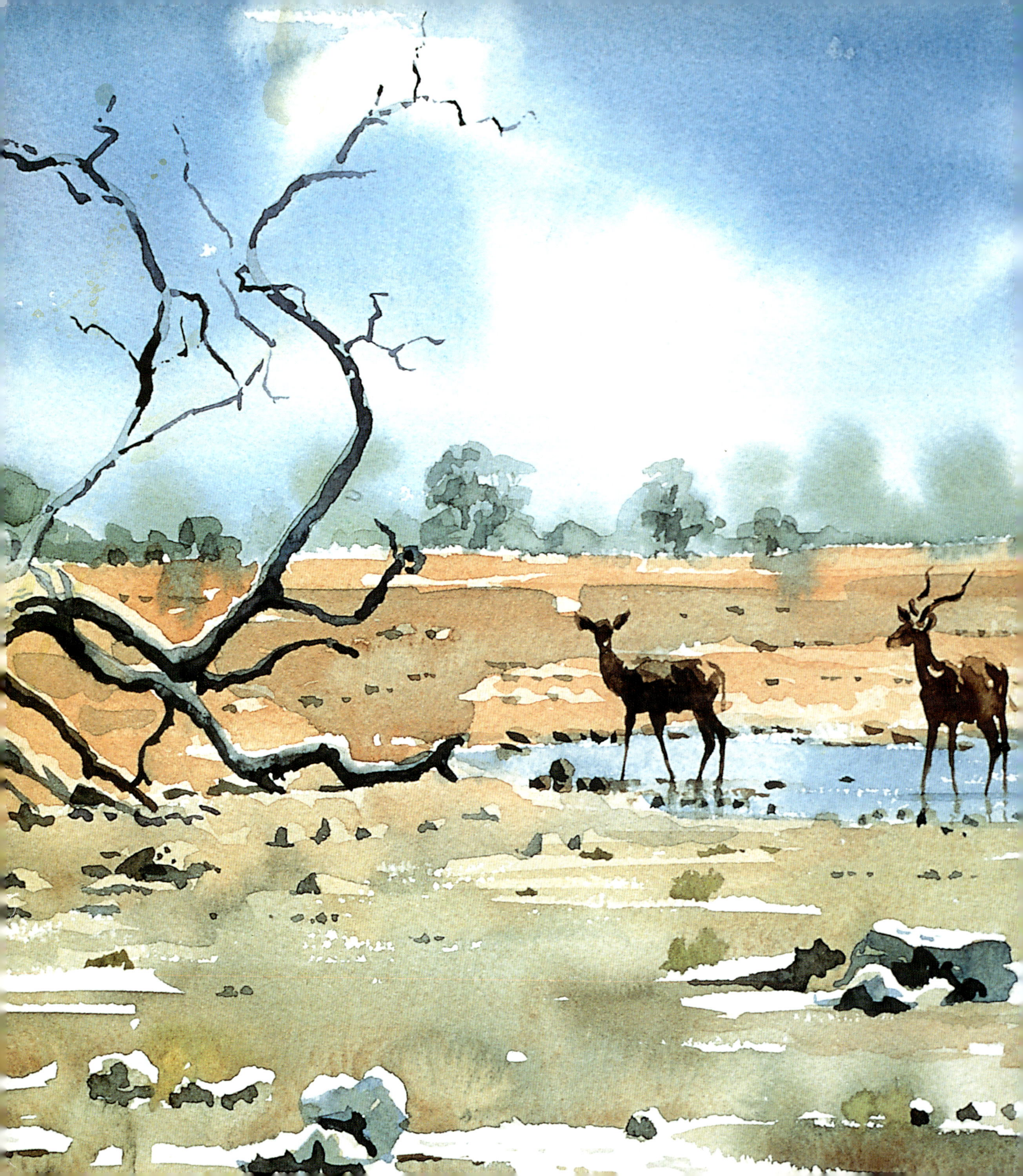

Collins

HAZEL SOAN'S

African Watercolours

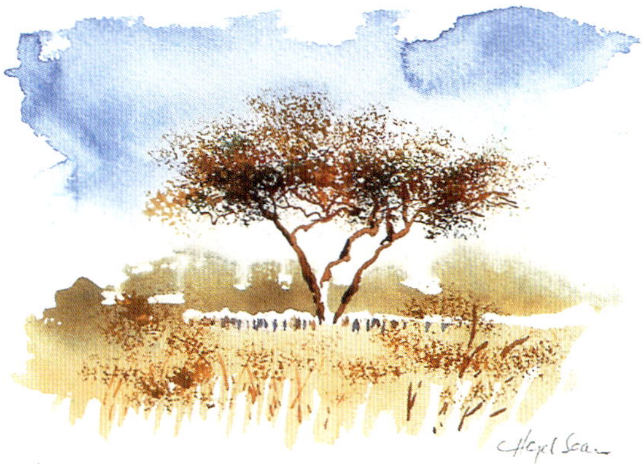

Yellow Ochre in the trees,
tapping violently in the breeze.

SEAN GOATLEY-SOAN

ESSEX COUNTY LIBRARY

Dedication
To John, for his ability to fix vehicles.

Acknowledgements
This is the book I always wanted to write so I would like to extend my grateful thanks to Cathy Gosling and Caroline Churton for enabling it to happen. Without John's skilful driving and adventurous spirit I could never have ventured into the wild places of Africa, so a big thank you to him. My thanks also to T. V. Bulpin for his book, which informed many of my travels, and to the National Parks of Southern Africa for their dedication to conserving this wonderful land. Especial thanks to Rondeberg Nature Reserve for their flowers. Lastly, a big thank you to Geraldine Christy, Julie Francis and the team at HarperCollins for pulling out all the stops to meet the deadlines.

First published in 2003 by
Collins, an imprint of
HarperCollins*Publishers*
77-85 Fulham Palace Road
Hammersmith, London W6 8JB

The Collins website address is: www.collins.co.uk

Collins is a registered trademark of HarperCollins Publishers Limited.

07 06 05 04 03
6 5 4 3 2 1

© Hazel Soan, 2003

Hazel Soan asserts the moral right to be identified as the author of this work.

All rights reserved. No part of this publication may be reproduced, stored in a retrieval system, or transmitted, in any form or by any means, electronic, mechanical, photocopying, recording or otherwise, without the prior written permission of the publishers.

A catalogue record for this book is available from the British Library

Editor: Geraldine Christy
Designer: Julie Francis
Photographer: Laura Knox

Hazel Soan's paintings on pp. 67 and 70-1 are reproduced courtesy of The David Shepherd Wildlife Foundation, and on p. 117 courtesy of Rosenstiel's.

A video to accompany this book is available from Teaching Art Ltd, P. O. Box 50, Newark, Nottinghamshire NG23 5GY

ISBN 0 00 714384 2

Colour reproduction by Colourscan, Singapore
Printed and bound by Imago in China

PAGE 1: *How Silently*, 18 x 23 cm (7 x 9 in)
PAGE 2: *Kudu at Goas* (detail)
PAGE 3: *Symbol of Africa*, 13 x 18 cm (5 x 7 in)
PAGE 4: *Wild Clash* (detail)

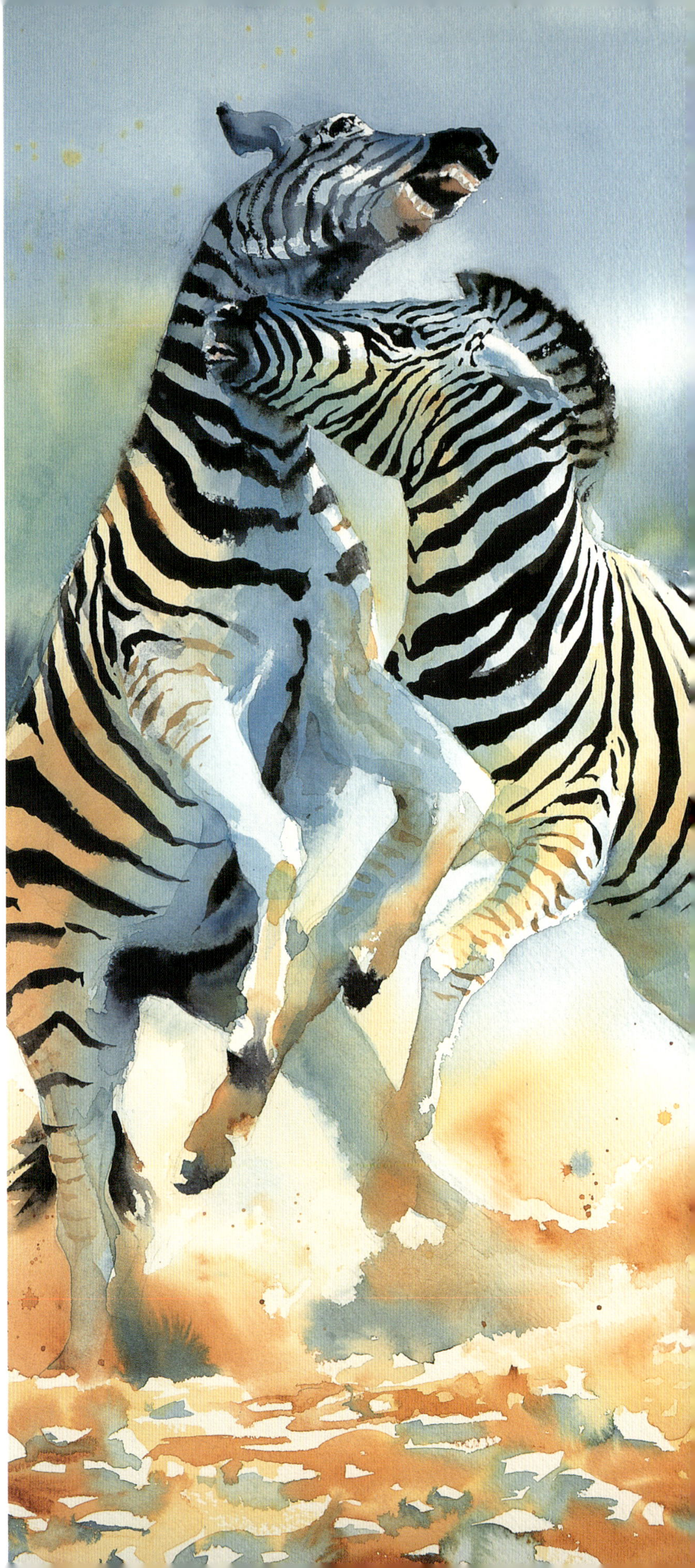

Contents

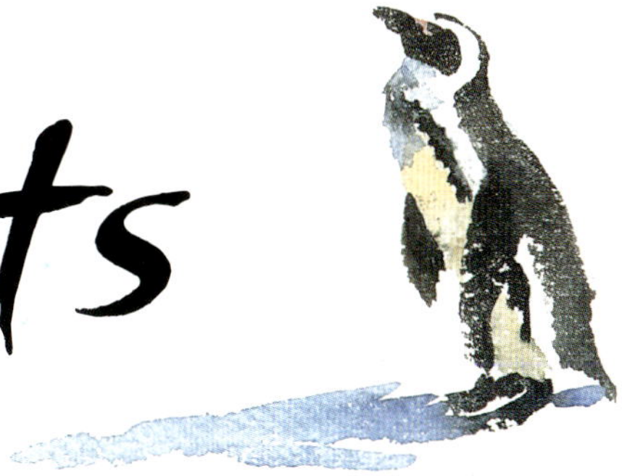

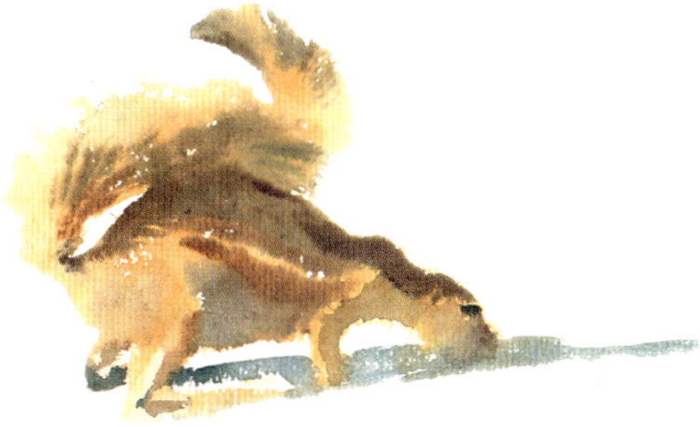

Introduction:

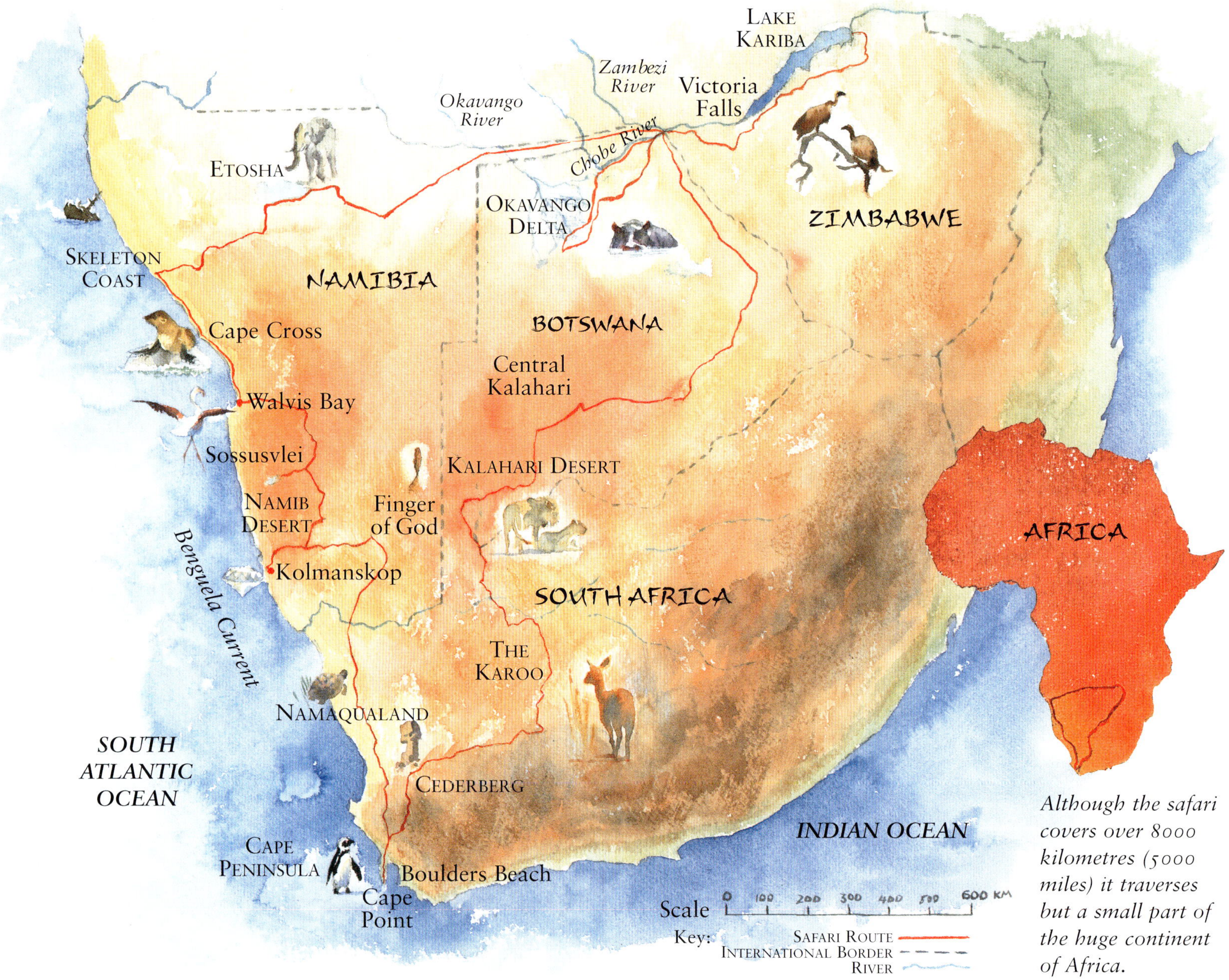

Although the safari covers over 8000 kilometres (5000 miles) it traverses but a small part of the huge continent of Africa.

A tale of two journeys

This book is about two simultaneous journeys – one, a safari through southern Africa; the other, an artistic journey through a range of subjects, showing different ways to see and paint them.

The art of travel

I love travelling and can think of no better way of really absorbing new or unfamiliar environments than painting them. You never truly know what something looks like until you attempt to draw or paint it. The curves, the shapes, even the colours of the landscape, wildlife and people are only properly seen when you try to record their impression on paper. Painting opens your eyes, and enhances the pleasure of seeing.

Watercolour is the perfect medium for the travelling artist because it is light to carry, dries fast, packs flat and uses water, which is generally available.

The safari

The journey begins at the Cape Peninsula in South Africa, where I have a studio overlooking the Atlantic Ocean. From there we travel north through the flowers of Namaqualand into the sands of Namibia and the Skeleton Coast. Then we head inland, eastwards, across Etosha to northern Botswana, the Chobe River and the Okavango swamps and then on, into Zimbabwe. At Lake Kariba the safari turns southwest, travelling through the Kalahari Desert of southern Botswana and across the Great Karoo of South Africa, finally returning to the Cape through the ancient mountains of the Cederberg.

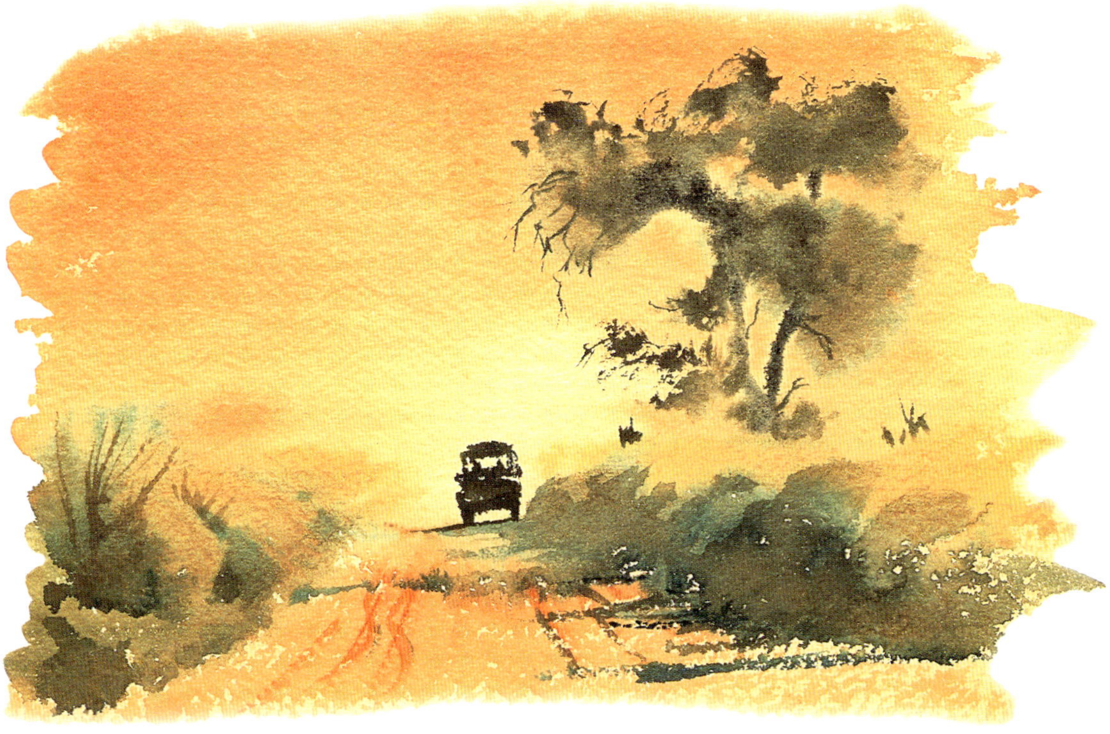

◄ LANDIE IN THE KALAHARI
13 x 18 cm (5 x 7 in)
Clouds of fine dry dust are thrown up by the vehicle as she travels along the sandy roads of the Kalahari Desert.

Africa travelled

Travelling in Africa is still an adventure. The vast empty spaces, long roads, amazing landscapes, abundant wildlife and the ready laughter of strangers make it a sheer delight for the wanderer.

It is easy to be overwhelmed by the awesome beauty; to be crushed by one's inability to compete with such grand Creation. But the artist is under no obligation to imitate what is seen: painting is a response to visual inspiration.

With watercolour you need only suggest something and the eye will complete the rest. You do not need to be literal, just allow the beauty of the medium the space to glow. Even the simplest sketch made in honest admiration is worthwhile. The pigments of watercolour are so lovely they need very little coaxing for pleasing results.

▼ YOUNG ONES
46 x 56 cm (18 x 22 in)
There are few things more delightful on safari than having to stop along a road for passing elephants.

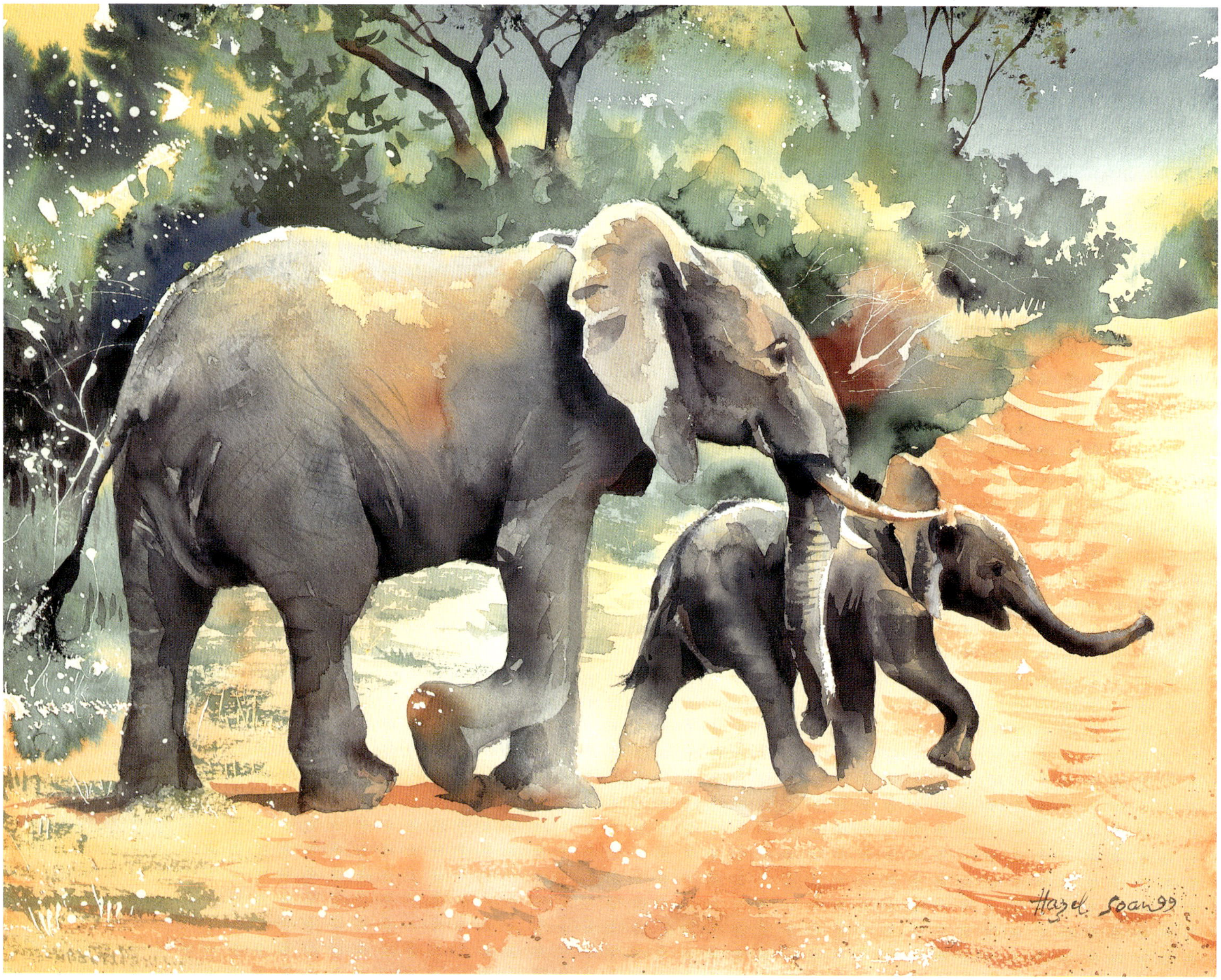

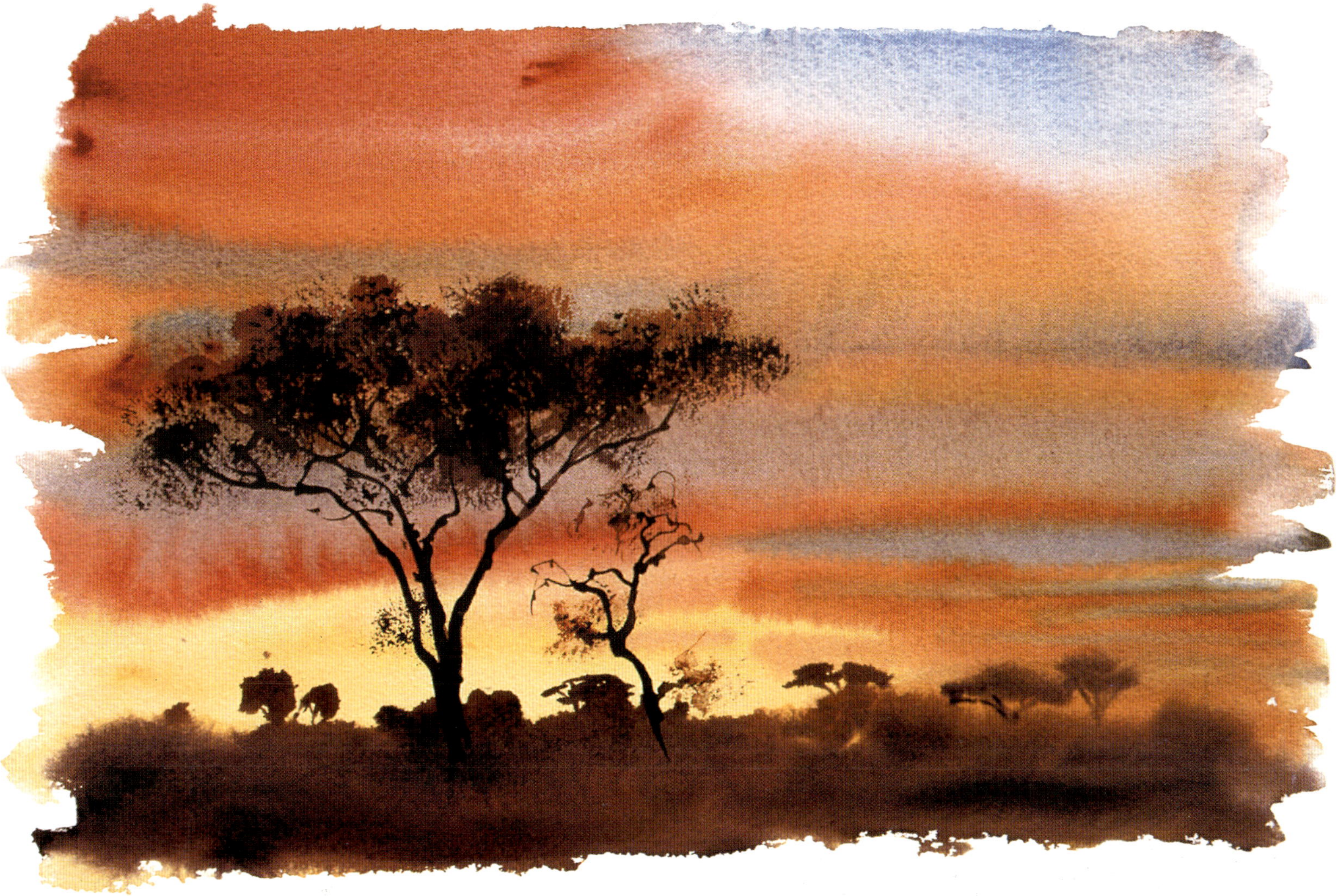

▲THE AFRICAN BUSH
28 x 36 (11 x 14 in)
The acacia tree is symbolic of the African Bush. After a striking sunset the stillness of the night steals quickly over the hushed land.

Watercolour unravelled

The journey unfolds in ten chapters, giving a flavour of the remarkable landscapes traversed. It is written from my own perspective and shows an artist's response to these striking environments.

After setting the atmosphere and scene I take the reader on an artistic journey. Each chapter reveals a vital aspect of watercolour painting, using the subject matter of the surrounding landscape for inspiration. The subjects painted in this book may belong to Africa, but the approach and techniques apply everywhere.

Most days on safari end with a good story around the campfire, so the chapters end with an amusing anecdote recalled from the journey set in a page from my African sketchbooks.

An artist's paradise

The sheer variety of habitats and strong, definite light make Africa an artist's paradise. As the traveller responds on paper so Africa returns a hundredfold the joy in what is seen. This book attempts to share that joy; it is a book I have wanted to write for a long time.

Dramatic Seascapes:

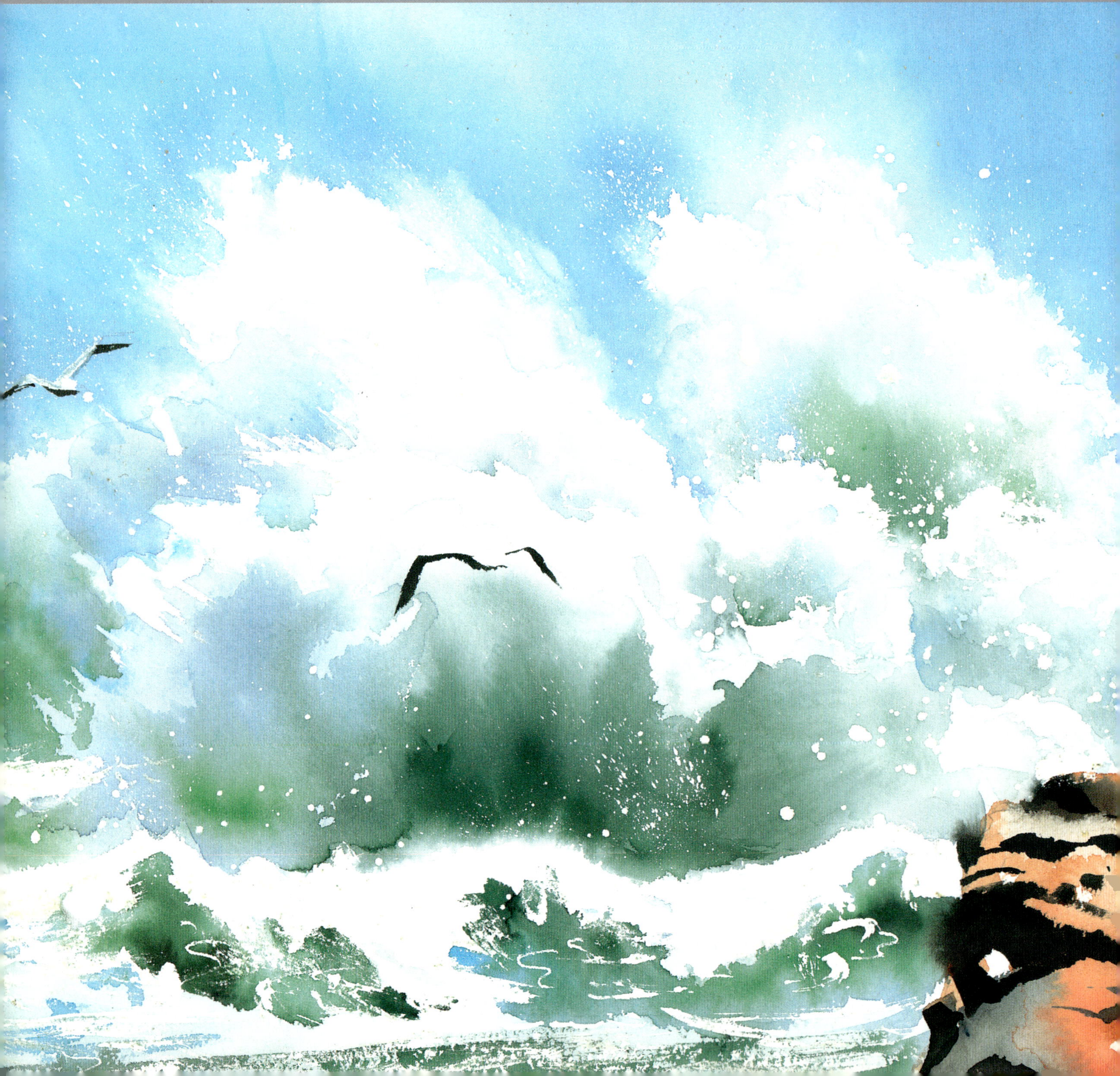

The Cape Peninsula

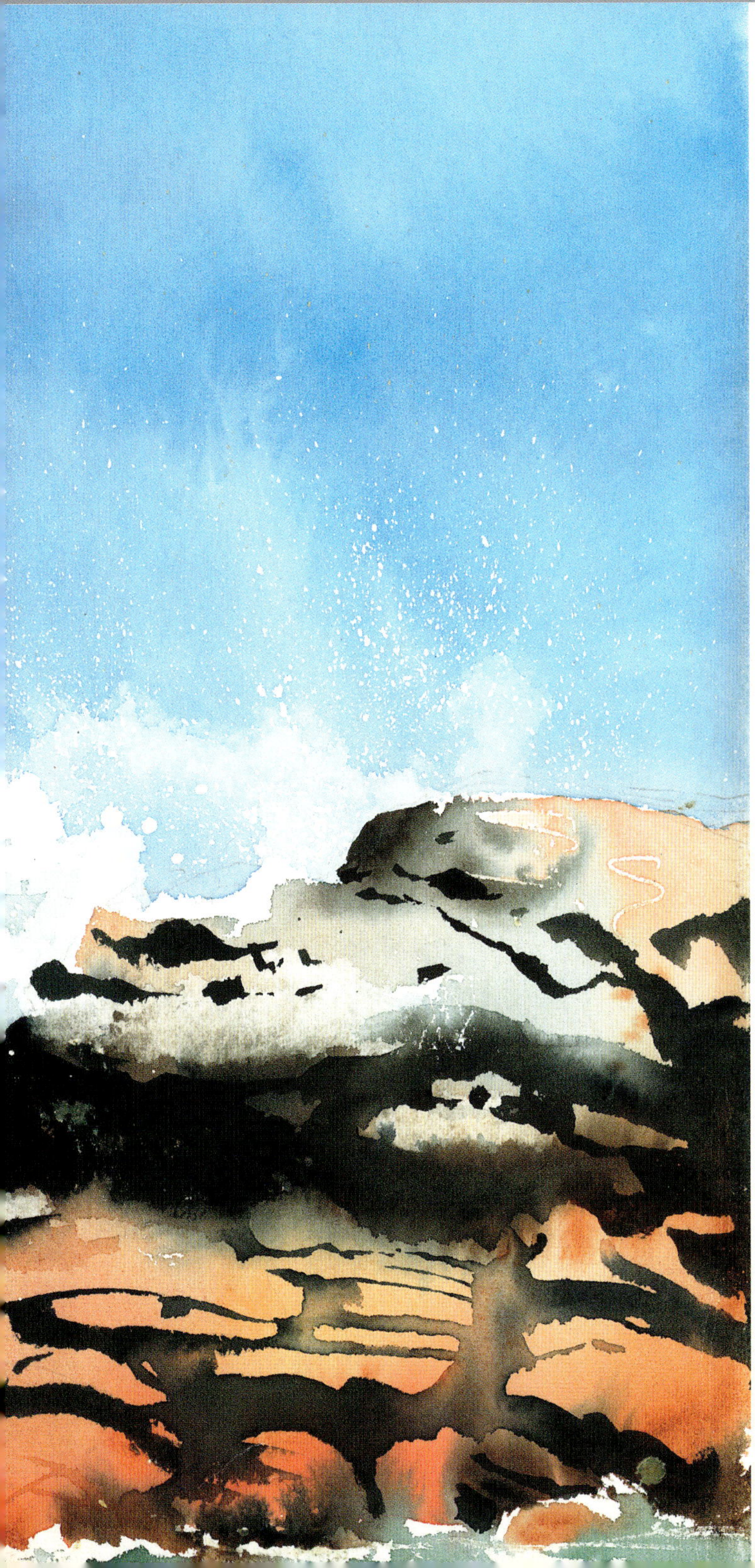

Creating the third dimension

Mountains green and turquoise
rise and fall and rise,
furling, thrashing, frothing,
with passion in their cries.
Holding vision captive,
relentless they advance,
a self-destructive army
bound in endless dance.

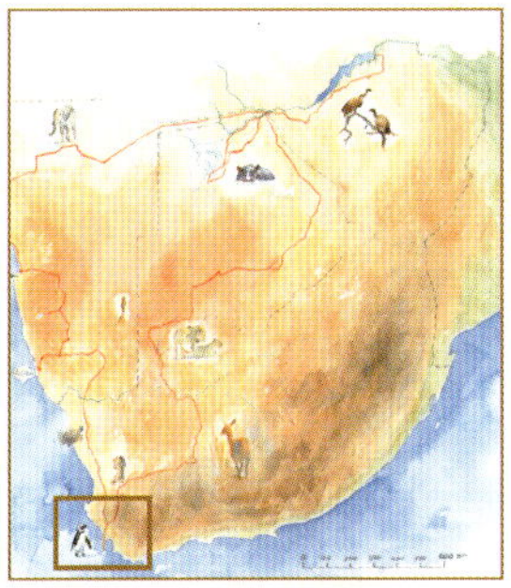

◀ CRASHING WAVE
38 x 56 cm (15 x 22 in)

The power of the elements

The journey begins at the temperamental tip of southern Africa, a maritime peninsula renowned for the profile of Table Mountain and the longed-for Cape of Good Hope.

Charm and drama alternate for attention around the entire perimeter of the Cape. Here, beneath a mantle of changing weather, lies a panorama of beguiling beauty. A majestic spine of mountains, distinct in the daylight, becomes soft and ethereal beneath the wreaths of cloud that roll in from the sea. Turquoise waters turn steely grey and placid waves become enormous white rollers in the merciless onslaught of the South Atlantic winds. A parade of dazzling white beaches contrasts with curious round boulders or jagged walls of red-brown cliffs.

Two great ocean currents, the cold Benguela and the warm Aghulas, meet here to do battle at the end of a continent, pounding the sandstone and granite bastions with relentless force and earning the 'fairest Cape' the forbidding sobriquet 'Cape of Storms'.

▼ THIS IS WHERE THE PROUD WAVES HALT
28 x 36 cm (11 x 14 in)
The monolithic cliff face and the fractured rocks at Cape Point make a strong diagonal composition.

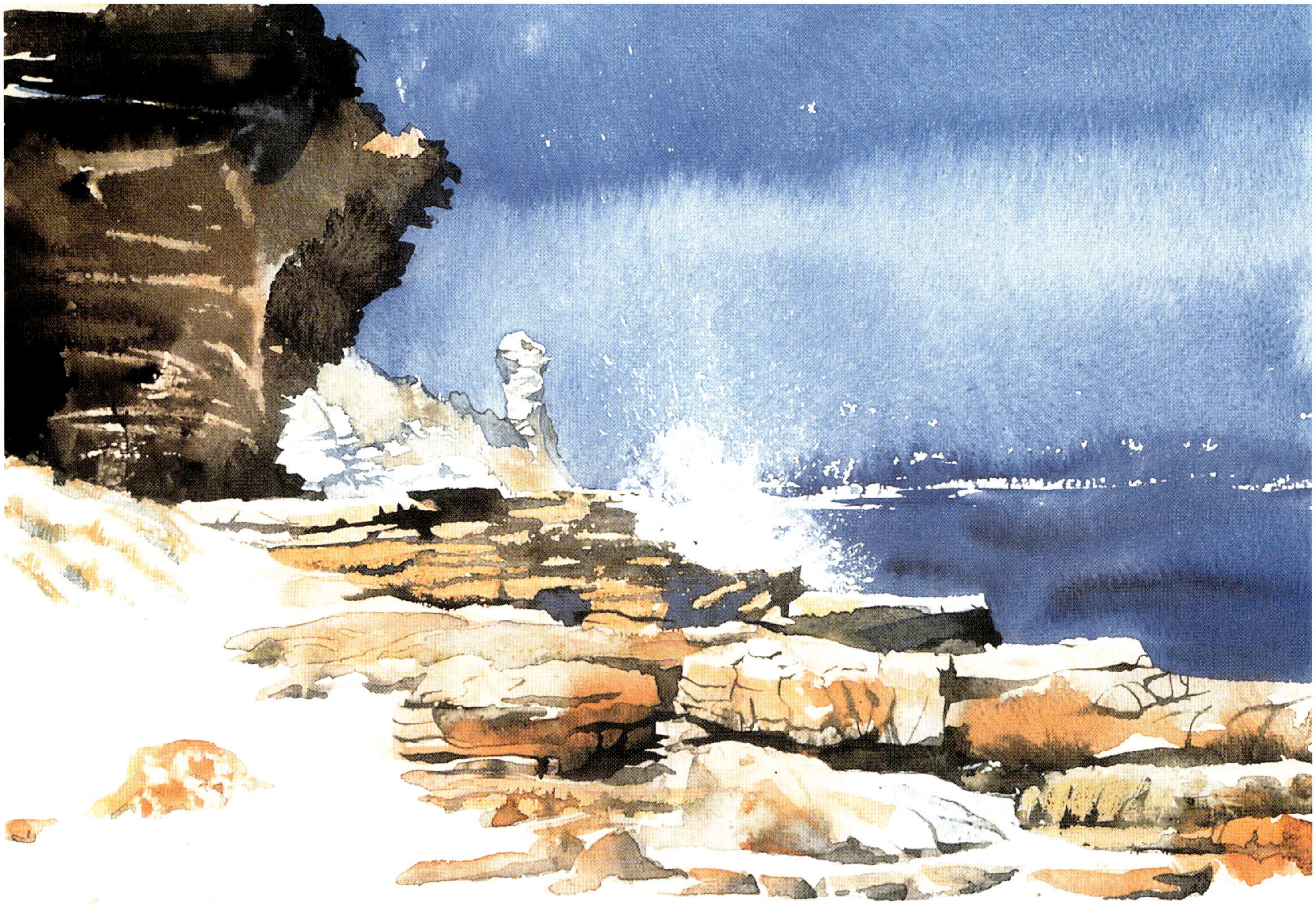

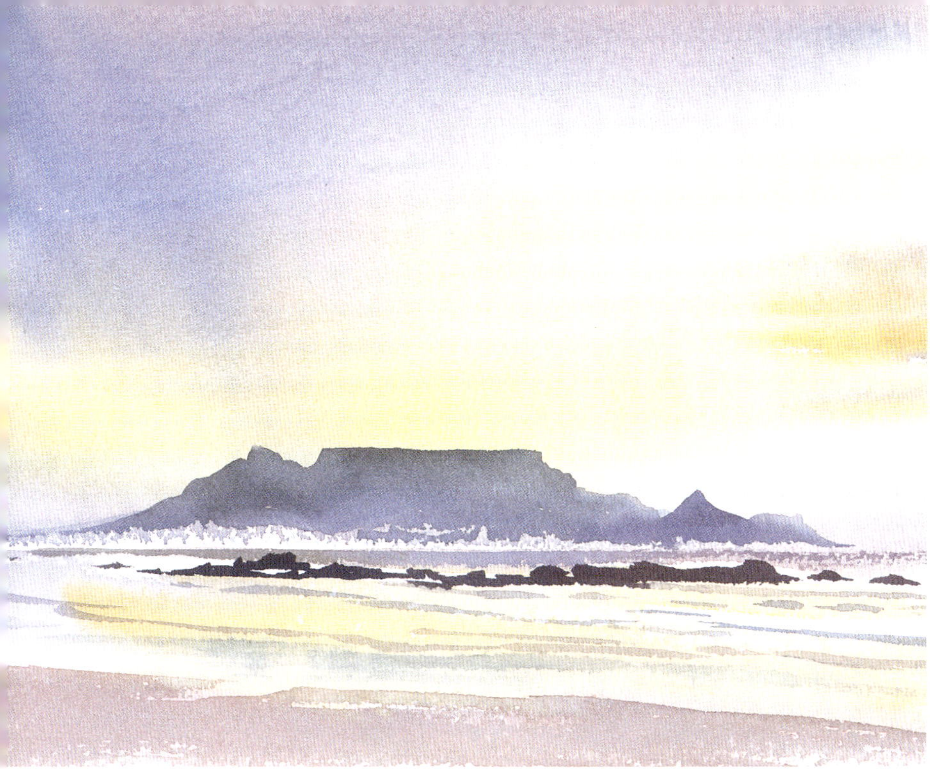

A special light

The peninsula is bathed in a unique light, reflected from the vast mirrors of water that encompass this finger of land. Positioned on a north–south axis it enjoys a sunrise and a sunset over the sea – a wonderful bonus for a painter.

Daylight is bright, but not harsh. The shadows are tinged with blue on the ground and mauve on the mountains, exaggerating the startling forms as the angle of the sun decreases. This combination of intriguing light and dramatic scenery makes the landscape appear both intimate and grand, inviting you to paint, and then rendering you dwarfed and breathless in the face of such magnificence.

▲ TABLE MOUNTAIN
28 x 38 cm (11 x 15 in)
Drama is not bound to dynamic scenery; it can also be found in the colours of skies and more serene views like this classic profile of Table Mountain.

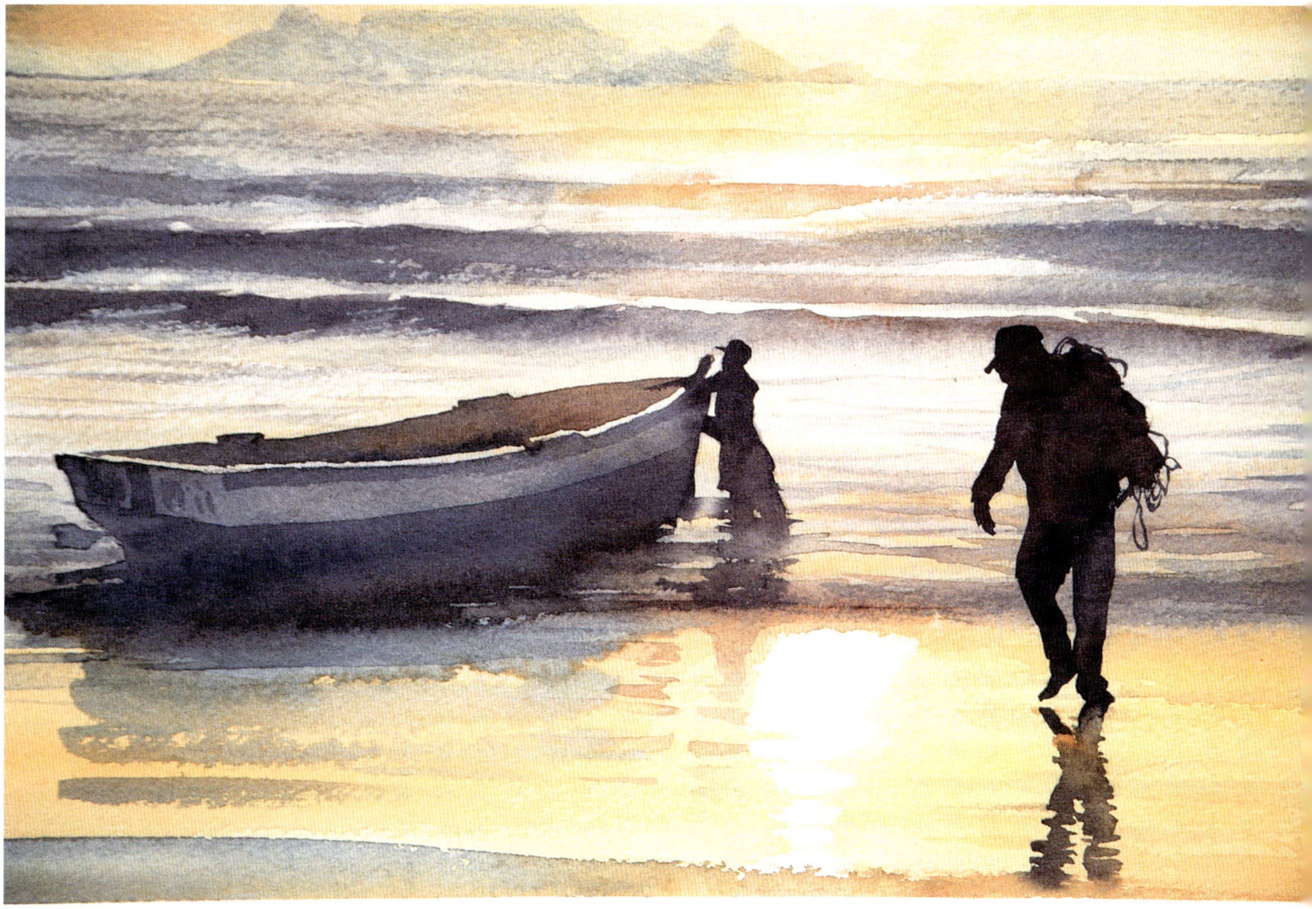

► FISHERMEN AT DAWN
20 x 28 cm (8 x 11 in)
Silhouetted by the rising sun, the fishermen haul in their meagre catch. Strong darks contrast with the untouched white paper left to portray the reflected glare of the sun.

Painting seascapes

Watercolour's translucent washes and variegated blends lend themselves perfectly to painting the changing face of the sea. The transparency of watercolour conveys the character of the water and the gentle blending of tones ably renders the forms of the shoreline's irregular rocks and cloud-clad mountains.

The two main ingredients of a seascape are usually those of sea and sky. Making sure these work together in the painting is vital. The sky will determine the sea's colour, but the sea is usually darker in tone. Linking the sea and sky with the same initial blue wash marries the two elements.

Space and distance

On the painted page a paler sky will recede and a darker sea will advance, thereby creating a sense of space in the painting. Strengthening the tones within foreground features such as rocks and grasses brings them forward.

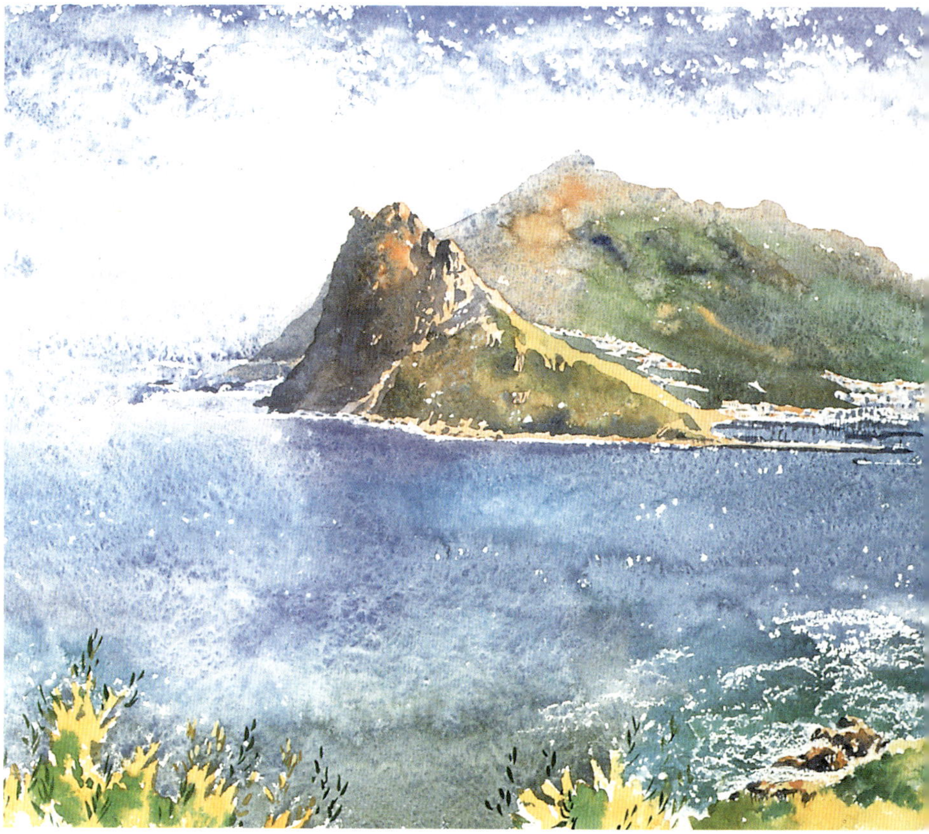

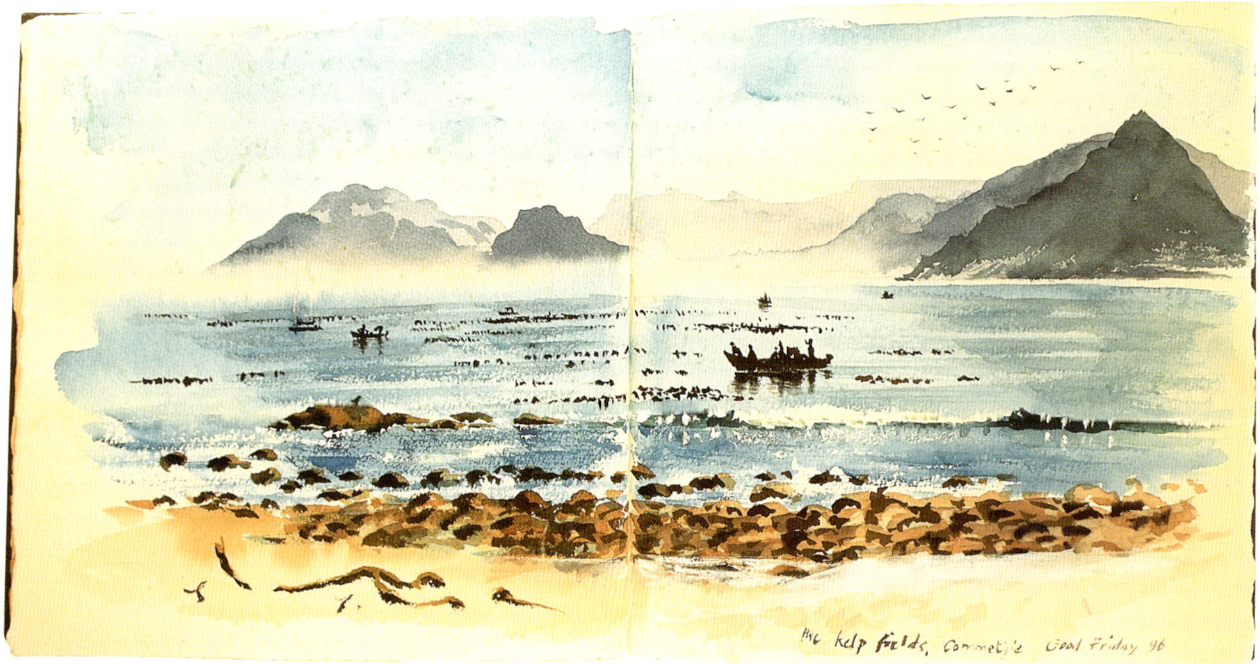

▲ HOUT BAY FROM CHAPMAN'S PEAK

41 x 51 cm (16 x 20 in)

The high horizon emphasizes the sense of vast space across the water.

◀ THE KELP FIELDS, KOMMETJIE

25 x 51 cm (10 x 20 in)

The dark foreground and silhouettes, and the gradual paling of tones in the background, create convincing distance in this view of Hout Bay from Long Beach.

▼ TUMBLING ROCKS

28 x 36 cm (11 x 14 in)

The rounded form of the prominent rock is emphasized by painting a strong tone on the shaded side. The distant hill retreats behind the mountainside by using a paler tone.

The impression of distance can also be enhanced by scale. A large foreground item against the horizon, for example, or the narrowing of wave lines as they retreat across the sea, will increase the impression of receding space.

Finding form

The intriguing shapes and massive bulk of the peninsula's mountains, coupled with the clutter of smaller rocks in the sand, offer the chance to explore three-dimensional form on both the grand and small scale. Sunlight aids the painter, highlighting the top surfaces and deepening the shadows, clarifying the tonal differences around the rotund or angular forms.

Tonal interchange is one of the most exciting aspects of painting, and seeing a feature come to life with the stroke of a darker tone is very satisfying. Three tones are all you need to achieve this: a highlight, a mid tone and a dark tone. By increasing the difference between the lightest and darkest tones you can emphasize three-dimensional form.

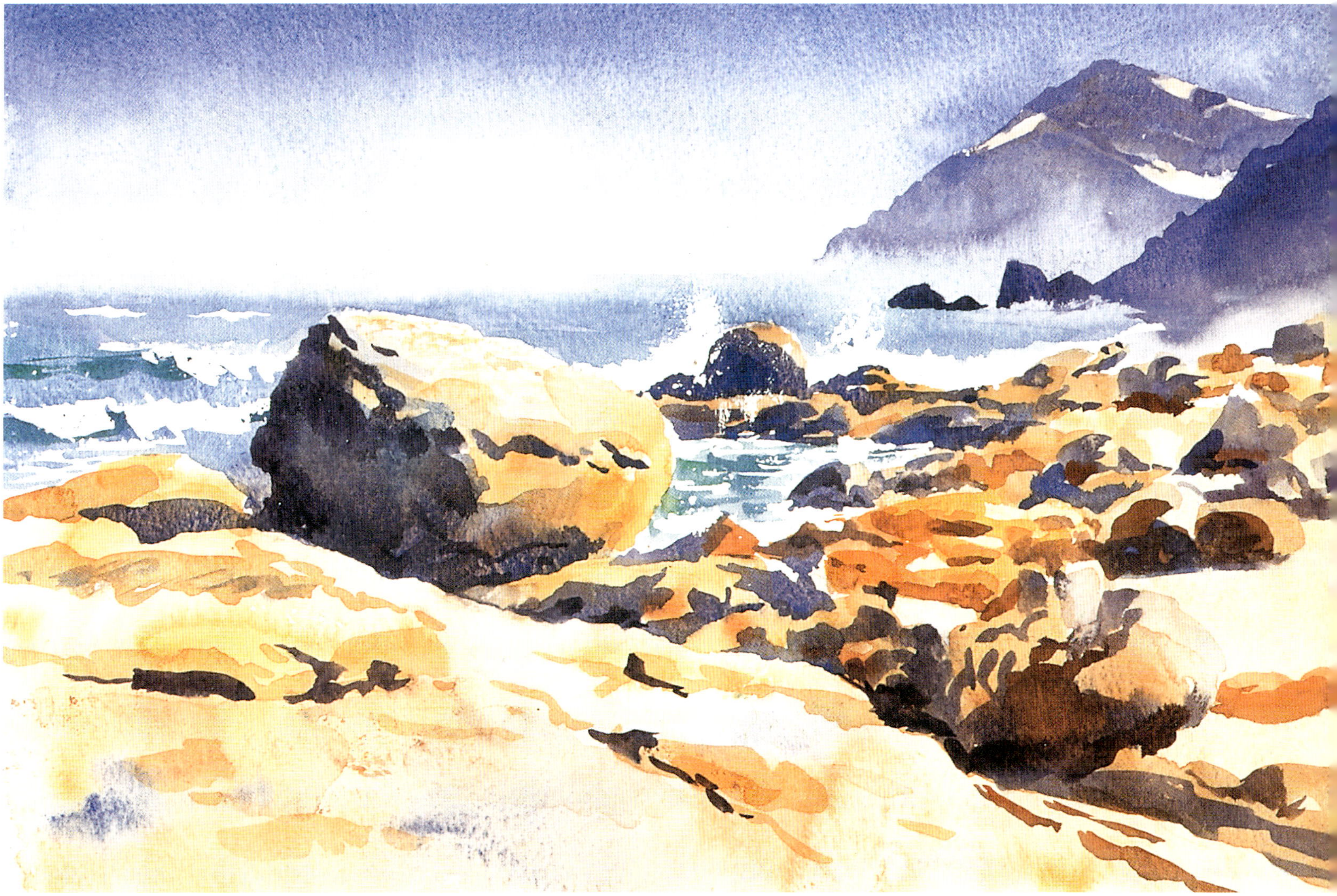

Making space

Not all form is concrete. Painters need to convey that there is space between things. This air is three-dimensional too and its implication is strengthened by the use of tone to create space in a painting.

a

b

c

d

e

▲ *In this sequence of waves (a–e) note the area under the falling crest of foam, where a dark tone is used to suggest depth. As the tone is darkened against the white foam, the arch of air becomes more convincing.*

Making waves

Even though watercolour paper is rarely pure white, the brightest whites and highlit areas in a painting are not made with white paint, but by leaving the white paper untouched. These areas of virgin paper are one of the most important keys to vibrant watercolour painting.

Keeping the painting fresh is paramount. Never overwork a lovely wash for the sake of accuracy and above all do not fiddle! Remember you are making a painting, not re-creating the world.

▲ *The crisp whites of a breaking wave are created here with the virgin paper and the tumbling froth implied with touches of colour dropped into dilute wet washes.*

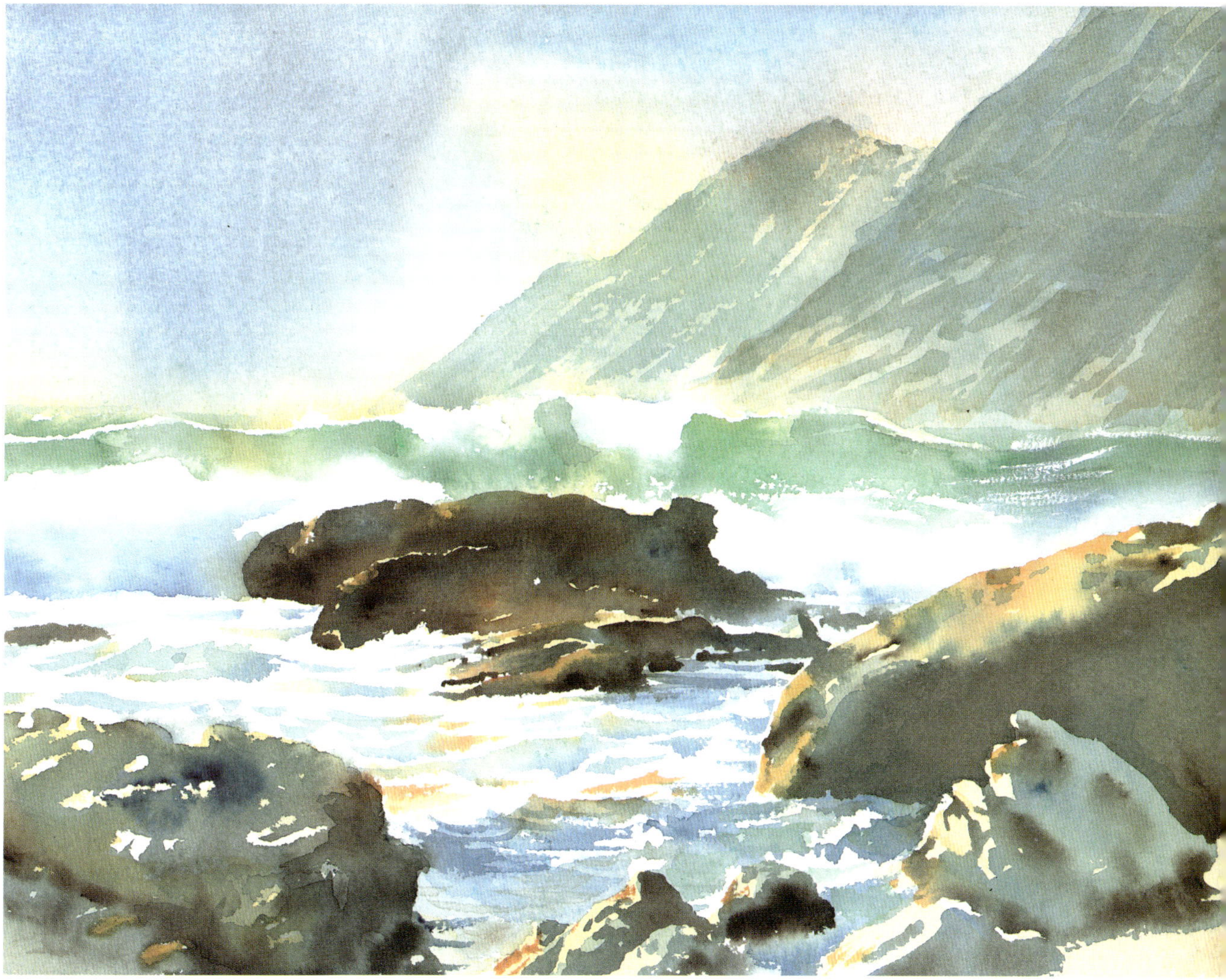

► THE CHURNING SEA
28 x 36 cm (11 x 14 in)
The sea is in constant motion; the painter encapsulates the essence of that movement rather than making a portrait of the scene. A painting has its own, very different, power.

Safari sketchbook

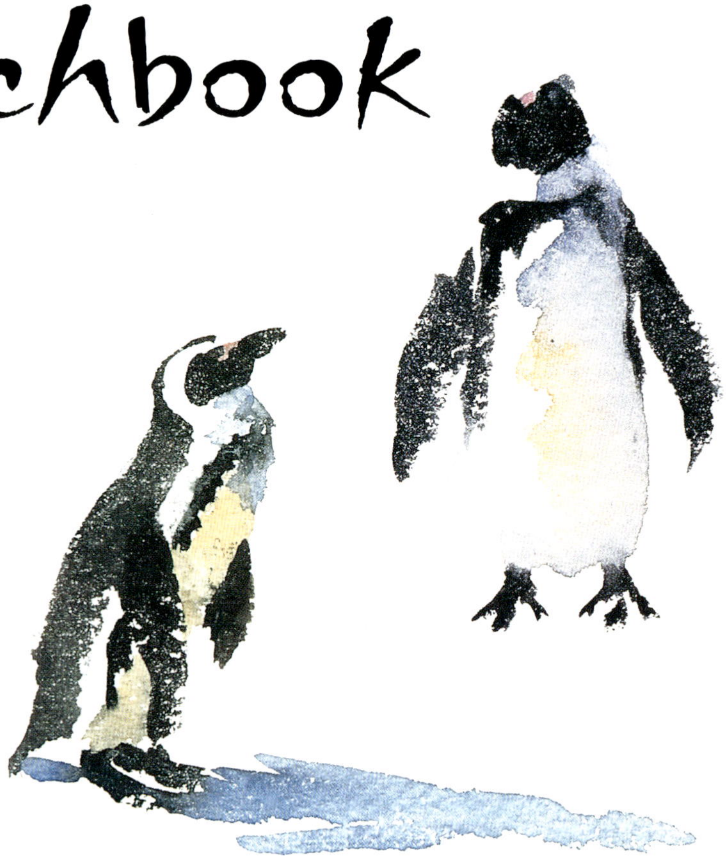

Cape residents

The Cape Peninsula is home to the African Penguin. At Boulders Beach a penguin colony has made its home among the rounded rocks. These characters even swim alongside the people in the sea.

Penguins are delightful to paint; they really are just black and white and their form can be hinted at with just a light shadow under the belly. Leave the virgin paper for the whites and mix your black from Indigo and Sepia - oh, and a touch of pink for the eyes!

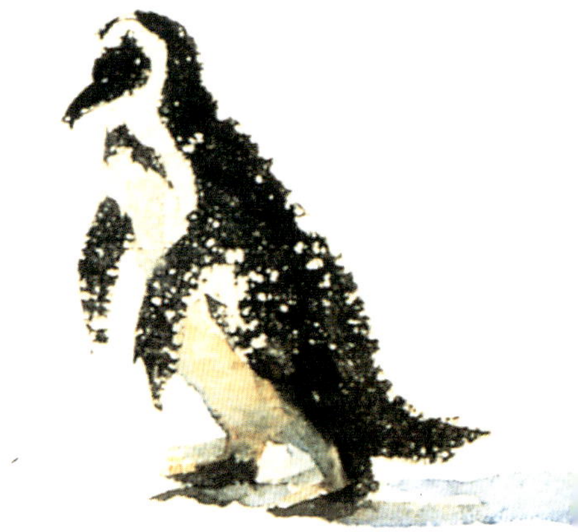

I loaded a size 9 brush with almost neat paint and painted the black markings with one brushstroke.

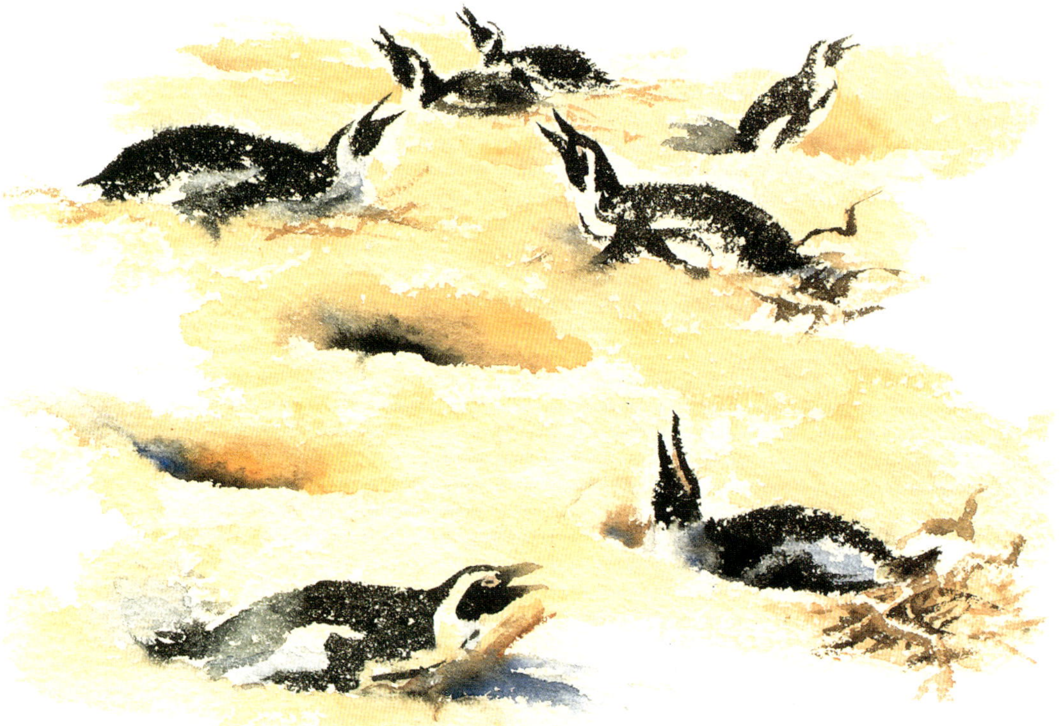

Nesting penguins

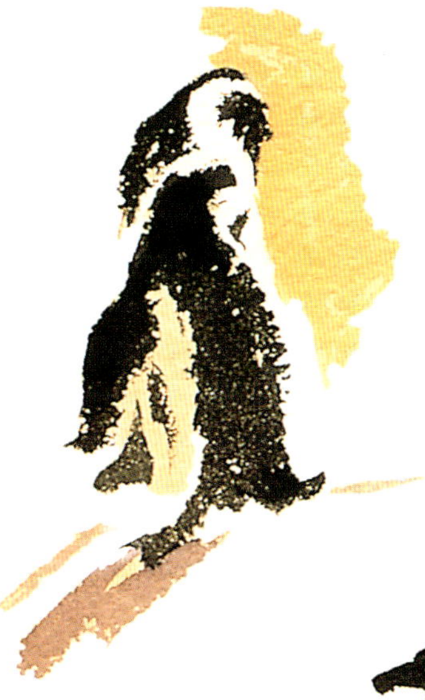

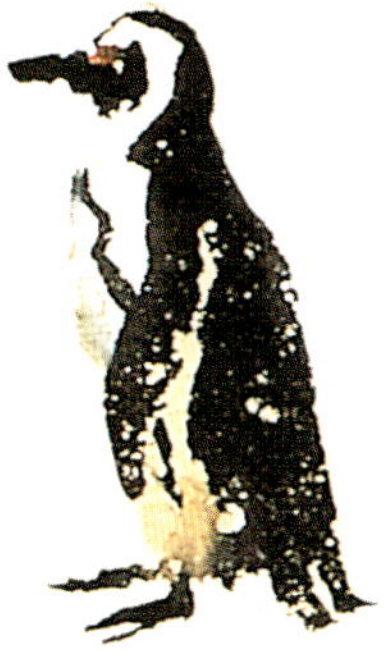

Campfire tale

A rocky start with a sweet ending

Painting is not always the tame pursuit it is made out to be. As I left the car to paint some rocks, a huge baboon came straight for my art bag. He seized the strap and would have run off with it had I not been so attached to my brushes and paints. I grabbed the other end of the strap and we faced each other in a tug of war across the boot of the car. It was foolish of me, I should have let go.

The monkey's eyes looked straight at mine; his were a deep yellow ochre, matched in colour by his sharp canines.

Suddenly the baboon let go, jumped off the boot and came circling round the car. I threw myself to safety through the driver's door. When I calmed down I found the cause of my encounter — a tempting end-of-packet sweet at the bottom of my bag.

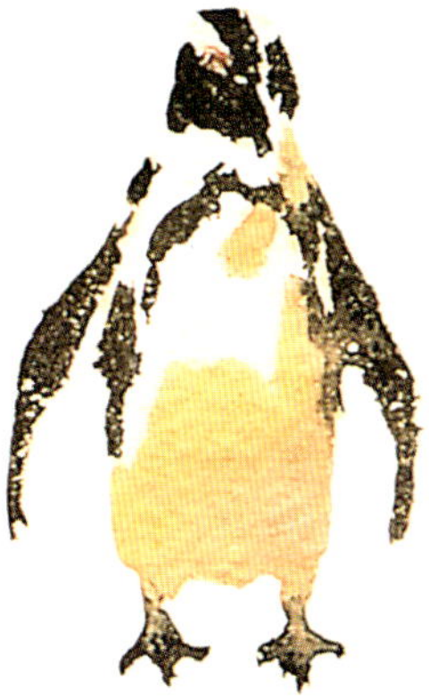

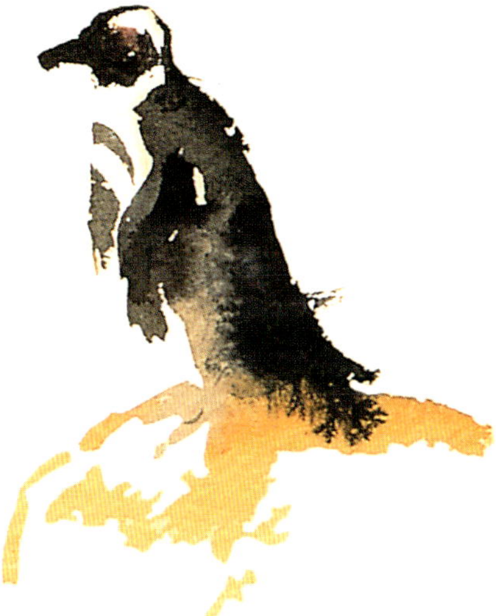

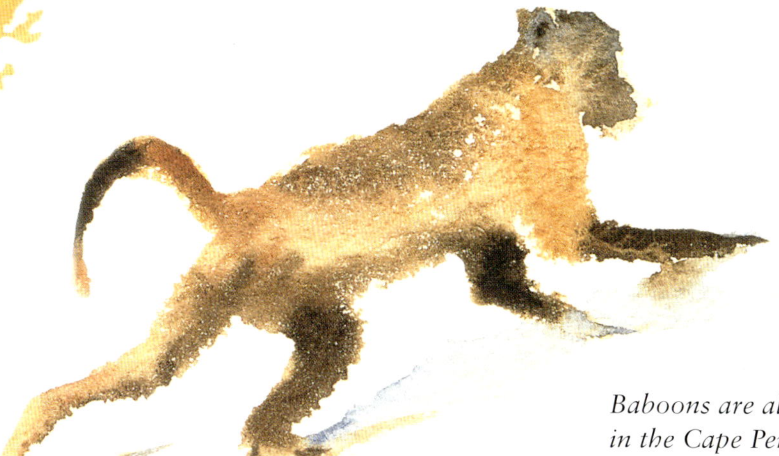

Baboons are also resident in the Cape Peninsula.

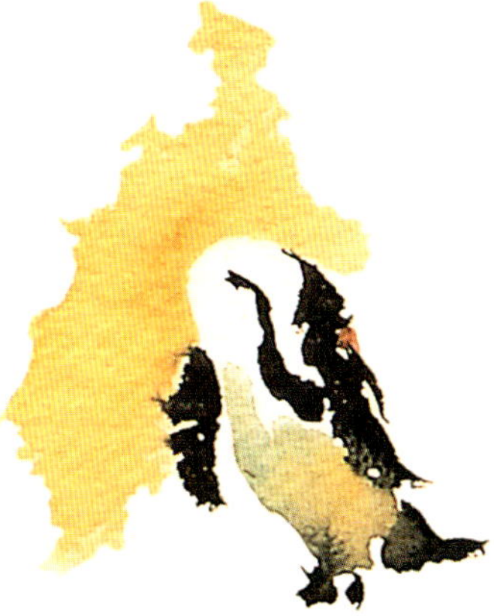

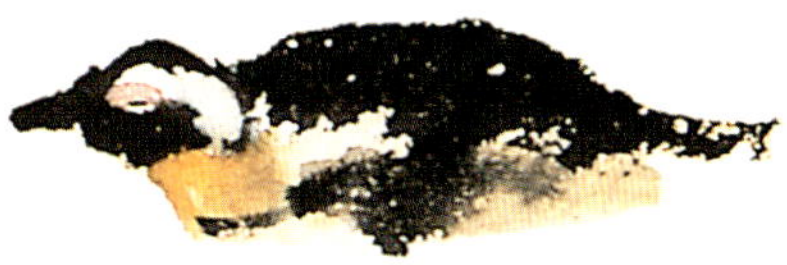

The Desert in Flower:

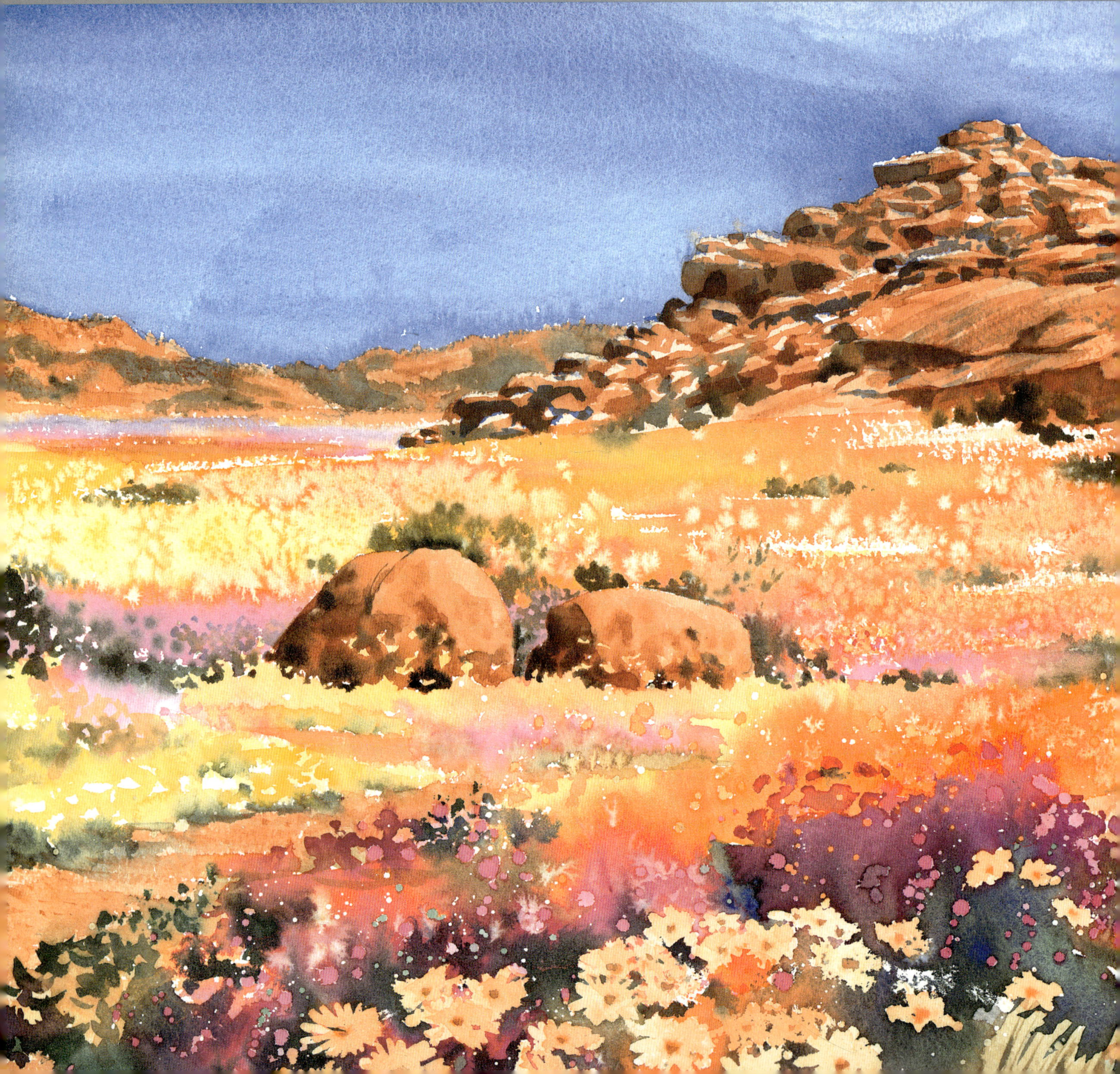

Namaqualand

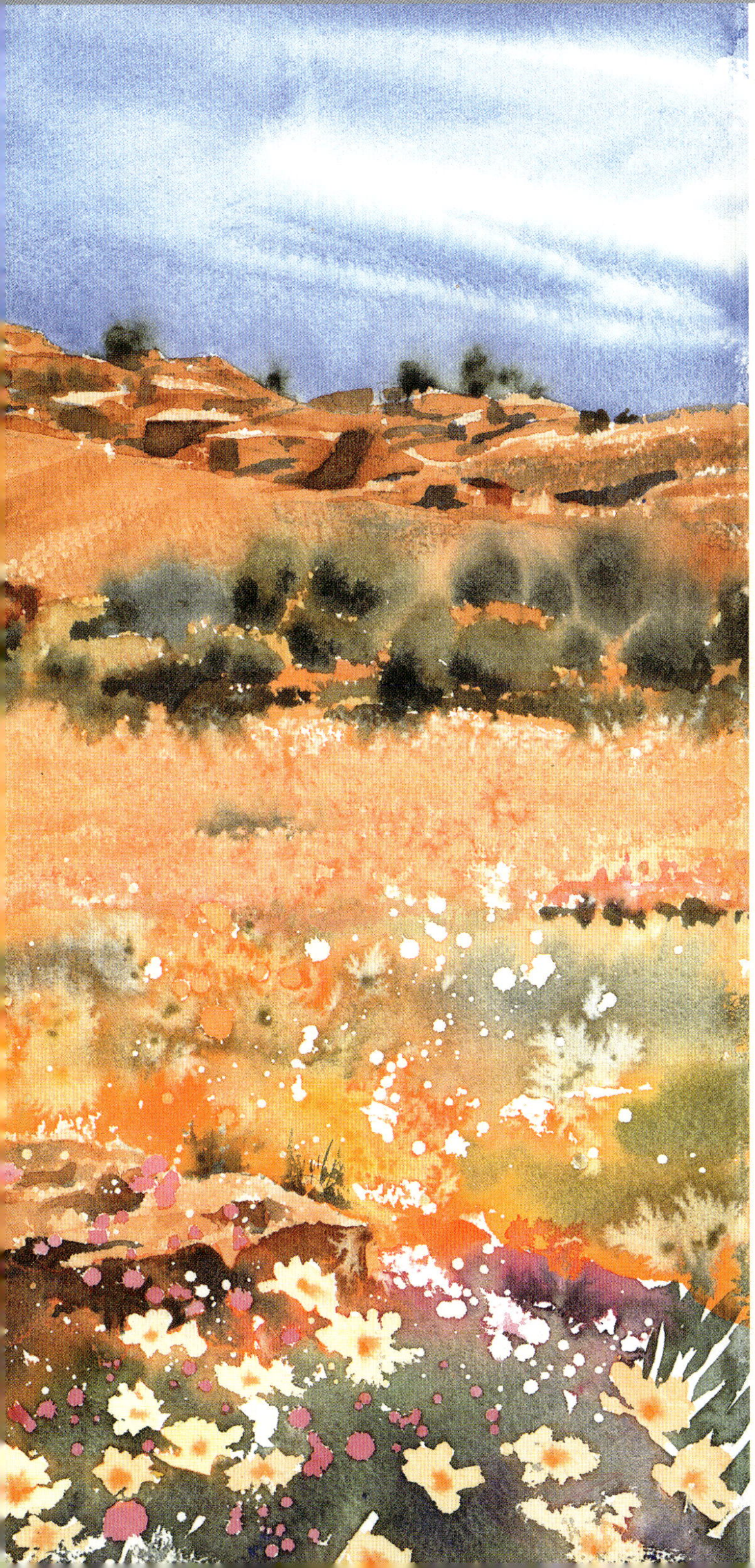

Releasing vibrant colour

Shimmering purple flowers,
faces drawn toward the sun,
dance with dazzling yellow daisies
over fields that run and run.
Floods of pink and orange
stretch as sheets between the hills,
shouting from the landscape
the repeal of winter's chills.

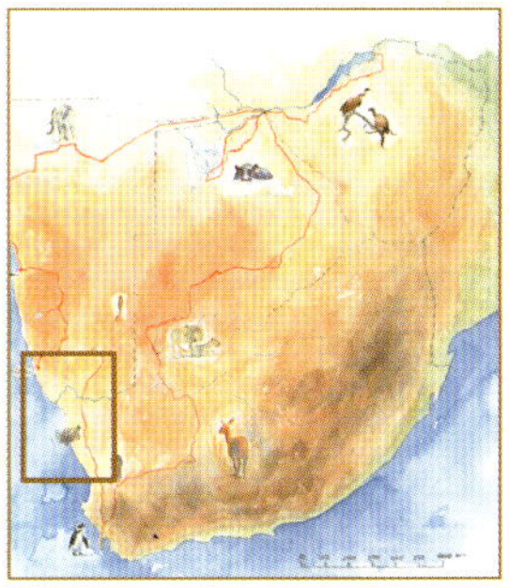

◀ EXPLOSION OF COLOUR
38 x 56 cm (15 x 22 in)

The desert's story

As you drive north the landscape changes dramatically. The blues and greens of the south are replaced by the desolate, sun-baked domain of Namaqualand. Ancient plateaux, rugged escarpments, granite domes and rocky hills are separated by strips of sand and undulating plains. The colour of the landscape turns bronze beneath an unforgiving sun and the rocky terrain is blistered and cracked with age. Minimal rains fall in winter and the few rivers dry up to leave ribbons of sand snaking through the summer landscape.

Long ago Namaqualand carried a diverse vegetation that was stolen away by the arrival of the cold Benguela current as it began to flow northward from its icy Antarctic home. The cold water resisted evaporation and the land became arid for lack of rain. A few hardy species survived, their seed lying dormant in the dusty ground or lodged in crevices until weather conditions became favourable.

Colour in the cauldron

With the warmth of spring a miracle occurs that transforms this barren vista into a flood of colour. Millions of African daisies bloom suddenly across the valleys and the hills in a spectacular affirmation of life. The seeds germinate with such speed that Namaqualand people say they can hear them stirring with life. The flowers bloom and carpet the landscape with orange, blue, white, yellow, purple and pink. Hillsides are overtaken with a riot of colour, valleys are covered with quilts of many hues.

▼ **THE DESERT IN FLOWER**
18 x 36 cm (7 x 14 in)
Burnt Sienna domes of granite, with bald, cracked heads, dominate the region. From this dry, rocky terrain millions of daisies spring forth, laying carpets of colour over the hills.

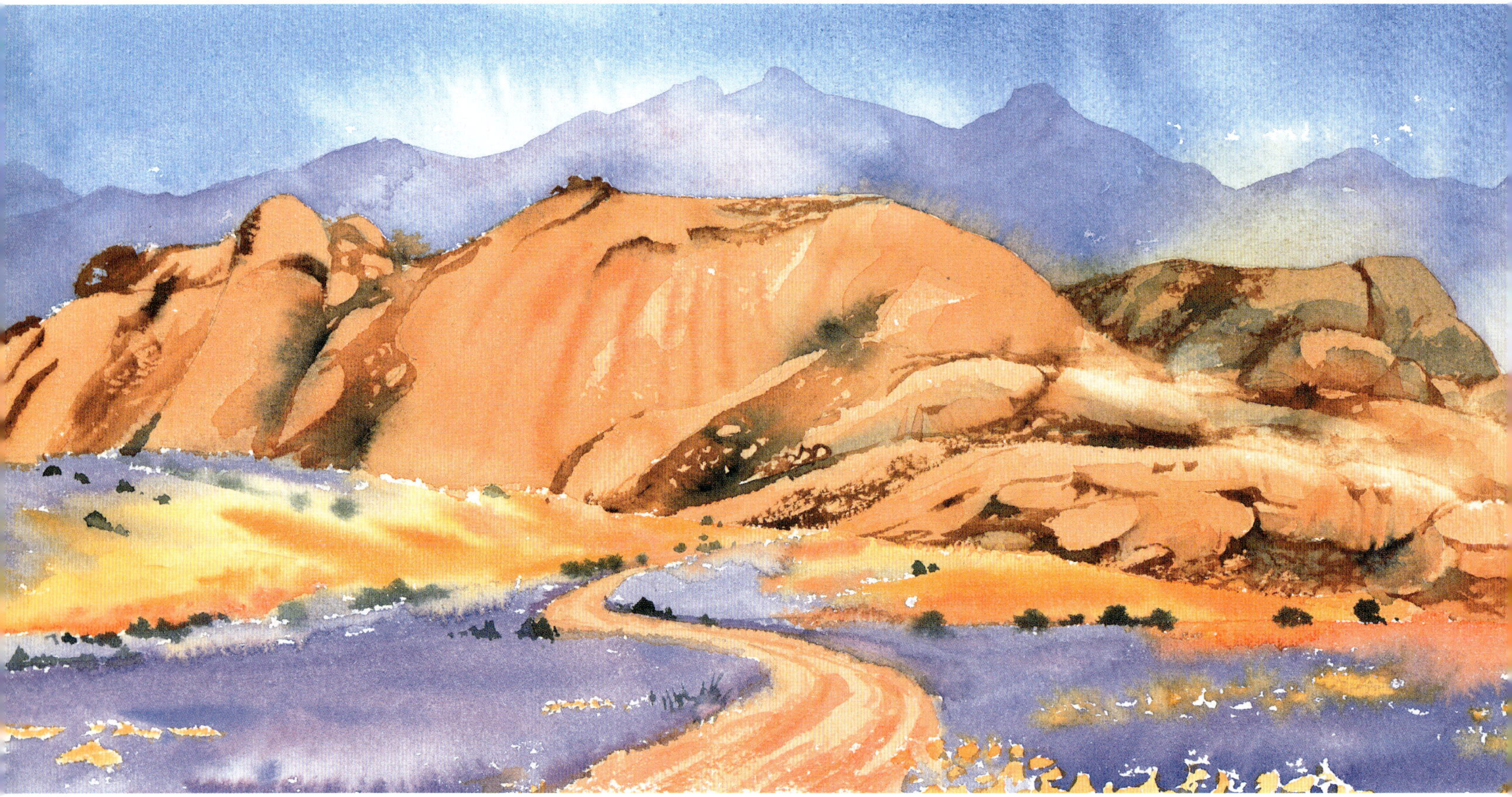

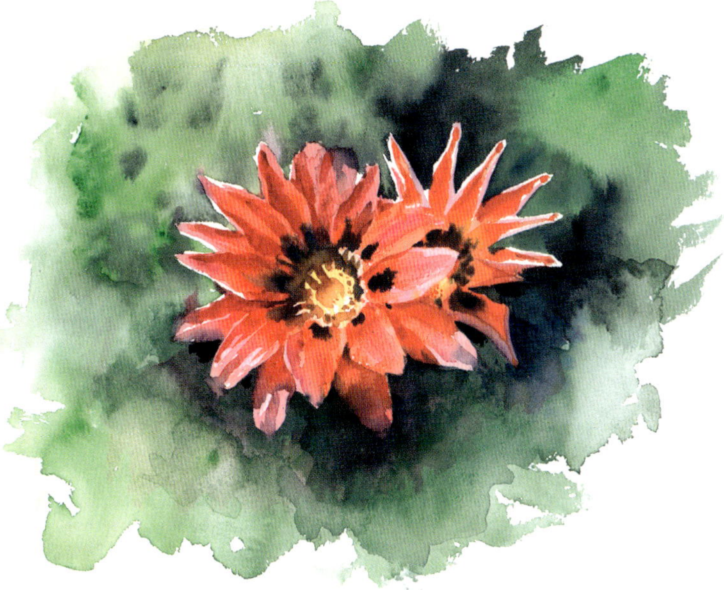

▲ *The blooms only open in the sun. The petals of these Gazanias curl up and close at dusk, and remain closed on overcast days.*

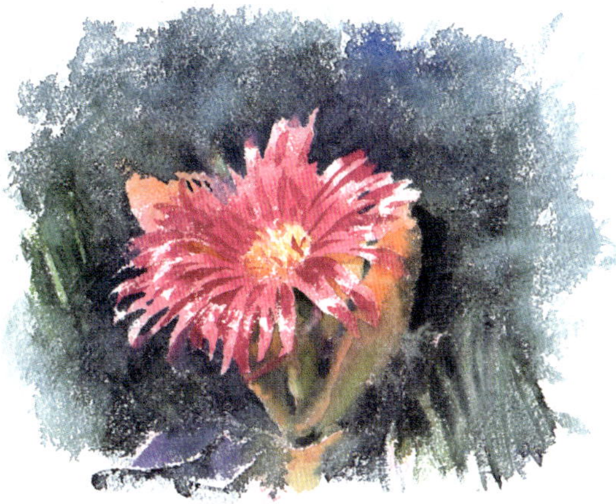

► *The vygies or 'figs' are almost luminous in colour. They sing out brightly against sandy backdrops.*

The flowers spread in swathes – strips of mauve between bands of yellow, patches of pink in fields of blue. In places it looks as if a white or orange sheet were laid across a valley. So tightly packed are the flowers that it is impossible to walk among them without crushing their lovely heads.

Amongst the daisies a variety of other flowers spring into life. Along the roadside plucky shrubs burst into bloom and even in the narrow crevices of the rocks, small clumps find nourishment enough to grow.

The passing of spring

The flowers vanish almost as quickly as they come. In a few weeks drought stalks the landscape and the dusty browns and reds return. At dawn the hills are bathed in blue, the yellow sun rises quickly, losing colour as it climbs, and the heat is palpable. It is soon too hot to paint outside. The shadows are hard, the overhead light flattens the form and every living creature seeks shade.

The contrast of the fleeting delicacy of the flowers with the immutable landscape becomes just a memory.

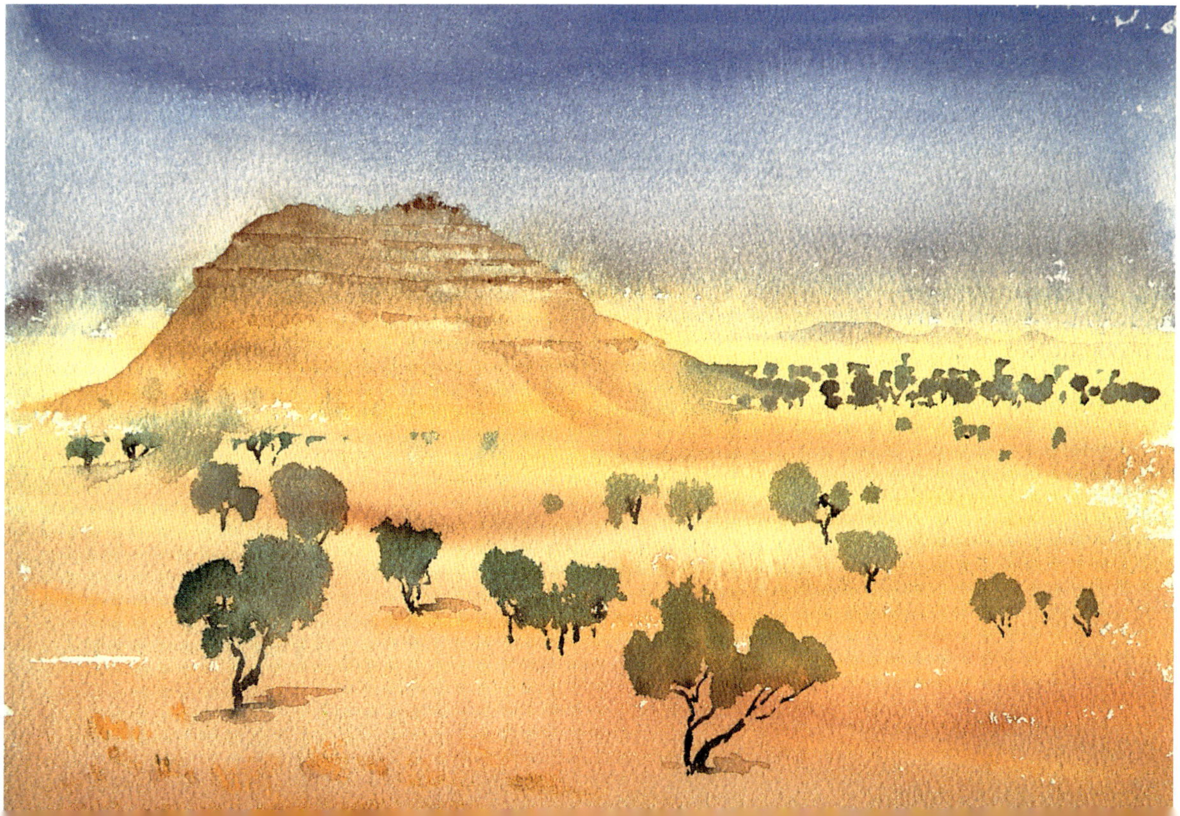

► BARREN LANDSCAPE
20 x 28 cm (8 x 11 in)
The flowers die and the desert rules, hiding the seeds of next spring's blooms beneath its parched dusty terrain.

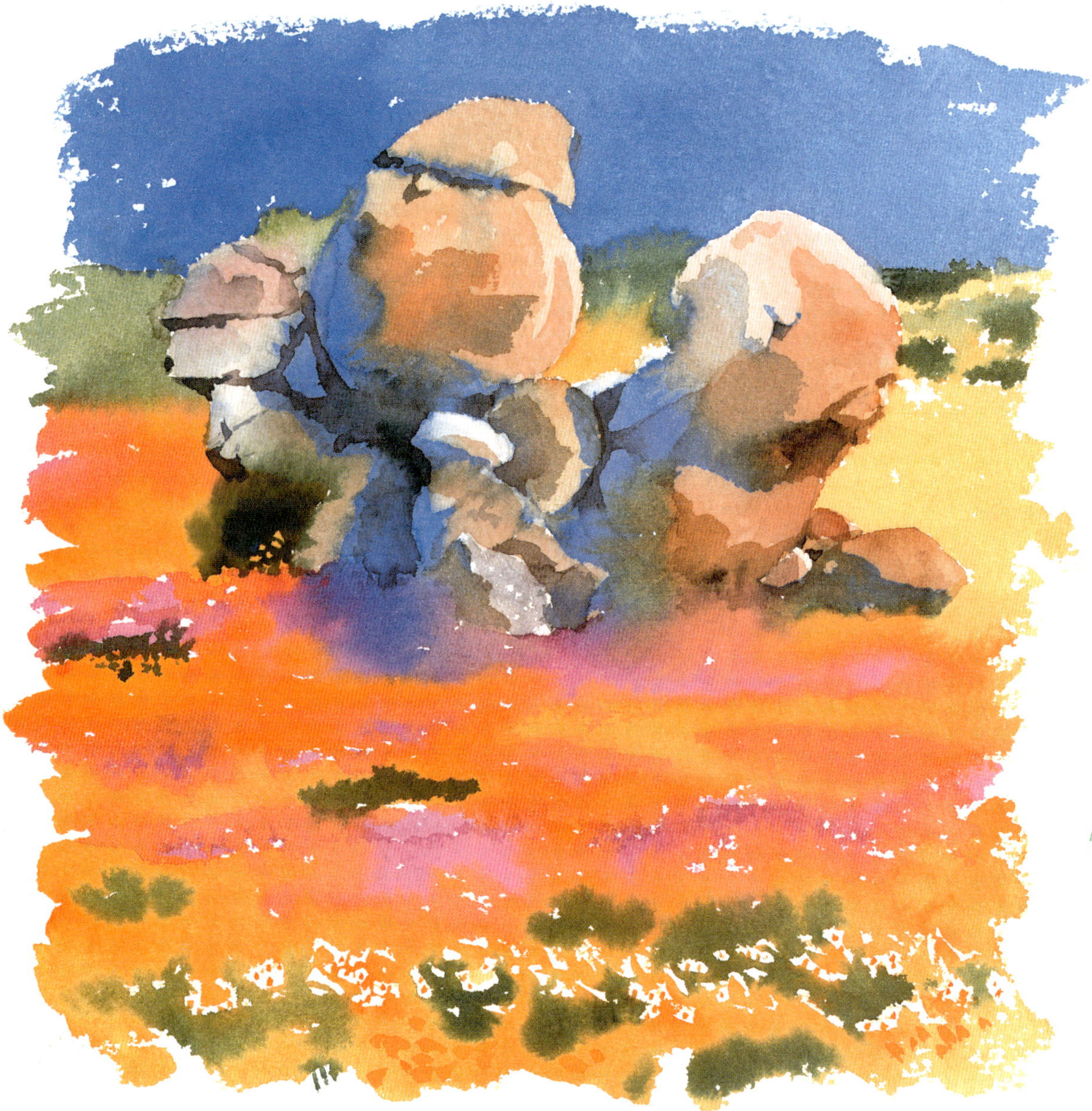

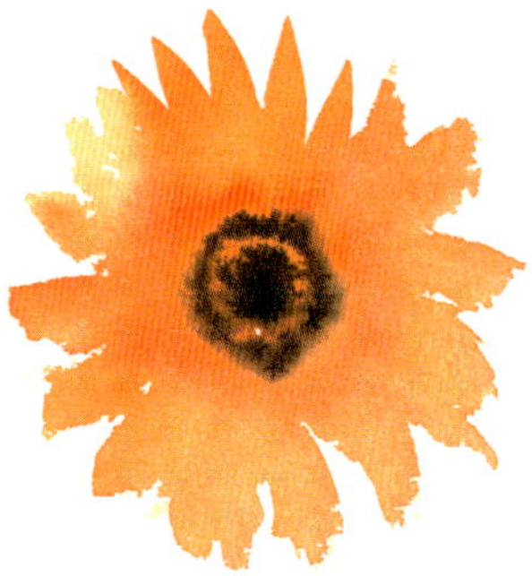

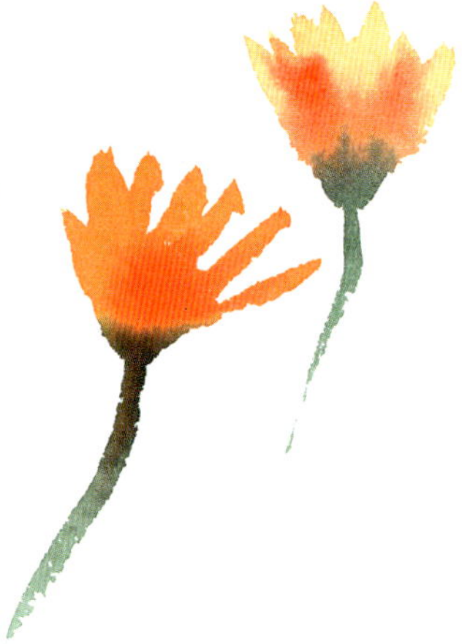

◀ GOD'S GARDEN
20 x 20 cm (8 x 8 in)
The carpet of orange and pink flowers becomes more vibrant backed by the bright blue sky.

Painting flowers

However fleeting, flowers always present the painter with a marvellous excuse to use a variety of bright, strong colours.

Flowers are well matched with watercolour techniques – the transparency of washes and the freedom of brushstrokes so closely relate to the translucence and extravagance of blooms. Layers of transparent watercolour mirror overlapping petals and fluid wet-in-wet blends help to suggest the movement of living things.

You do not need to paint every detail, sacrificing freshness for accuracy. Leave some of the painting to the imagination and enjoy the texture of the watercolour washes and the vibrancy of the pigments.

Vivid colour

Colours are relative. A bright colour will dominate the colour beside it and appear more bright against its duller partner. Divine creation uses this comparison to great effect. For example, the dull greens of

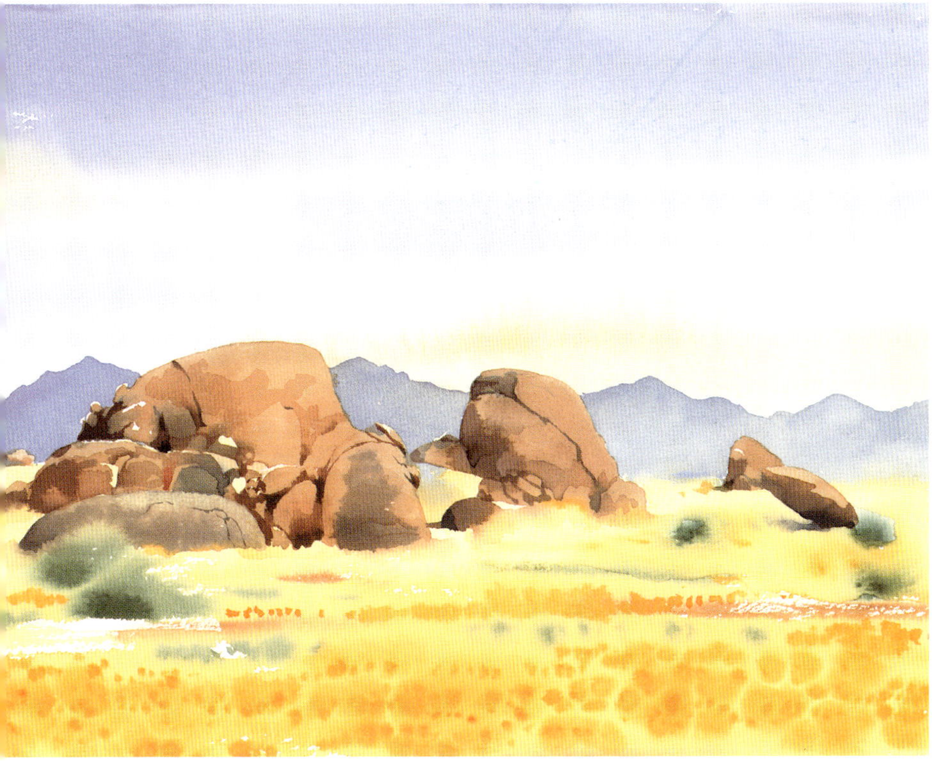

leaves serve to brighten the colours of the flowers they support, attracting the insects.

Contrasting colours help each other to shine more brightly. A clump of purple flowers looks more vivid in a field of yellow daisies than in a field of green grass.

Depth and distance

The form of the landscape beneath the mass of flowers needs to be gently implied, however strong the colour. If you are painting an individual flower use darker tones in the centre or interior of the bloom to suggest depth.

Paler tone helps to create distance in painting, but you can also make use of perspective by a reduction of scale. Paint the flowers in the foreground larger or in greater detail than the flowers beyond. As the flowers recede paint them with smaller, less distinct shapes, until they become just a blur of colour in the distance.

▲ THE FIELD OF GOLD
25 x 36 cm (10 x 14 in)
Here the bright yellow flowers follow the curve of the landscape, becoming lighter in tone as they retreat over the rise.

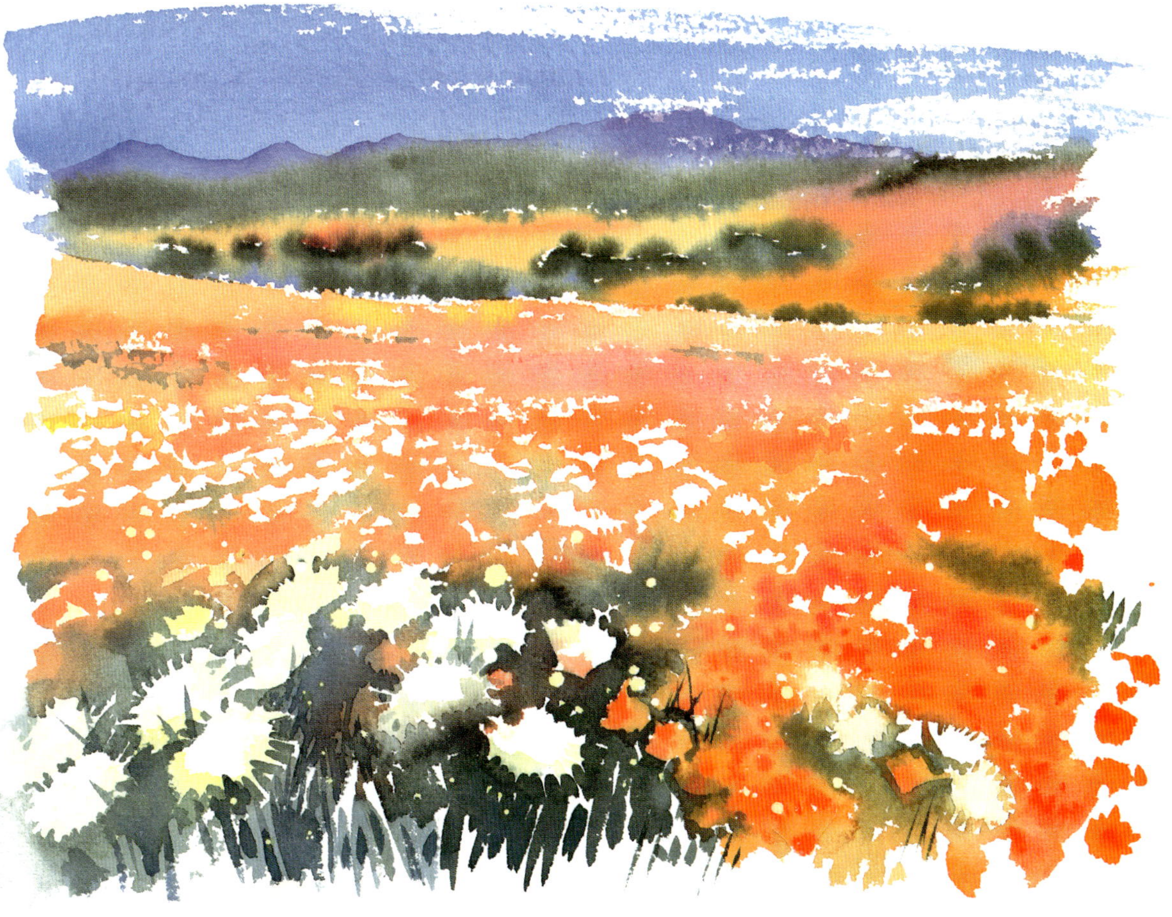

► SEA OF ORANGE
23 x 30 cm (9 x 12 in)
Distance is implied by a comparison of scale. The size of the blooms diminishes as the field of flowers rolls into the distance.

Releasing vibrant colour

Colour is one of the most enjoyable aspects of painting and watercolour has dozens of mouthwatering pigments. Flowers are the perfect subject for this exploration. To get the maximum impact out of a colour you need to lay it on the paper with confidence. First, therefore, let us take a look at different brushstrokes.

Colour at a stroke

The shape of a round sable brush is perfect for painting petals and leaves. Mix a generous quantity of pigment with water in the palette and load the brush with colour.

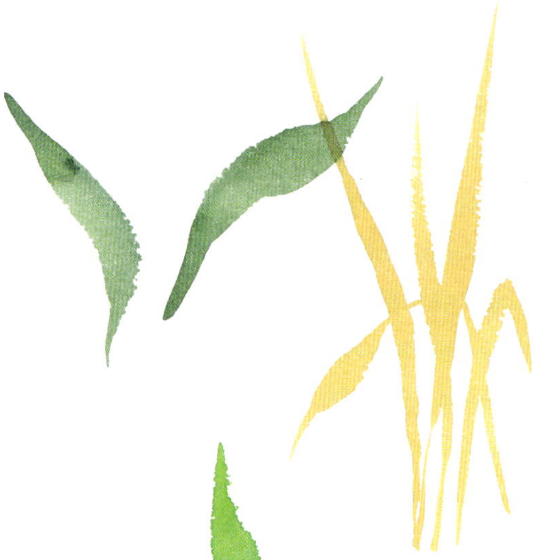

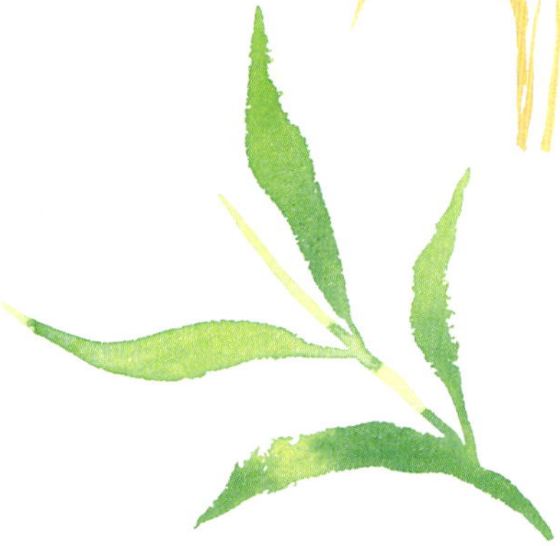

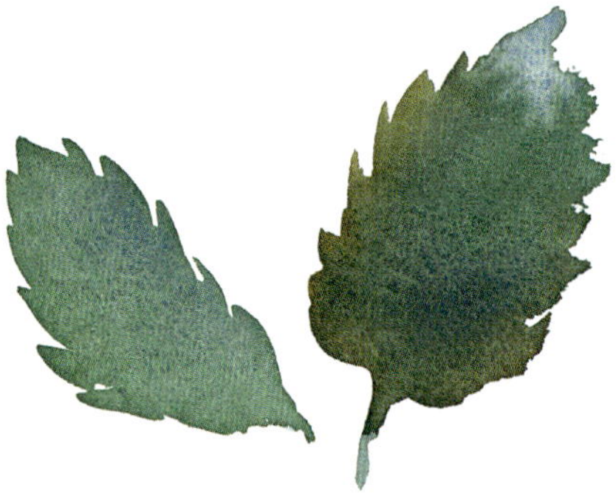

▲ *Start at leaf tip or stalk. Gradually press down, releasing the colour and lift with a slight twist at the end. Use the same stroke to lead the leaf out from the stem while it is still wet.*

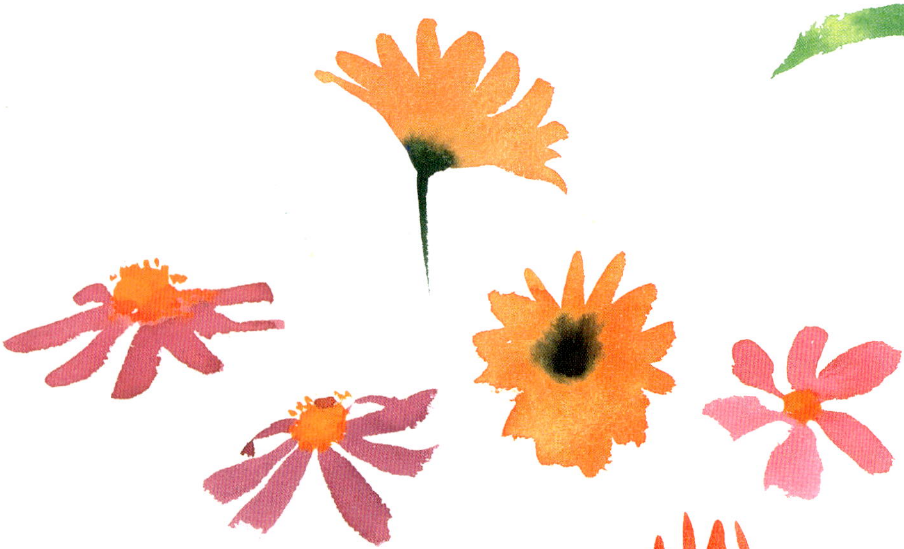

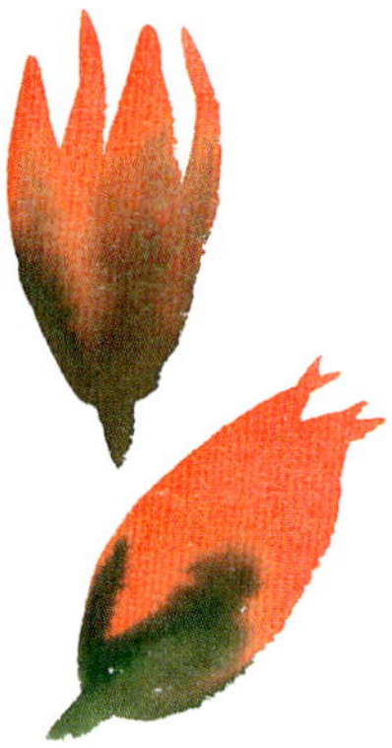

▲ *Start the brush at either the base or the tip of the petal. Try to touch in the centres and sepals before the petals dry so that the colours blend.*

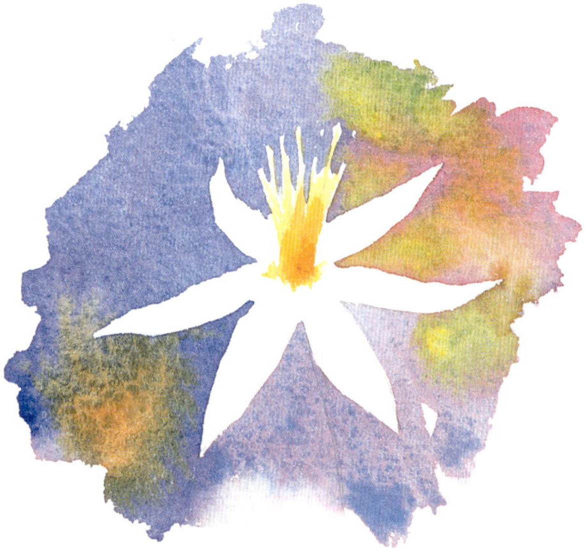

▲ *White flower shapes can be created with the surrounding background colour.*

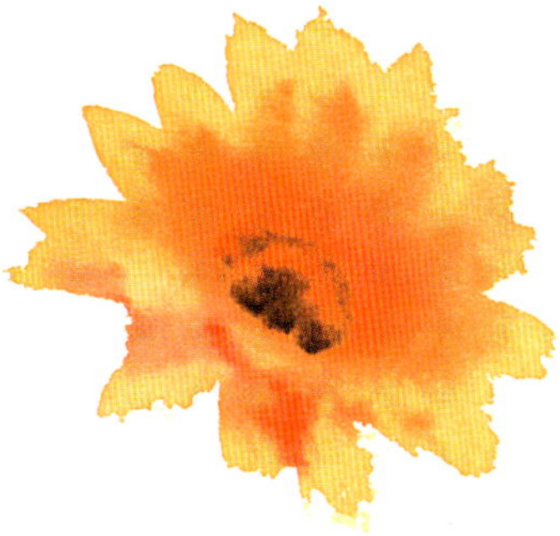

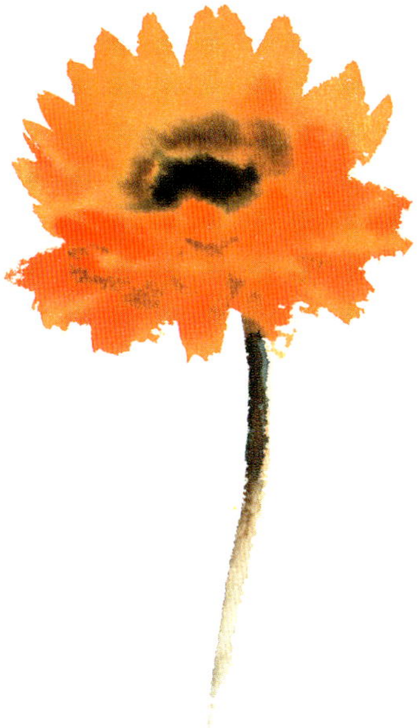

Flower forms

Wet-in-wet technique is perfect for creating the form of the flower. The secret of success is in the amount of water you mix with your pigment. Try not to make the colours too dilute. If your first wash is very wet the colour you add next needs to be almost dry or it will spread too far into the wet wash.

▲ The dark centres of flowers and underlying petals can be painted entirely wet-in-wet.

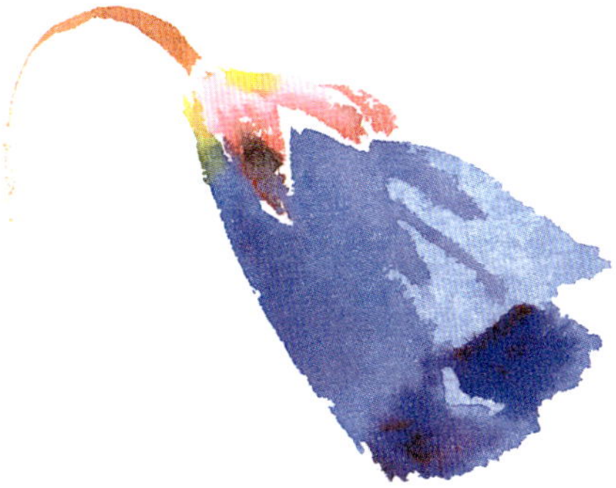

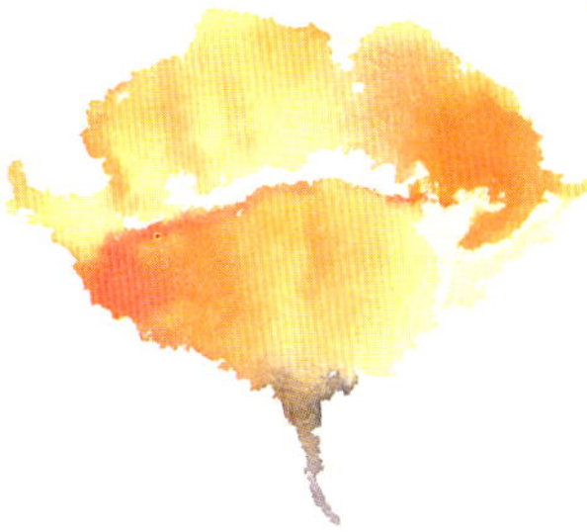

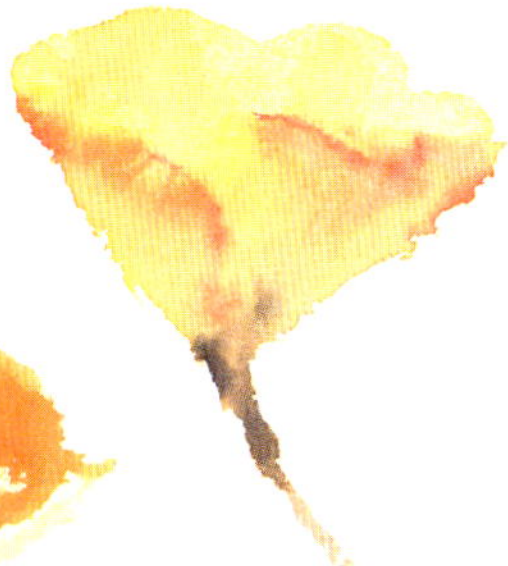

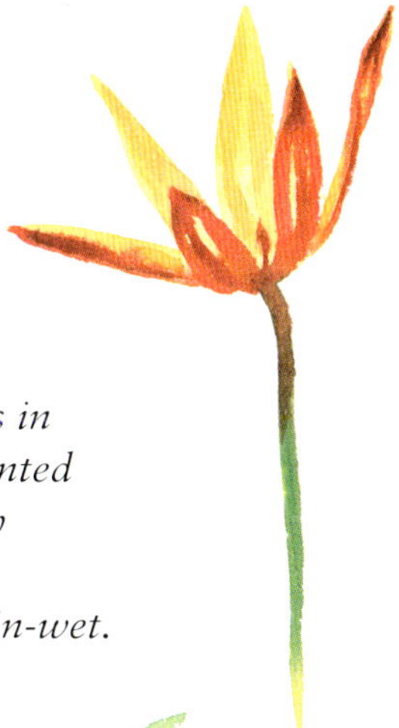

▲ Darker petals in front can be painted wet-on-dry, with coloured edges touched in wet-in-wet.

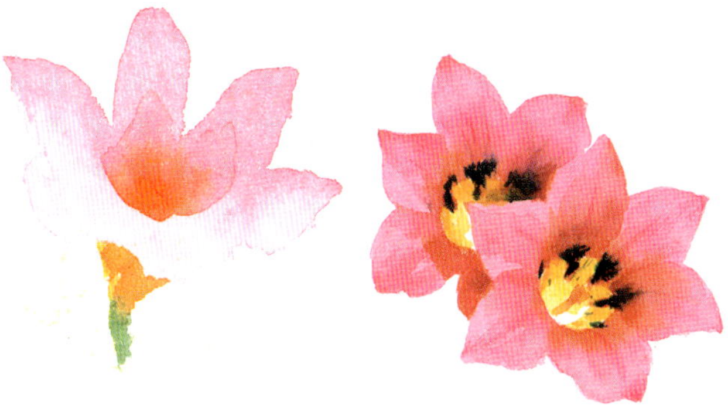

▲ To create a crisp edge against a darker centre, allow the wash to dry, then re-wet the centre with clean water and add the next colour from the edge wet-in-wet.

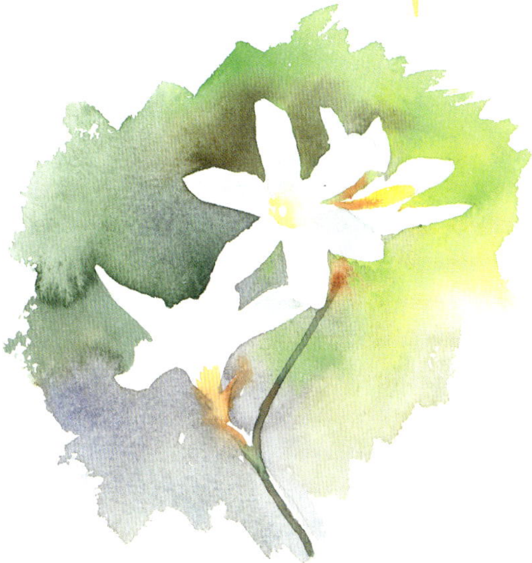

► Cobalt Blue mixed with Yellow Ochre makes a gentle grey for the shades in white flowers.

Colour in action

If the three primary colours – red, yellow and blue – and their secondaries – orange, green and purple – are drawn into a circle, the red will face the green, the blue will be opposite the orange, and the yellow will confront the purple. These pairs of colours are called opposites or complementaries.

All these colours influence each other visually. They interact by pushing each other away from their own colour towards the opposite side of the circle or spectrum. A colour will therefore look its brightest when it is painted in the company of its opposite colour.

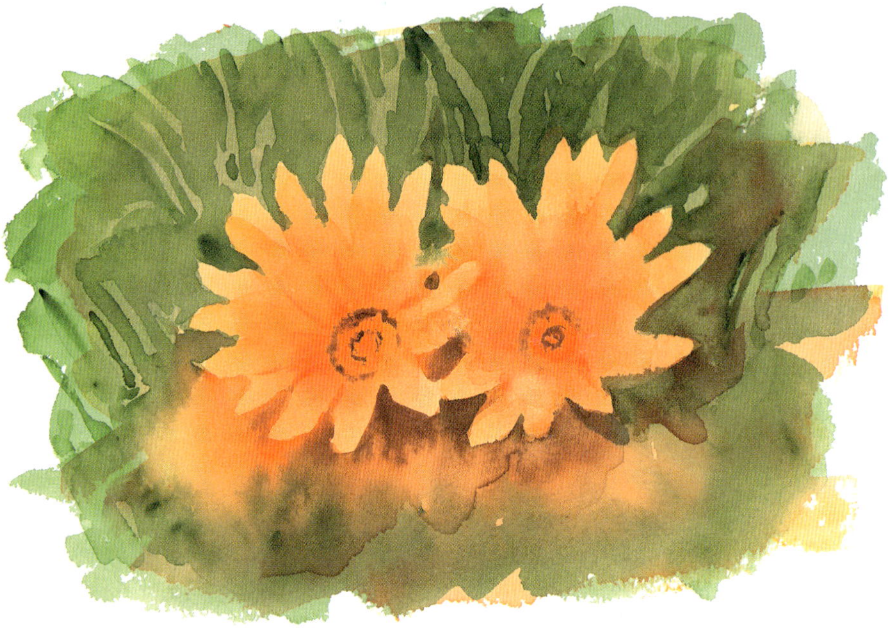

▲ *The orange flowers set in yellow green foliage look bright, but you can make them more vibrant by using the interaction of opposite colours.*

▼ *The flowers in blue green foliage look brighter and more orange because blue is the opposite or complementary colour to orange.*

▲ *Pairs of opposite colours: red and green, blue and orange, yellow and purple.*

Hidden hues

Deliciously bright colours make an obvious choice for the painter's brush, but you can find rich colour even in apparently dull subjects. You may not see these colours at first, but ask yourself, 'Does this brown or grey veer towards red, green, or blue?', and as you decide so you will begin to notice more colour.

The transparency of watercolour means you can make tertiary colours by overlaying tints of complementaries. Experiment with two opposite colours, both by mixing them together and by overlaying transparent washes. You will find that you create different results with each method.

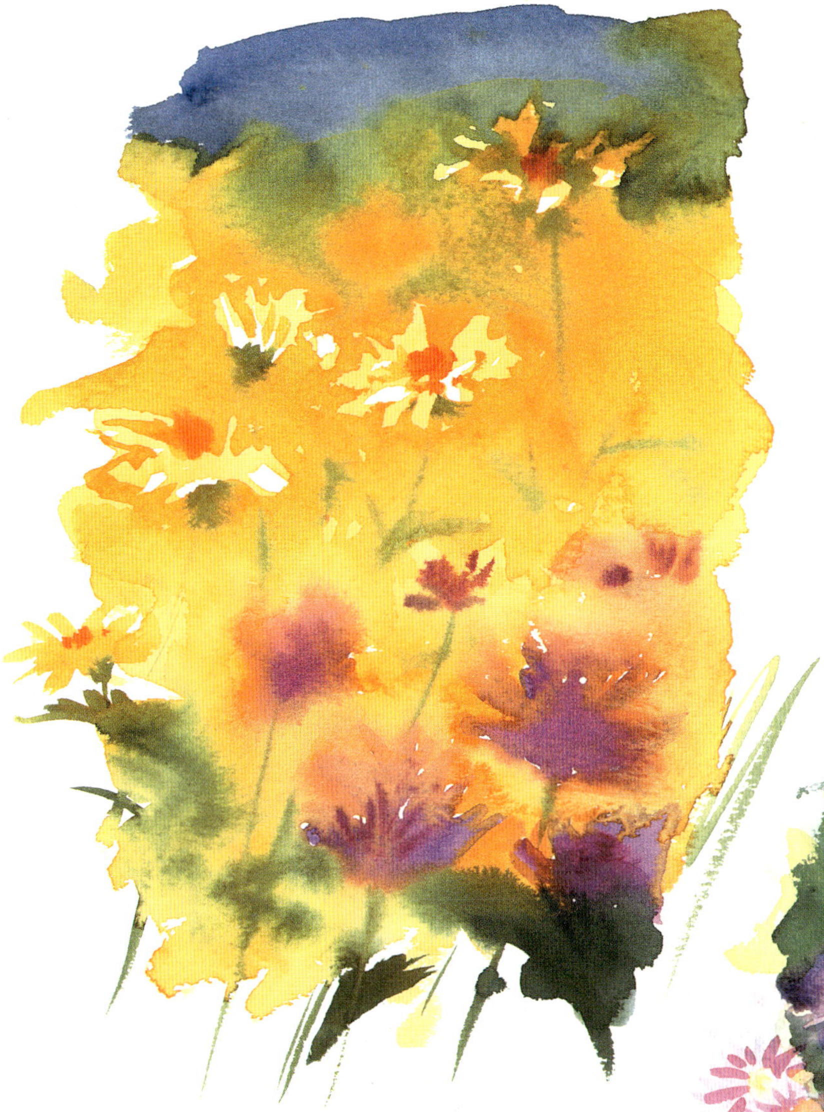

▲ *The intrusion of purple flowers into a complementary yellow field of daisies makes both colours appear more vivid.*

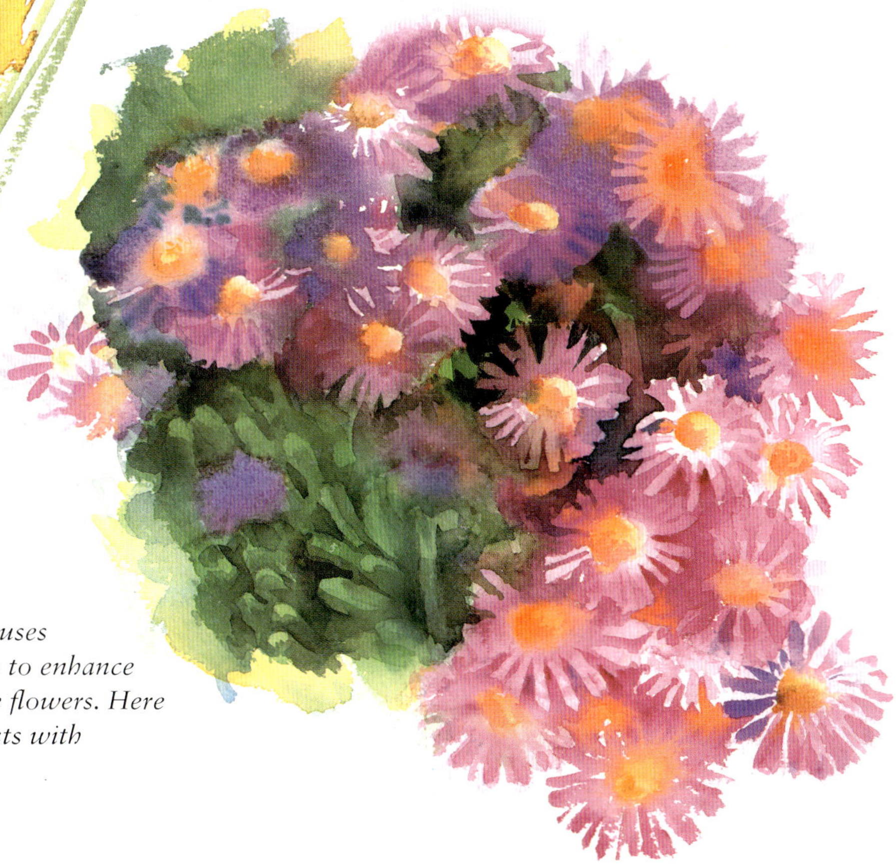

► *Nature often uses opposite colours to enhance the colour of the flowers. Here Magenta contrasts with yellow green.*

Safari sketchbook

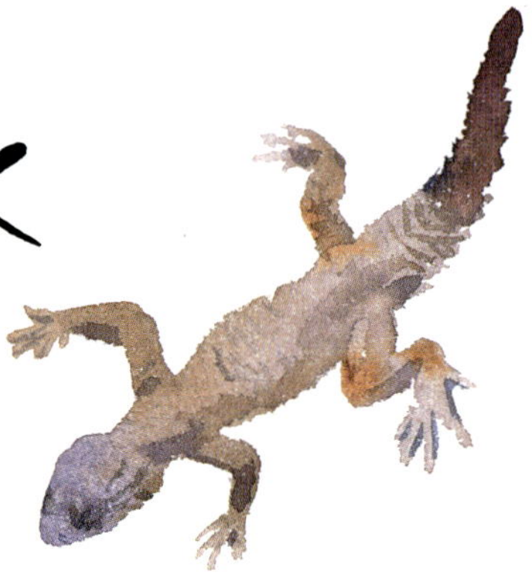

Diamonds in the desert

In 1908 a railway labourer chanced upon a diamond near the desolate sandy coast north of Namaqualand. A rush of prospectors followed.

Kolmanskop became the centre of a diamond-mining area and grew into a rich little town in the desert. Eventually the diamonds were exhausted. The people left and the sands of the desert blew in.

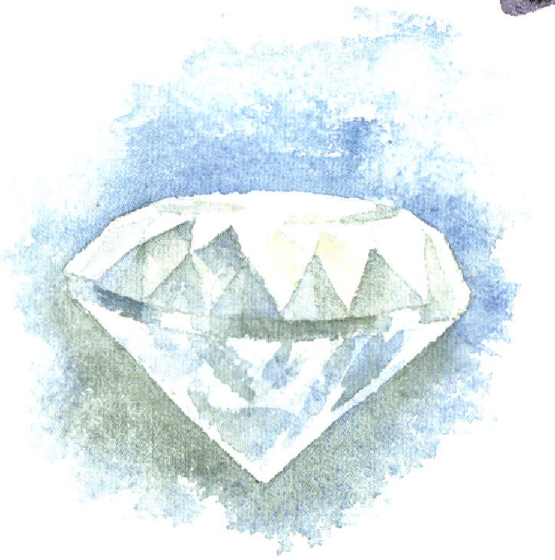

No-one could believe they had not noticed the diamonds before – they could be collected in handfuls.

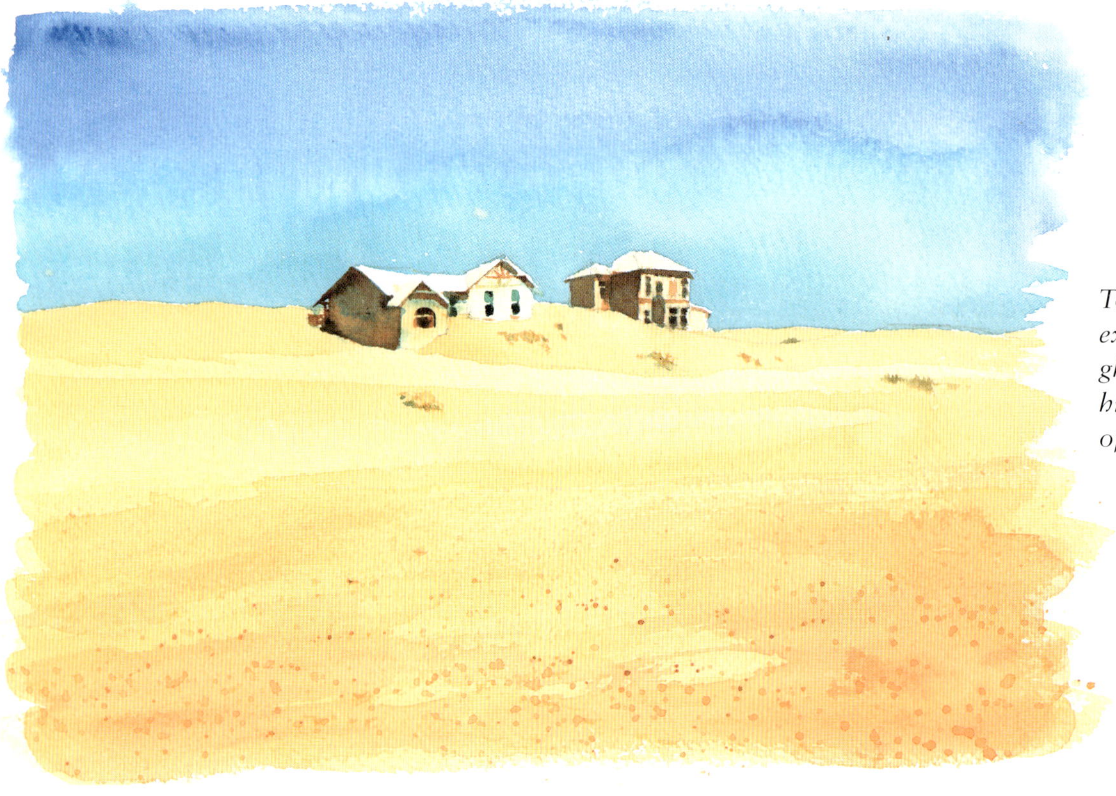

Today Kolmanskop exists as a surreal ghost town half-hidden beneath heaps of yellow sand.

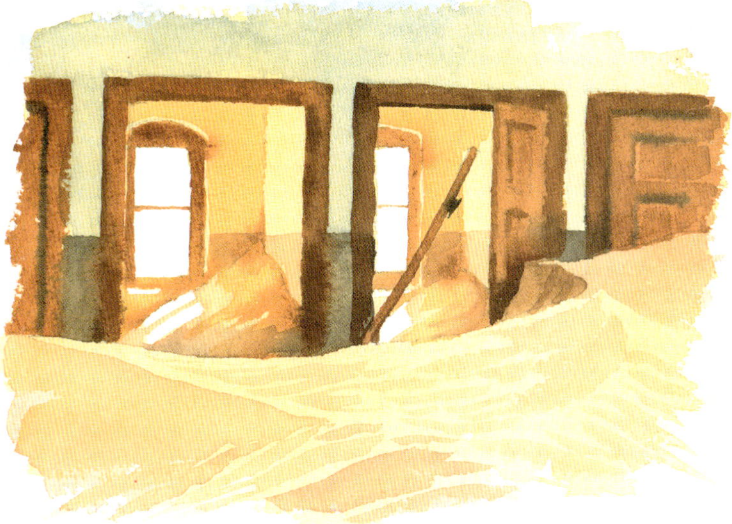

Kolmanskop even had a hospital that served champagne and caviar to its patients and a miniature railway to ease the passage around town!

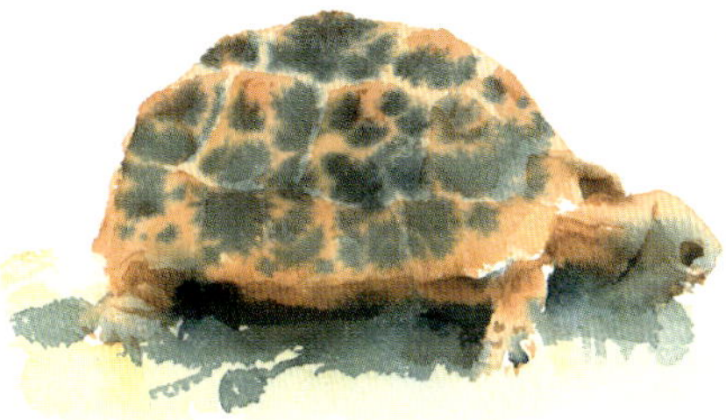

CAMPFIRE TALE

Finger of God falls down

Just across the Namibian border there stood a remarkable pillar of stone called Mukurob, the Finger of God. It consisted of a cone of slate topped with a precariously balanced finger-shaped column of rock 34 metres (112 ft) high. I had always wanted to see it, but when we reached the spot it was nowhere to be seen, just a pile of rubble at the base of a cone-shaped mound and freshly shredded plants sticking out like crushed limbs.

Disappointed though we were, we realized we were the first to witness this geological collapse, so, shooting off some camera film, we headed hastily back to the nearest town. We rushed excitedly into the newspaper office with our breaking news, only to discover that Mukurob had fallen down three weeks before. We were too late again!

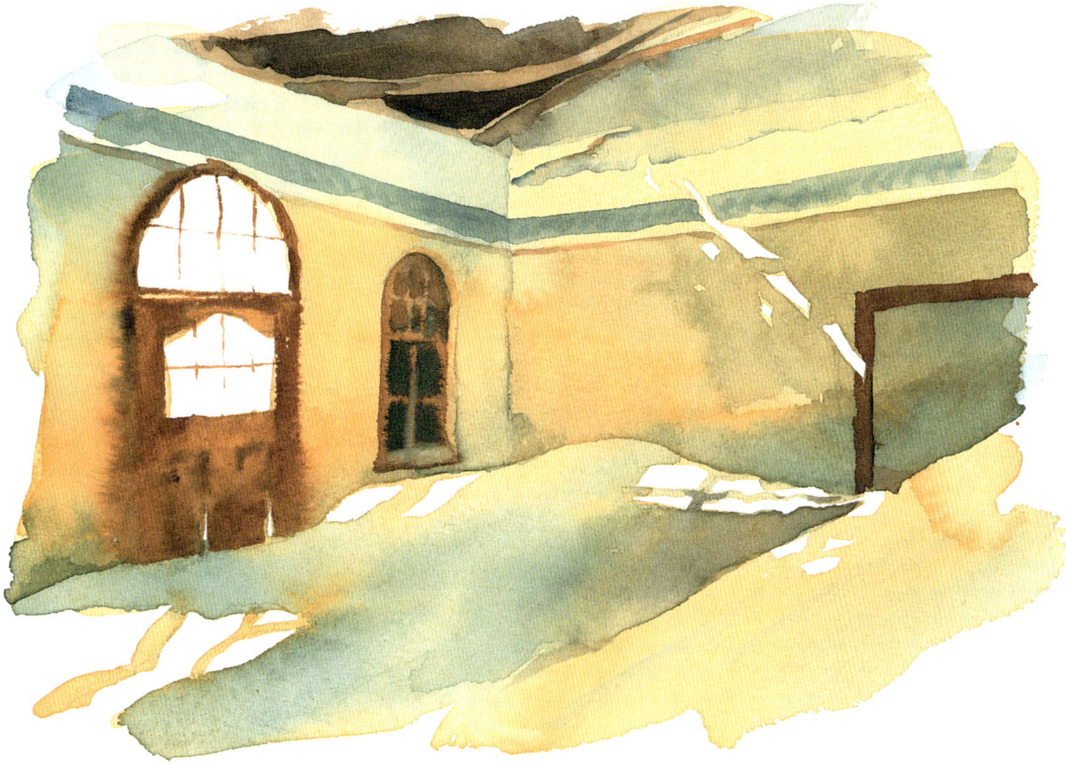

The sand blew into every crevice, preserving the comfortable homes and painted walls from decay.

Red Dunes, Cool Mists:

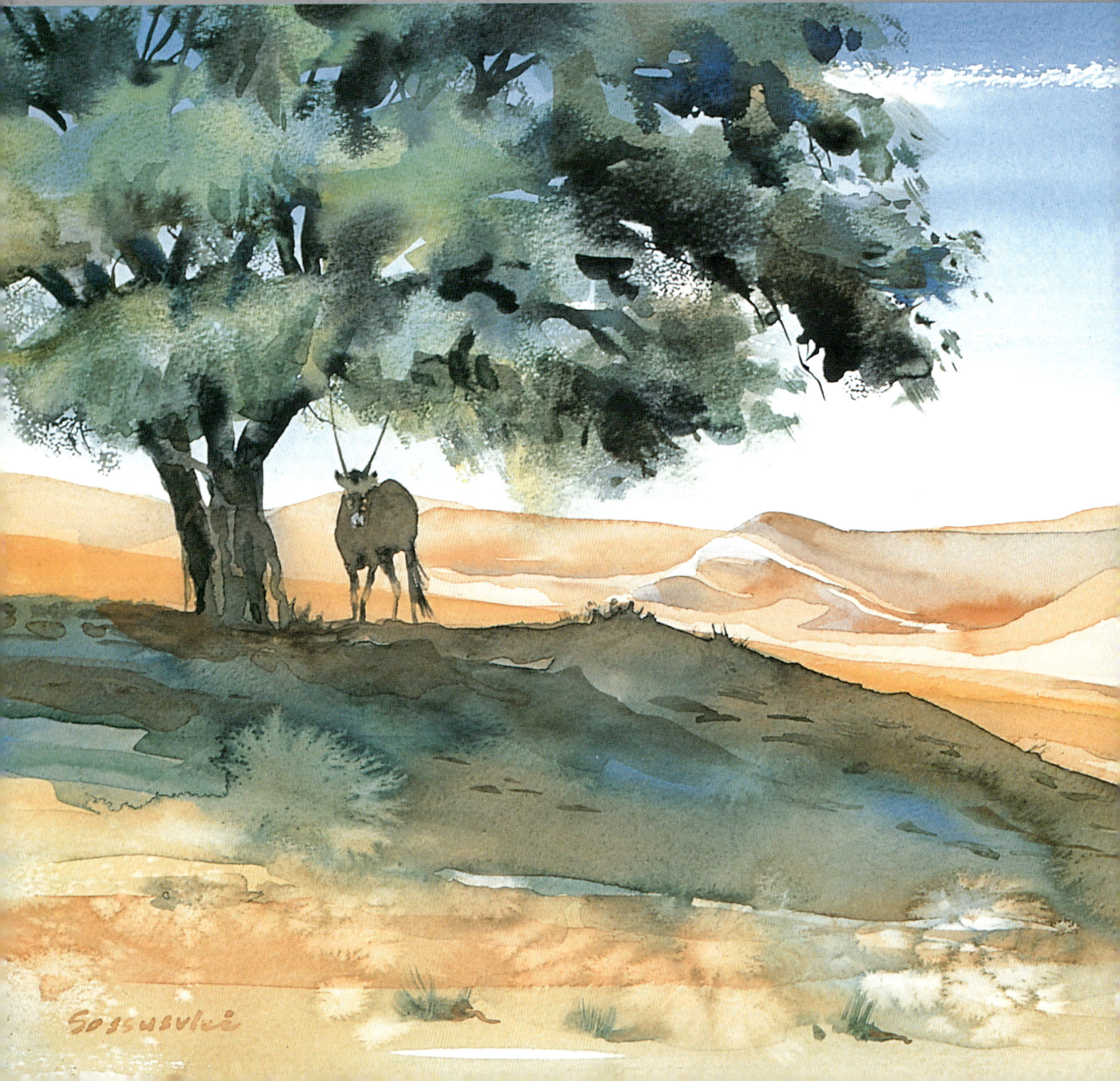

The Namib Desert

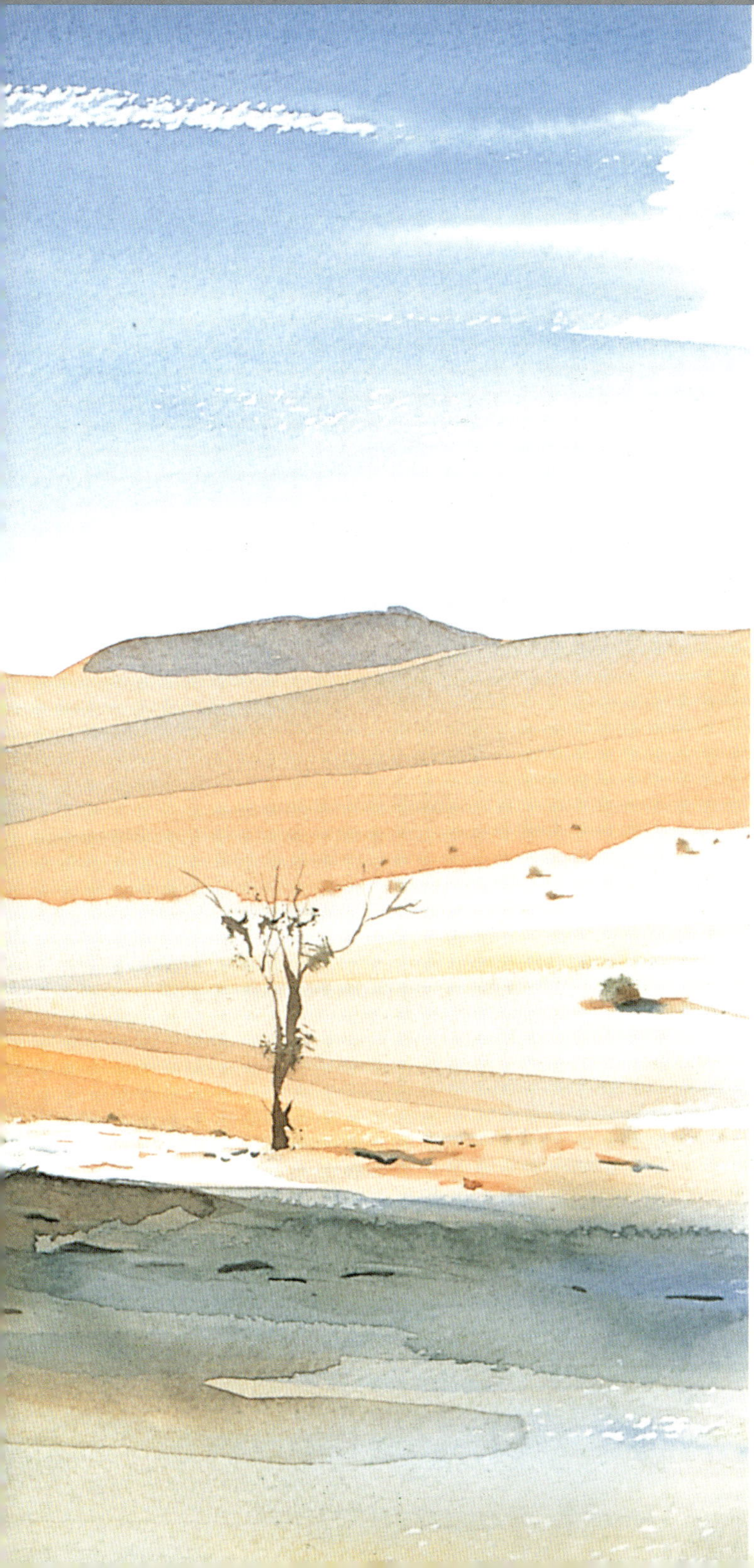

The strength of simplicity

Under the Namib's myriad stars,
beneath Orion's Belt,
out of endless desolation
the night begins to melt.
The sabre horns, majestic stride,
the silent line, the line of pride,
the wary eye, the lapping tongue,
the graceful oryx, one by one,
taking of the desert's gift,
the desert's juice, the will to live.

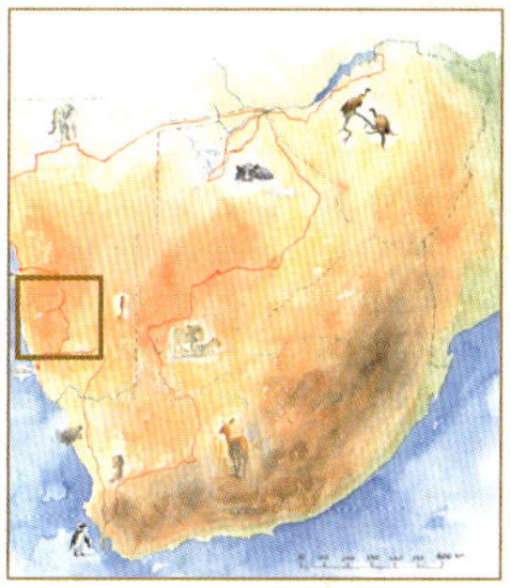

◀ LONELY REFUGE
38 x 51 cm (15 x 20 in)

The dune sea

The Namib Desert, ancient and extremely beautiful, lies on the coastal side of southern Namibia. Towering red sand dunes and gravel plains create a vast, unrivalled wilderness.

Millennia ago the cold waters of the Benguela Current turned the Namib into a desert region and one of the most remarkable places on earth was formed. For the visual connoisseur this solitary wilderness is unmatched. It is not only the exquisite beauty of the dune sea that so captivates the soul, but the extraordinary life that flourishes in this desolate home. It is deceivingly welcoming, like entering Eden, and yet there is no rain, no water, only unrelenting heat, veiled mists and an ocean of sand.

In the middle of this desert wave upon wave of magnificent red dunes advance across the landscape from the western seashore. The panorama changes in appearance throughout the day as the different faces of the dunes are bathed in sun or shade. Climbing them is exhausting, but well worthwhile for the view across the dunescape from the top.

▼ SONG OF THE DESERT
20 x 28 cm (8 x 11 in)
Iron oxidization and particles of garnets paint the gigantic dunes a deep red-orange. They are the highest dunes in the world, reaching almost 300 metres (1000 ft) in height.

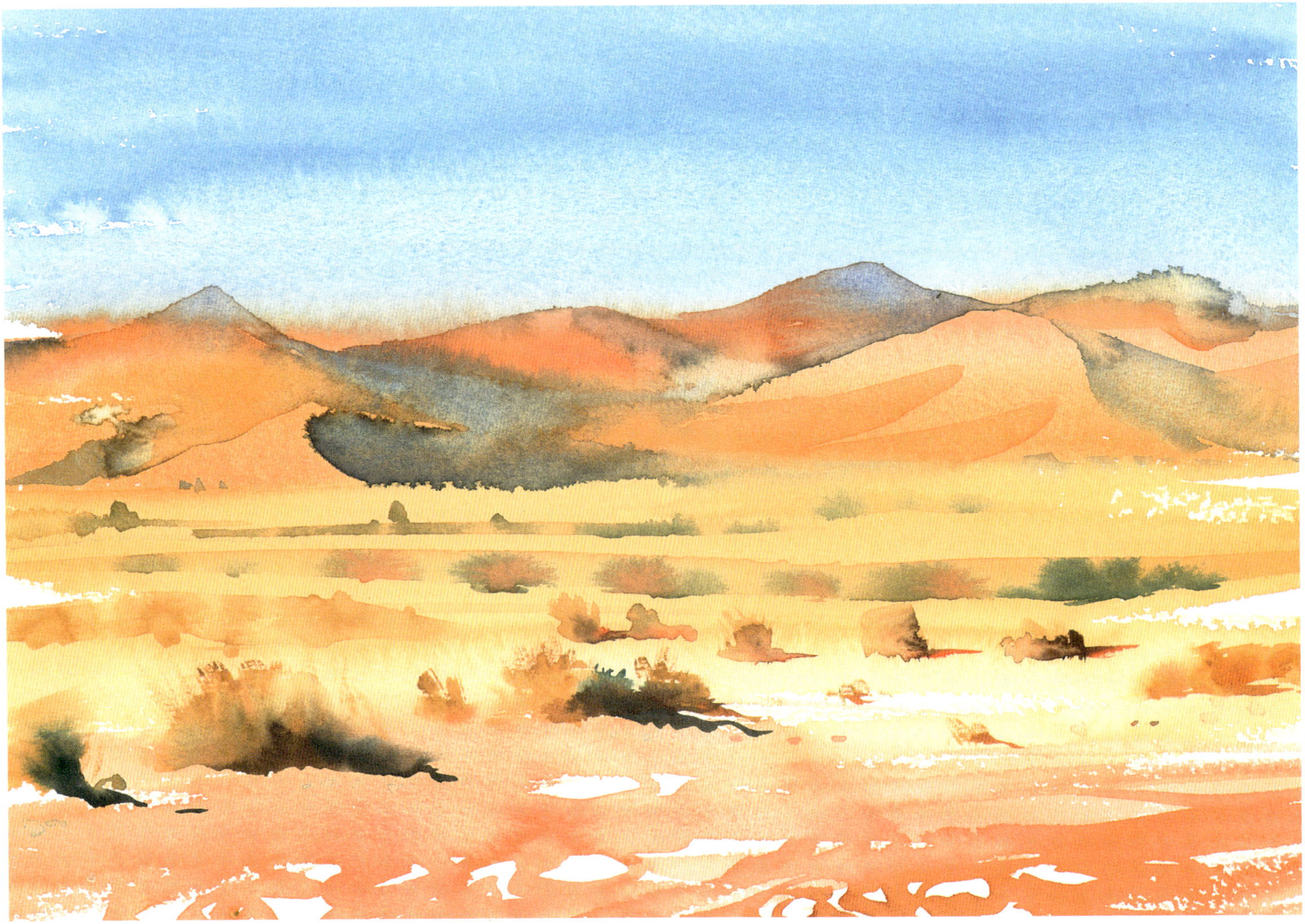

▶ SOSSUSVLEI
28 x 36 cm (11 x 14 in)
The dry, cracked surface of the pan appears pure white beneath the sun. The curved shapes of the dunes, with their razor-sharp edges, are breathtaking.

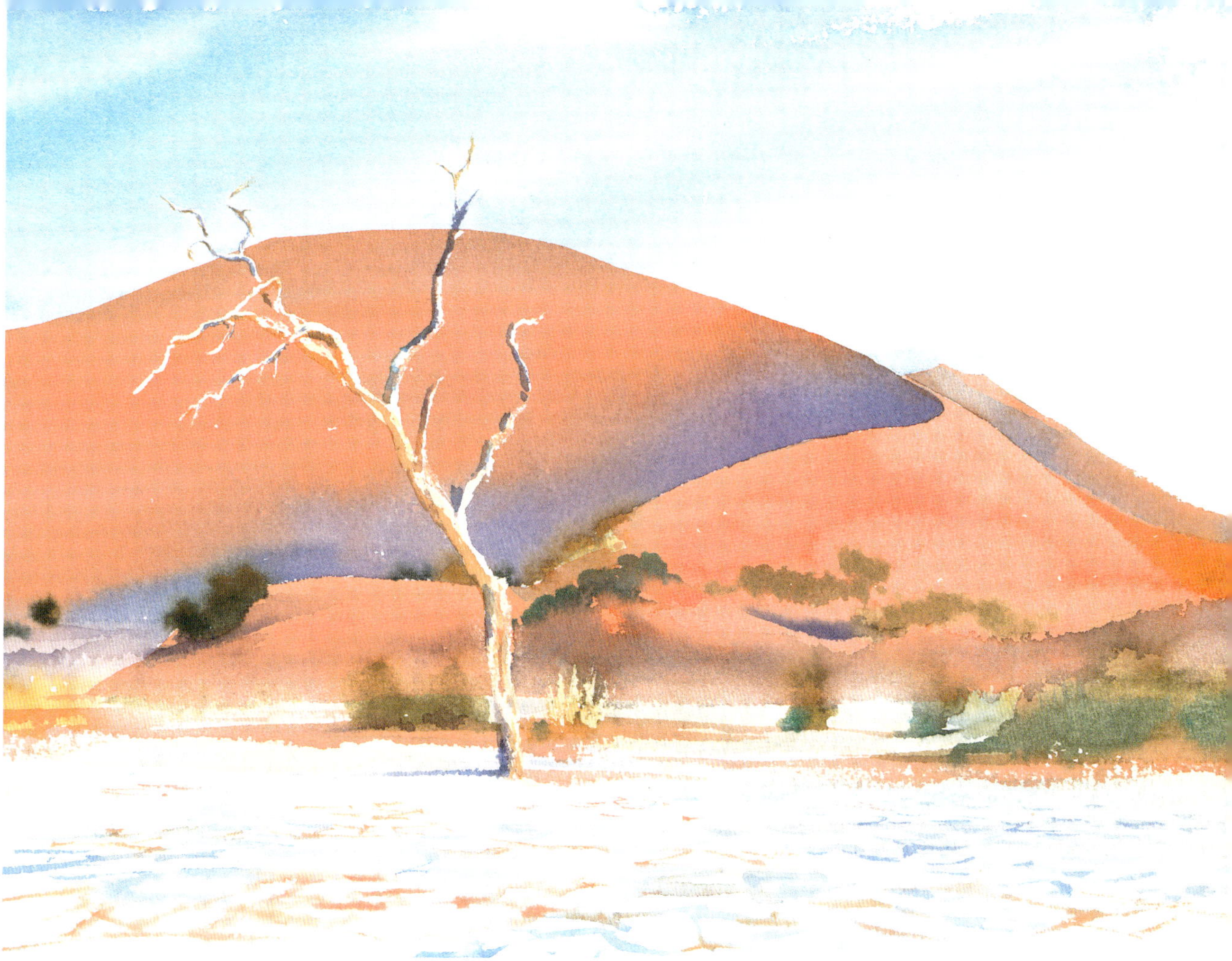

▼ ORYX IN OCHRE
20 x 25 cm (8 x 10 in)
Subjected to temperatures that are often above 40 degrees Celsius, the oryx has refined a system of self-cooling the blood by running it through a network of capillaries in the nose. This enables the animal to flee at speed without the blood rising to a fatal temperature.

Sossusvlei

A wide gravel plain, bordered by dunes, leads to the end of an occasionally running river. The river's futile hope of reaching the sea is thwarted by the mountains of sand, and the water is trapped in the desert, creating a miniature lake. For most of the time it is dry, however, and Sossusvlei is a dazzling white pan, a crazed pavement, surrounded by the implacable dunes. A few ancient trees are testament to a wetter time.

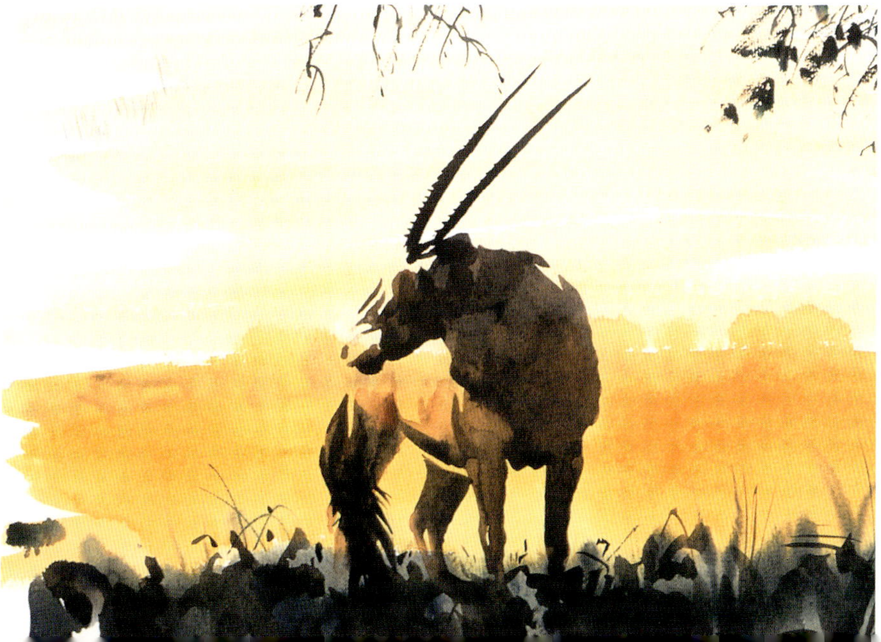

Thirsty mammals

In this arid and primeval home life still exists. Oryx, springbok, jackals and ostrich can be seen crossing the dunes, their spoor imprinted in the soft red sand. The animals, always few in number, make defined shapes against the background of orange. The scrubby trees that run along the ancient watercourses provide shelter for these animals in the blistering heat of the day. Wreaths of early morning mist delineate the dry riverbeds and allude to the secret, underground rivers.

Painting the dunes

If it is possible for the eye to be saturated with beauty it is here in the Namib. The astonishing red dunes, interrupted by a few solitary trees, scarred by tyre tracks or punctuated by the passage of a lonely animal, are powerful in their clarity. The landscape is clean and uncomplicated; it may be grand, but it is also simple. In painting, simplicity has a unique strength and this landscape lends itself to simple, but striking, compositions.

Isolated features

It is easy to want to overcomplicate a picture, but a single feature in a wide, empty composition makes a powerful painting. A dead tree or a wandering animal is all that is needed to turn a simple landscape into a dramatic painting. Even in a less deserted setting the presence of a figure or a simple man-made structure will animate an empty scene.

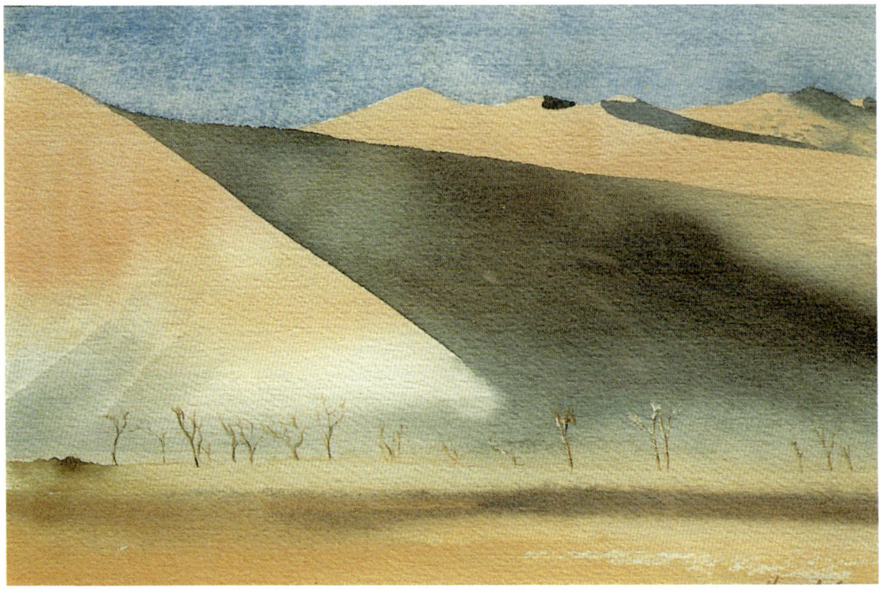

▲ MIST BENEATH THE DUNES

20 x 28 cm (8 x 11 in)

The clean edges of the dunes and the spindly trees are a delight for the precision tip of the sable brush. The swathes of mist are painted by lightening the shadow wash at the base of the dune.

Leading lines

To lead the eye into and around a painting artists seek flow lines in the composition. It is easier to find these flow lines in an uncluttered setting. In a desert landscape

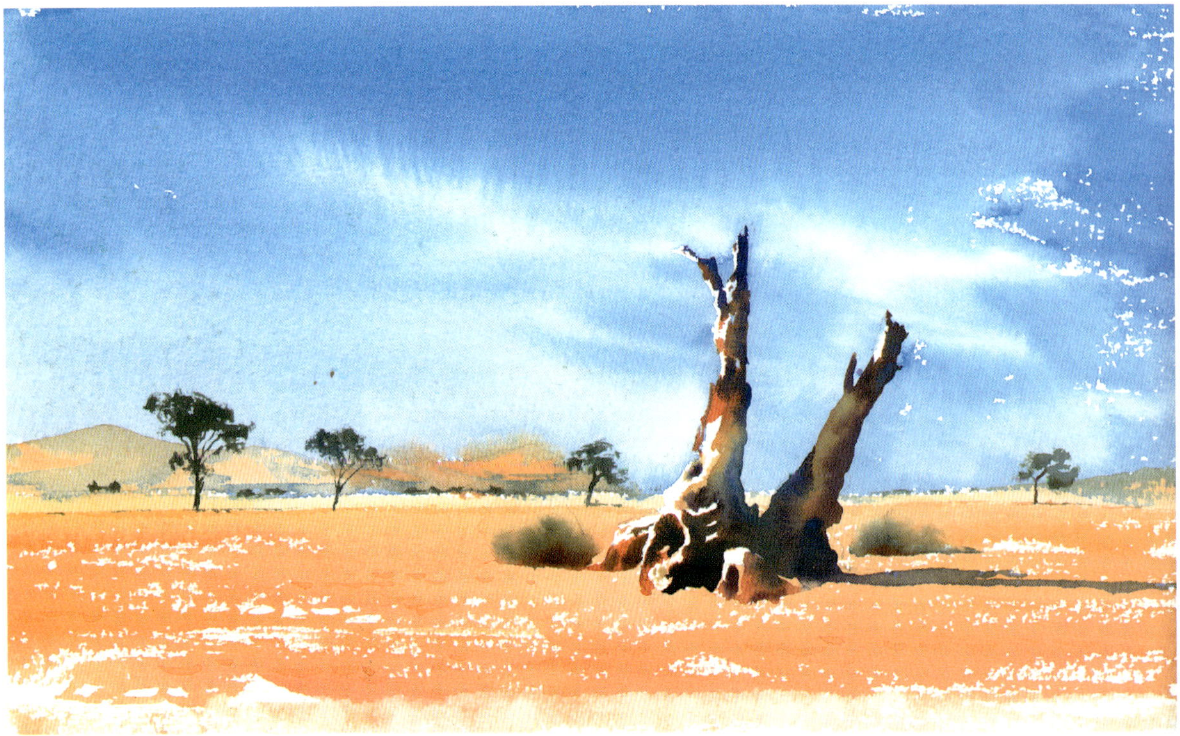

◀ SPLENDID ISOLATION

20 x 38 cm (8 x 15 in)

A simple, but strong, composition is created by the presence of the dead tree stump. Place your hand over the stump and then reveal it again to see its full effect on the painting.

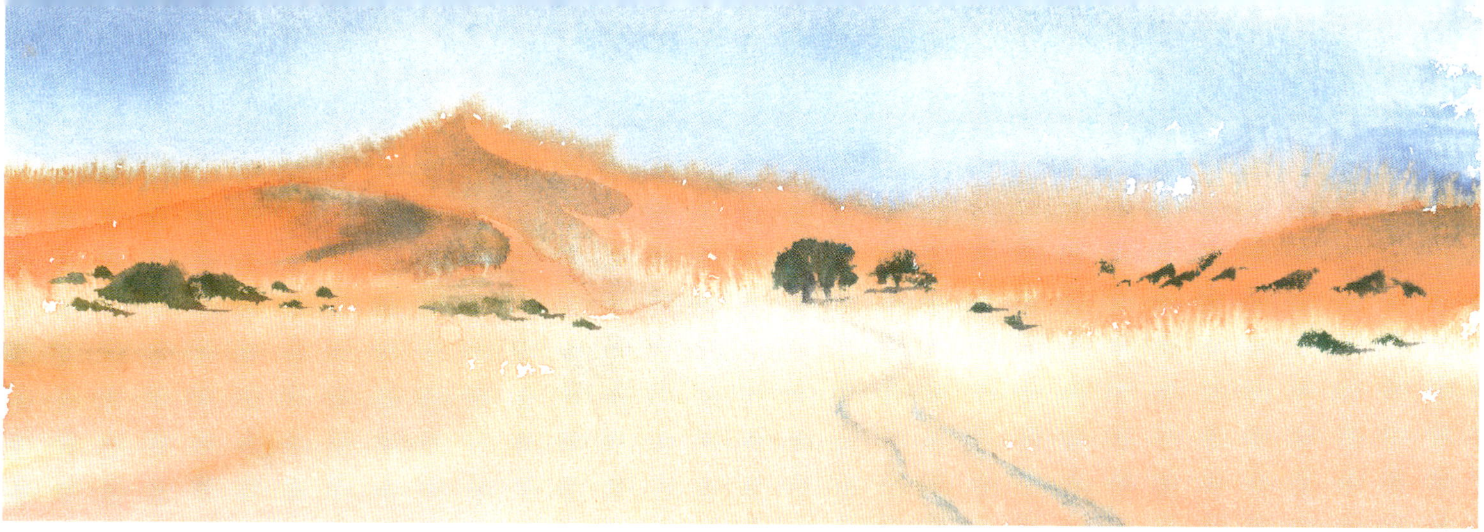

▲ TRACKS IN THE SAND
10 x 36 cm (4 x 14 in)
The set of tyre tracks provides a sense of mystery as it leads the eye into the depths of the painting.

the curves of the dunes, tyre tracks or dried river beds act as leading lines within the painting. Individual features can have the same effect; dead branches, shadows, grasses or footprints, strategically placed, act to draw the eye into the composition. In any landscape look for anything that has a linear quality that can be used to lead the eye into the centre of the painting or to move it from right to left, top to bottom.

Do not be afraid to move elements around a little to enhance the composition of your painting. Leave out whatever does not interest you or anything that may distract the viewer. Draw attention to that which you enjoy.

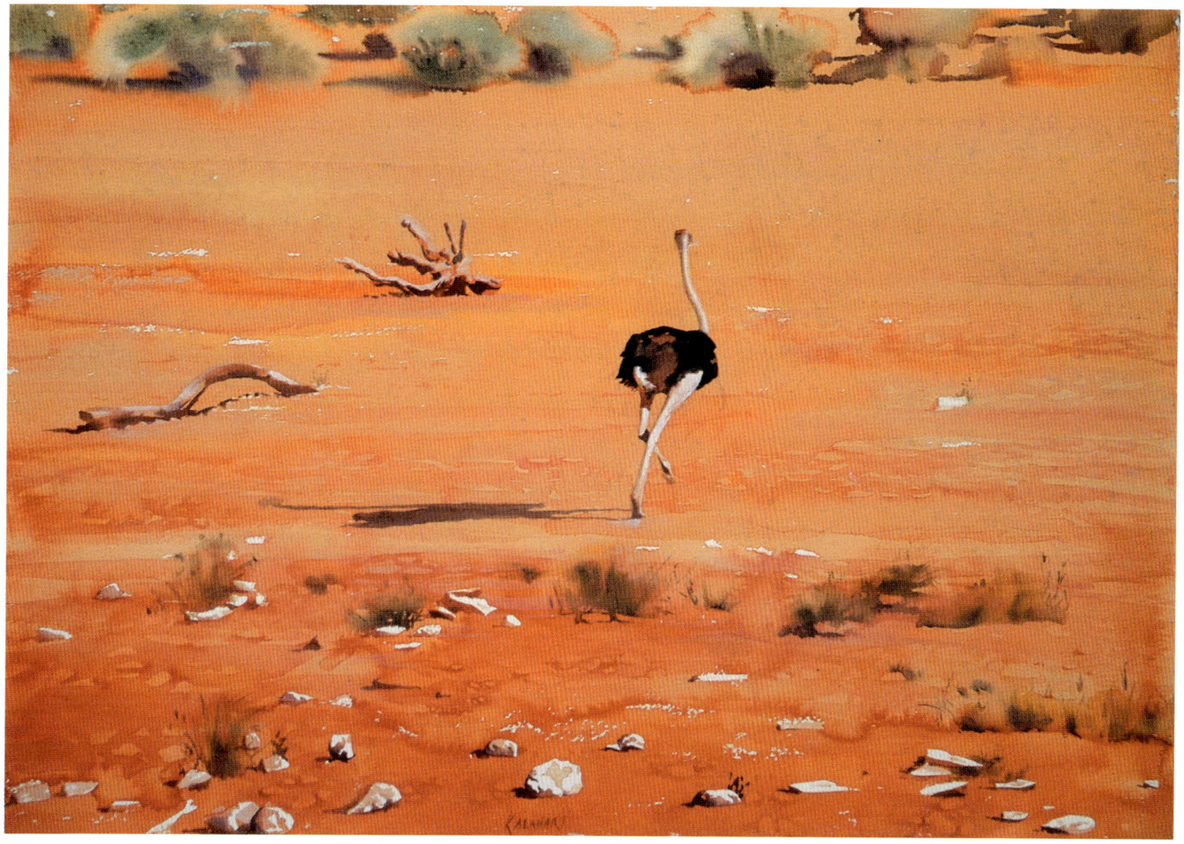

► FLIGHT ACROSS THE DUNES
56 x 76 cm (22 x 30 in)
A field of brilliant orange is broken by the ostrich caught in his dash across the dunes. Placed on the diagonal, he leads us right across the painted space.

The strength of simplicity

The previous chapters have shown the importance of creating form and enhancing colour, but successful paintings need a good composition too, an interesting design on the paper. Composition is also the art of selection: viewing the wide world, choosing what counts, and then reducing those features to fit your small piece of paper in a workable balance of shapes and lines.

Horizontals and verticals

Start with the horizon. Your eyelevel, wherever you choose to place it, will be crucial to the rest of the painting. It is better usually to place the horizon above or below the centre line, otherwise it tends to divide the painting into two equal halves.

Having established the position of your horizontal lines you now need to decide where to place the main verticals of your composition. Start with one item breaking the line of the horizon; again it is better not to place it dead centre, but to place it to the right or the left. Try to feel where in the painting it creates the best balance.

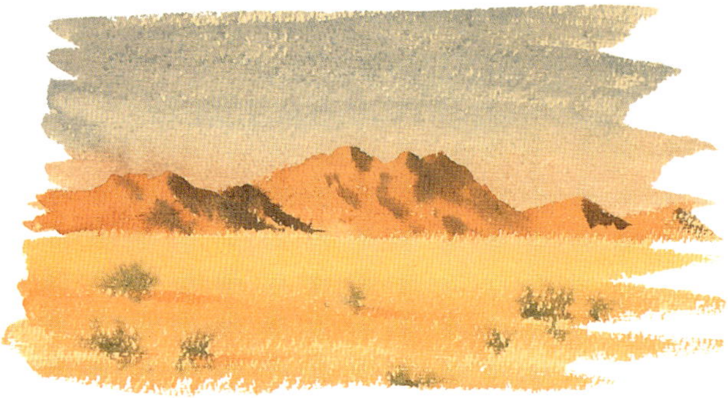

◄ Here the horizon line is just below the centre line, allowing the mountains to cross into the upper half of the painting, making a satisfying balance of the three main elements.

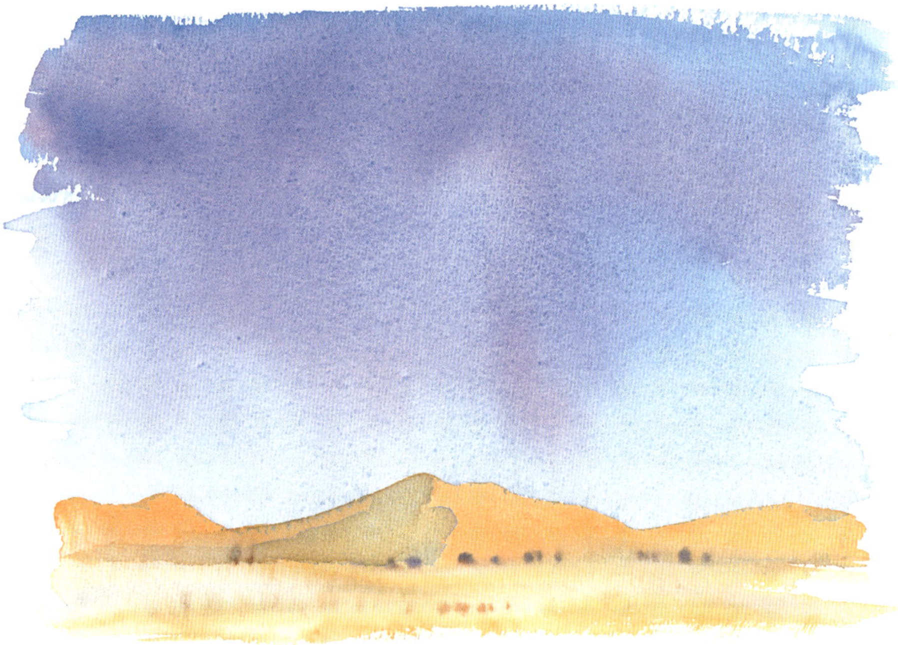

▲ A low horizon creates a large expanse of sky with a narrow strip of land. This is ideal for an empty landscape or a sunset, where the interest is in the sky.

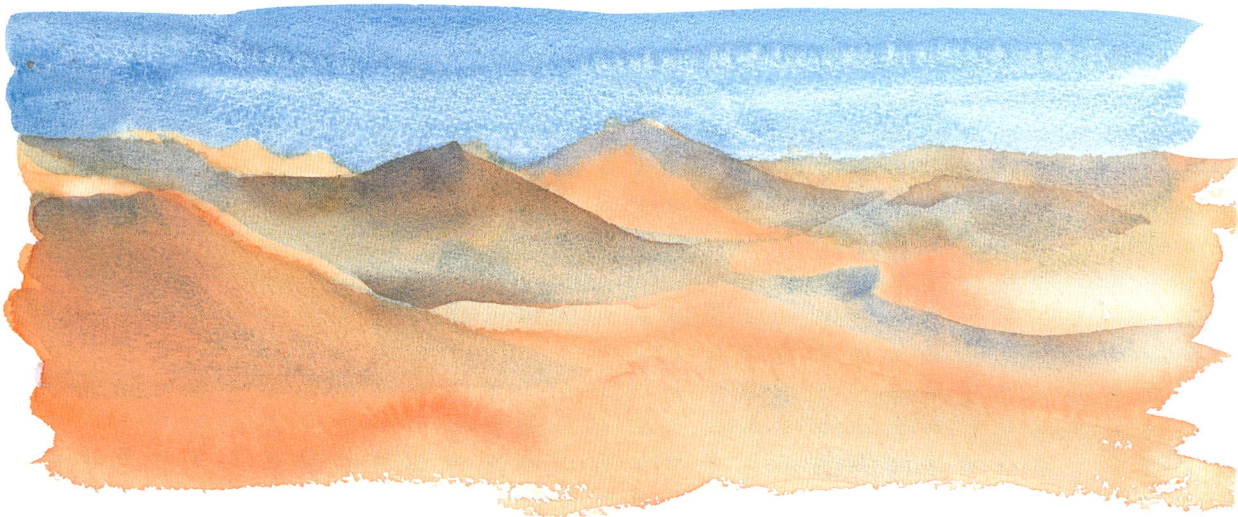

◄ A high horizon means you are effectively looking down on your view. A wide painting creates a panoramic vista.

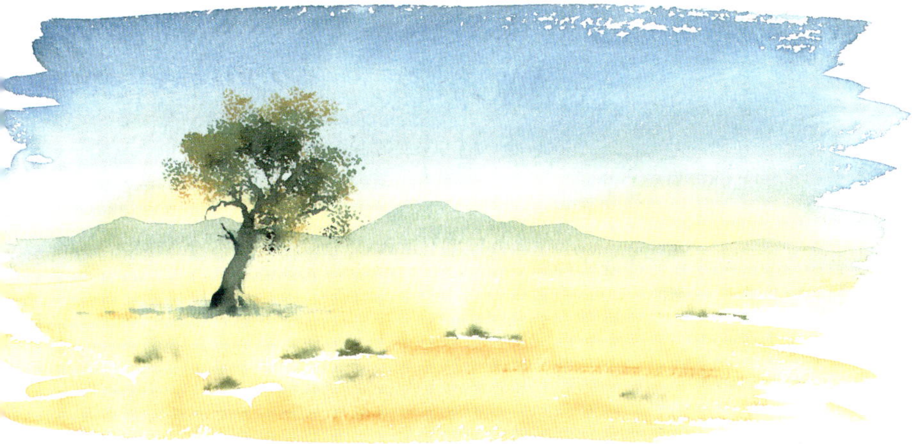

▲ *A single tree breaks the skyline and relieves the monotony of this empty landscape.*

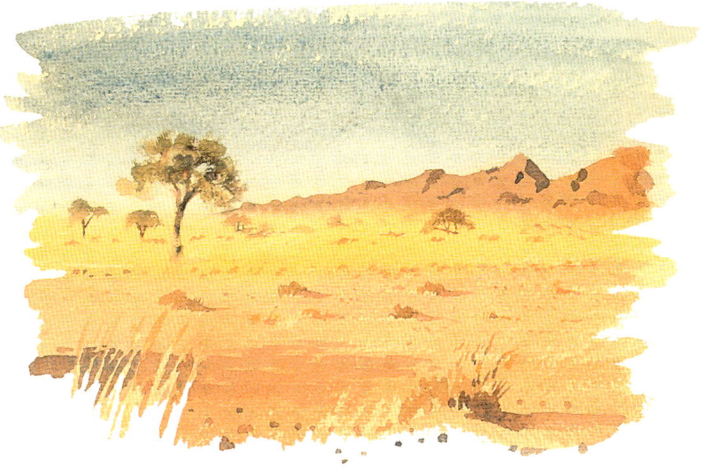

▲ *The tree breaks the horizon to the far left and is balanced by the mountains to the right.*

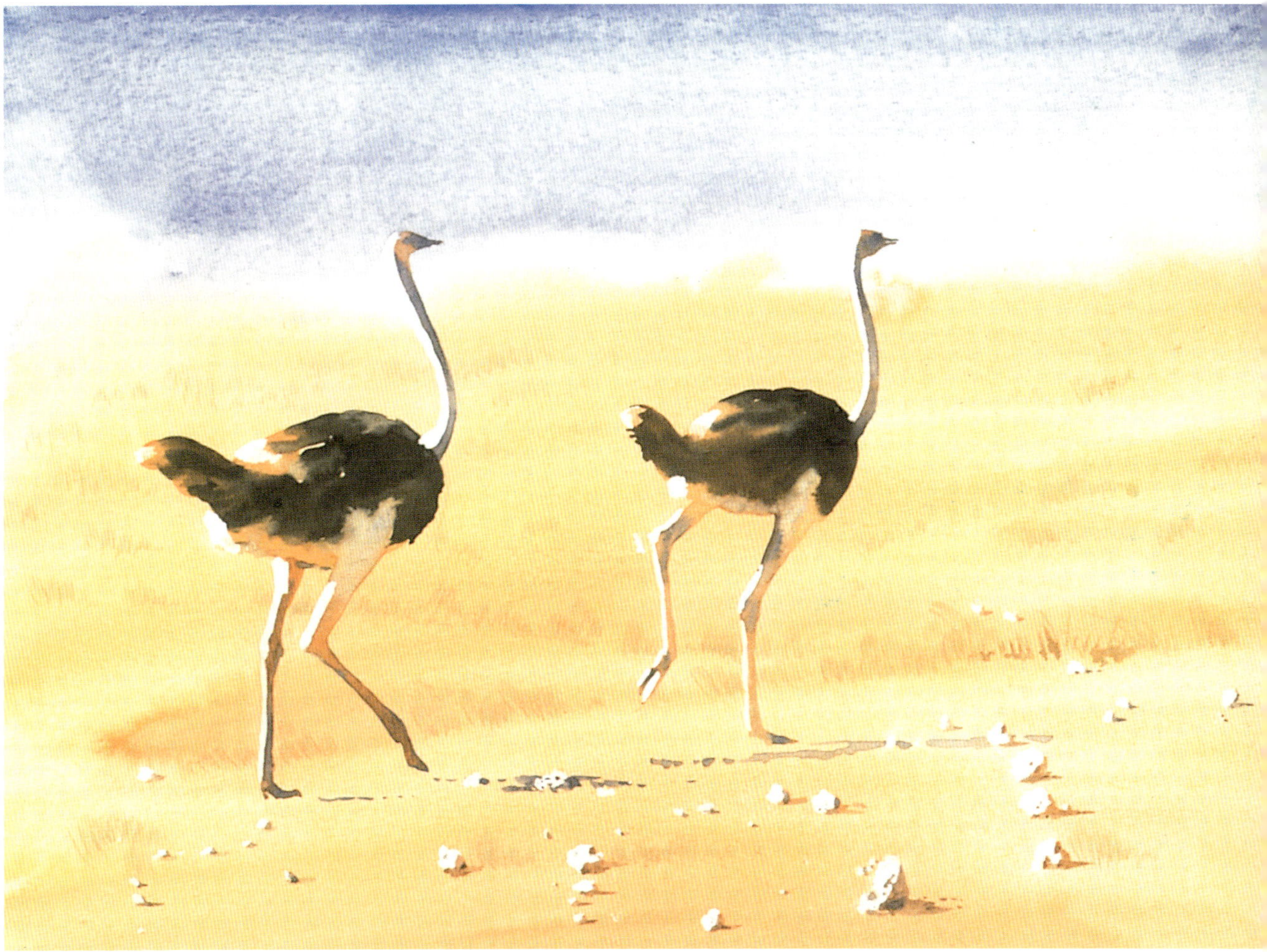

► DESERT STRIDE
20 x 28 cm (8 x 11 in)
The duo of ostriches break a blurred horizon to create a simple, yet striking, composition. The arid terrain is suggested by a few stones in the foreground.

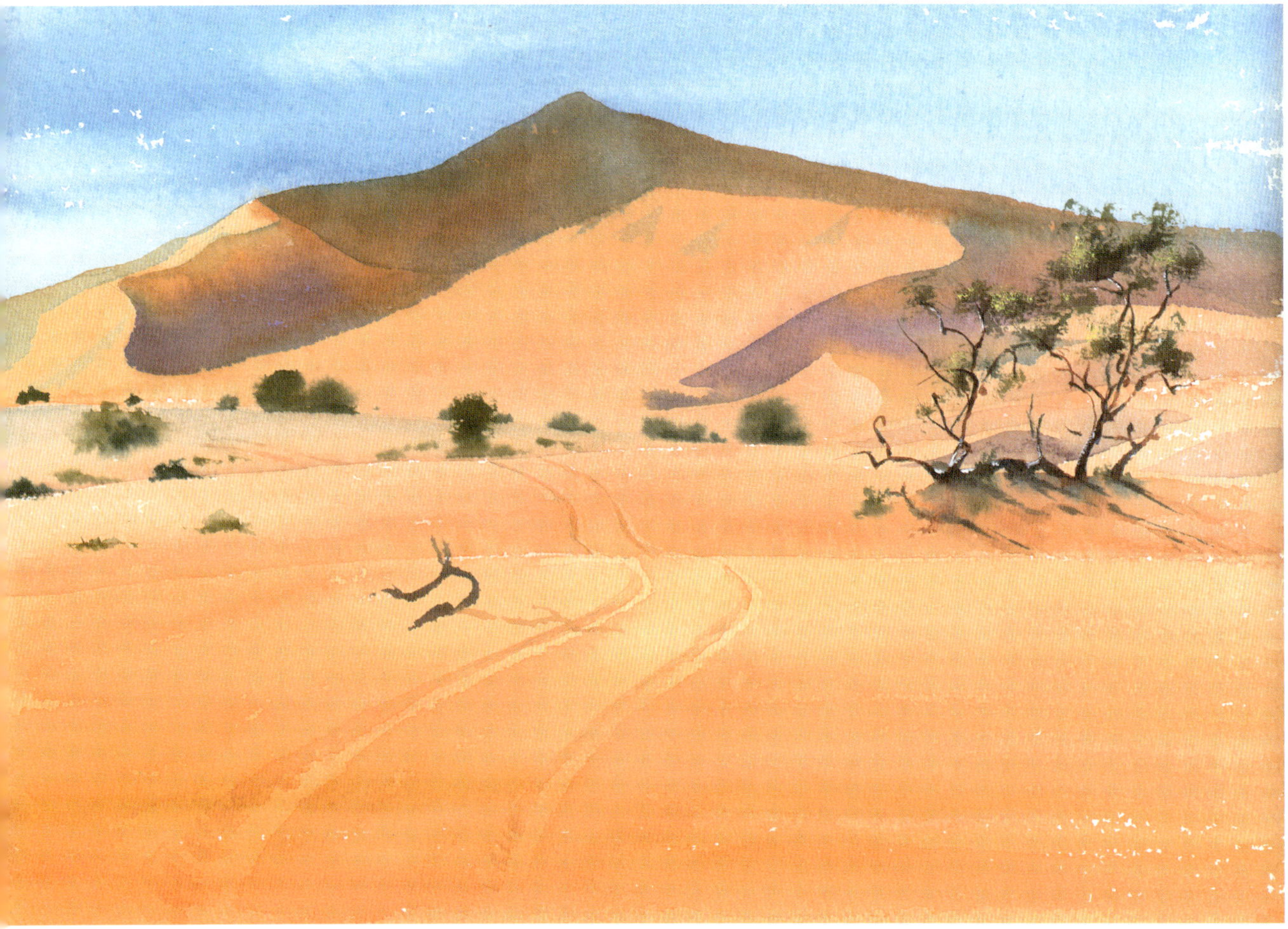

◄ THE DUNE SEA

28 x 36 cm (11 x 14 in)

The track of the tyres leads the viewer over the waves of sand towards the mighty dunes. The eye is drawn back across the painting by the strong emphasis of stark trees on the right.

▼ *Lead lines do not need to be obvious. In this quick sketch the avenue effect of the trees takes the eye from the foreground back to the dune in the distance.*

Leading the eye

Often the desire to turn a view into a painting occurs because you are attracted to a good composition already existing within the landscape. It may be a satisfying balance of shapes, colours or tones, or it could be natural 'lines' that lead the eye to a feature in the landscape, or 'flow lines' that carry the eye through the scene.

To draw the viewer into a painting artists use 'leading lines', and merely suggesting them is enough to direct the eye.

Careful positioning of the main features will make stronger compositions. Plan your painting to take advantage of your main interest. Place the focal point where you want the viewer to enter the picture.

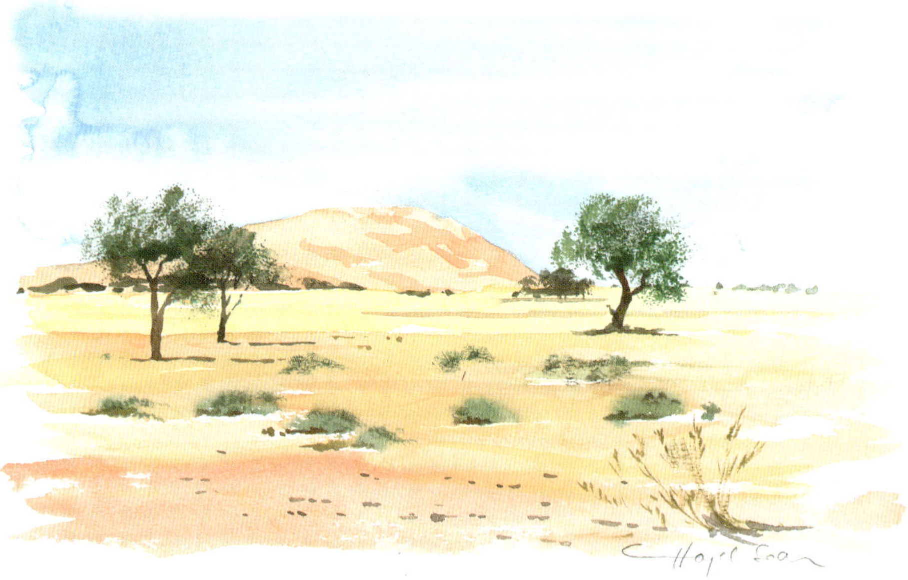

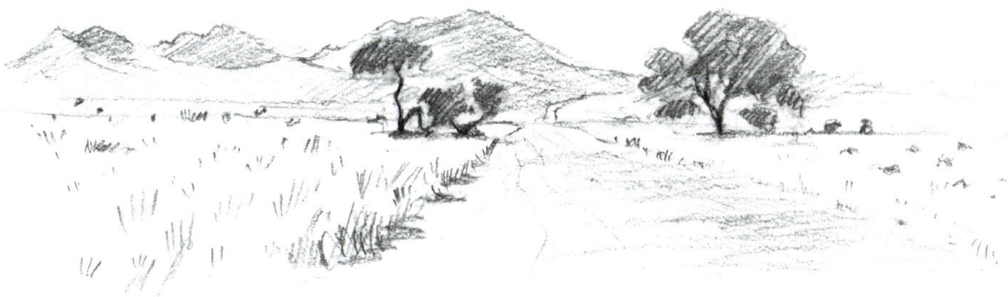

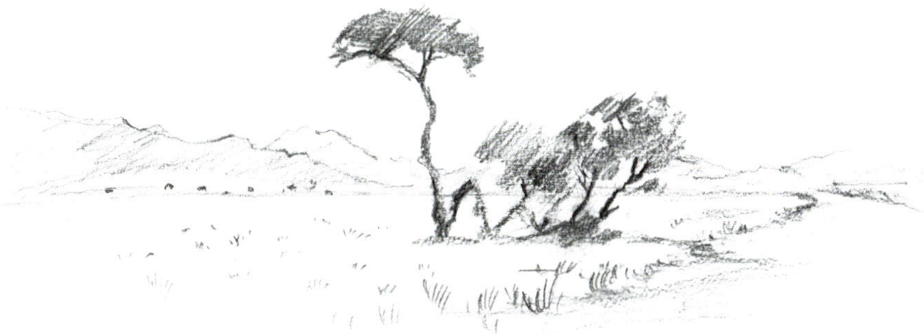

You may need to be selective, which means leaving out elements that distract the viewer. This is especially important if you are painting from photographs; the tendency is to include everything, as the camera does. You will find it is easier to be selective if you are working directly from life, especially as lack of time and changing light force you make decisions faster.

Attracting attention

A moving or active feature in a landscape will act as a pivotal point in the painting. The eye will follow the direction towards which the moving object is going or looking. If the direction of movement is towards the centre of the painting it will lead the eye into the rest of the picture, but if the direction of movement looks outward it will lead the eye out of the painting.

▲ *Selection may involve homing in on your subject. These sketches are made from two photographs taken from the same spot. In the second I zoomed in with a long lens and, by focusing in on a point of interest, found a more dynamic composition.*

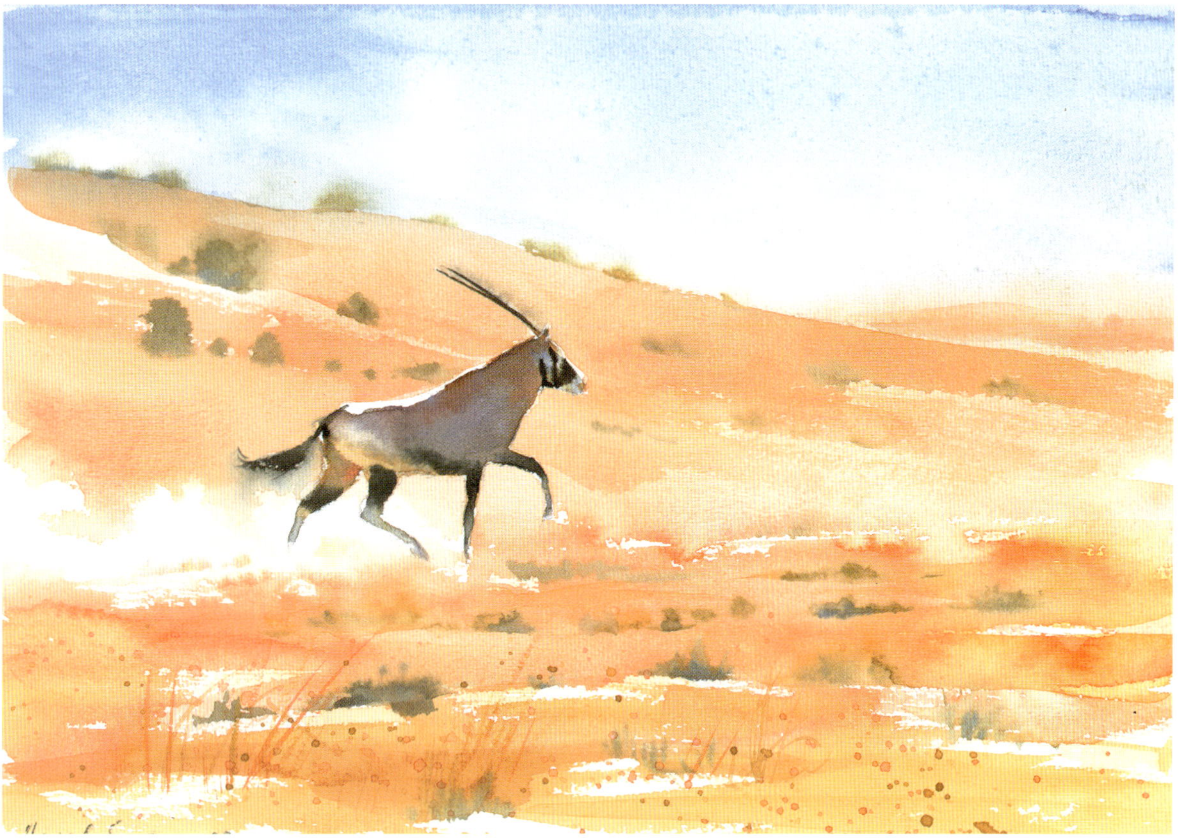

► THE SOUND OF SPEED
25 x 36 cm (10 x 14 in)
Placing the oryx on the left, running to the right, ensures that the eye is carried into the painting and not out of it.

Safari sketchbook

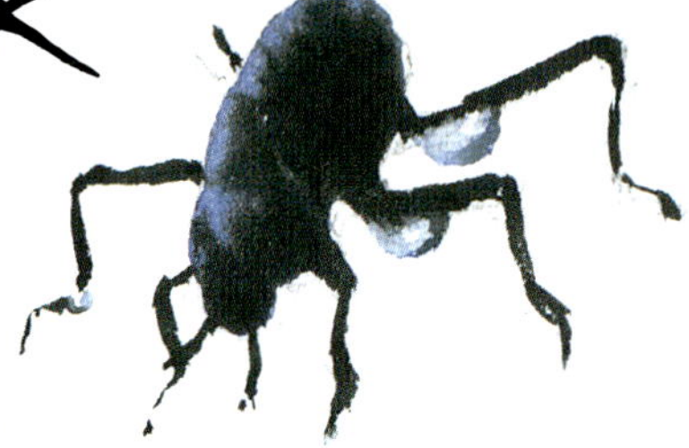

Fog-basking beetles scramble to the crest of the dunes and stand head downward facing the wind, allowing the fog to condense on their bodies and run directly down into their mouths.

Life-giving mist

Nothing should live in this desert – it is so hot that any liquid falling on the sand instantly evaporates – yet an astonishing number of life forms exist. Their provision is found in the mist that rolls over the dunes from the coast.

The welwitschia plant derives its water from the mist, its taproot probing 20 metres (60 ft) deep into the ground. Just two enormous leaves grow constantly outwards and fray into long ribbons with the wind.

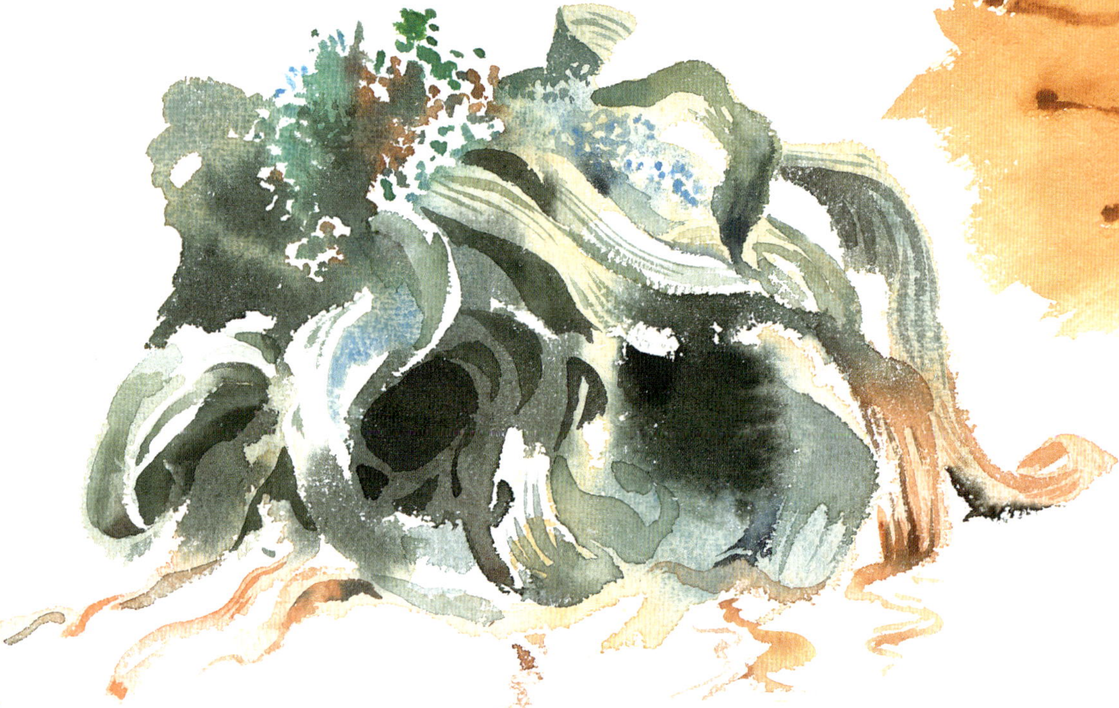

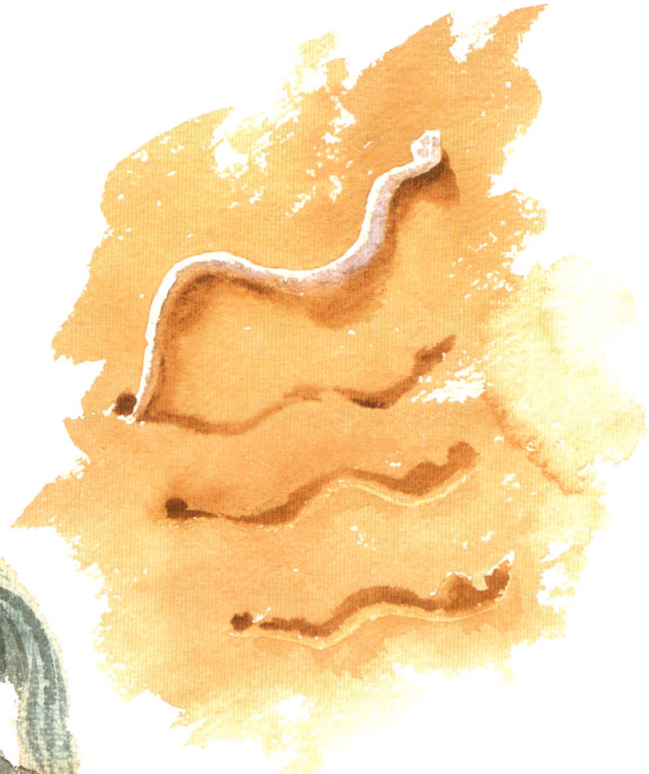

Sidewinder snakes lie in the mist and lick their own bodies.

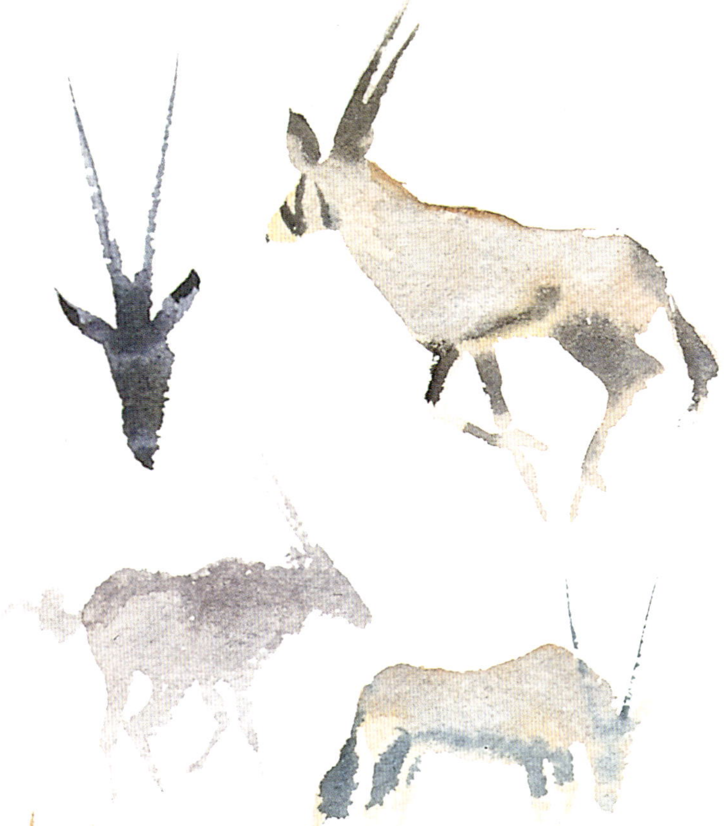

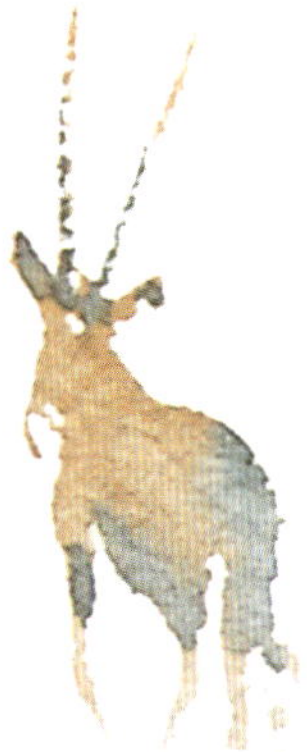

CAMPFIRE TALE

A celestial happening

The sun had set and we were enjoying supper under the indigo sky. The moon rose in the east and the stars began to shimmer in the clear desert air. As we watched the moon climbing in the sky its perfectly round shape became distorted on the lower side. It began to look as if part of the moon was dissolving. We watched puzzled, and then perturbed. In the comfort of urbanity the steadfast orbits of earth and moon are taken for granted, but here in the eerie loneliness of the desert anything seems possible and we began to feel the fear of primitive man. Were we witnessing an alteration in the heavenly spheres?

Imperceptibly slowly the moon, like cheese, was nibbled away by darkness until suddenly, to our relief, the invading shadow took on the obvious curve of an intervening planet — Earth! The reassurance that we were witnessing an eclipse dawned on us like healing balm and made us realize just how vulnerable early man must have felt in his lack of cosmic knowledge.

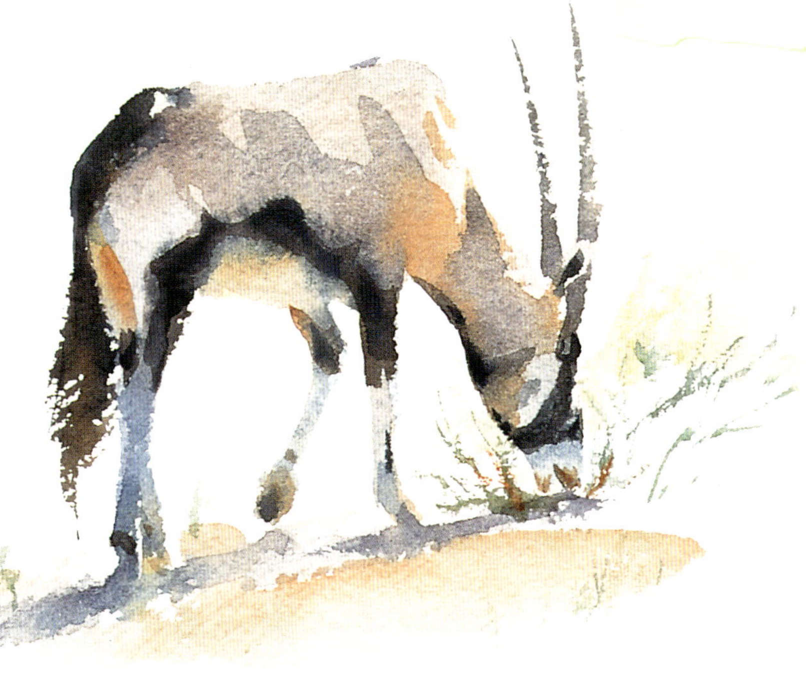

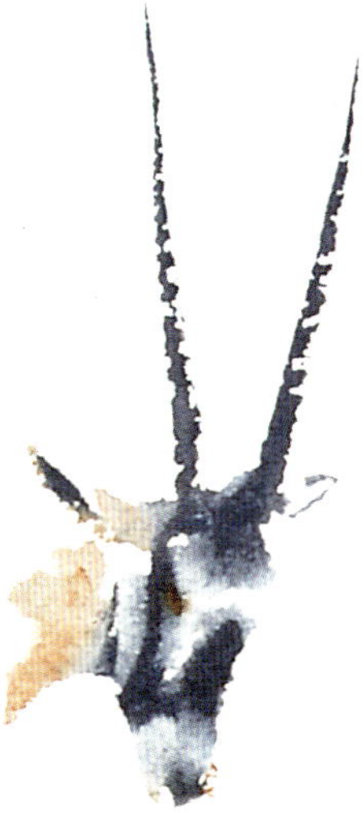

With a lack of water holes, the oryx often derives its liquid from the juice of the narra melon.

Desolate Coastline:

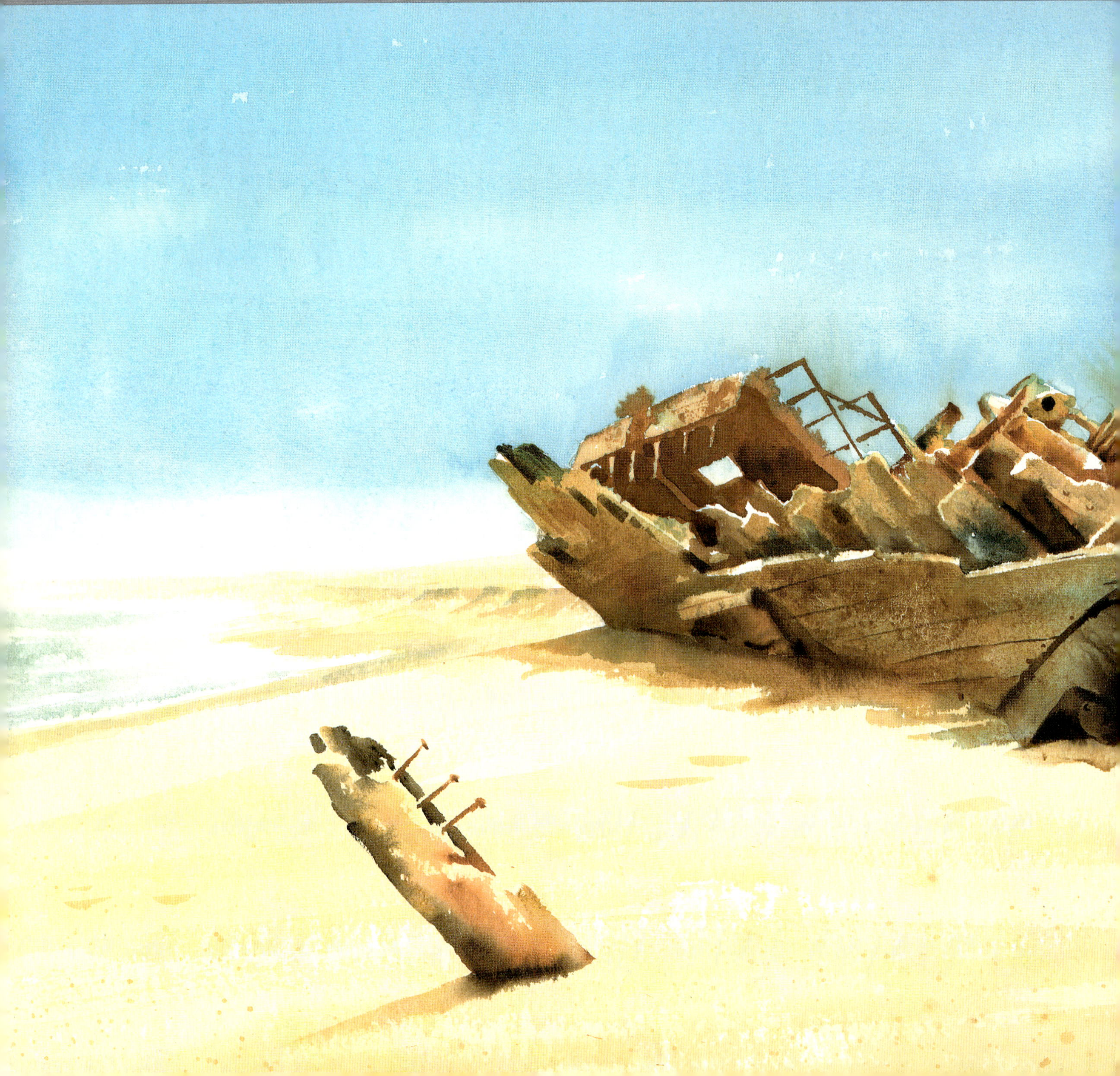

The Skeleton Coast

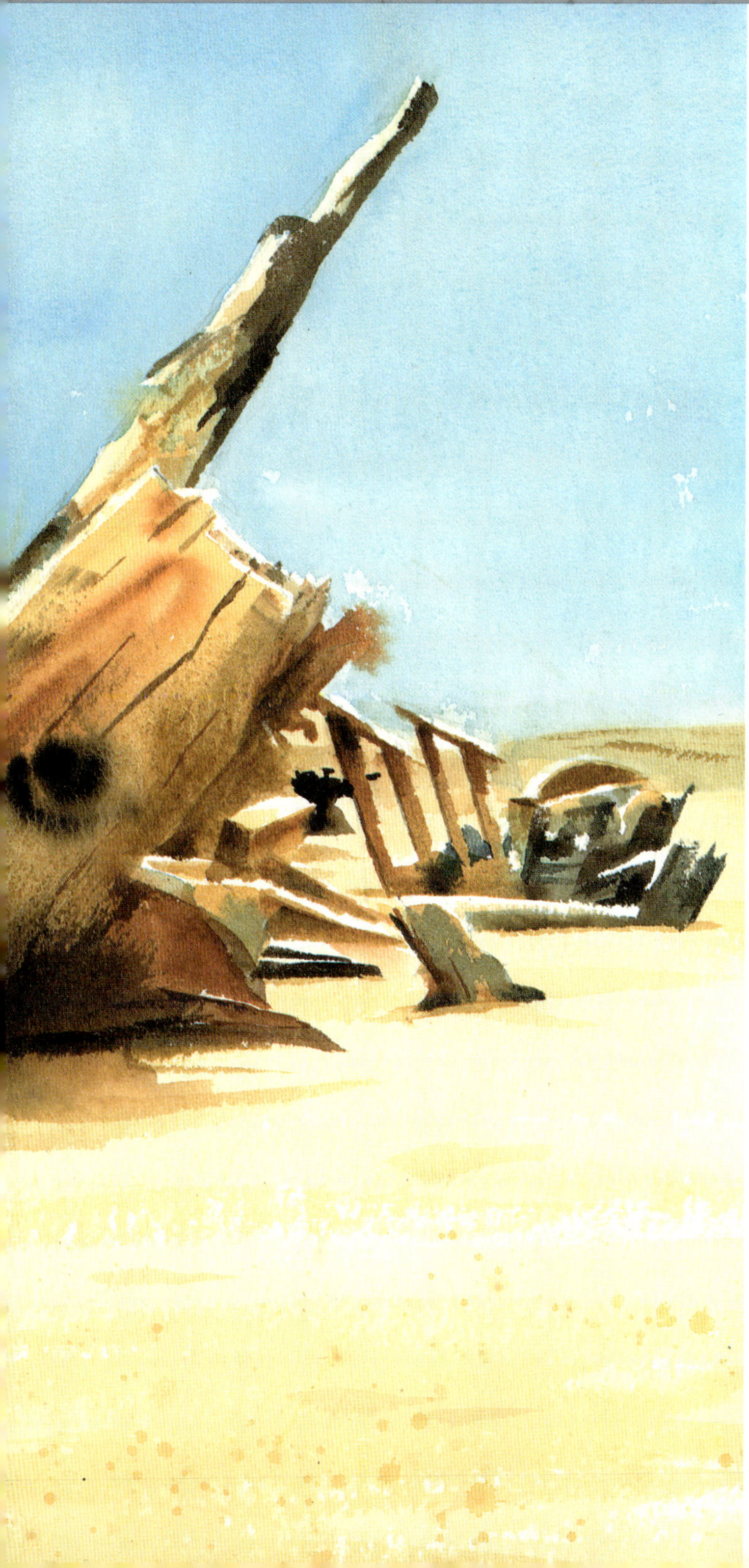

Conveying an atmosphere

Feckless coastline hide your grin,
shield the horror held within.
The many skulls you dare to hide
were lovers of a carefree bride.
Shame on you, you coast of death:
your spine, their bones;
your mist, their breath.

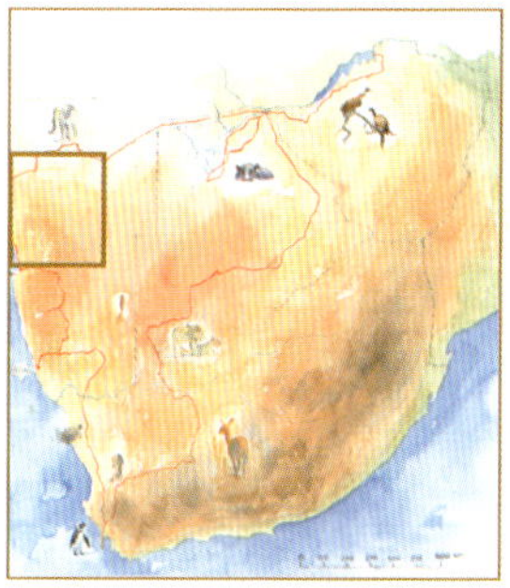

◄ SILENT ECHOES
38 x 56 cm (15 x 22 in)

Shifting sands

As the desert coast continues northward the dunes are interrupted suddenly by the bed of the Kuiseb river. The landscape remains desolate and the splendour of the dune country disappears and gives way to a bleak emptiness.

Shipwrecks dotted along the coastline are testimony to treacherous seas and shifting sandbanks. Mists sweep in across the cold sea, intensifying the formidable solitude. Sunbaked by day, shivering by night, this barren terrain does not welcome life; no rain falls and there is no surface water other than a few salty springs.

Oases of life

Africa is always full of surprises and along this forbidding shore one or two pockets of life appear like oases in the desert. At Walvis Bay the buried delta of the Kuiseb River forms a lagoon that teams with aquatic birds. Flamingos and pelicans wheel across the sandbanks, making a spectacular display of silhouettes against the setting sun. To the south, the lagoon is

▼ **SHIPWRECK**
28 x 36 cm (11 x 14 in)
It is said that a picture speaks a thousand words. There can be few more eloquent subjects than the skeleton of a ship that has been wrecked.

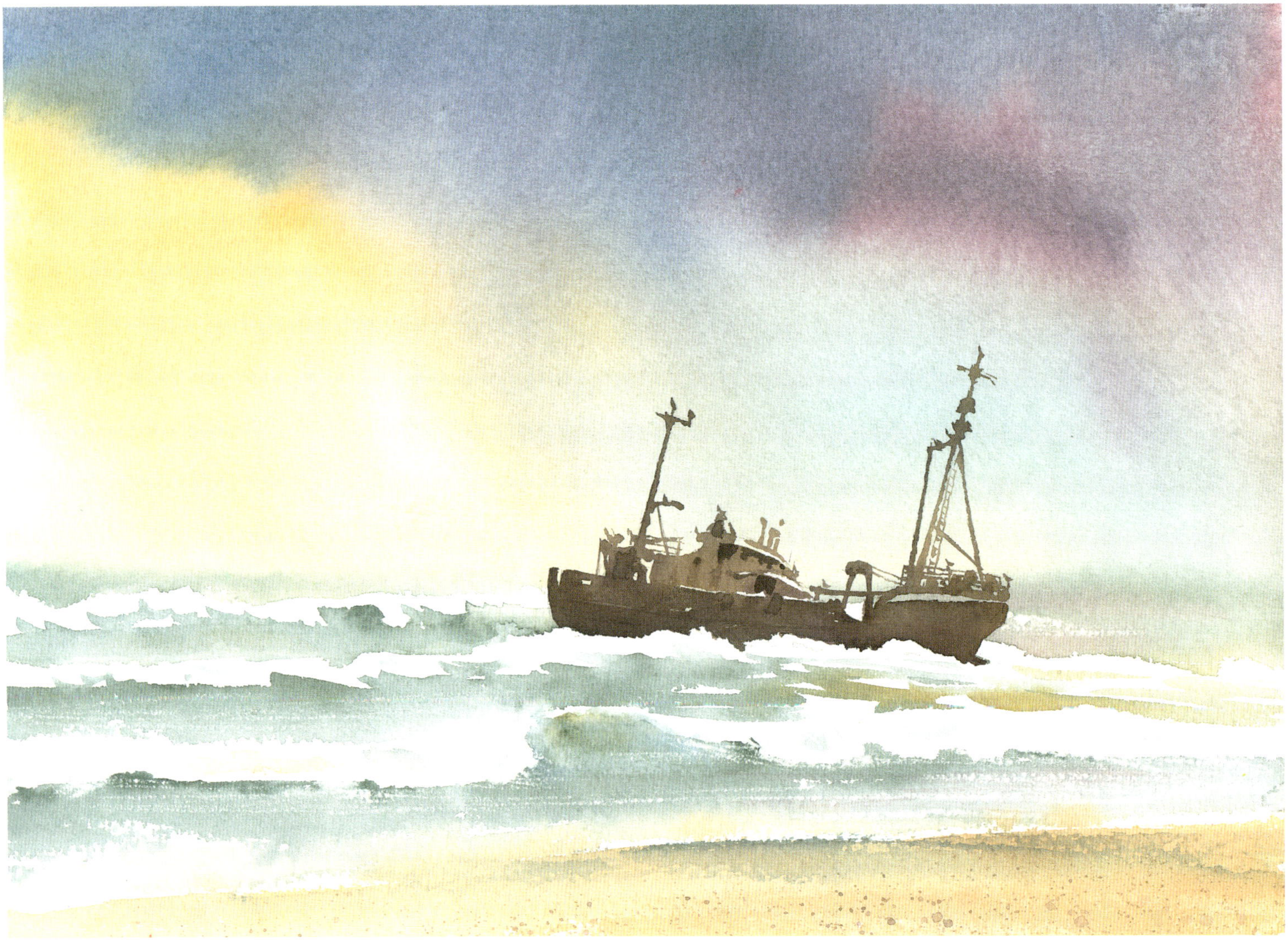

► OASIS IN THE DESERT
56 x 48 cm (22 x 19 in)
The late-afternoon sun warms up the colours of the west-facing dunes as the pelicans fly in to gather in large noisy groups in the lagoon at Sandwich Bay.

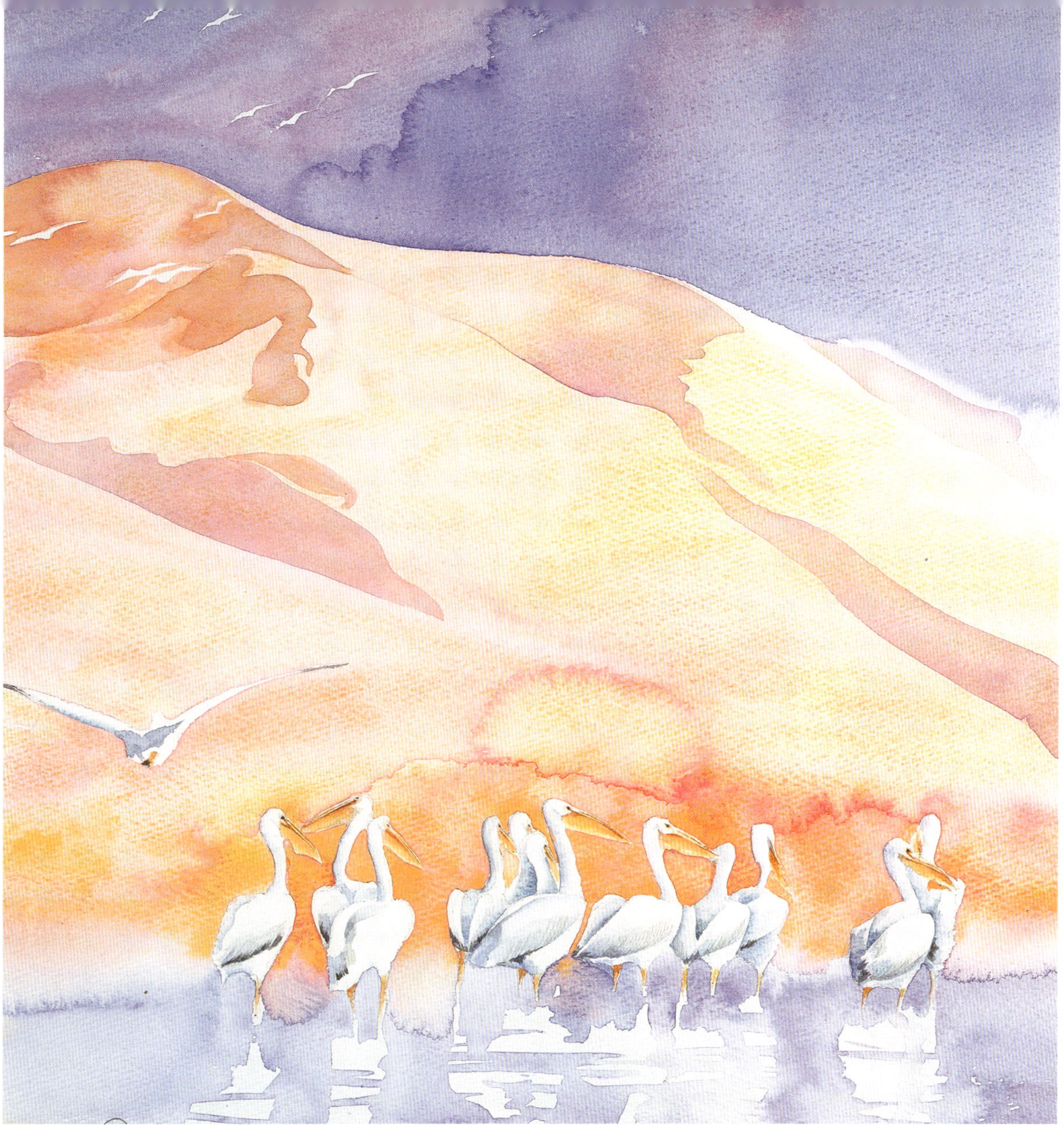

▼ *The lumbering seals appear quite comical on land, but on entering the water they become at once sleek and graceful.*

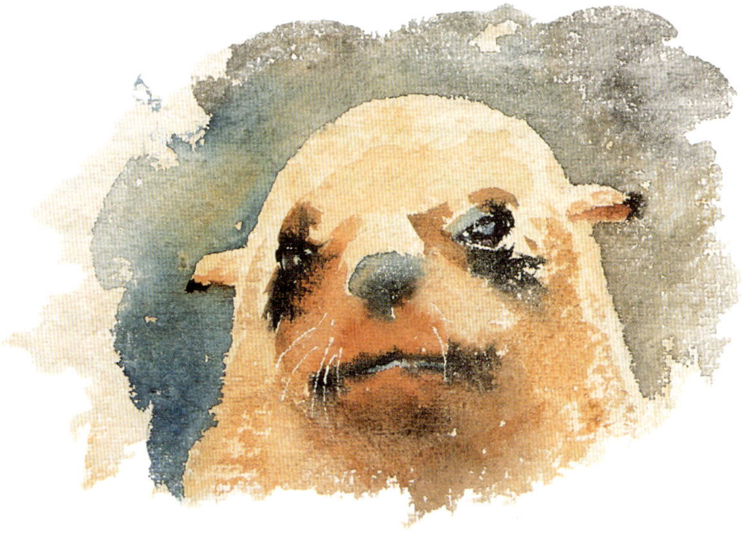

backed by yellow dunes. Pelicans fly overhead while their shadows undulate across the parabolic curves below.

On Cape Cross, further north, tens of thousands of Cape fur seals flourish in the cold waters of the Benguela Current. They crowd together on the islets, heralded by a pungent aroma and a cacophony of barks. Having a whole coastline to colonize, they choose instead to live so closely packed together that they have to clamber over each other to reach the sea.

Tangible atmosphere

In this landscape the oranges give way to ochres and browns. The blue of the sky becomes colder, and French Ultramarine is exchanged for Manganese Blue and Coeruleum. A thousand miles from the lush greens and blues of the Cape, earth colours eventually predominate, creating a cooler atmosphere in the paintings.

Beyond the sporadic outbursts of wildlife there is little to paint but the shipwrecks and the sea. The reds of the flamingos' wings and the yellow of the pelicans' beaks are welcome touches of colour in this bleak terrain. One moment you can see forever and then suddenly the mist rolls in, obscuring all but the sand at your feet. Occasionally the odd jackal provides a subject to paint as he skitters across the sand or skulks, head down in search of titbits, padding noiselessly in this silent place that is his home.

Stormy skies, with the lights and darks of rolling clouds, are desirable interludes in this featureless land, bringing with them the hope of colourful sunsets and the chance to use wonderful wet-in-wet washes, backruns and a contrast of tone.

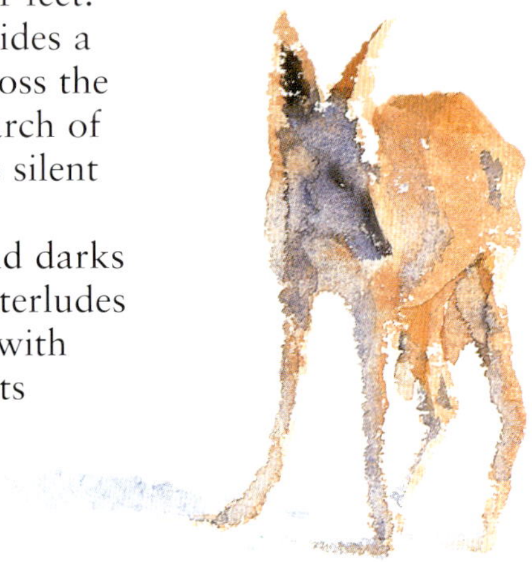

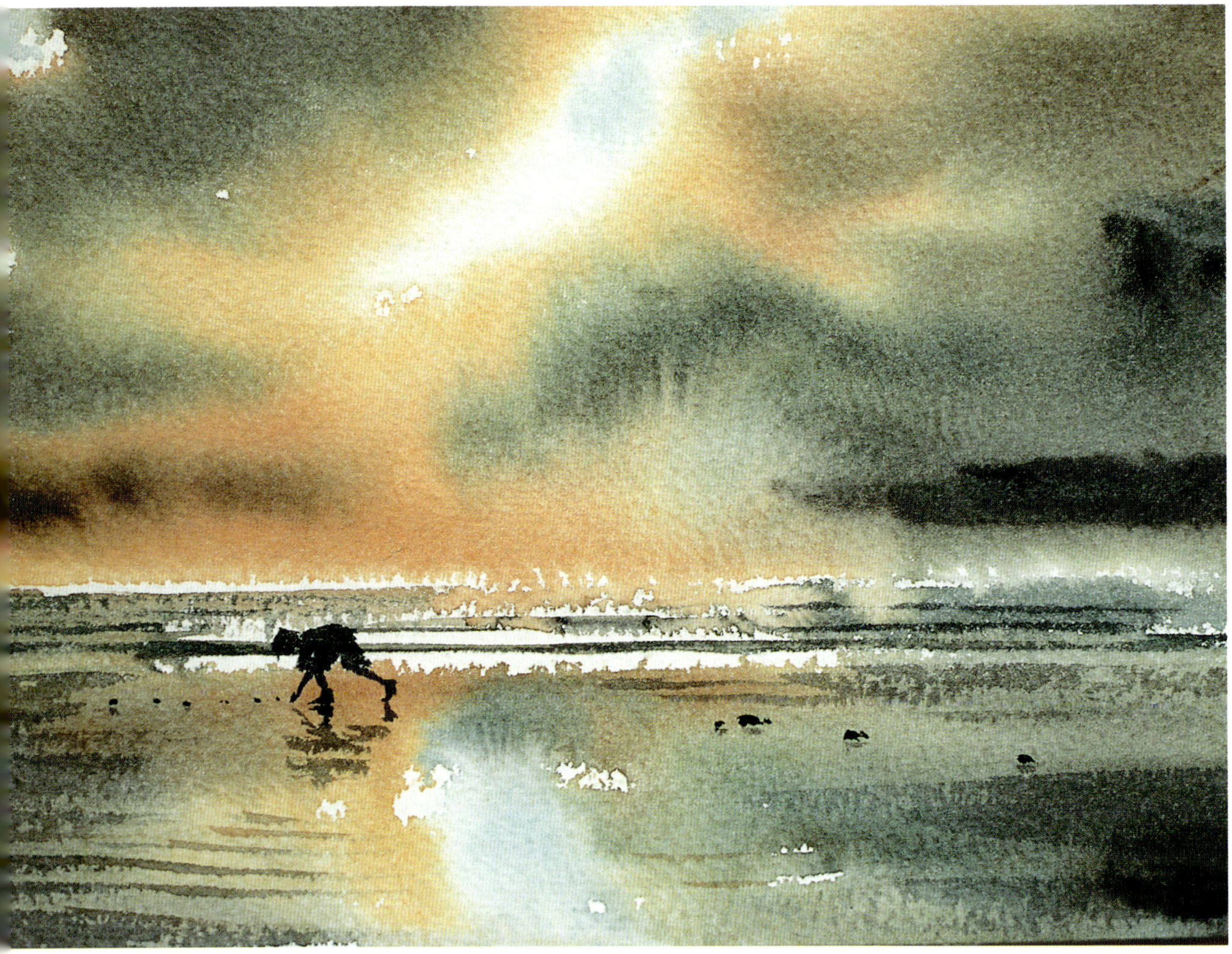

◀ THE CLOUDS ARE BREAKING
28 x 36 cm (11 x 14 in)
Raw Sienna, Sepia and Indigo are blended in a variegated wash to create the soft forms of the clouds and their reflection in the wet sand. The warmer colours break into the dark sombre tones, creating an atmosphere of hope within the gloom.

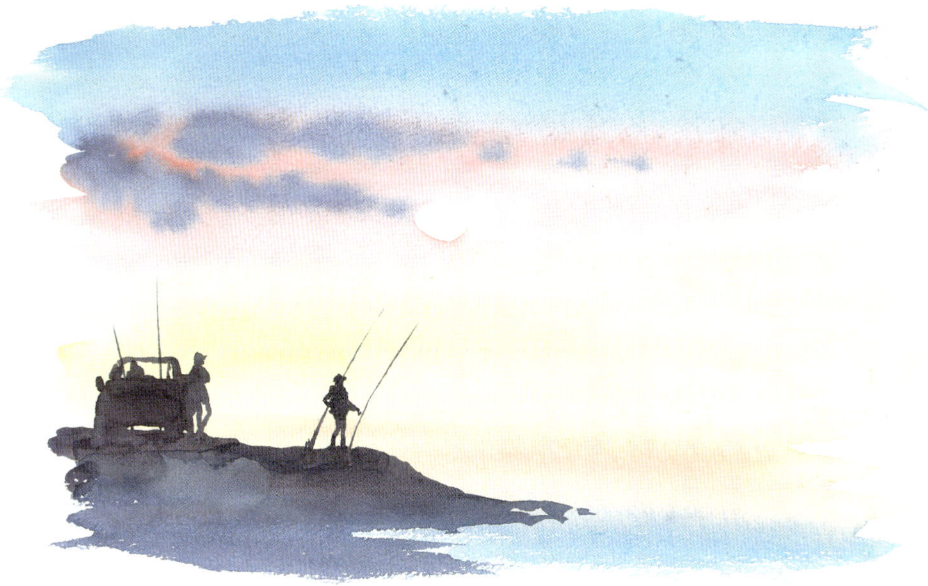

Blurred horizons

Although the sun is hot, the proximity to the cold ocean dampens the paper and the watercolours take noticeably longer to dry. The horizon is indistinct, blurred by the pounding surf and the threads of hazy mist. Here, too, the colours of the sea and sky can be blended wet-in-wet, or the horizon can be softened by lifting out the pigment with a sponge when the washes are dry.

The sense of atmosphere along the Skeleton Coast is profound. It is eerie rather than gloomy, mysterious but not recondite. By painting with stark shapes and similar tones, using cool colours from the palette, the sense of atmosphere can be conveyed in the paintings.

▲ THE PATIENT DUSK
18 x 30 cm (7 x 12 in)
The pale translucent colours of the sky and the intrusion of the fishermen on the bluff carry an appropriate sense of isolation.

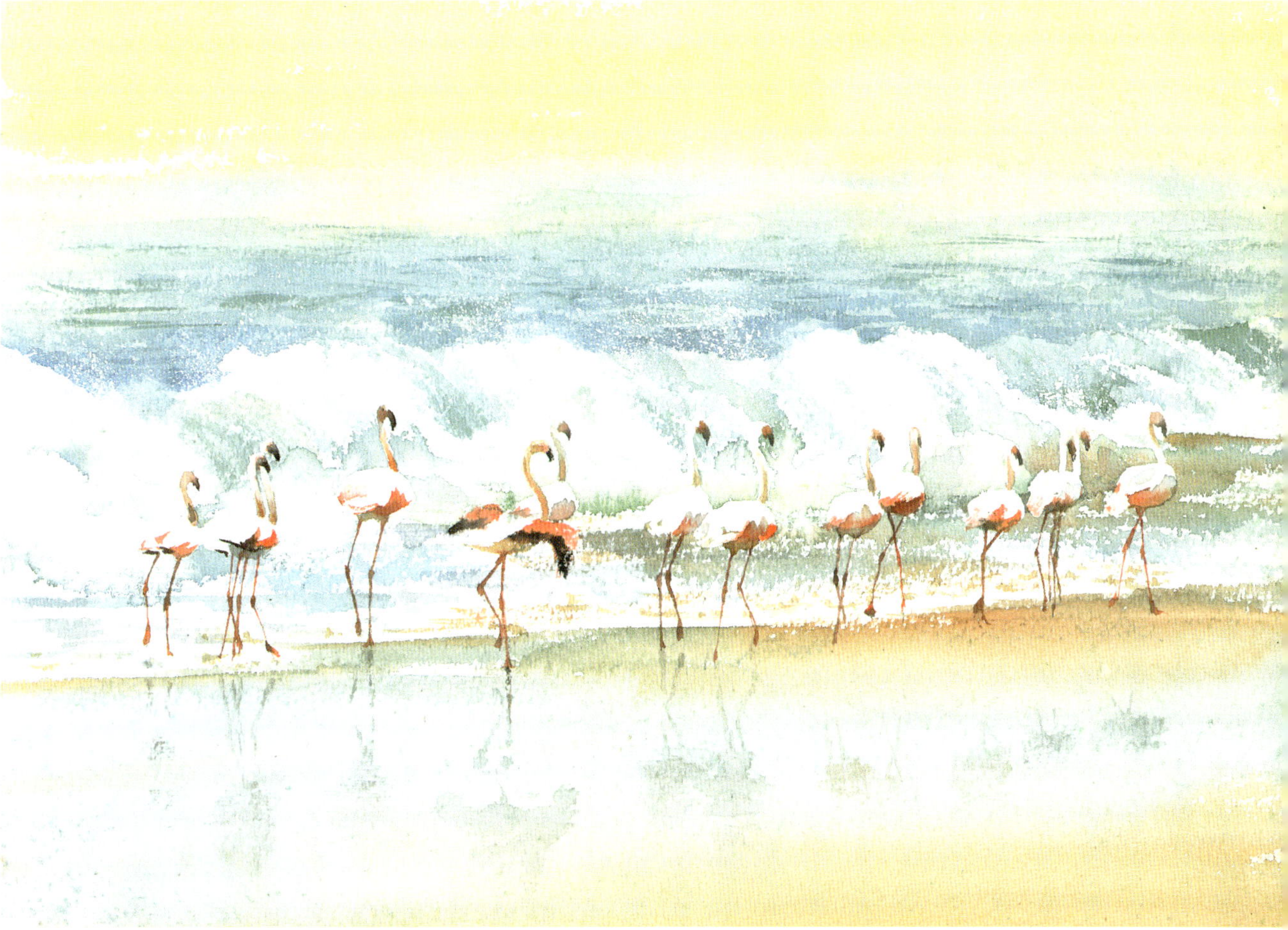

► PARADE
25 x 38 cm (10 x 15 in)
The graceful lines of the birdlife are a welcome contrast to the empty landscape. Simple backgrounds mean you can concentrate solely on the shapes and forms of the birds.

Conveying an atmosphere

All the elements of watercolour covered in the preceding chapters – tone, colour, composition – help contribute to the atmosphere conveyed by a painting, but there are also other factors you can use to influence the mood you want to create.

Evocative subject matter

Certain subjects are more suggestive than others. In the desolate landscape of the Skeleton Coast the empty space, overcast skies and scattered shipwrecks contribute directly to the mood portrayed.

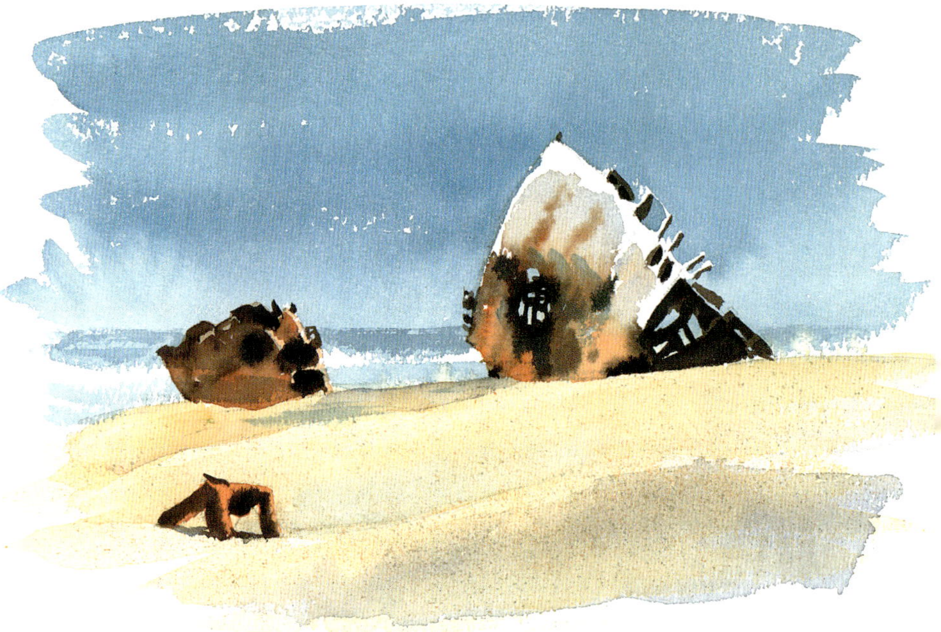

▲ *A shipwreck spells doom and despair.*

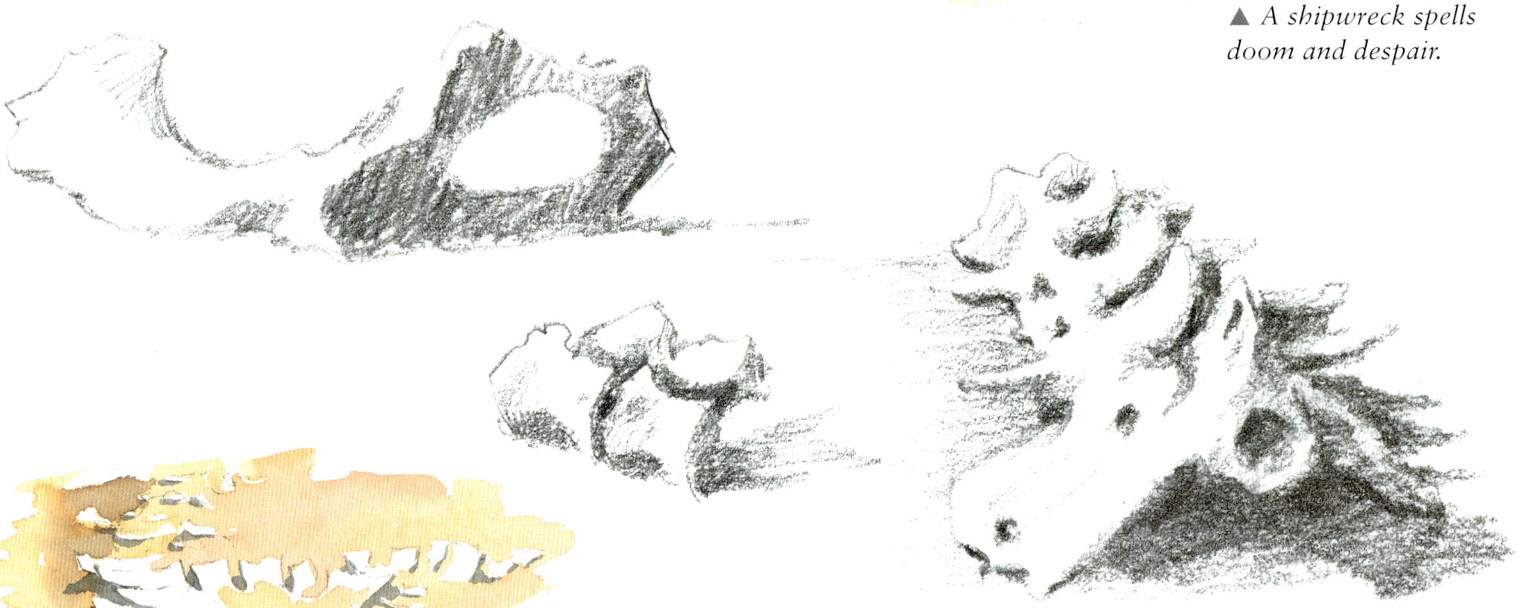

▲ *Bleached bones bring to mind the fragility of life.*

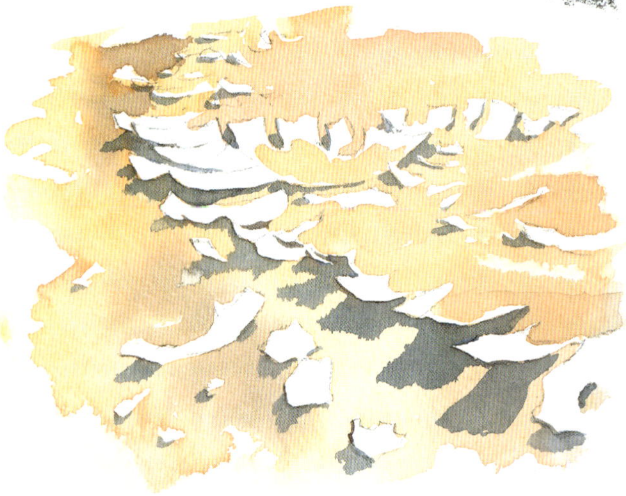

◄ *A cracked layer of dried silt takes on the appearance of skeletal remains and carries ominous overtones.*

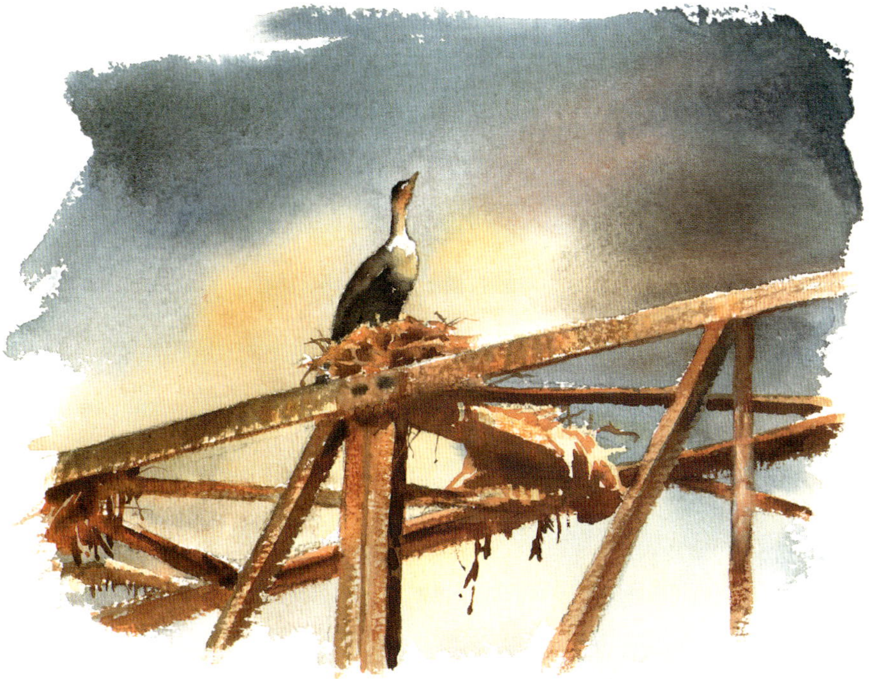

Angle and scale

The angle at which you look at an object can add or detract from its prominence and so influence the atmosphere you wish to convey. A foreground object viewed from a low angle will loom against the horizon and thus dominate the painting. The shipwreck in the painting opposite, for example, would have less prominence if viewed from a higher angle.

The scale of items in a painting can be used to dramatize atmosphere. By making a foreground feature large you give it a greater presence than it would otherwise have. Alternatively, if you want the landscape to dominate, keep the features within it small and they will become less significant, enlarging the scene.

▲ *Both the low angle of view and the darkening sky create a prescient mood to this painting of a cormorant nesting in the ruins of a rusting mine shaft.*

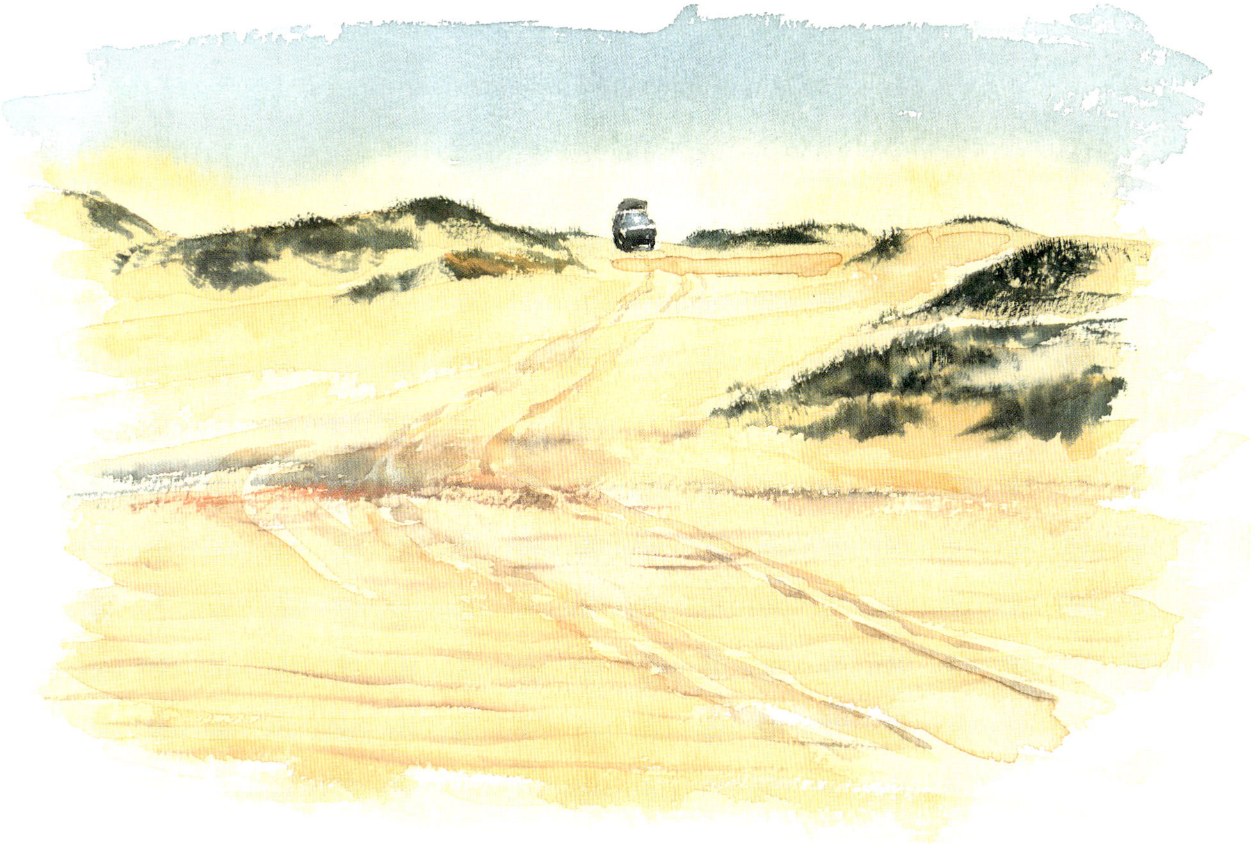

► *The small scale of the vehicle in the vast landscape creates a sense of isolation.*

Mood and temperature

The mood of a painting can also be controlled by the use of colour. Red, orange and yellow are traditionally happy, upbeat colours; green is calm and restful; blue can be gentle, but also hints at seriousness or melancholy; while black seems to suggest a more sombre note.

In painting colours are often referred to by their temperature. The reds and oranges, and colours that veer towards those hues, are warm colours, while blues and colours that tend towards blue are cool colours. A Yellow Ochre wash under a painting will warm up the atmosphere, while a pale blue wash will cool it down.

▼ BEATING WINGS
10 x 23 cm (4 x 9 in)
The reds and oranges of the sunset are palpably hot compared with the blue of the lagoon in the painting below.

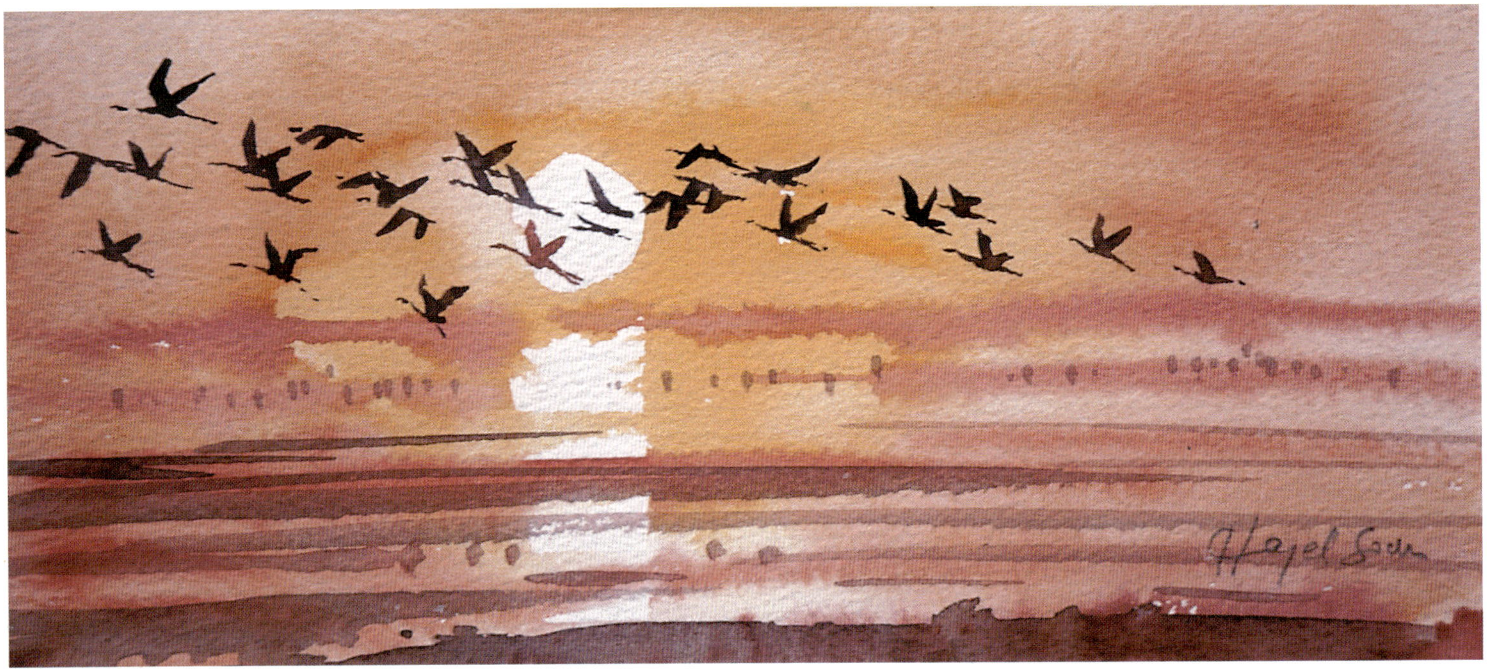

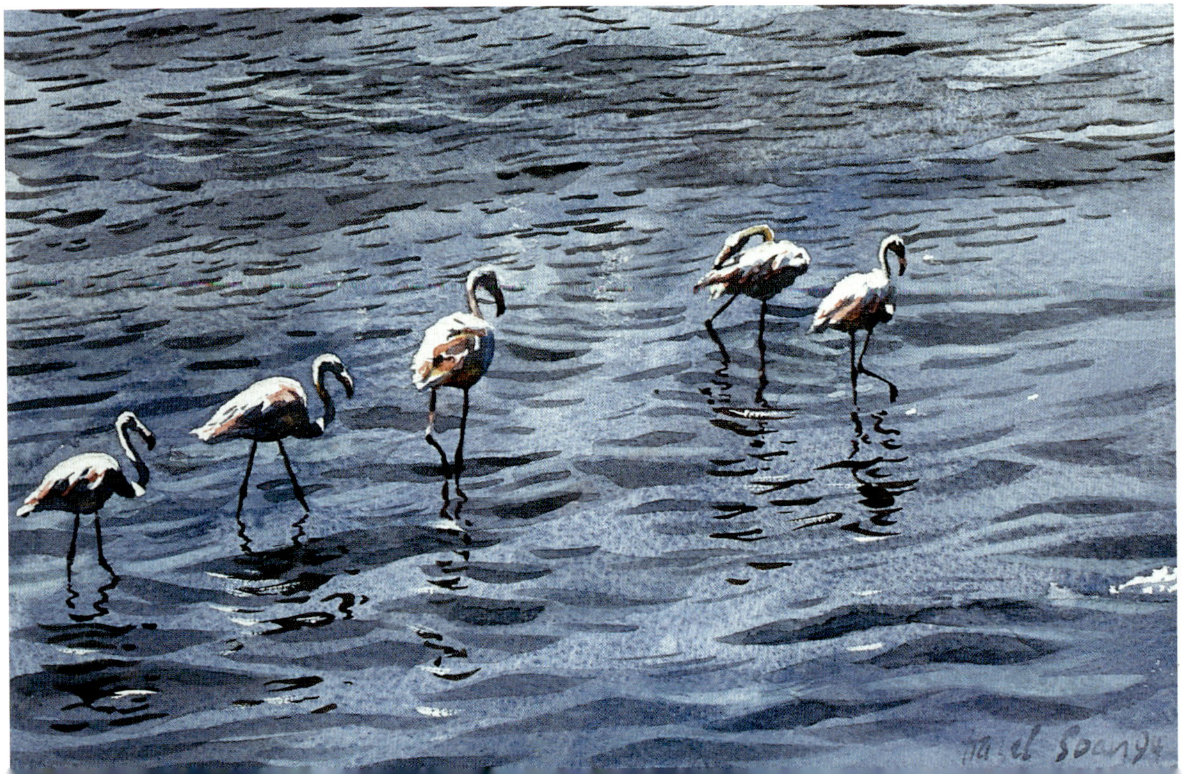

◄ BLUE LAGOON, WALVIS BAY
20 x 28 cm (8 x 11 in)
If a painting is a field of similar colour the atmosphere is readily conveyed. Here the high eye level brings the water across the entire picture plane. The colour of the sky above is reflected in the sea.

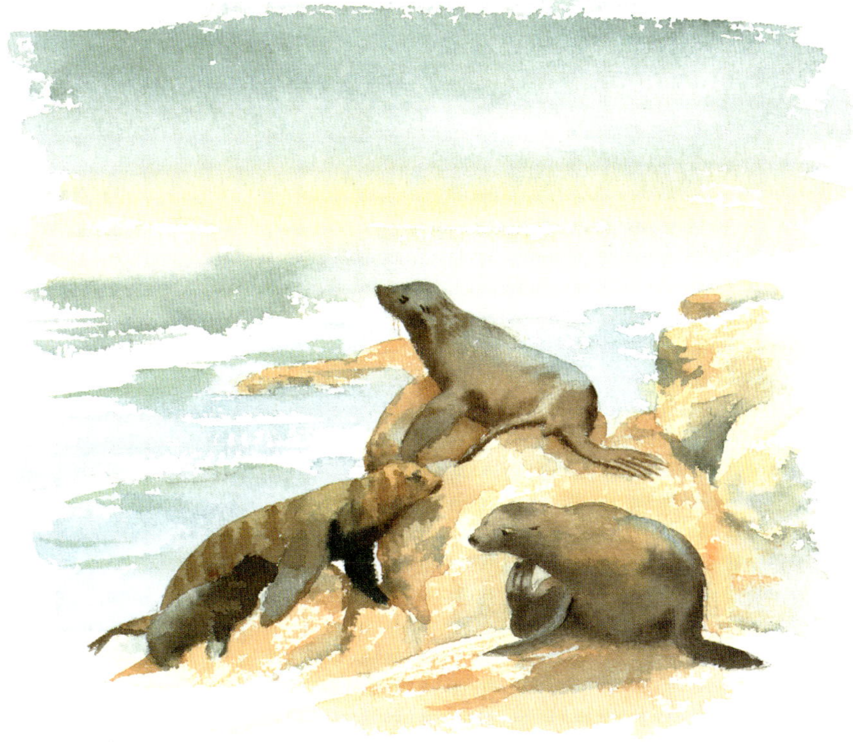

▲ *A cool blue (Prussian Blue) with a slightly warmer yellow (Yellow Ochre) and an overall pale tone create a gentle mood to this sketch.*

▼ *By using much stronger hues the intensity and drama of a sunset is portrayed.*

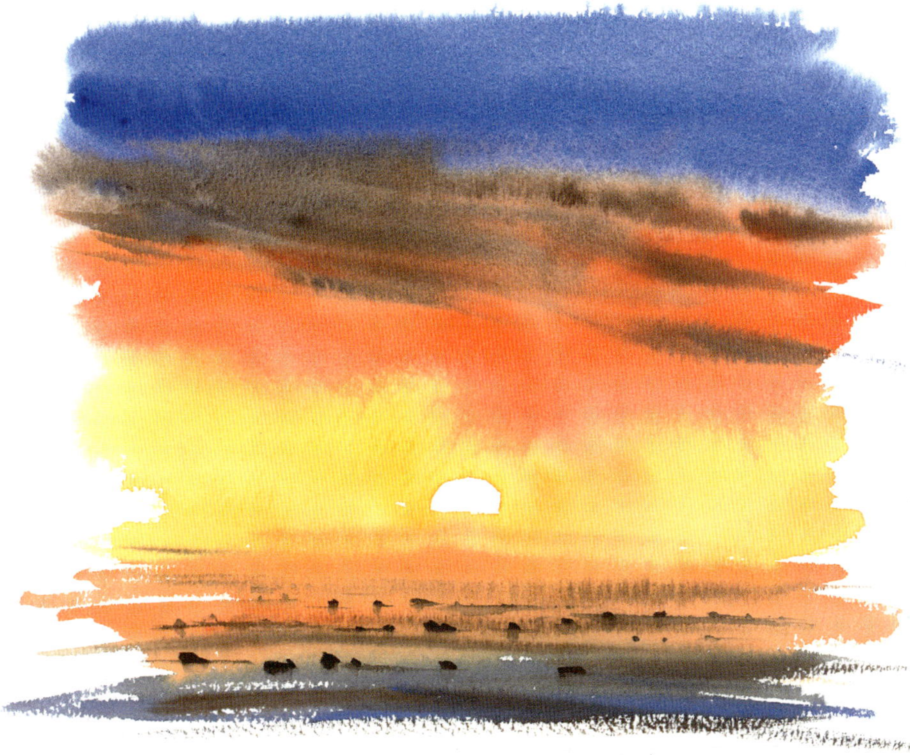

Strength of tone

Just as colours influence atmosphere, so tone plays its part in creating the mood you want to convey. Light tones represent a gentle, calm, or lighthearted mood, whereas dark tones contribute to a sense of gravitas, strength or drama.

Depending on how much water you add to your pigment, you can vary the tone of any watercolour hue by an enormous range. Some colours, especially the opaque colours, will even change in temperature as they are diluted.

Try to imagine the sunset painted with pale hues and the seals painted with stronger tones. What a different mood each painting would have.

In any palette it is a good idea to have a choice of a warm and cool version of any hue. Listed below is the set of colours I most often carry on safari.

Warm version	Cool version
Cadmium Red	Alizarin Crimson
French Ultramarine	Prussian Blue
Indian Yellow	Aureolin
Sap Green	Viridian
Burnt Sienna	Raw Umber
Sepia	Indigo

I also always carry Yellow Ochre, which I probably use more than any other colour as it can create both a lovely warm wash against blues or a cool counterfoil to reds.

When you blend a warm colour such as Cadmium Red with a cool colour such as Prussian Blue you can create lovely dark tones that convey a sense of black.

Safari sketchbook

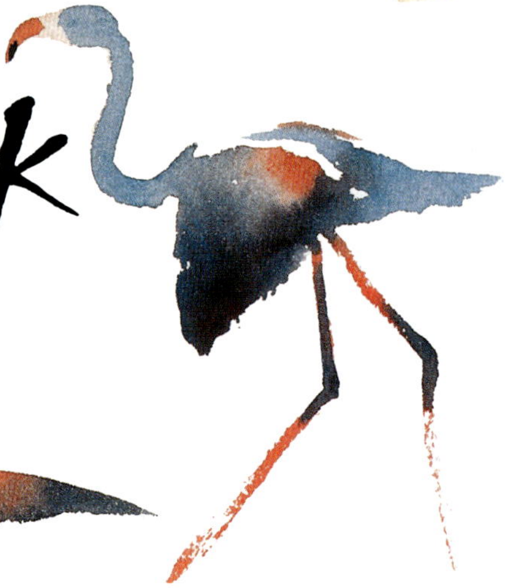

Wings over water

All day the graceful shapes of the flamingos parade on the lagoons. Their elegant proportions make them particularly attractive to paint. The pelicans appear more clumsy than the flamingos as they land and take off upon the shallow water. I love the way the body shapes of both these big birds change so dramatically with wings outstretched in flight.

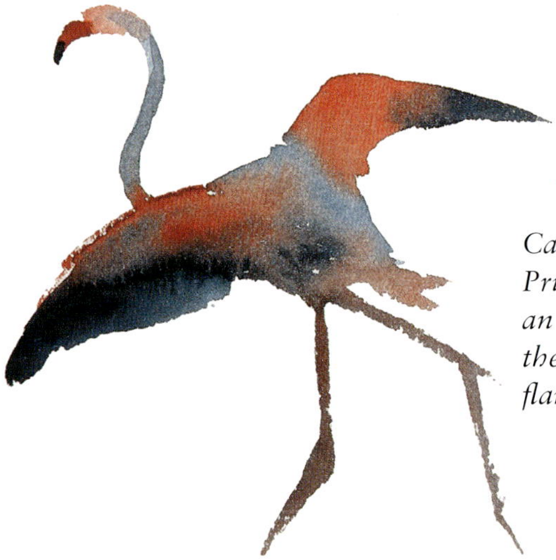

Cadmium Red and Prussian Blue blend to an elegant black for the wingtips of these flamingos.

Prussian Blue and Raw Sienna create the cool waters of the lagoon.

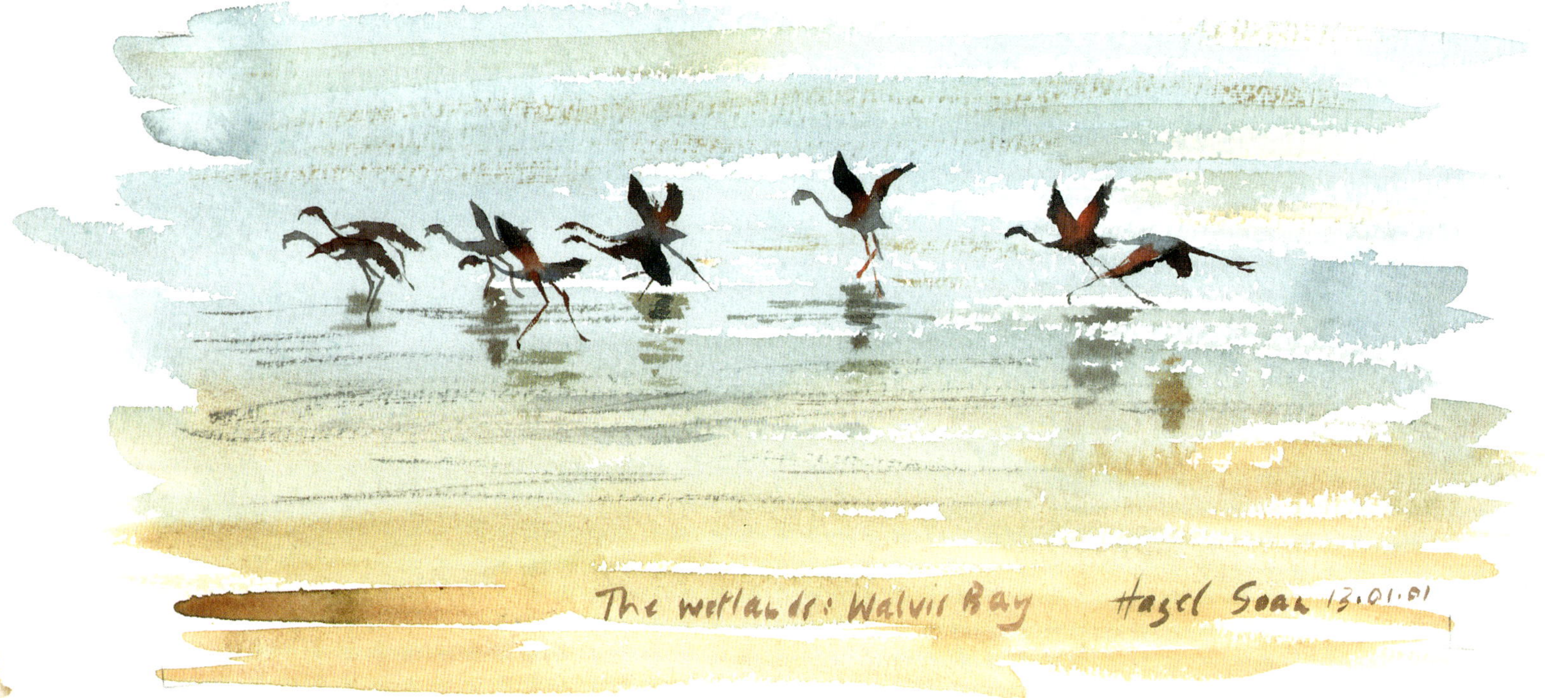

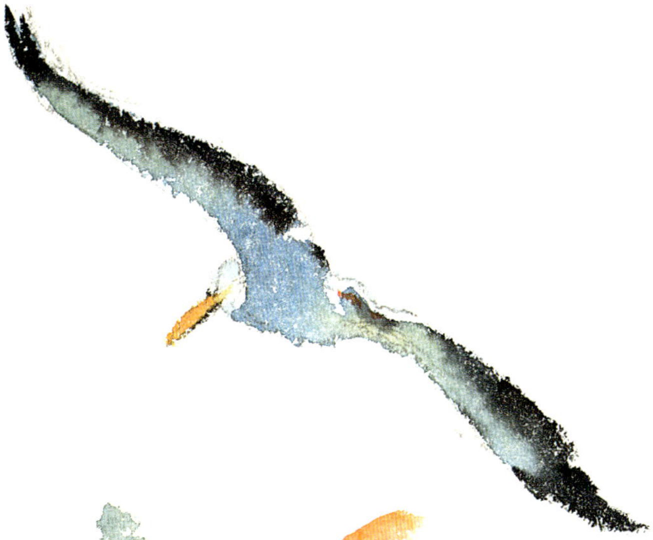

Campfire tale

SOS

In 1943 my great-aunt Dorcas was shipwrecked on the Skeleton Coast. The Dunedin Star was sailing south, fairly close to shore, aware that U-boats were an ever-present threat, when suddenly she struck an object. In the pitch dark the captain managed to beach the boat offshore before she filled with water and at dawn the 21 passengers and some crew were landed ashore. However, this proved a mistake as it was impossible to rescue them by sea as the surf was treacherous. An attempted rescue was made by air, but the aircraft stuck fast in the salty pans. Another ship was sent, but the surf was too rough to reach the castaways. For fourteen days they languished without shade in the cruel heat, blasted by sandstorms, frozen by night.

Eventually, in an amazing story of courage and bravado, a landbased convoy of trucks and cars managed to forge their way hundreds of miles across the perilous wasteland and rescued the despairing band. Scattered bones and derelict ships tell of other travellers less fortunate.

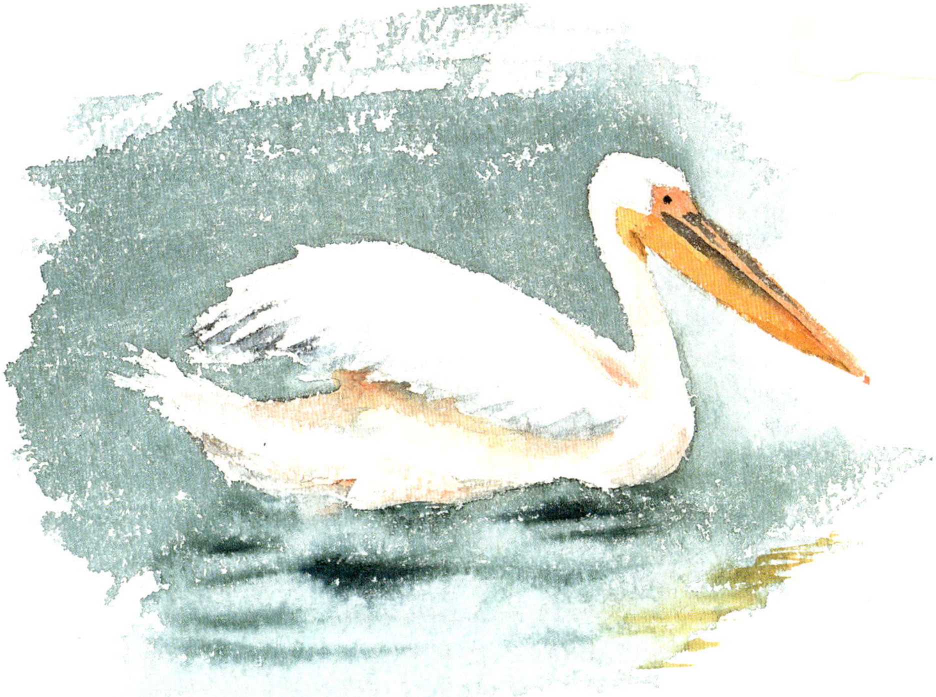

A Viridian and Coeruleum wash brings out the crisp white feathers and orange beak.

Heat and Dust:

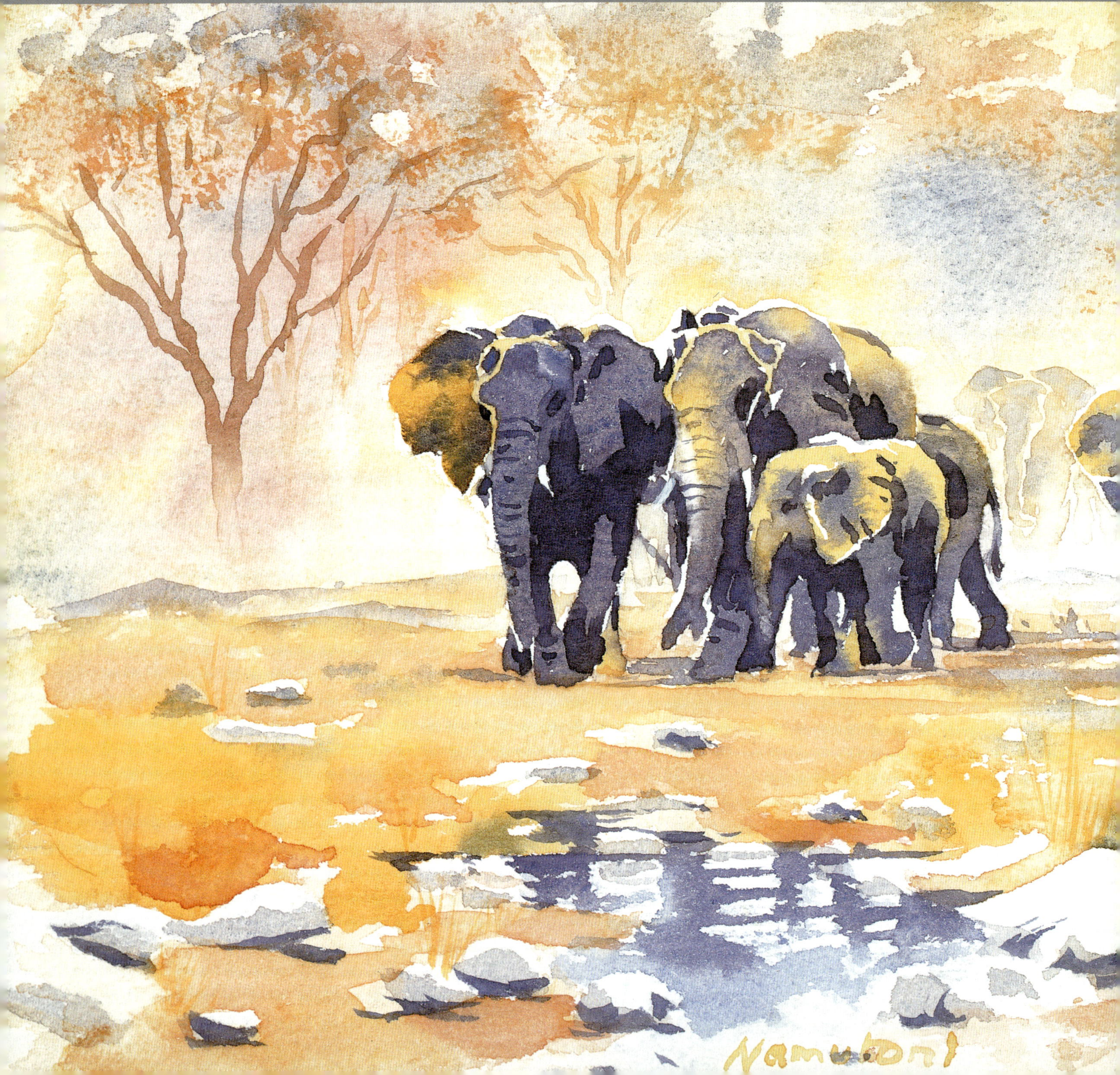

Etosha

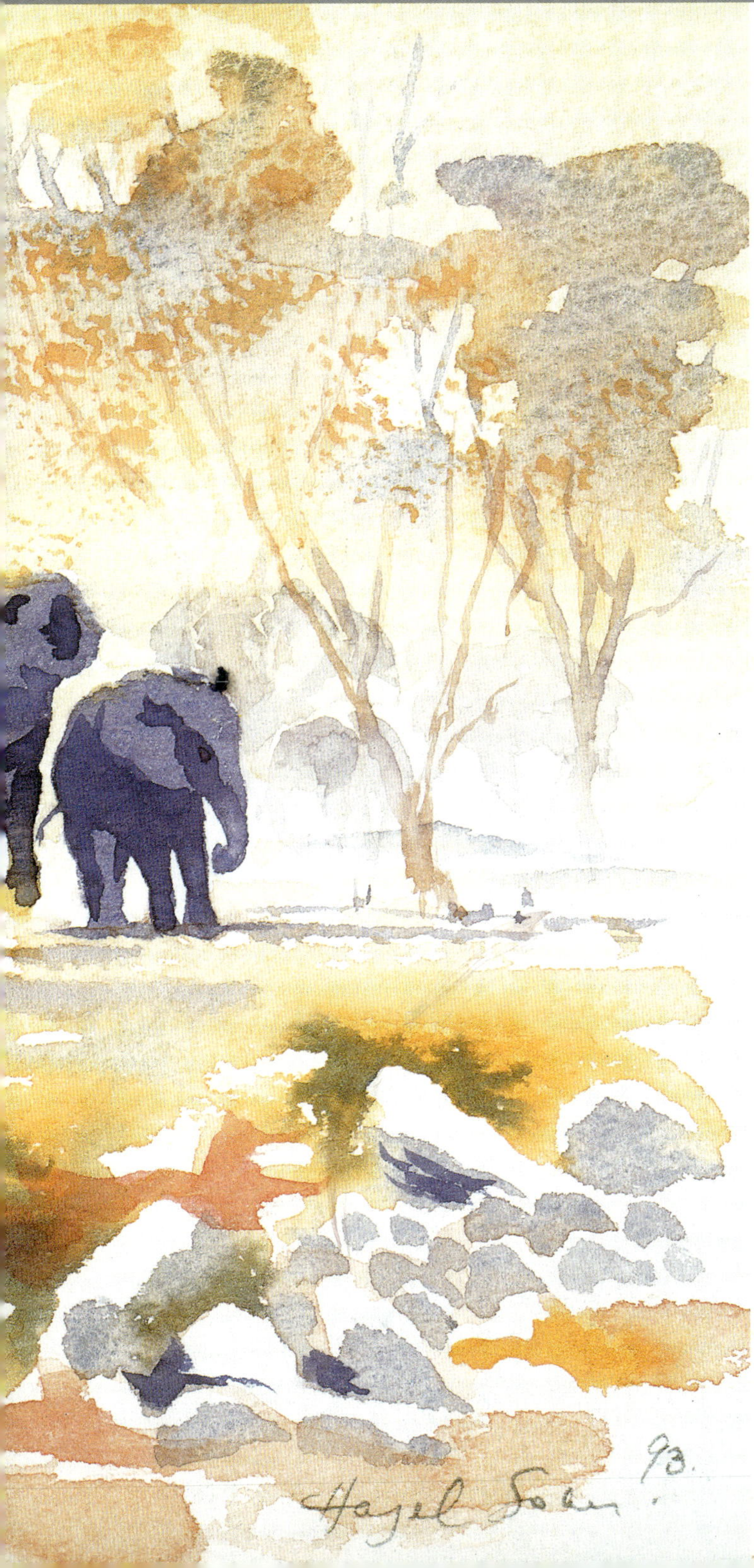

The suggestion of movement

The chattering parley of the bush,
the rising heat from dawn to dusk,
enlivened by the clattering hoof,
the rub of flesh, the touch of tusk.

The noisy silence of the bush,
murmuring from dusk to dawn,
extinguished by the lions' roar,
the thud of hoof, the clash of horn.

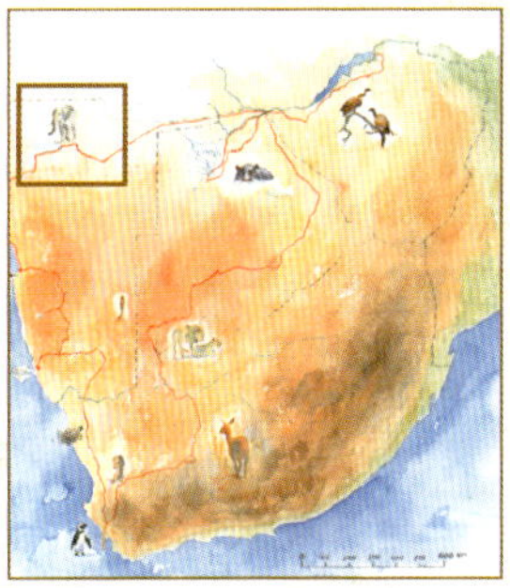

◄ THIRSTLAND
36 x 46 cm (14 x 18 in)

A dry white lake

Turning inland from the Skeleton Coast the gravel roads head towards Etosha, a great salt pan almost 160 km (100 miles) long and 56 km (35 miles) across. This vast shallow depression occasionally fills with water, but for most of the year it is dry and caked with salt, a ghostly, dazzling white lake, shimmering with heatwaves and mirages, casting white dust over the surrounding bush.

Around the lake are natural springs flavoured with mineral salts, which provide nourishing waterholes for wild animals and copious vegetation. Elephant, rhino, cheetah, zebra, giraffe, lion, oryx, kudu, springbok and many other species gather to graze and drink at these lush spas. Birdlife is also abundant, with larger aquatic birds like flamingos and pelicans migrating here after summer-season rains.

The dusty grasslands bordering the pan afford wide panoramic views, making this wonderful country for game viewing. A dark 'bush' in the far distance approaches and becomes a lone bull elephant heading for water. Animal footprints cross the dry cracked floor of the pan, occasionally breaking the hard crust to reveal the sticky mud beneath. Salt pans are not places to get stuck in a vehicle; the salty mire sucks in the turning wheels, refusing to let go.

Life in the herd

The vast empty spaces give the animals plenty of room to roam in herds. In the daytime heat they move at a leisurely pace but, if disturbed, clouds of dust rise into the air, cutting the sunbeams into shafts of light. Herbivores such as wildebeest, zebra, springbok and oryx often mingle together in a sea of hides and hooves.

▼ KUDU AT GOAS
28 x 36 (11 x 14 in)
Usually there is little rain in Etosha and the waterholes are the only places the animals can quench their thirst. These female kudu come warily to drink, their heads upright, ears alert. They are shy and easily disturbed.

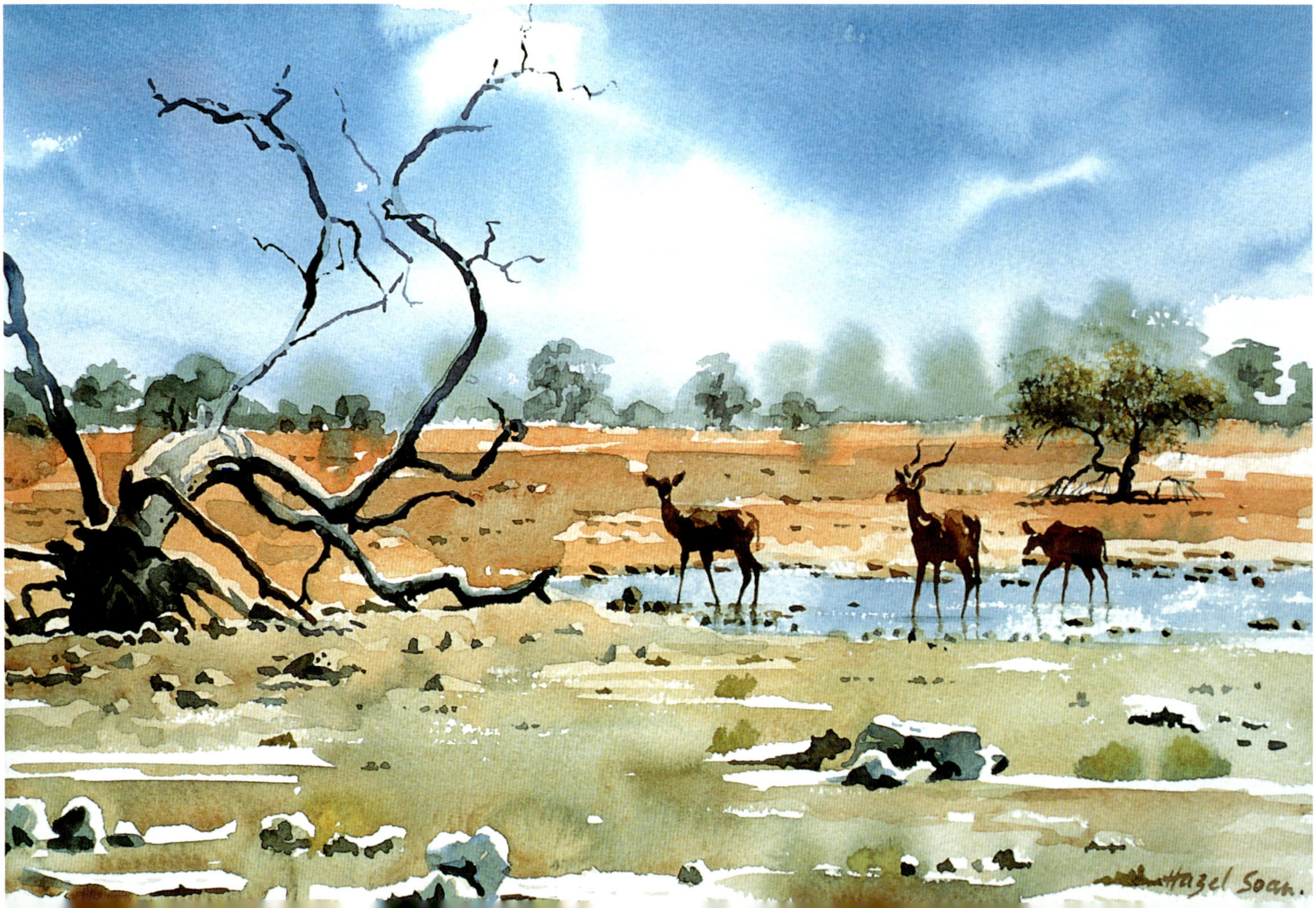

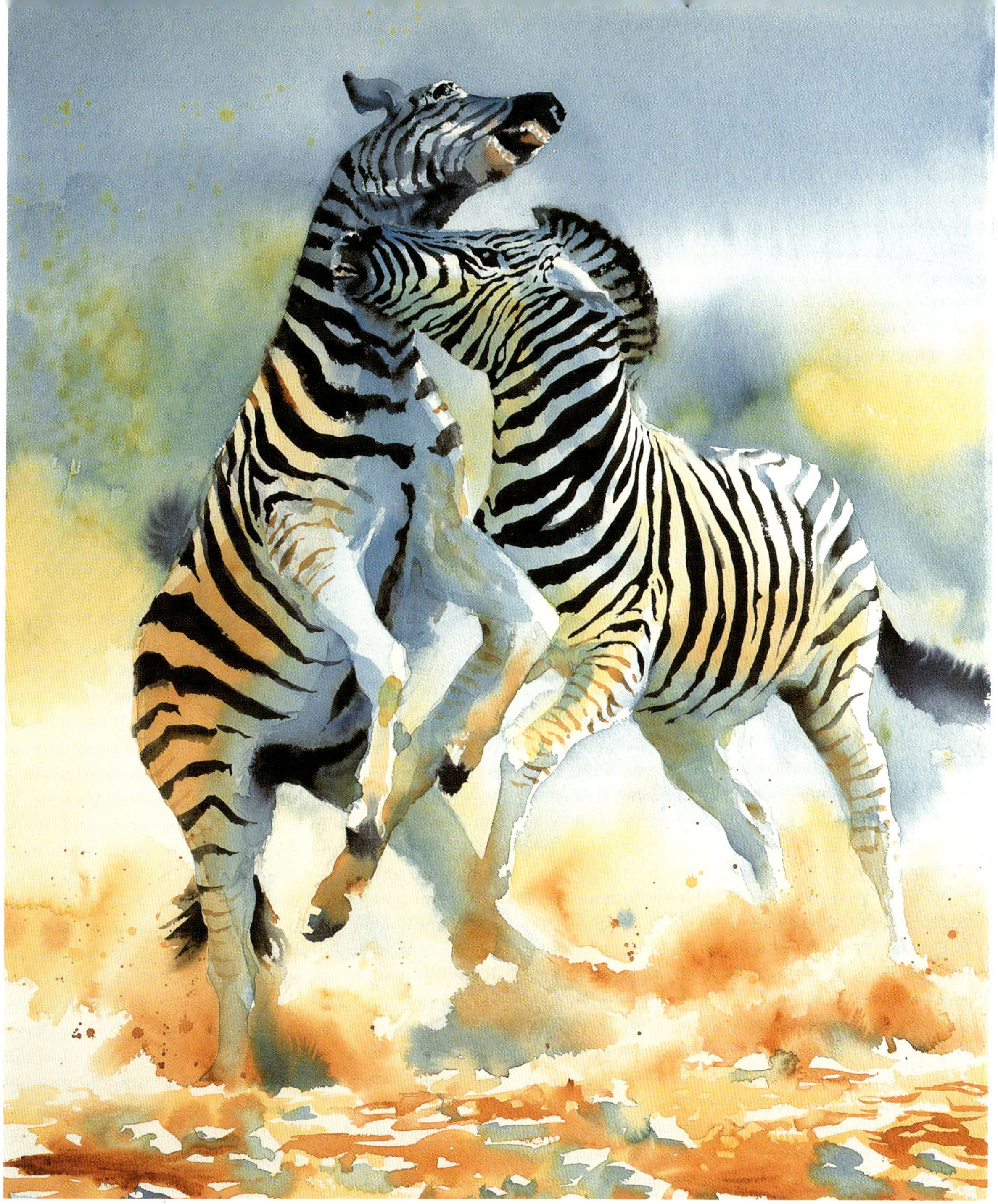

► WILD CLASH
76 x 56 cm (30 x 22 in)
The clash of hides and hooves can almost be heard in this painting of two stallions sparring for dominance in the herd. The direction of the stripes around the zebras' bodies creates strong three-dimensional forms.

Life at the waterhole seems ordered; smaller animals make way for larger species, small groups from larger herds take it in turns to drink. Zebra and other animals approach the waterholes in single file along well-worn game paths. The ordered hierarchy of the herd is disturbed by endless bickering and spats break out between young stallions kicking up the ghostly white dust.

The dust colours the elephants also, as they dry off their hides after a dip, flinging a covering of the dry powder over their bodies with their trunks.

Painting wildlife

The overall shape of the animal is more important than the details. There is rarely time to draw, so it is better to go straight in with a loaded brush, paint the whole shape in one or two fast brushstrokes and then touch into the wet wash the colours, stripes, spots and shadows of the animal with drier, more intense paint. The gentle blending of the watercolours wet-in-wet gives the impression of fur and hair and adds life to the form.

Observation is an essential part of the process. Looking and pencil sketching before painting helps summarize the shape in the mind's eye, making the mark on paper more informed.

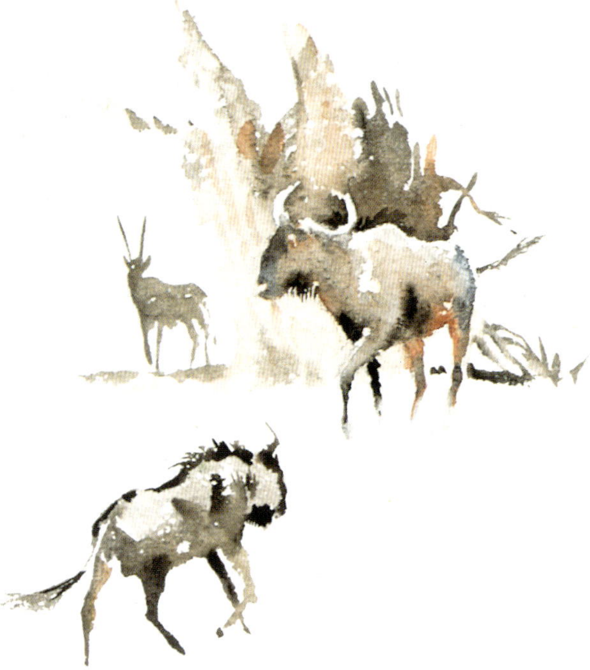

◄ *Just one colour, two at most, is a good way to start. Here the wildebeest are painted with Sepia and a little Burnt Sienna.*

▼ *To place highlights make a pencil sketch first. The highlit areas on the giraffe are left out of the background wash; the shadows and markings of the giraffe are painted over it.*

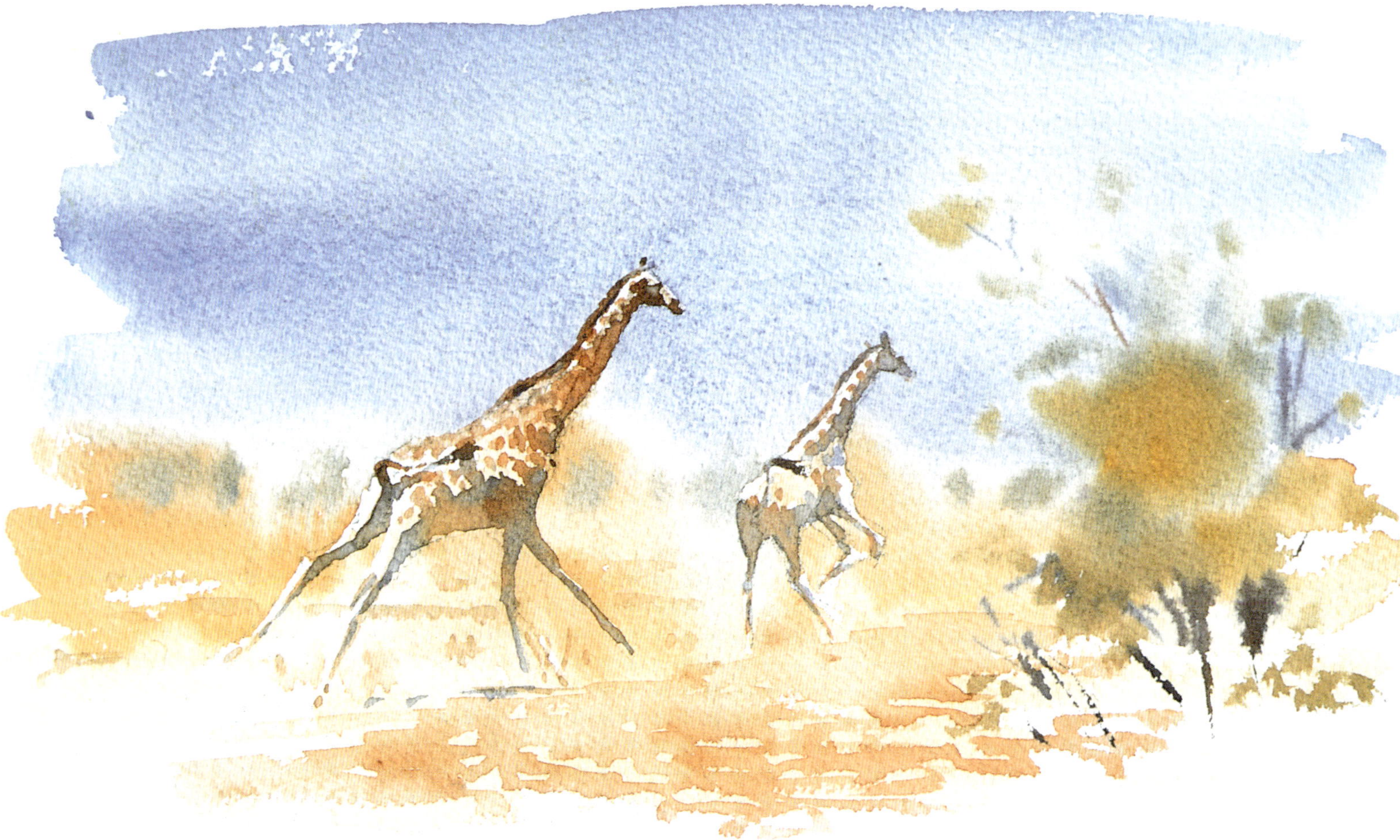

► BURNISHED GOLD
28 x 36 cm (11 x 14 in)
The glorious golden harmony of an African evening is painted with Yellow Ochre and a purple made from French Ultramarine and Alizarin Crimson. The wet-in-wet washes are perfect for suggesting the blur of rising dust.

▼ SAFE IN HER SHADOW
18 x 25 cm (7 x 10 in)
The background wash demarcates the rhinos' highlit backs. On the flat surface of a painting the background and foreground are of equal importance for the image to work.

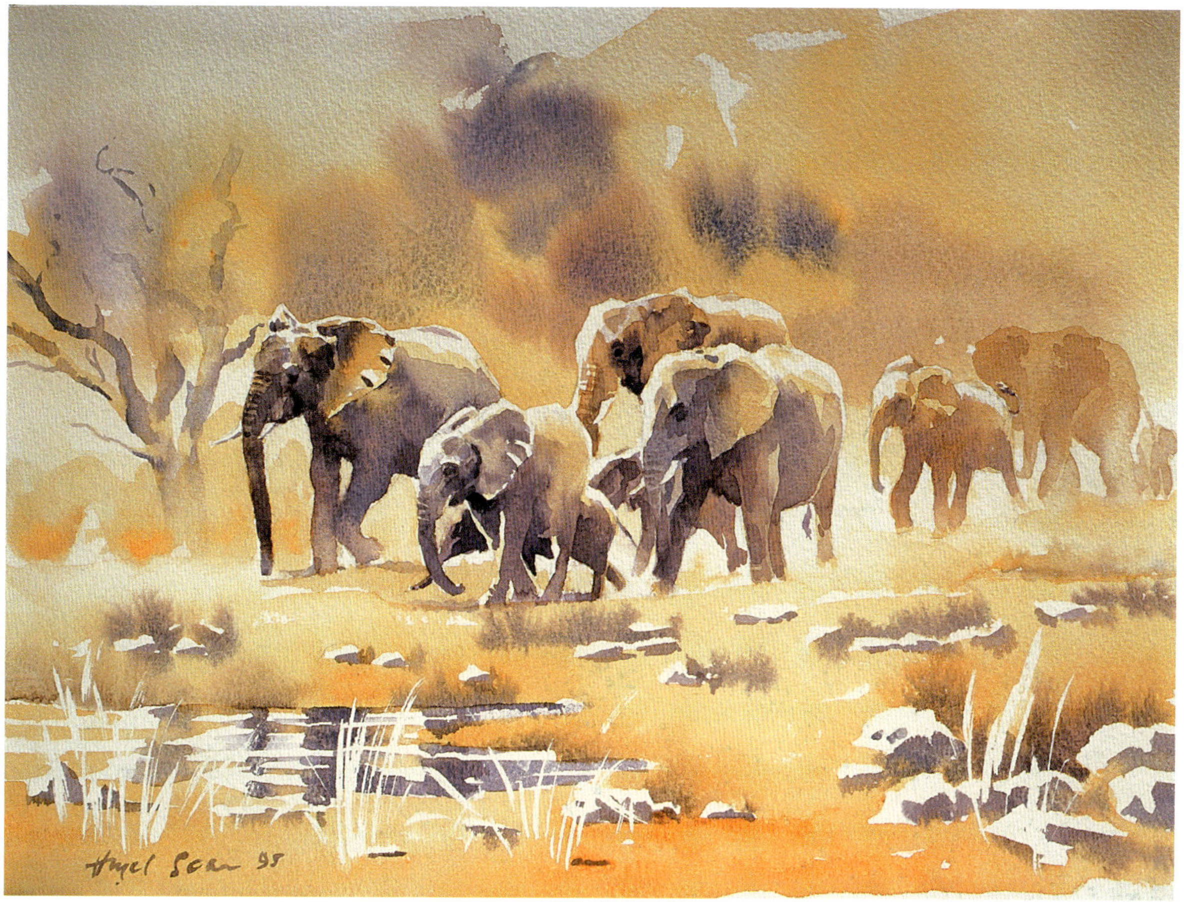

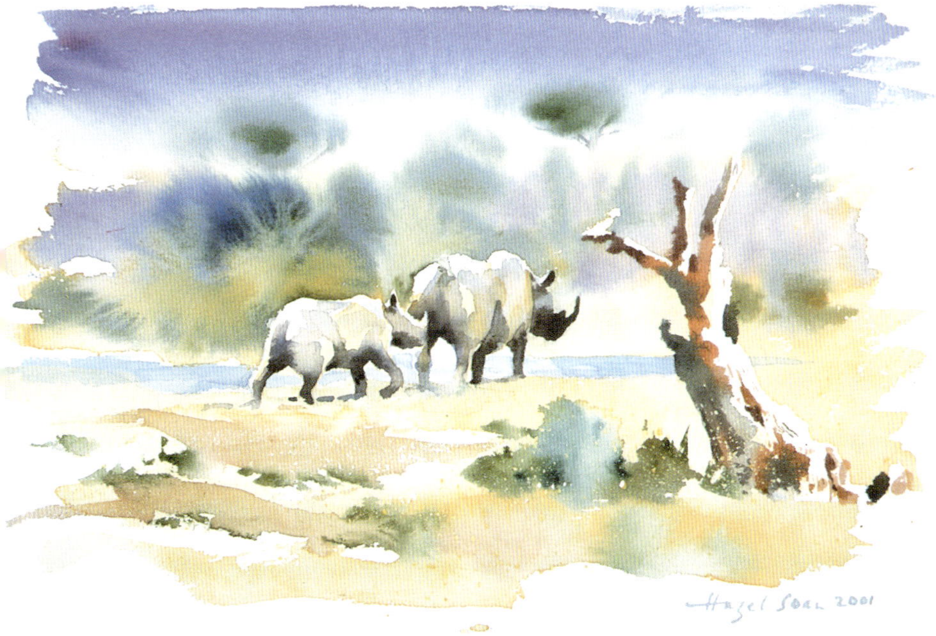

Animals in situ

Some of the waterholes are surrounded by thick scrub, tall grasses and even reeds, making satisfyingly dark backgrounds behind the pale glowing hides of the wildlife. If the creatures are backlit by the sun they become outlined with halos of white or golden light. In watercolour these outlines of light can be left as margins of untouched white paper, making it easier to paint the animal while the background is still wet or vice versa.

If small areas of background and animal washes do run into each other let them be; they help prevent the painting from becoming static. If you lose a highlight to a stray wash scratch it back with a sharp blade when the painting is dry.

The suggestion of movement

Until this chapter the subjects chosen – landscapes, ocean views, rocks, flowers – have sat relatively still. But often the source of inspiration is fleeting or moving and there is very little time to grasp the essence of something that catches the eye. This applies to changing light conditions as well as to living things.

Watercolour is a great medium for painting moving creatures. It is made for speedy application and the brushstrokes, blurs and blends readily suggest movement in the painting.

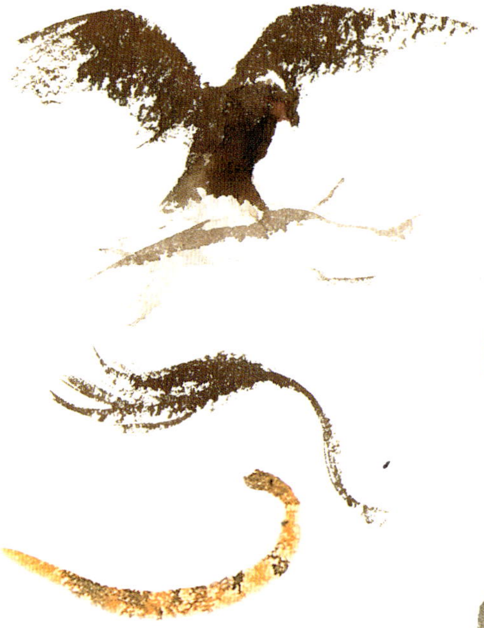

▲ A dry brushstroke will come in handy for the swish of a tail, the hint of a mane or a bird on the wing.

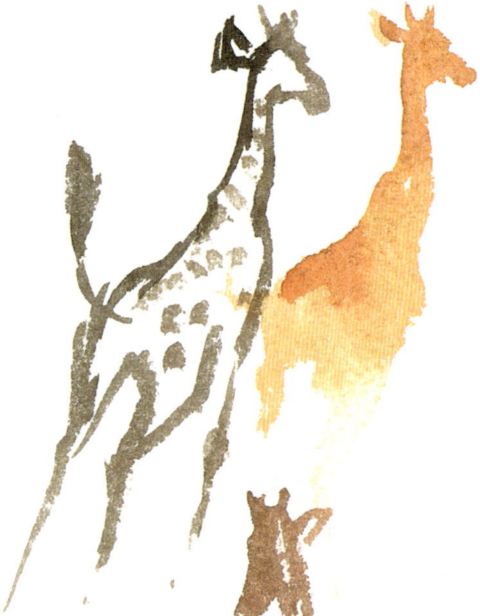

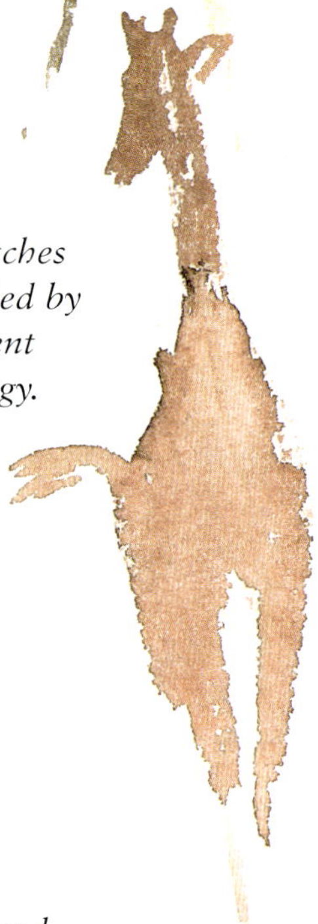

► In these giraffe sketches the movement is implied by shape alone. A confident brushstroke adds energy.

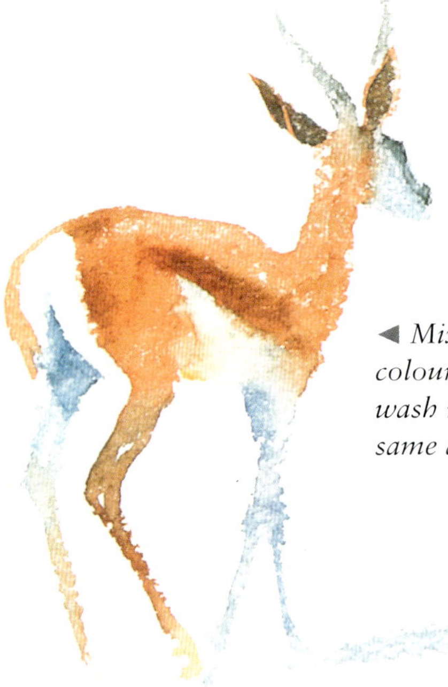

◄ Mix the strength of colour you want in the first wash rather than cover the same area twice.

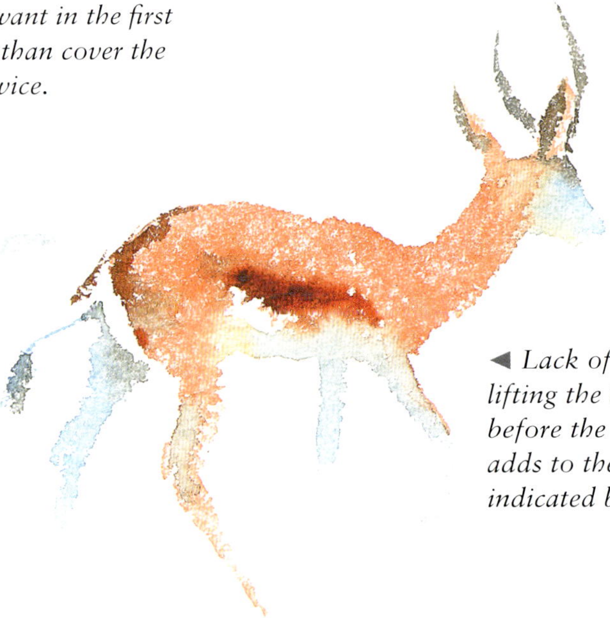

◄ Lack of definition and lifting the brush off before the end of the leg adds to the motion indicated by the pose.

► *The background shapes the zebra so that only the shadows and stripes need be painted to make an expressive little painting. Each stripe is playing its part to describe the form.*

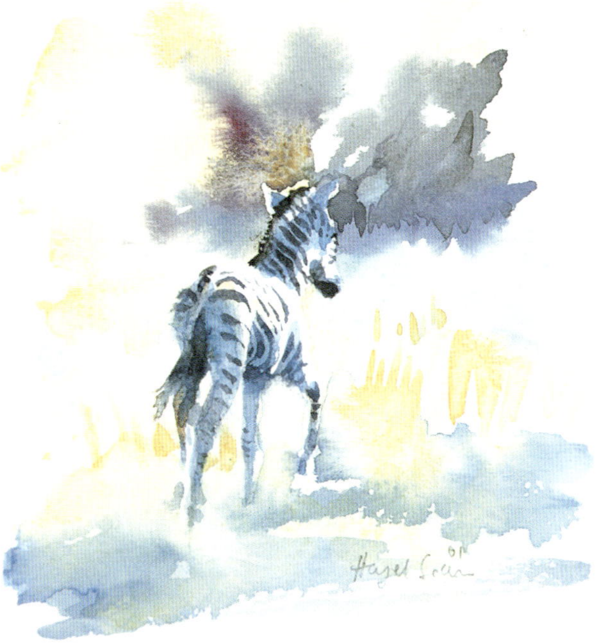

Meaningful brushstrokes

The most successful watercolours are those that say the most with the minimum of means. The paradox of watercolour painting is that the more concentration and effort you put into laying just the right colour, in just the right place, at just the right time, and with a meaningful brushstroke, the more effortless and spontaneous your watercolour will appear.

A good way to avoid aimless brushstrokes is to 'paint by numbers' – choose a simple subject, then limit yourself to 20 or 30 brushstrokes and you will be sure to make each one serve its purpose. A watercolour completed in fifteen minutes has actually taken a lifetime to create.

▼ RETREATING HERD
23 x 36 cm (9 x 14 in)
In this painting mass movement is implied with just a few bent legs and raised feet.

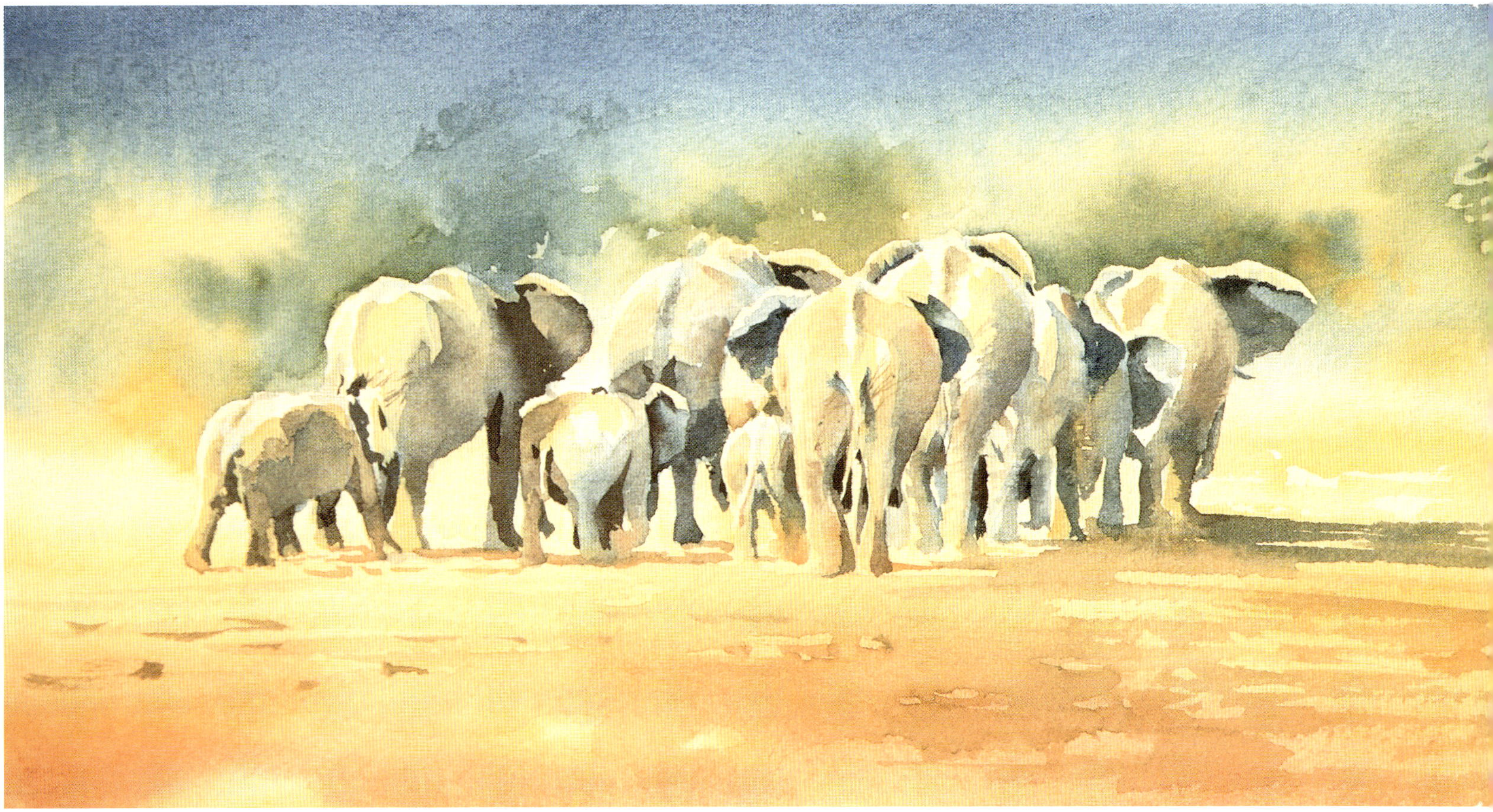

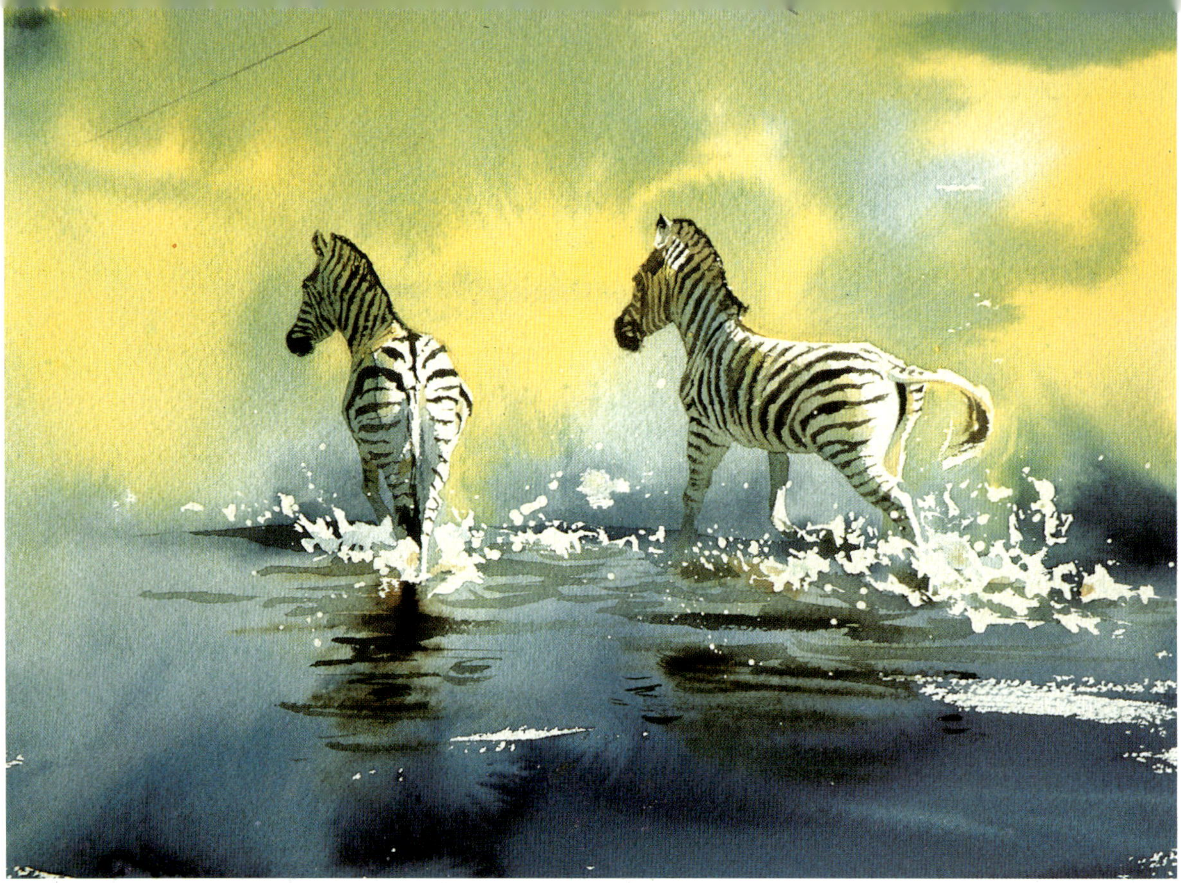

◄ A BIGGER SPLASH
25 x 36 cm (10 x 14 in)
The splashes of water made by the zebra as they make a hasty exit from the waterhole are made by using masking fluid.

▼ TAKNG FLIGHT
18 x 10 cm (7 x 4 in)
The background and lower legs of the fleeing giraffe are vigorously lifted out with a damp sponge, creating the effect of rising dust.

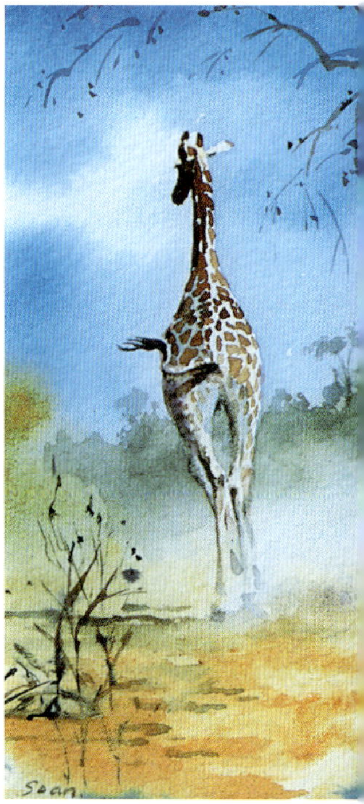

Active assistance

There are several methods you can use to help you lay your watercolour with more confidence or to correct mistakes.

Many artists use masking fluid on a painting from the outset. This latex fluid can be painted on the areas of your painting you want to keep as white paper. Only paint over it when it is dry and rub it off when you have finished the painting.

Some people worry that watercolour, once laid, cannot be removed. This is true of some staining colours, but once a watercolour is dry you can lift off colour with a clean, slightly damp sponge. Use a gentle, circular rubbing motion and dab off the loosened pigment with a tissue.

Cropping

Working on paper makes it easy to crop an image if part of a painting goes wrong. Sometimes there are even two cropped images to be found within one painting. To crop successfully cut an adjustable paper window for the area you want to keep and mark the four corners with dots.

Working from photographs

There is no shame to be had in working from photographs. Some living creatures move just too fast to allow you to make even a brushstroke! The camera can serve as a reference medium for the shapes of animals in flight, their environment and details of animal markings.

The secret is not to be a slave to your photographs, but to make them work for you. Try to paint as swiftly from them at home as you would have done from life had you been painting on location. The colours of photographs are seldom as you remember them, so, think back and re-envisage the event, the atmosphere and the colours. Recall the reason why you took the photograph and keep that in your mind as you paint.

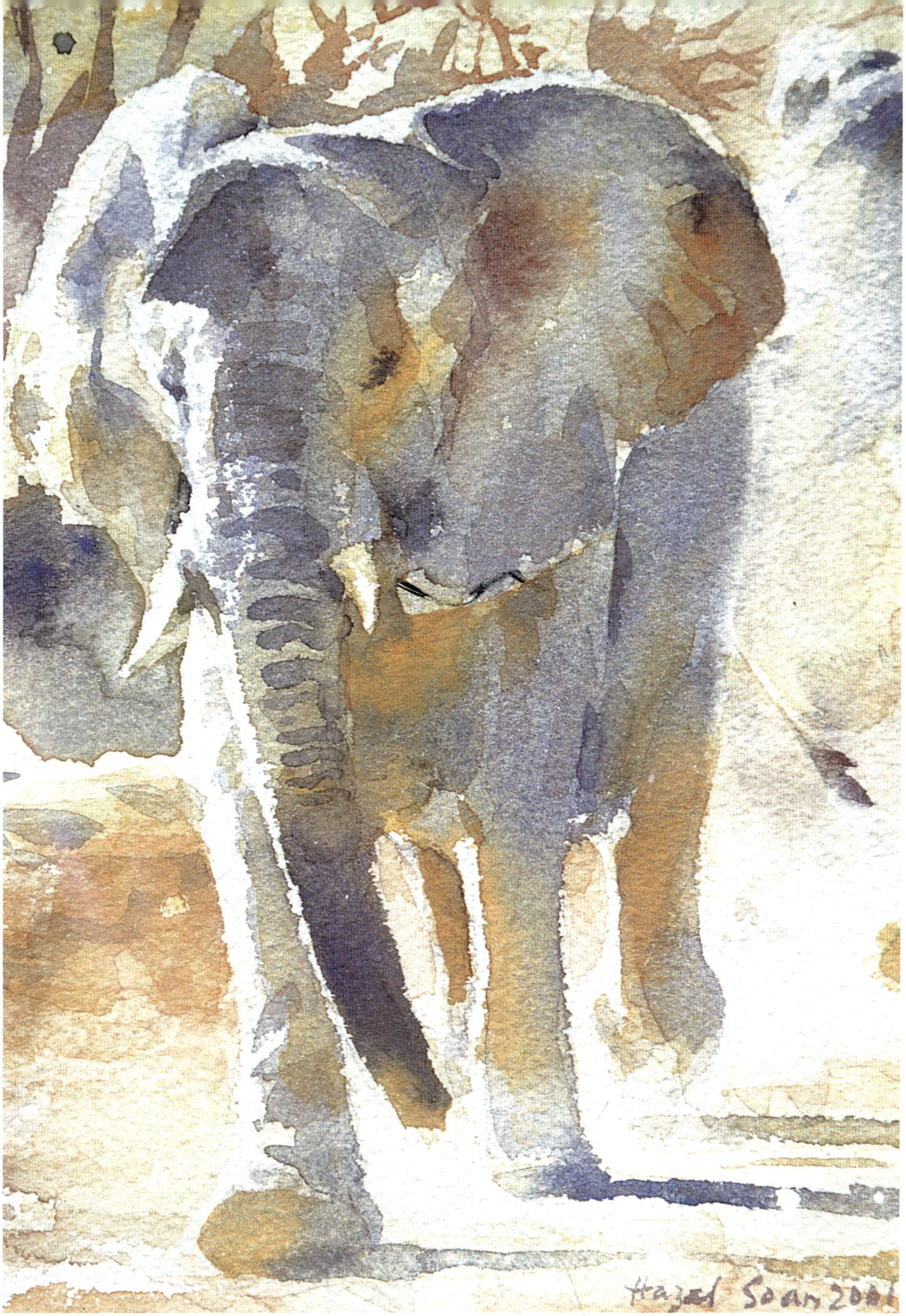

► **HEAT AND DUST**
23 x 15 cm (9 x 6 in)
This elephant belonged to a larger herd coming down to water, but the painting was overcrowded, so the image was cropped. Look closely and you can see where the elephant behind has been lifted out.

Safari sketchbook

Waterhole sketches

In this land of heat and dust you can settle yourself at a waterhole and wait for the wildlife to come to you. Animals rarely stand still for very long, but they do for a time while they are drinking. This is an excellent opportunity to make sketches of their shapes and body markings. When one animal moves on another usually steps in to take up a similar position, and in this way you can paint one animal from many models!

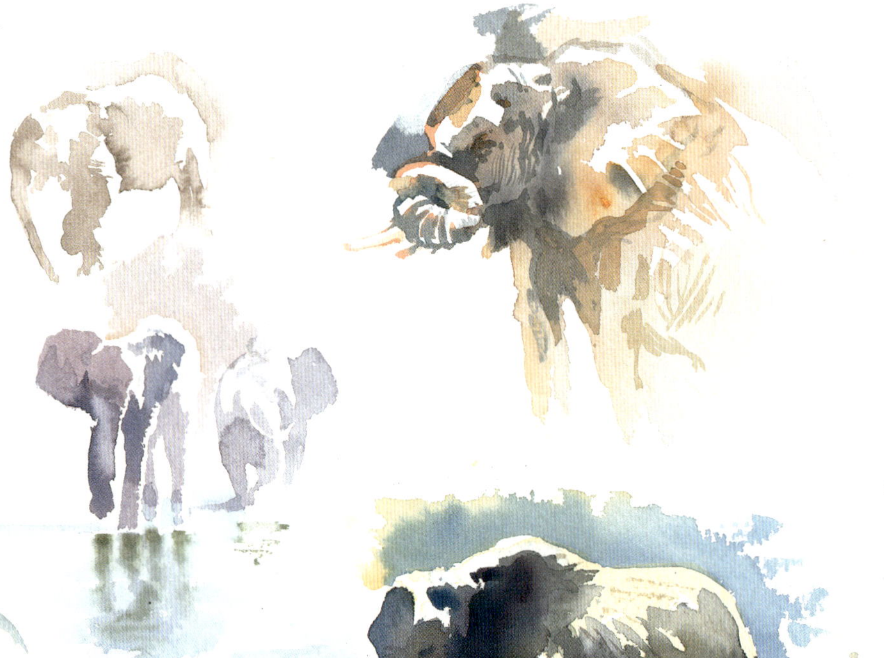

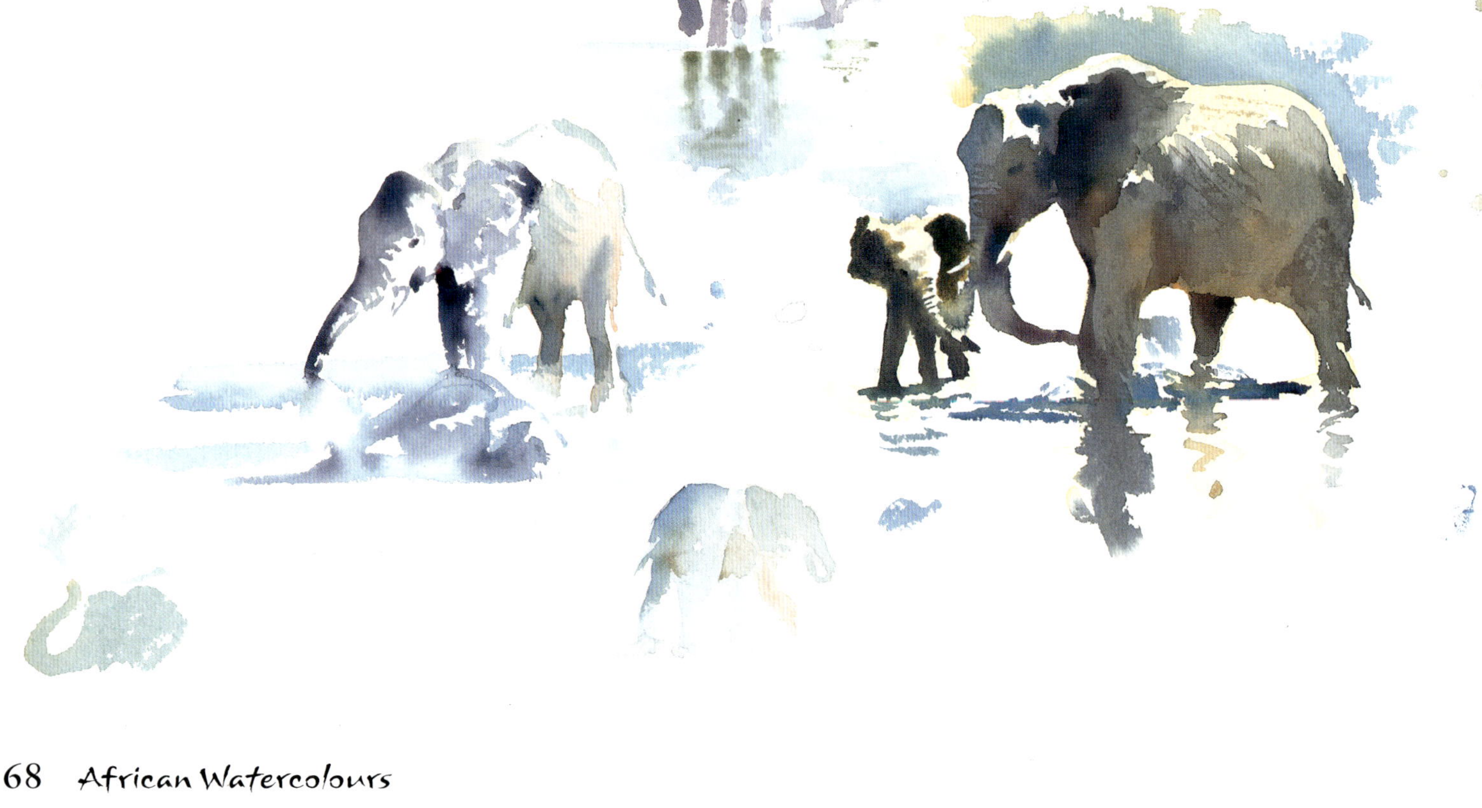

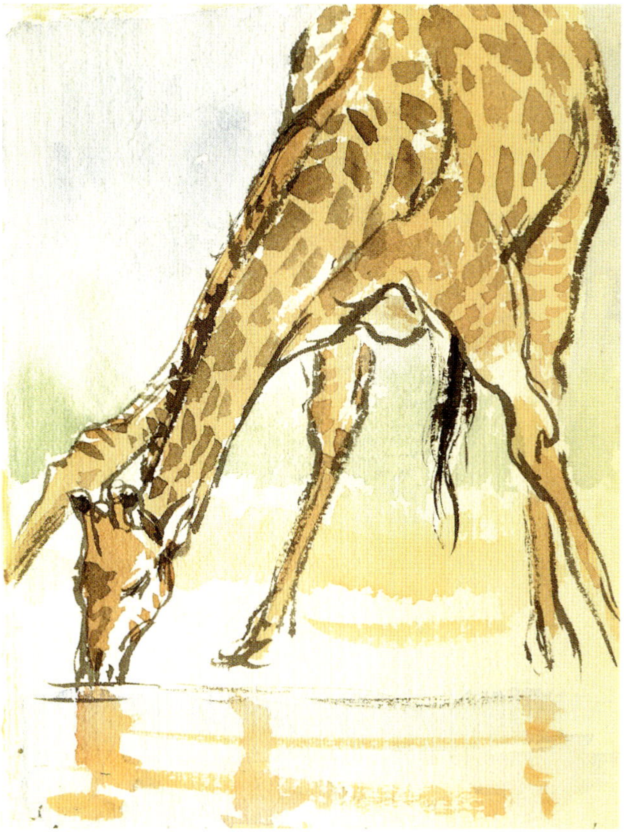

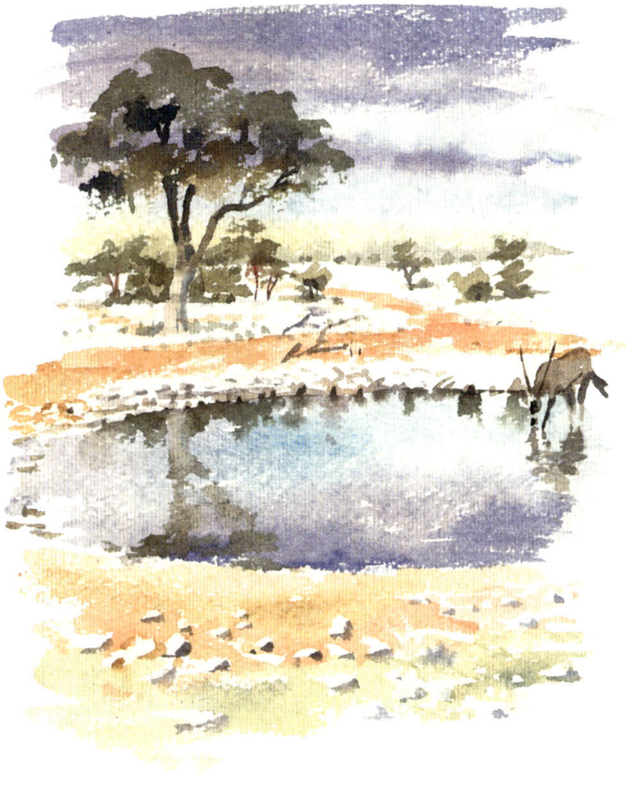

CAMPFIRE TALE

A friend in the wild

One night during a long drought I saw a lioness waiting quietly by a waterhole. A few metres away a rhino and her youngster were coming down to drink. They were aware of the lioness, but obviously not bothered as they wandered around the hole. Eventually the young one lay down and the mother lay on guard beside him.

A small group of giraffe approached. They were apprehensive and, smelling the scent of danger, watched warily. One by one, they bravely began to lower themselves into their awkward and vulnerable stance in a bid to quench their thirst. But before they reached the water they were suddenly alerted and rocked jerkily up.

Then the mother rhino, who had been watching, rose to her feet and trotted meaningfully around the waterhole towards the lioness. The startled predator thought better than to call her bluff and shot off into the night. The rhino returned to settle down with her child, while the relieved giraffe descended from their great height and began gratefully to drink.

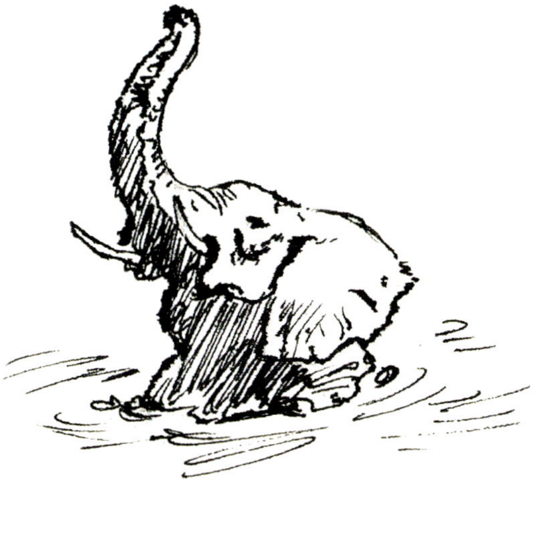

Rivers of Life:

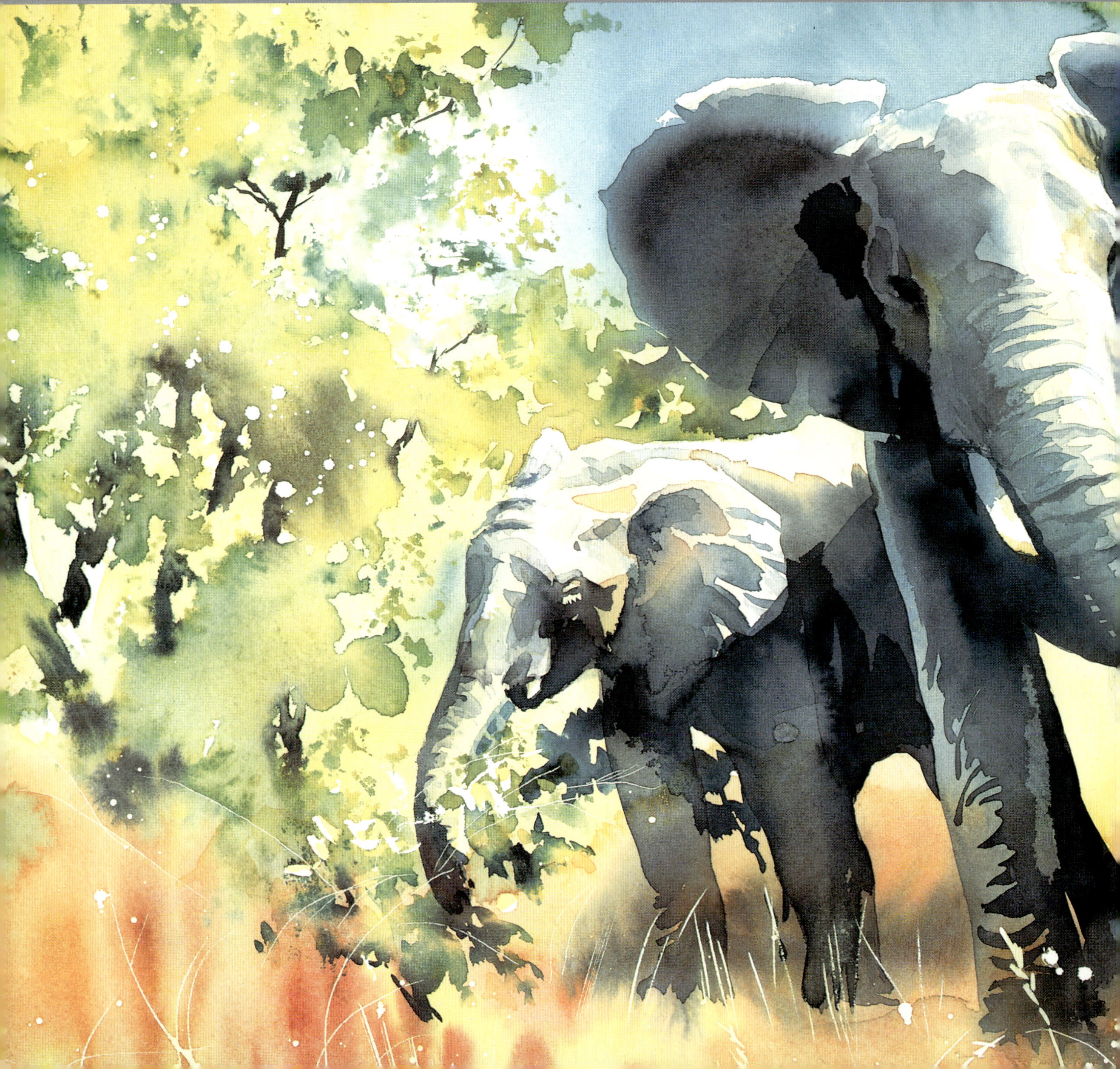

The Chobe

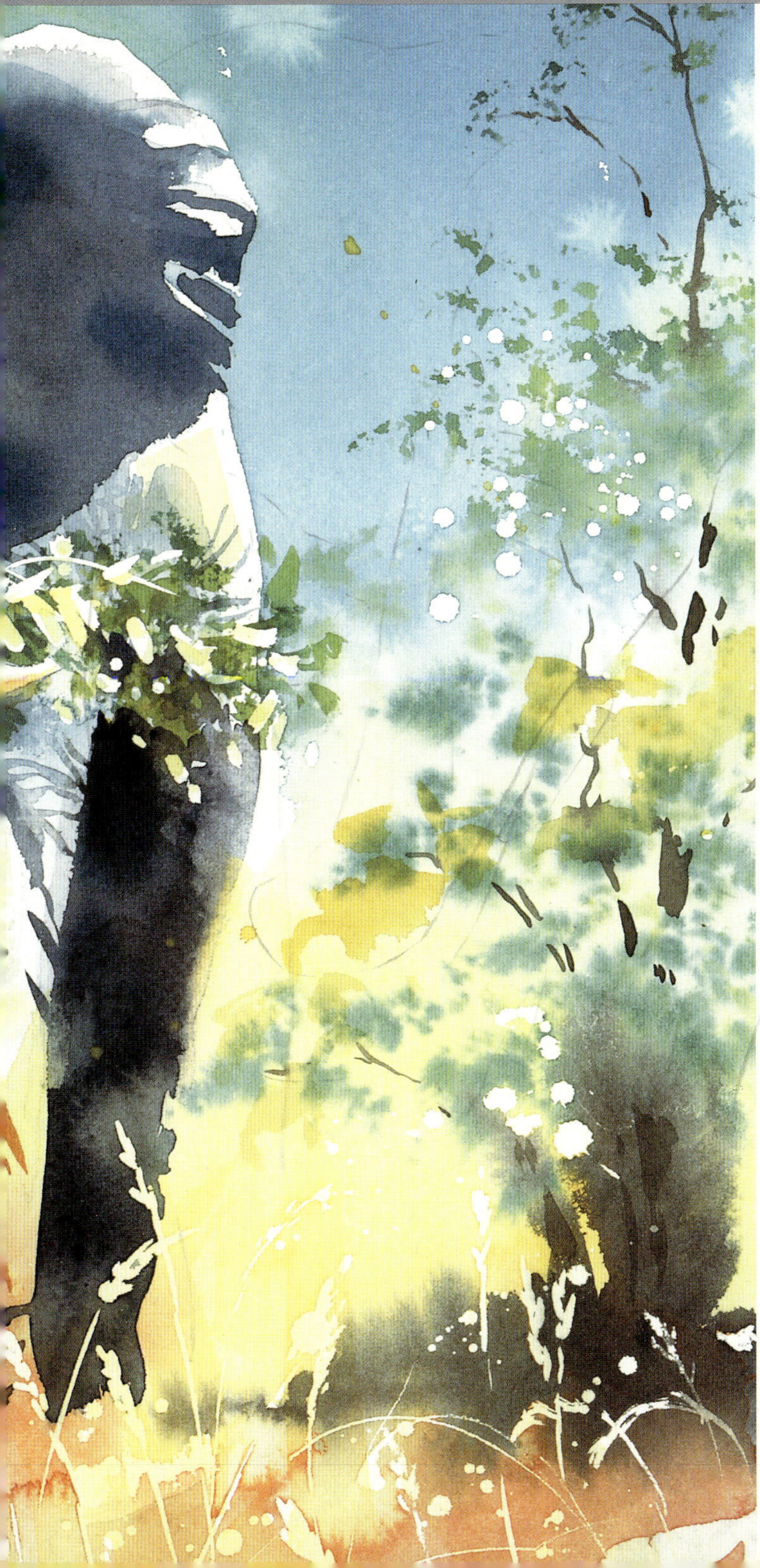

Deep darks and reflections

Cerulean snake
slithering through Africa,
cooling the sunbaked sand;
green is the colour
of the cloak you trail,
life the gift
in your healing hand.

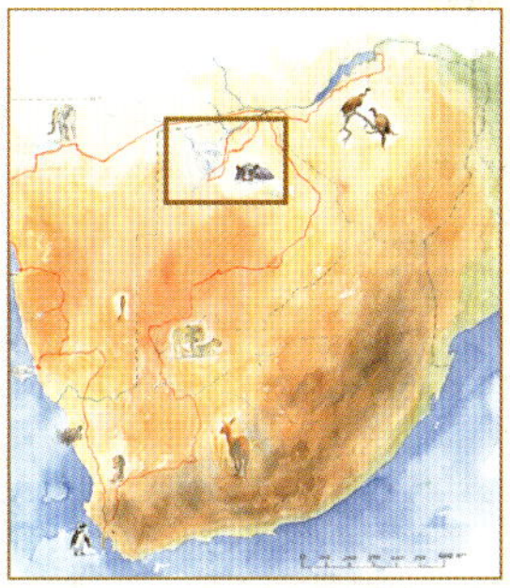

◀ **AFRICAN FEAST**
56 x 71 cm (22 x 28 in)

Seasonal migration

As the journey heads east the safari leaves Namibia and enters Botswana. Very little of this country has seen human inhabitation. Here vast tracts of true Africa remain largely undisturbed and Chobe National Park is a paramount example. No fences restrict the flow of the animals from crossing park boundaries, or prevent access to camping areas.

This area is populated by huge concentrations of game, especially elephants. In the winter dry season the pans dry up and the animals gradually leave the interior and seek the life-giving waters of the Chobe River or the permanent water of the marsh at Savuti. A tide of buffalo descends in thousands on the floodplains at Serondella, while breeding herds of elephant gather along the river's banks. Wildebeest, zebra and other ungulates congregate in mixed herds on the marsh. The gatherings of game make easy pickings for the predators, and prides of lions have their fill.

In late October the clouds begin to build and the first heavy rains start to fall. Roads become quickly impassable. Almost overnight the over-grazed earth becomes a paradise of lush grass; food and water are in abundance. The animals rejoice in their freedom to spread out and, as the season continues, the young are born. Only the predators are tested; now they must hone their hunting skills to catch the widely broadcast game.

▼ THE FLUSH OF YOUTH
15 x 23 cm (6 x 9 in)
The young herbivores grow up quickly. Within moments of being born this impala is already on his feet.

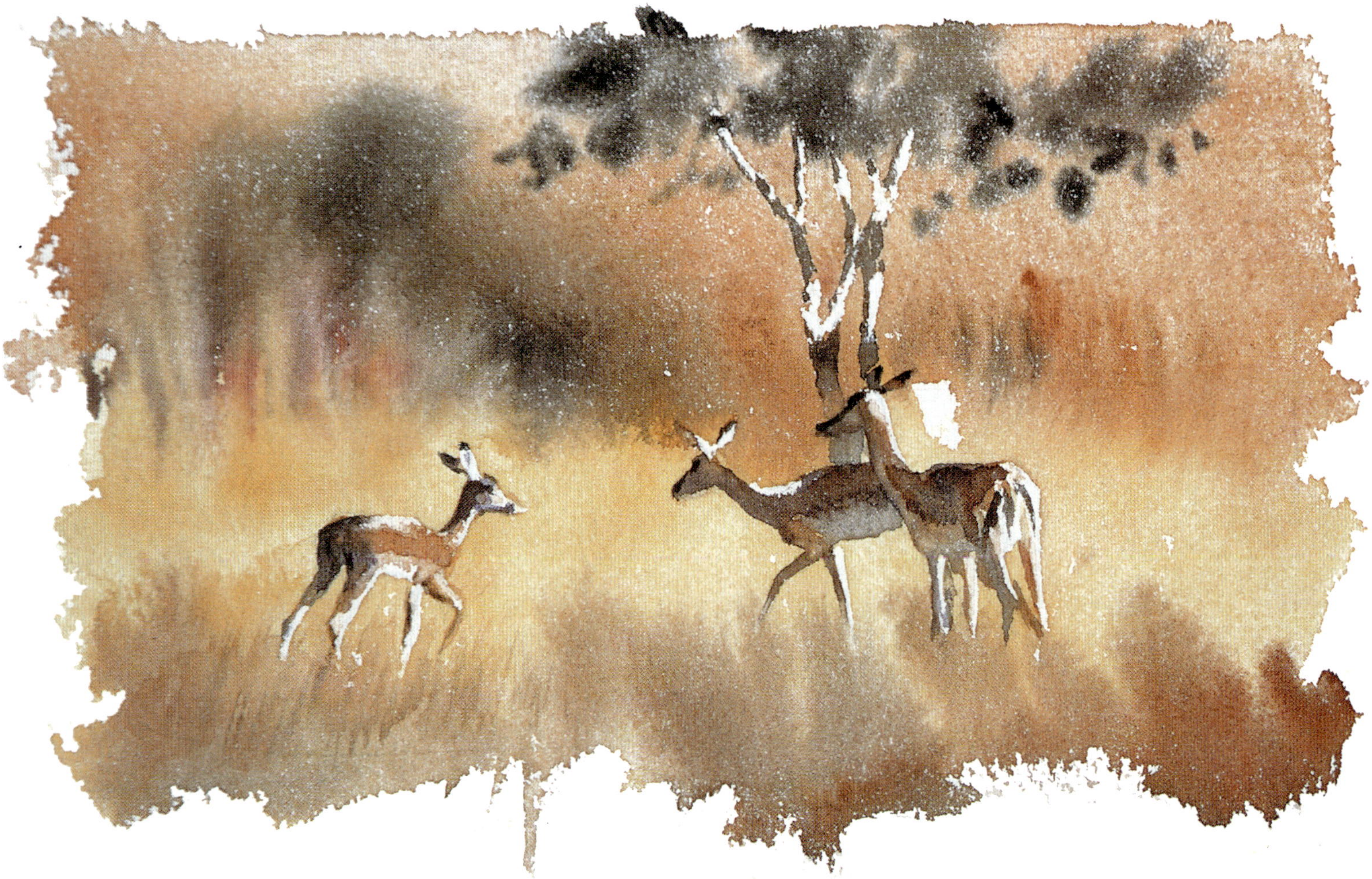

▶ RITE OF PASSAGE
18 x 23 cm (7 x 9 in)
Elephants keep regular times as they come down to the river to drink and bathe.

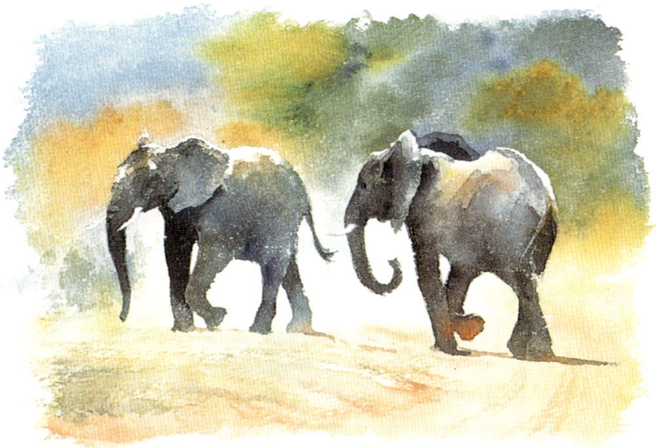

▼ INTO THE AFRICAN NIGHT
30 x 36 cm (12 x 14 in)
As quickly as they arrive, the elephants disappear into the night, their bulky shapes quickly camouflaged by the surrounding bush.

Gentle giants

Elephants throng the floodplain. The young are ushered into the river in almost daily routine by the caring aunts and loving mothers. The herd immerse themselves in the cooling water, fondling each other gently with their trunks.

This awesome animal weighs up to seven tonnes and eats over 100 kg (220 lb) a day. Elephants spend much of the time browsing on their way to water. The sound of branches snapping and ripping heralds their otherwise silent approach.

Amongst the reeds, pods of hippo lie immersed in the water, their ears, eyes, noses and backs visible above deep reflections. On the low sandbanks crocodiles bask in the sun or slither snake-like into the dark water.

Sunset

Come evening this land of deep blues and emerald greens takes on the opposite hues of orange and red. The landscape is thrown into dark silhouette against a rich red and gold backdrop. The echo of the fish eagle fades, the huge glowing circle of the sun dissolves and utter blackness descends on the river and its banks. The noises of the African night begin to fill the warm air – the call of frogs, the rustle of cicadas, the whoop of the zebra, the howl of the hyena and the distant roar of the lion.

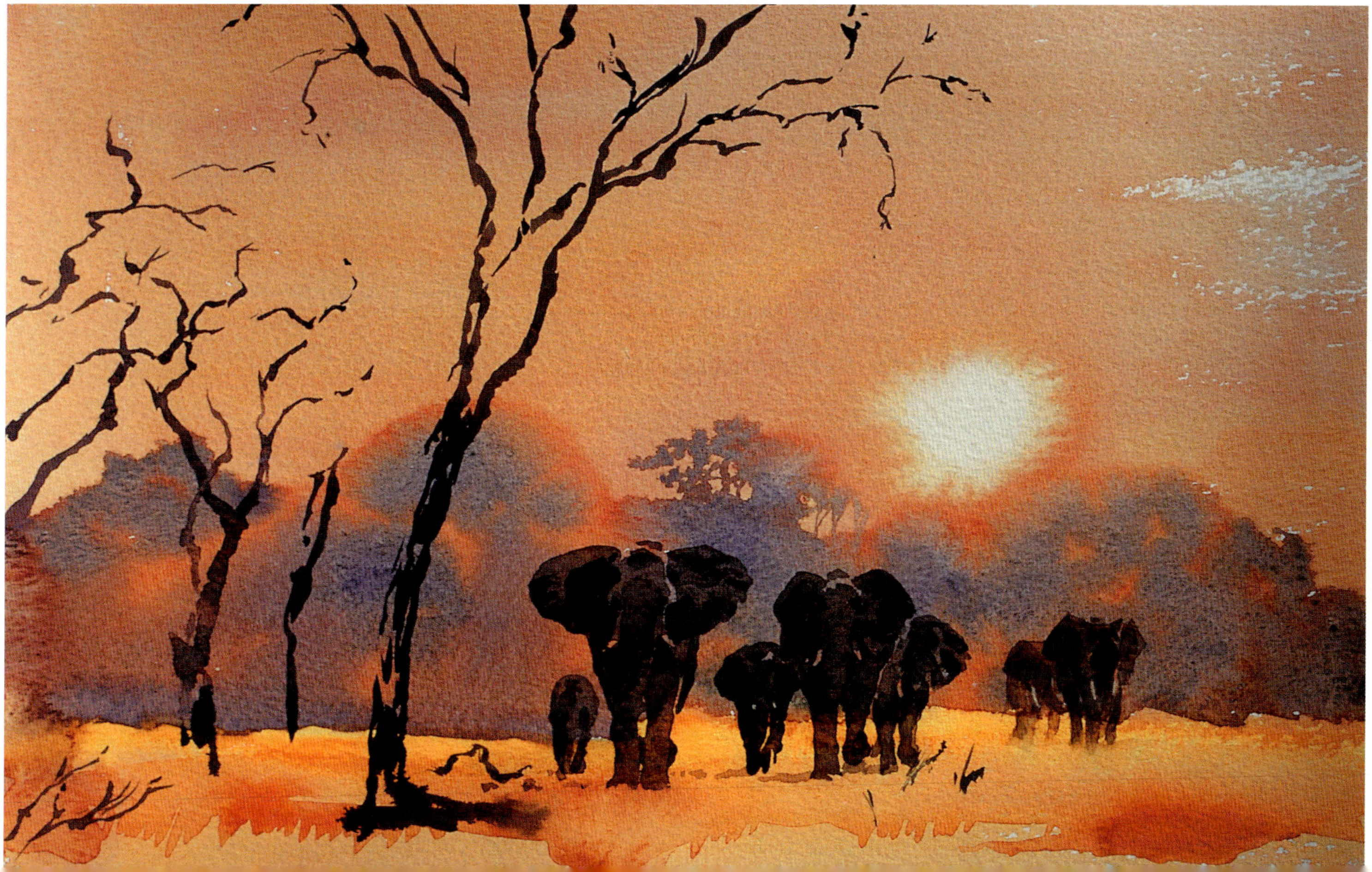

Contrasts of tone

The tones and colours of the foliage bordering the life-giving river are rich and deep. The greens are lush, the yellows clean and the blues intense. Hidden crimsons sing out from the shadows. The strong tonal differences between the sunlit yellows and the deep blues, browns and mauves bring clarity and definition to the paintings.

The wet hides of the elephants emerging from the water gleam blue in the shady glades, while the hippo revel in deep purples tinged with pink. The shiny highlights and deep darks give the painter a chance to mix rich quantities of colour in the palette and to compare strong highlights with deep darks.

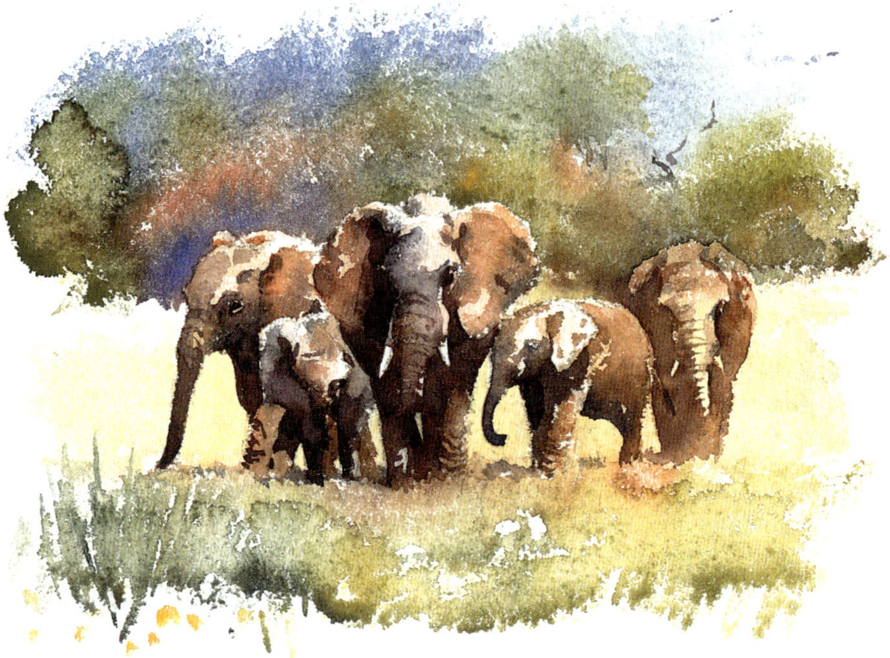

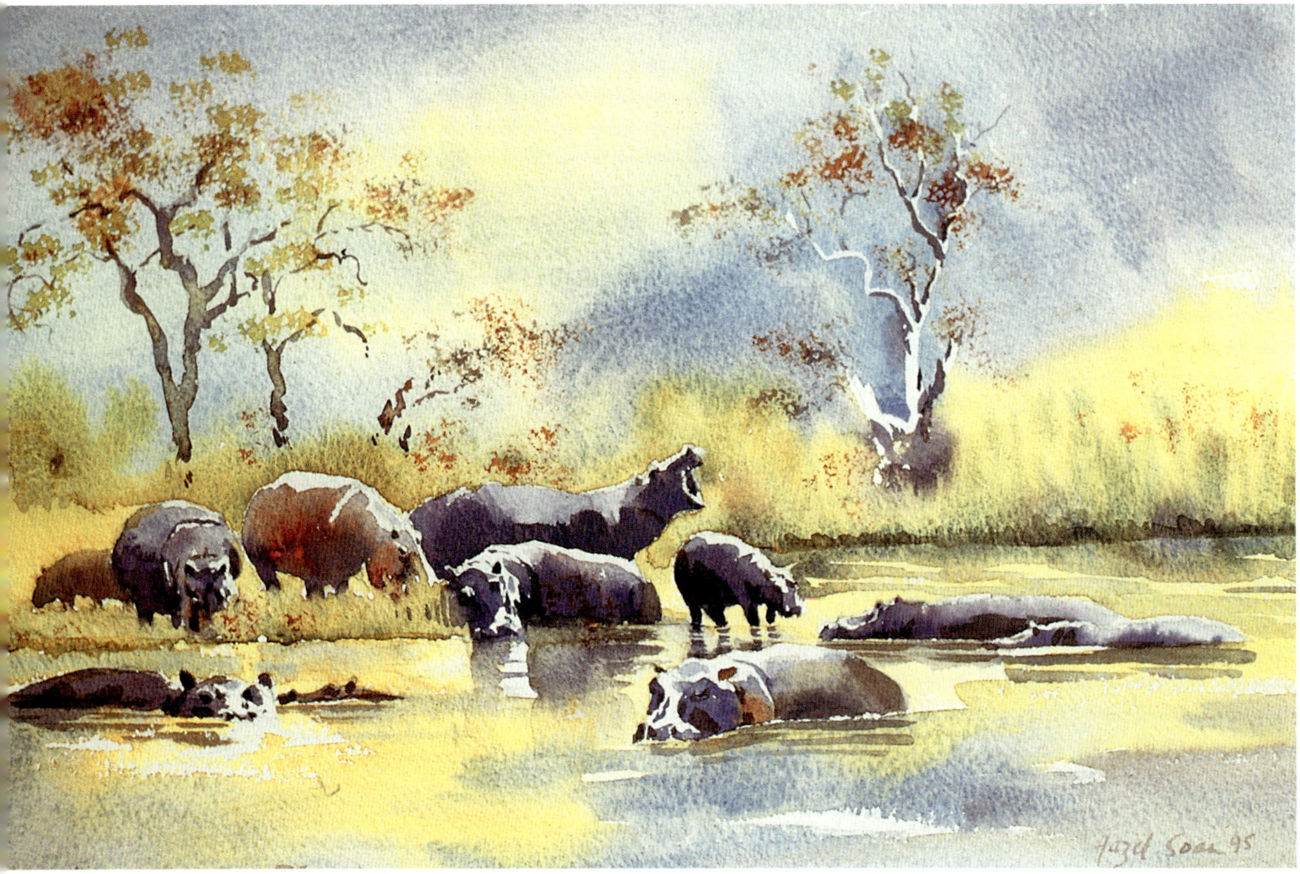

▲ HEADING FOR WATER
18 x 23 cm (7 x 9 in)
Cadmium Yellow shimmers in the landscape beside the Alizarin Crimsons, Ultramarines and Burnt Siennas of the elephant hides.

◀ HIPPOS IN THE SHALLOWS
28 x 36 (11 x 14 in)
The sheen of the wet backs of the wallowing hippo contrast brightly against the dark undersides. During daylight hippo spend most of their time under the water, coming out on the banks late in the day.

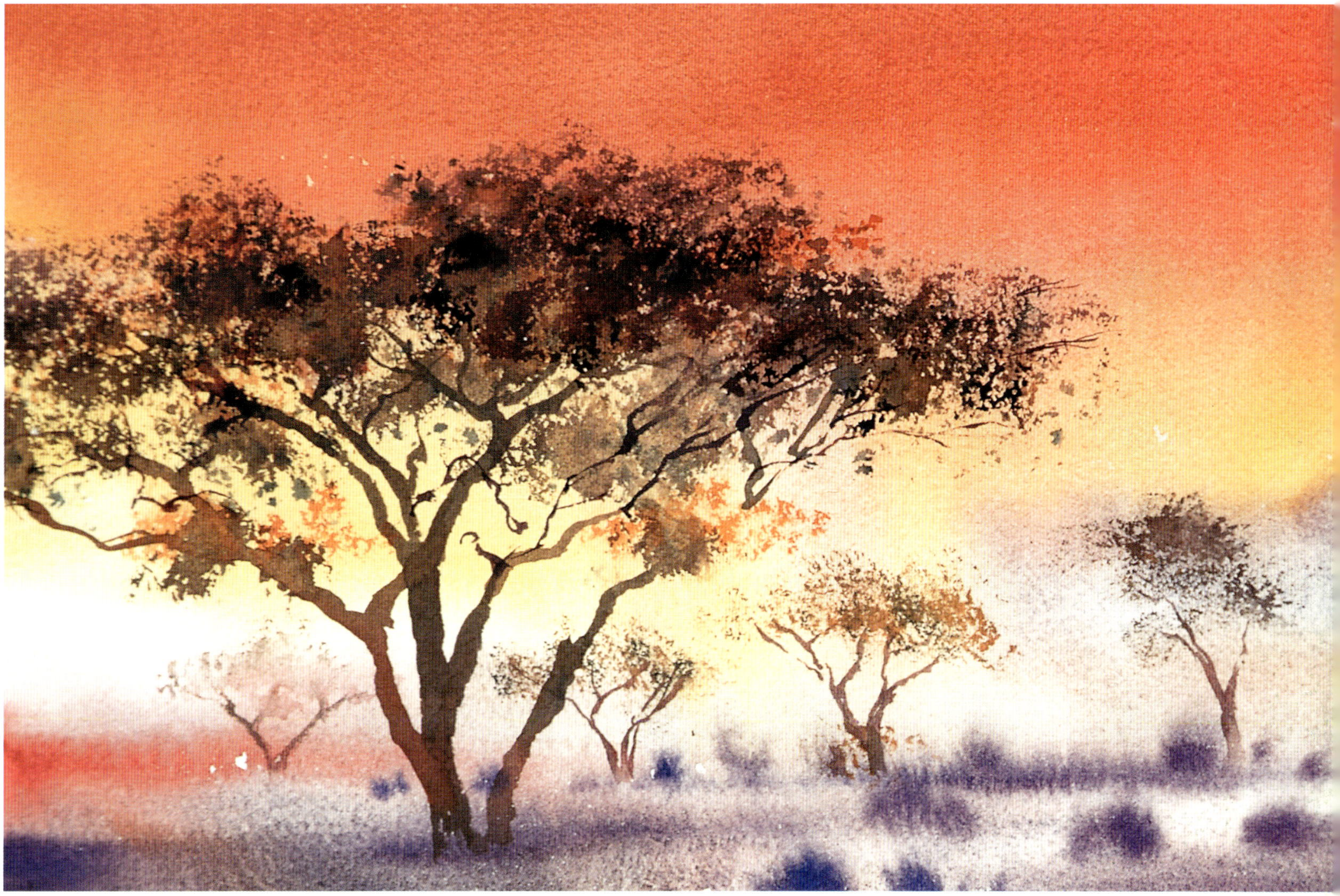

▲ SUNDOWN, BOTSWANA
28 x 36 cm (11 x 14 in)
Colourful blacks and dark tones can be created by blending the three primary colours. The silhouette of the acacia tree is painted with a mixture of the red, yellow and blue of the sunset.

Fire and water

Perhaps the greatest contrasts of tone occur at sunset, when the blazing sun, mirrored by the lazy river, descends swiftly to its nightly home and the bush is cast instantly into silhouette. Black is rarely used in watercolour, but on this occasion it is often warranted. Although watercolours take a long time to dry at this time of the day, some of the most thrilling colours in the palette can be used with great intensity. It is often better to watch, waiting until the sun has actually set, before making the painting, The colours in the sky continue to burn bright long after the sun has gone.

With the pale light of dawn the tonal contrasts mellow. The surface of the wide Chobe River stirs gently with the flow of the stream and the mild breeze. As the animals come down to drink they cast soft reflections at the water's edge, which can be gently portrayed with wet-in-wet blends. Where the reflections are cast in dark, distinct ripples the tip of a round brush or the end of a flat brush can be used to paint the ripple lines.

Deep darks and reflections

The mirror effect of reflections and the contrast of tones make good compositional design. The repetition of the colours above and below the waterline creates unity and the different values add impact.

Still water

When the water is still the reflections are uninterrupted by ripples. They may be soft and blurred or more defined, like mirror images. Wet-in-wet washes, blending softly into the water, create a hazy, indistinct echo of the banks above. Wet-on-dry washes create a crisp mirror-like reflection.

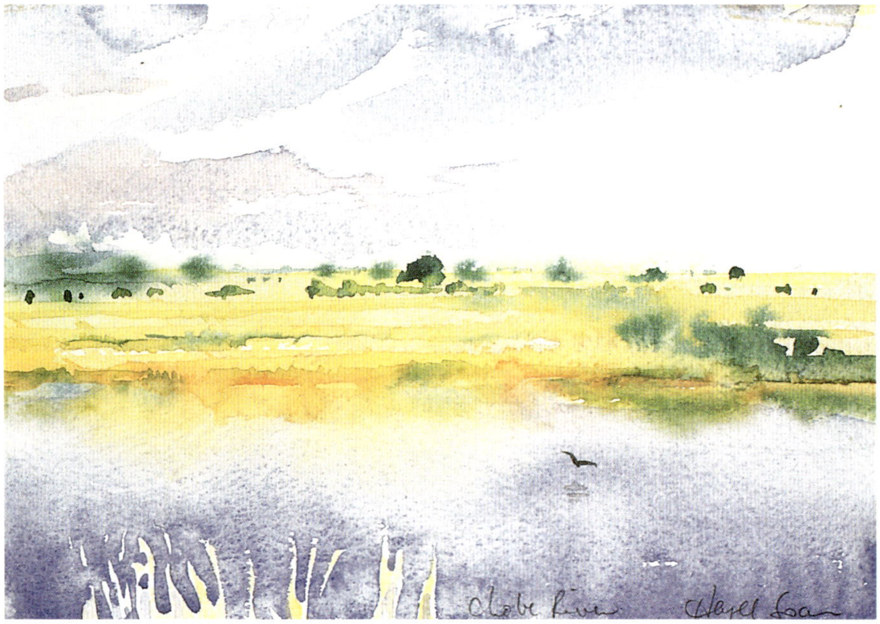

▲ ACROSS TO ZAMBIA
20 x 28 cm (8 x 11 in)
Brush in the reflection colour along the waterline while the wash for the water is still wet.

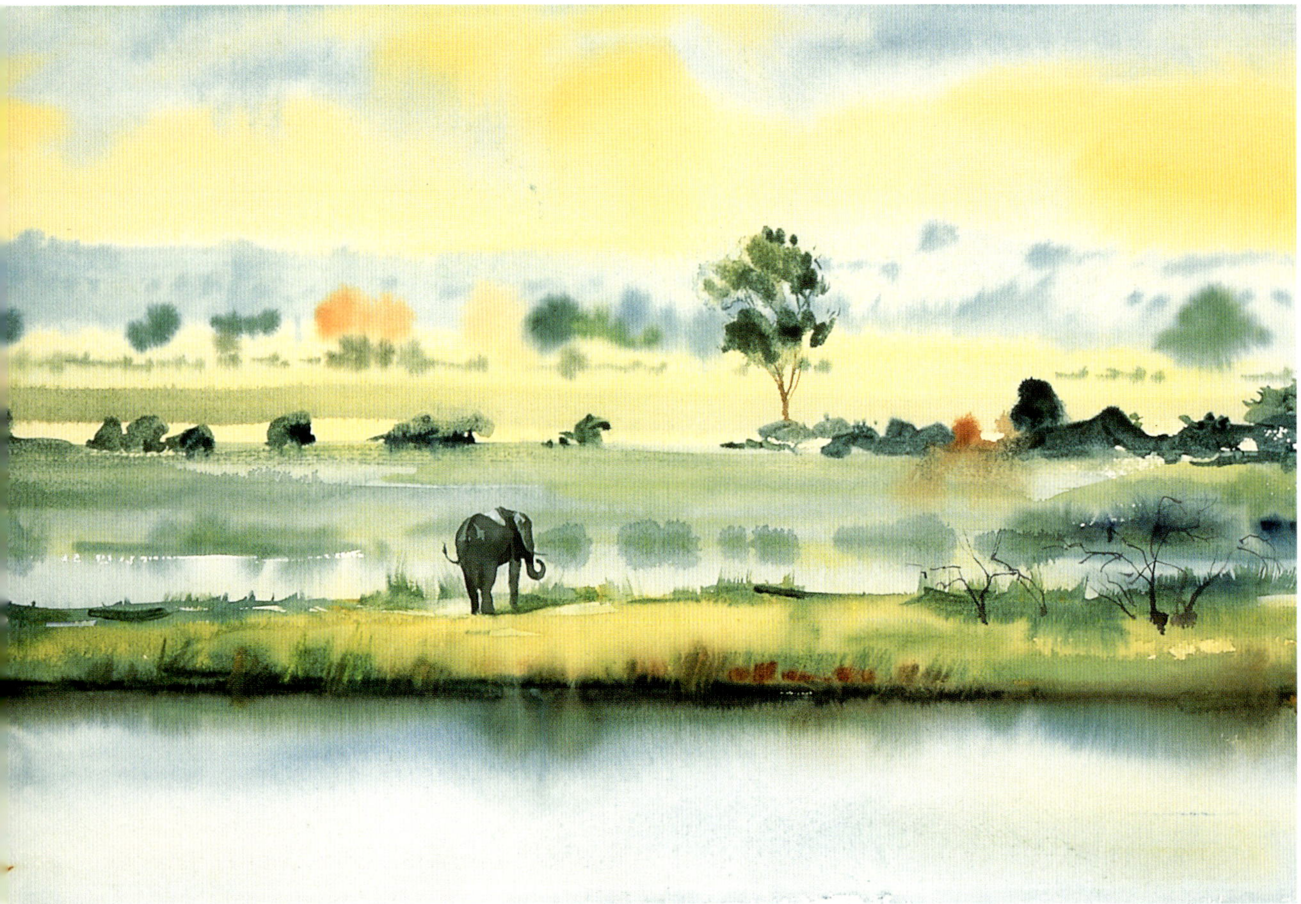

◀ LAZY RIVER DAWN
36 x 56 cm (14 x 22 in)
The river is still, and the reflections blurred. The wet-in-wet blends have been intensified under the bank by plunging almost neat colour into the damp wash.

▶ SERONDELLA SUNSET
10 x 13 cm (4 x 5 in)
Water mirrors both the land and the sky above. In this sunset the reflection was painted in tandem with the sky so that the colours tally.

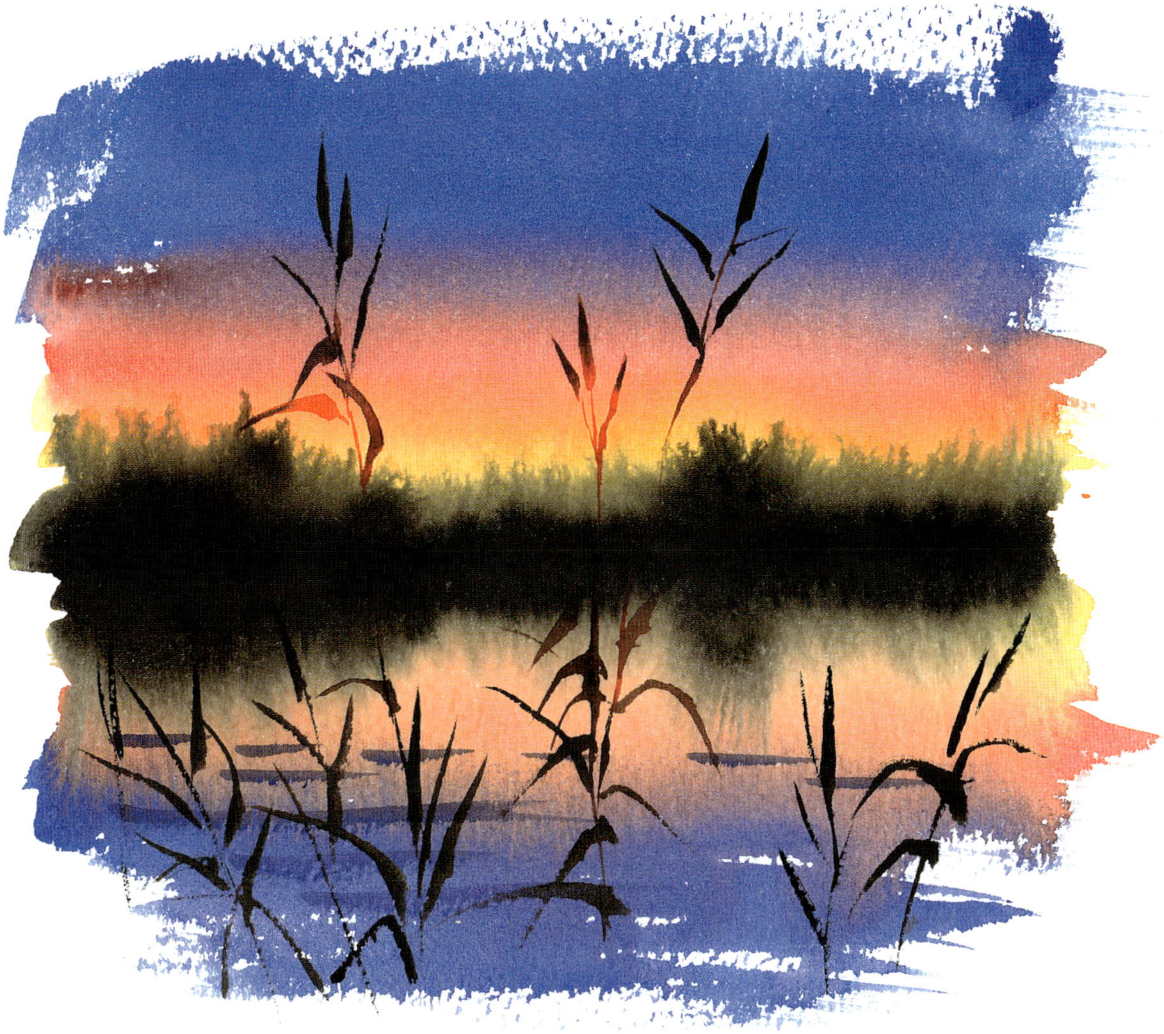

▶ NEWBORN
18 x 13 cm (7 x 5 in)
In this reflection of the wildebeest mother and child the spaces between the legs are also echoed in the nearly still water.

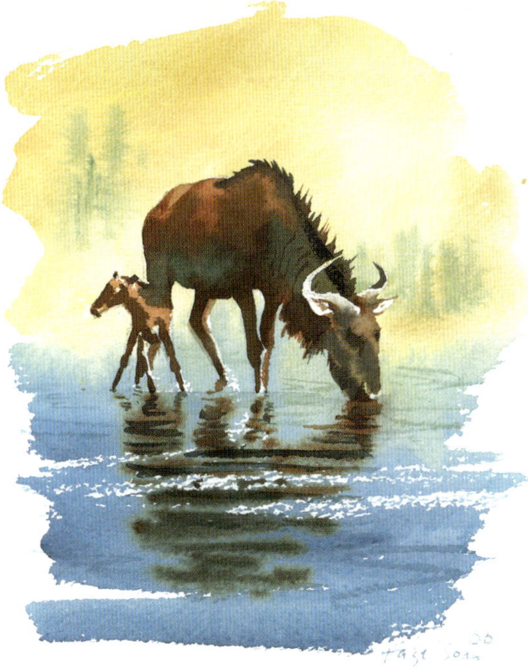

Reflecting the source

The reflection mirrors the world above and usually it is beneficial to paint the reflection after or at the same time as the feature being reflected. However, if you are blending the reflection into a wet wash it may spread beyond the desired area, so sometimes in watercolour it is better to paint wet-in-wet reflections first and then position the trees and animals above the shapes the blends have suggested.

If your watercolour looks fresh but the reflection and source do not quite marry, leave it alone and avoid the temptation to fiddle for the sake of accuracy.

Painting ripples

Water is seldom still. The movement in the previous chapter was linked to the wildlife; almost always its expression was twinned with a lightening of tone. Here, in the river landscape, the movement of water introduces ripples, which come to life in multiple lines of deeper, darker tones.

The two faces of the ripple act as mirrors; one side reflecting the sky, the other the landscape. Different water conditions display a variety of ripples, which can be painted with different techniques.

Disturbed water

Reflected colours and tones enable the painter to indicate the state of the ripples on the surface of the water. When still water is disturbed by an isolated incident, such as a herd drinking, elephants bathing, or the passing of a boat, evenly spaced ripples spread out across the mirrored surface in a series of parallel lines.

Further agitation breaks up the reflections into a jumble of darks and lights. Short, broken ripples can be represented with linear marks or dashes, and crescent or chevron shapes.

If the strokes are swift and animated they will carry more life than a brushmark that looks laboured.

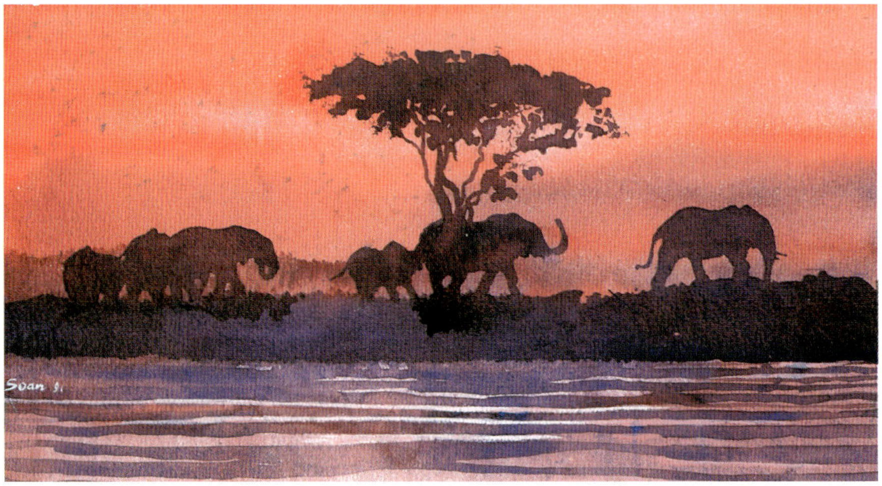

▲ DUSKY HOME
13 x 23 cm (5 x 9 in)
The even end of a flat brush is ideal for the longitudinal shapes of ripples. Narrowing the lines as they recede creates depth.

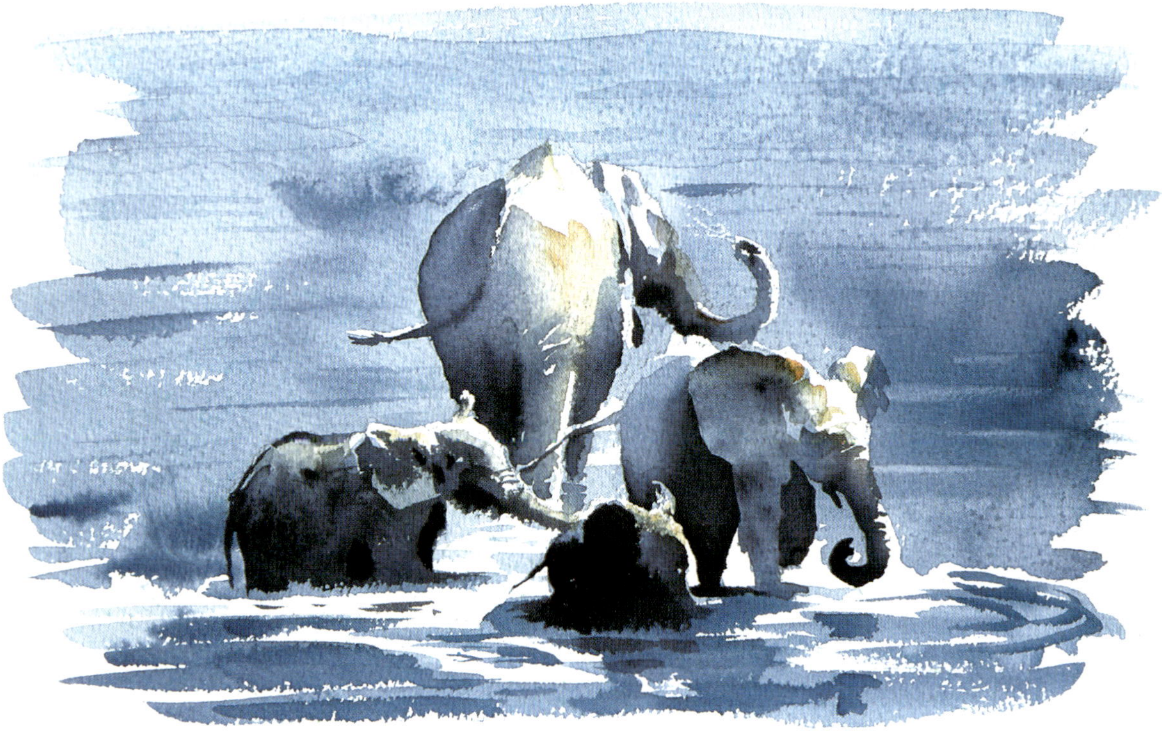

◄ TANGLE OF BODIES
23 x 28 cm (9 x 11 in)
Uneven white highlights are left around the elephants' legs to signify the churned-up water.

► The sparkle of ruffled water can be represented by dragging a wide, flat sable brush across the tooth of the paper.

Ripples of light

Flecks of light dancing across the surface of the water can be painted with a dry brushstroke, leaving white highlights within the wash. Test out your stroke first to ascertain how much water to pigment you need before launching into your painting.

Sometimes, rather than paint dark ripples onto light water, you may want to create light ripples in a darker wash. Thin ripple lines can be lifted out of a wash by loosening the pigment with the tip of a damp brush and then dabbing the colour off with a tissue.

You can also scratch off pigment in horizontal lines with the edge of a blade to reveal the white paper beneath. Alternatively, you can paint the ripples onto the wash with white gouache or Chinese White. Check that you use enough pigment or the white lines may dry paler than they appear when wet.

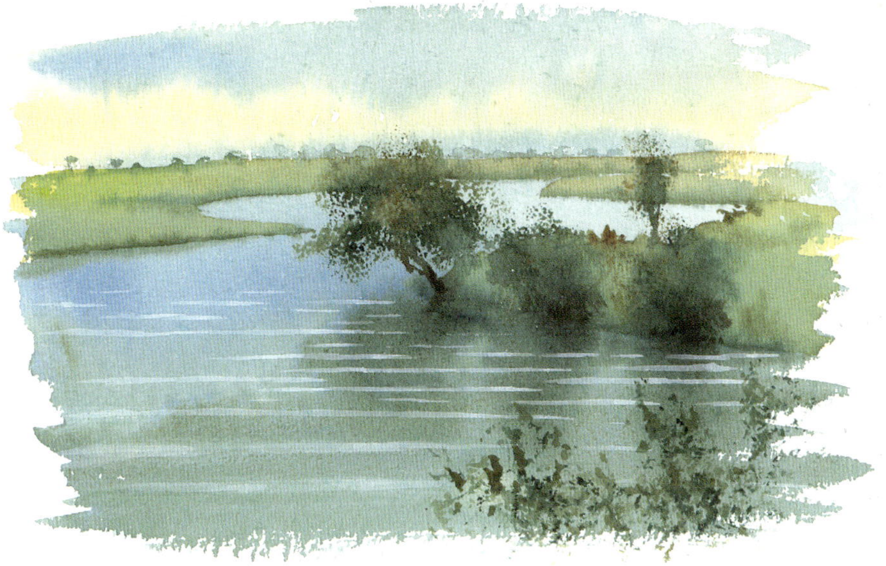

▲ These ripple lines are painted with opaque Chinese White watercolour and a flat brush.

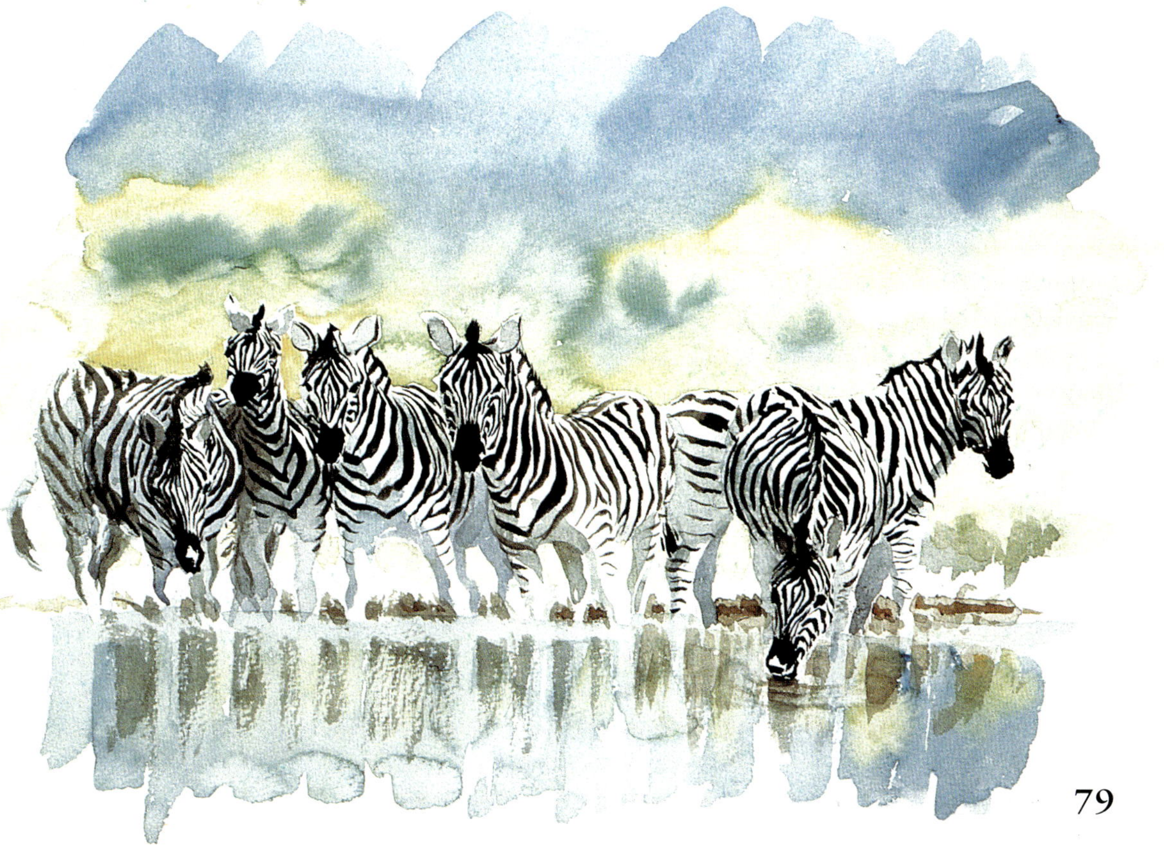

► BY THEIR STRIPES
38 x 56 cm (15 x 22 in)
Here the marks made with a dry brush are used between the reflections of the zebras' legs to give energy to the wash.

Safari sketchbook

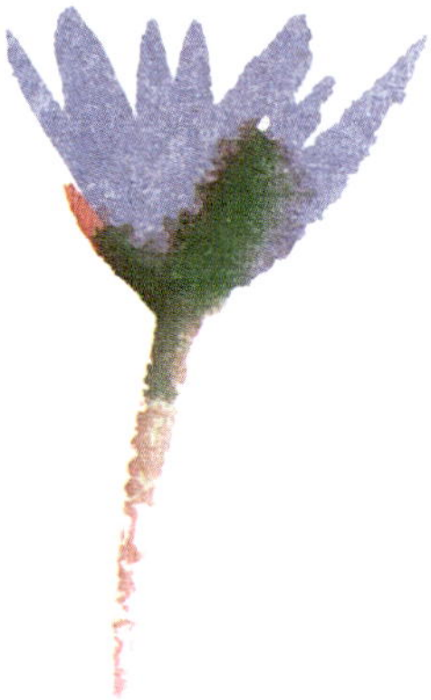

Rivers of land

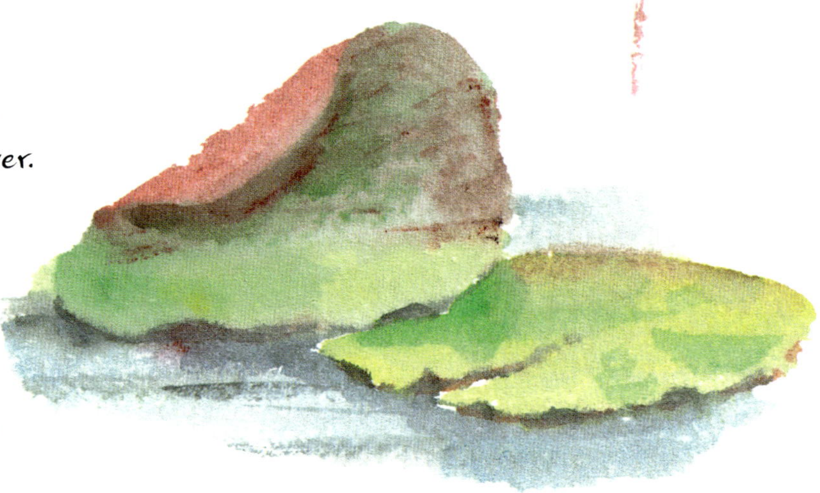

The Okavango Delta is an unrivalled wildlife paradise lying to the south of the Chobe River. Born in the mountains of Angola, the Okavango River flows east to the edge of the Kalahari and there divides into braids of small channels, lakes and swamps to form an inland delta that finally vanishes in the sand. This is a fragile wilderness, a finely balanced natural ecosystem that changes with the seasons.

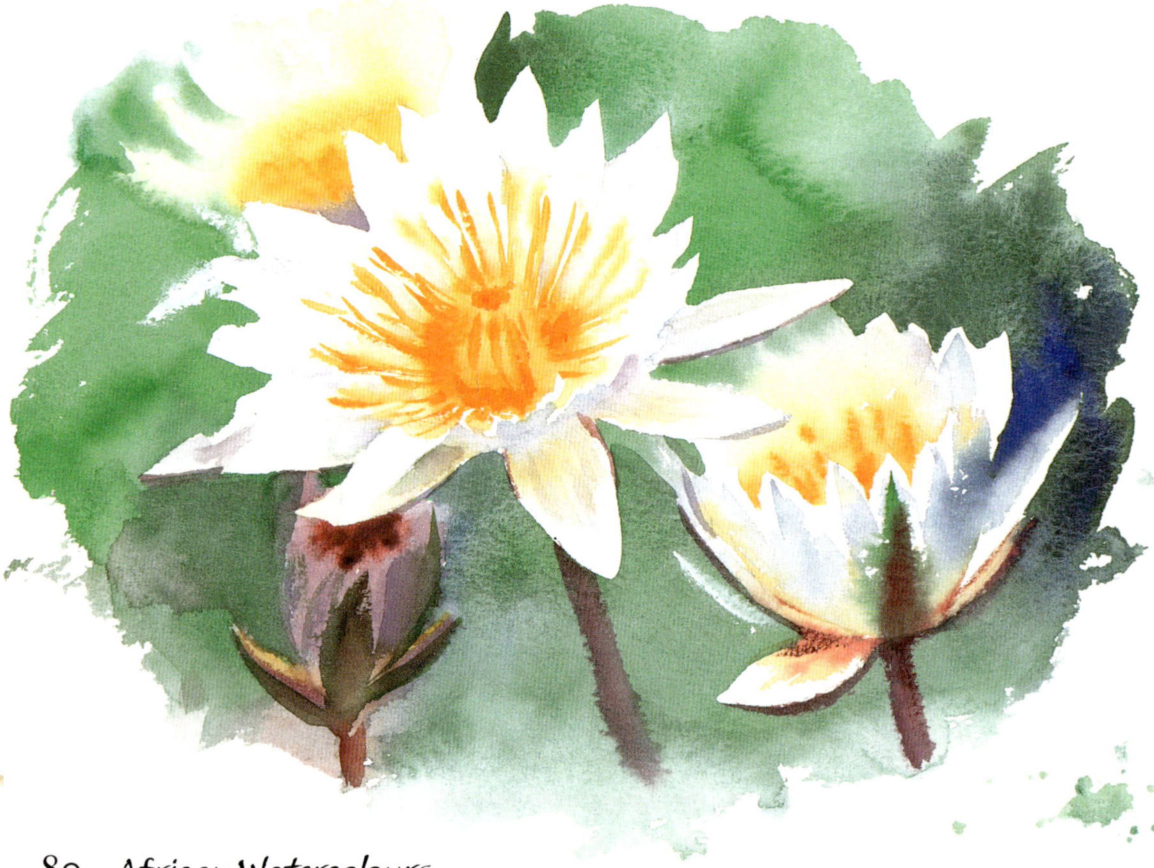

The streams and waterways are crystal clear, bordered by papyrus and decked with exquisite mauve and white waterlilies.

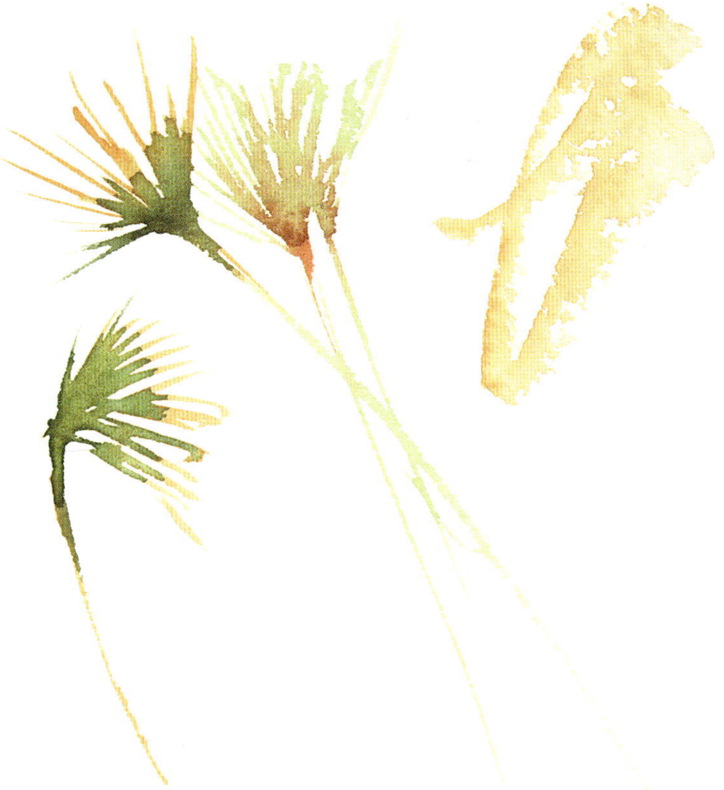

CAMPFIRE TALE

The roar of the lion

I woke to the spine-chilling belly call of a lion at close proximity to our camp at Savuti. I was eager to paint the bush at dawn, but waited in the ensuing silence until it seemed safe to duck out of the tent. I could see the print of the lion's huge paws in the soil and the deep imprint of hooves of an impala in flight. The spoor led a good way off to the north.

I took my paints and, walking a short distance in the opposite direction, found a good place to paint. I had not long started when I heard an over-calm voice behind me urging me to retreat slowly, back to the camp. I glanced to my right. Just six metres (20 ft) away a huge black-maned Kalahari lion stood watching me. I remember thinking how calm he looked, unlike me.

I backed off, he made no move, and then he turned and sauntered off. We traced his spoor and found he had circled right around the camp. Thankfully both the impala and I got off lightly that day!

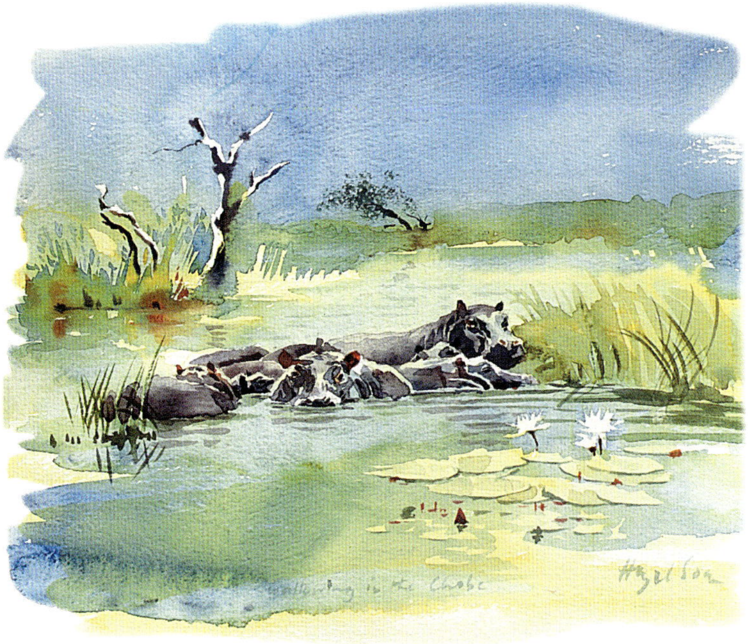

Crocodile and hippo live among the reeds that border the multitude of islands.

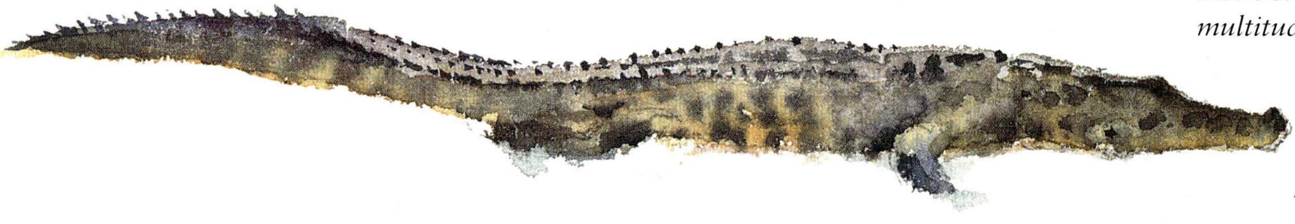

The Lake of Drowned Trees:

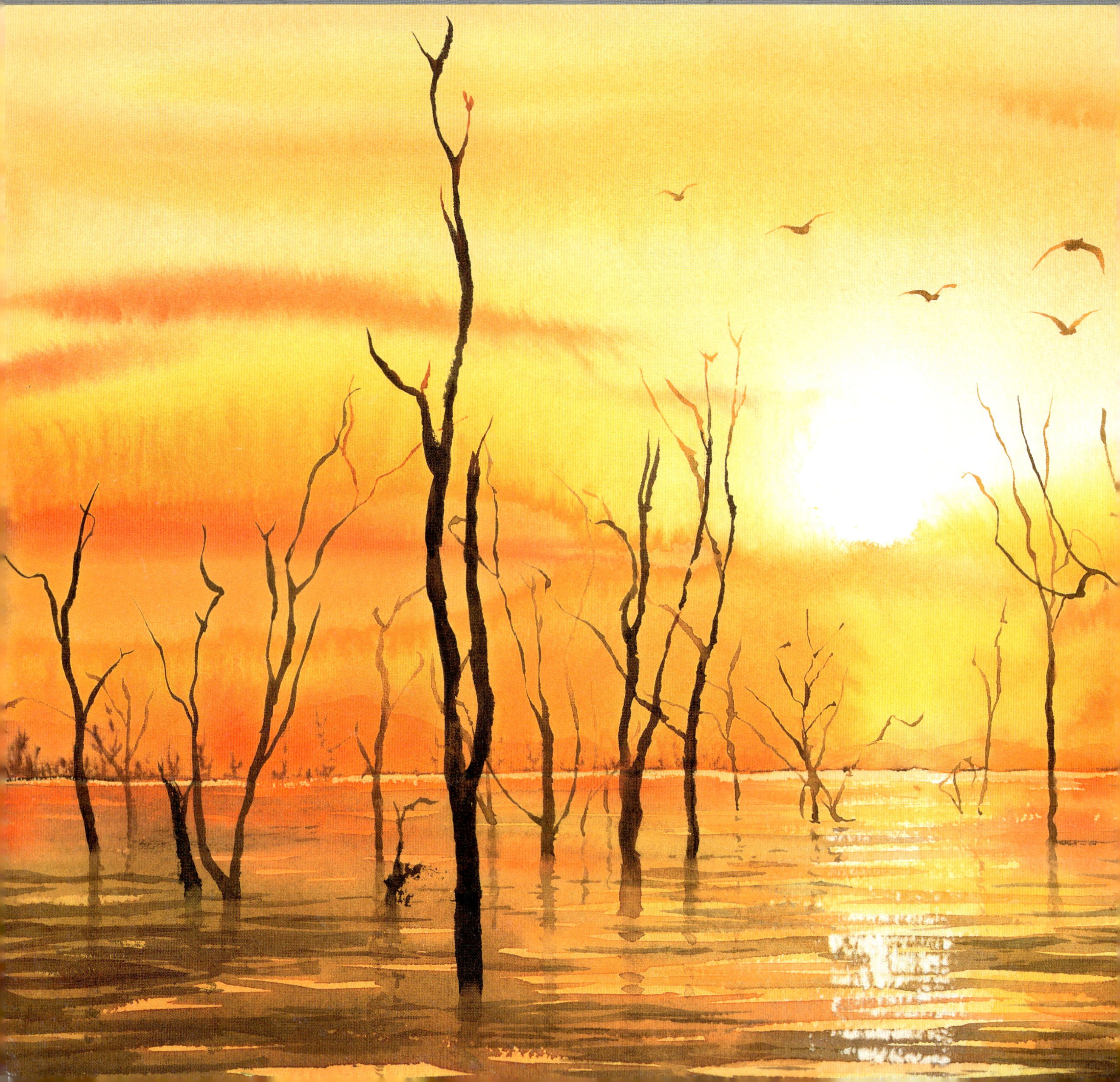

Kariba

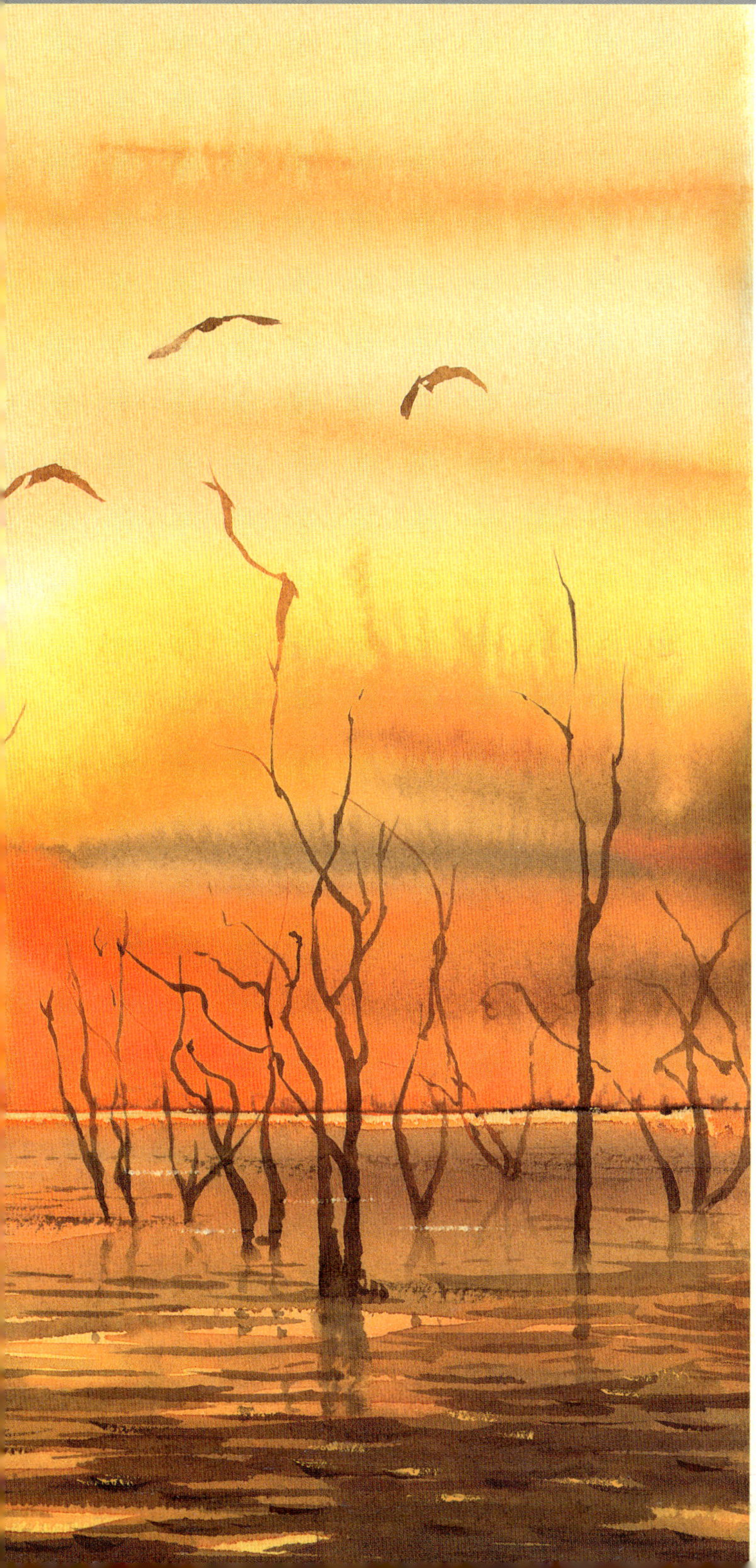

Exploring shape and line

Tall and trim, sharp and fine
lines, rigid with the passing time;
monographs to Noah's flood
shedding arboreal blood.
High above the eagle soars,
sears the skies above the shores;
charting branches for his perch,
remembering the olive search.

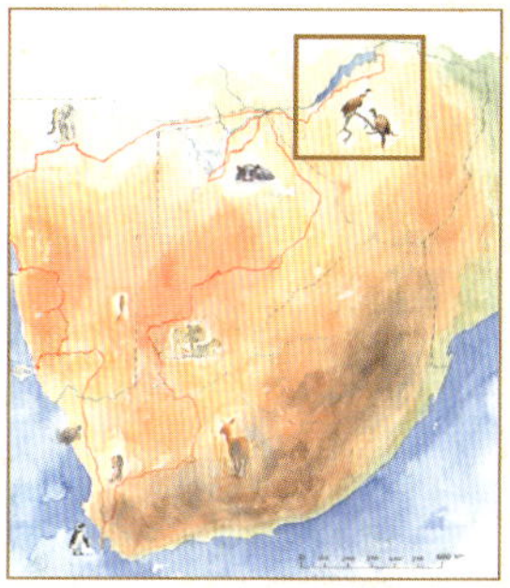

◄ SUNSET AT LAKE KARIBA
38 x 56 cm (15 x 22 in)

Floating islands, sunken trees

Crossing the border into Zimbabwe, the journey reaches Lake Kariba. This was the world's largest man-made lake at the time it was created in 1959. The Zambezi River was dammed by a huge crescent wall where it narrowed in a gorge after thundering over the Victoria Falls. When the water level rose more than five thousand animals had to be evacuated to safety.

The islands of the lake are cloaked with luxuriant grasses and support abundant game and a rich aquatic birdlife. Along the shoreline eerie landscapes of dead trees, drowned when the valley was flooded, shelter hippo and crocodiles or provide dramatic perches for huge fish eagles.

The trees, stripped of their bark, have grown white with time, creating an uncanny parade of spiky, angular shapes against a flat horizon. At sunset the trees make bizarre silhouettes against skies reddened by the dust-laden air, marching in random formation across the rosy lake.

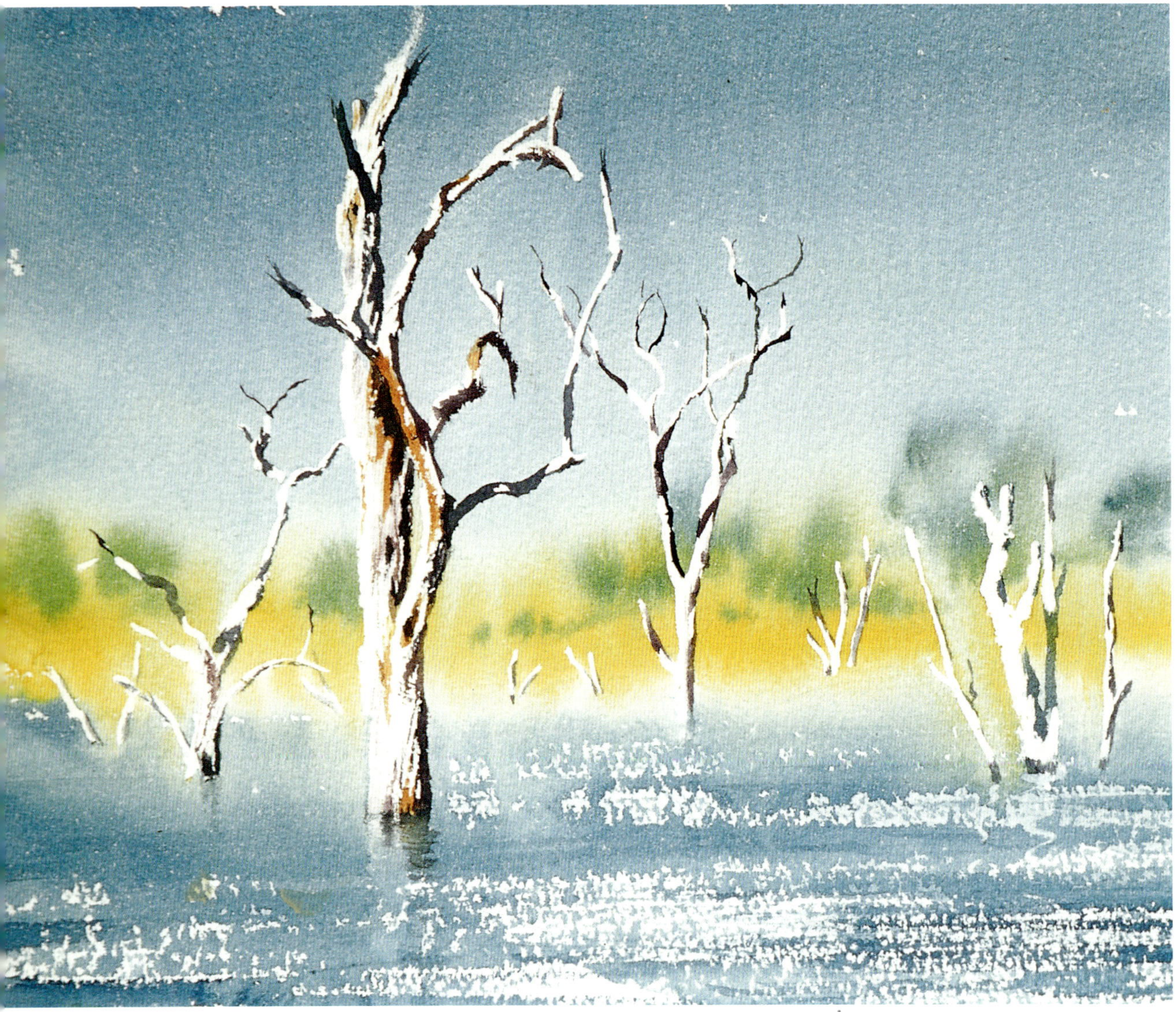

◀ GHOSTLY TREES
25 x 30 cm (10 x 12 in)
The light is dazzling, mirrored in the vast lake. Dry paint is dragged across the tooth of the paper to create the sparkle on the water.

▶ HIPPOS ON THE BANK
23 x 28 cm (9 x 11 in)
The round purple shapes of the hippos contrast beautifully with the ochres and golds of the dry grass.

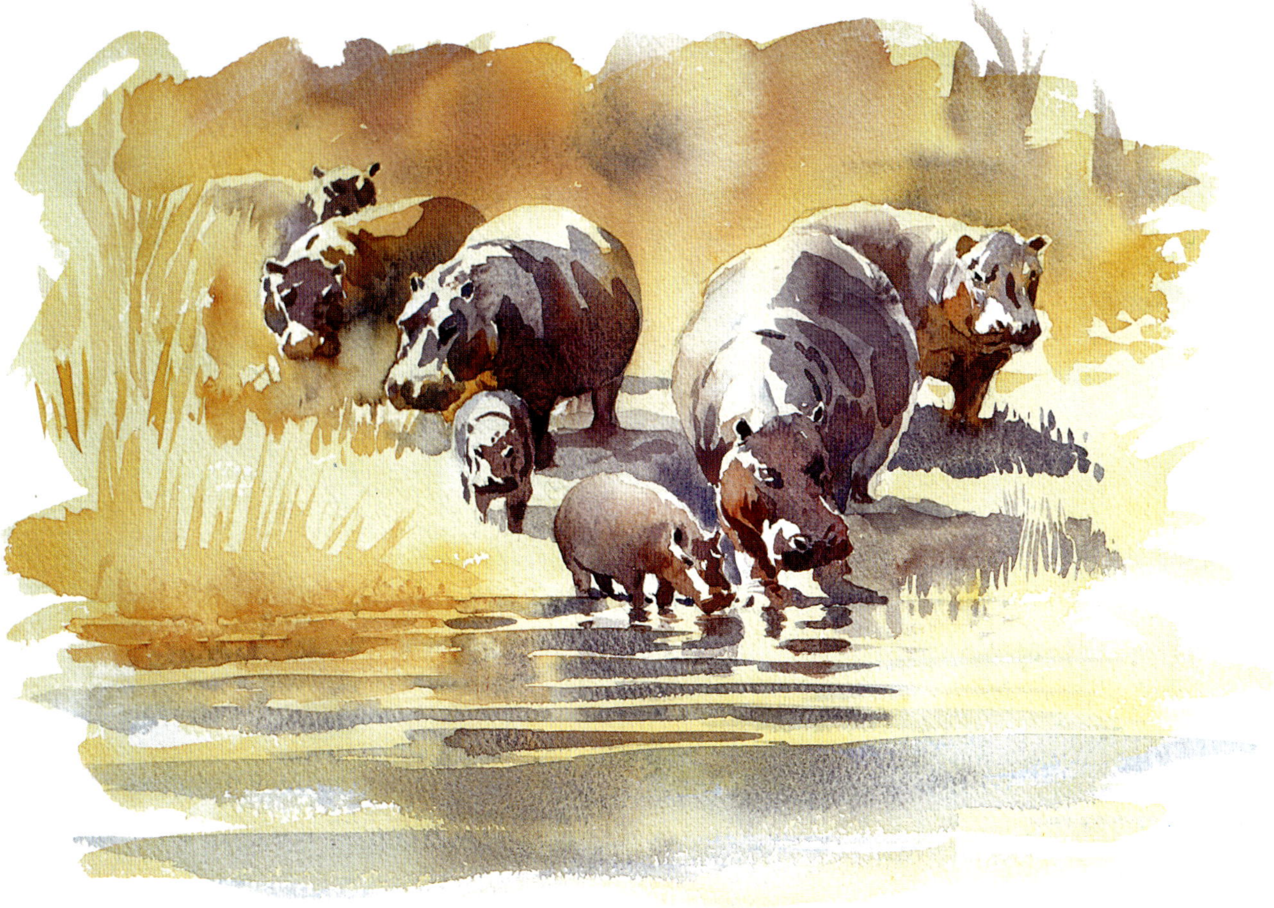

▼ THE SILVERY SEA
18 x 51 cm (7 x 20 in)
The lake sparkles, a blue expanse broken only by the stark branches of the dead trees and the light dancing over it.

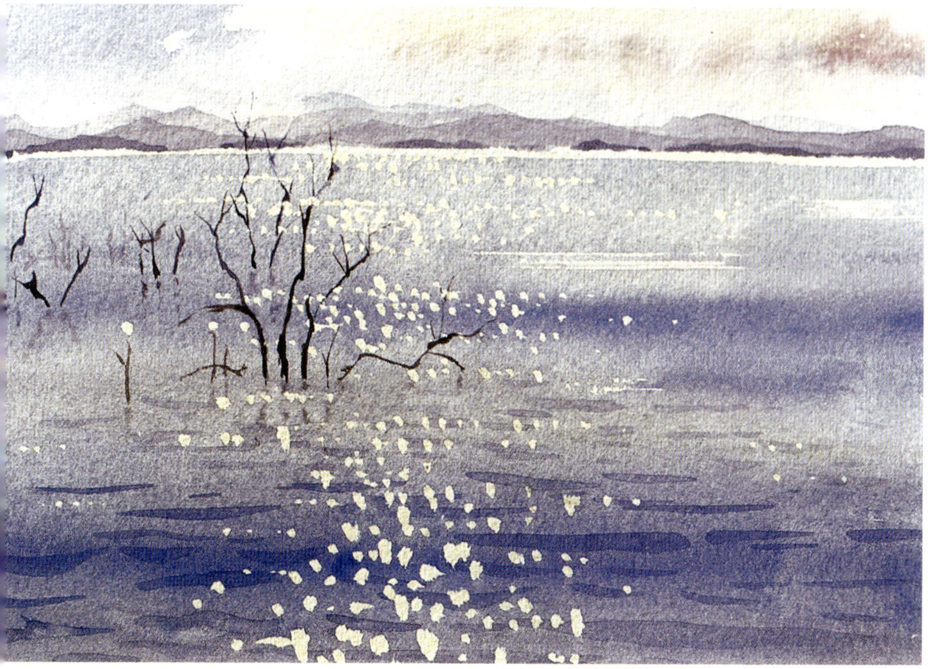

Silence in a silvery sea

The lake is explored by boat. Gliding silently past elephant, buffalo or impala peacefully drinking and bathing is a memorable experience. Without the hum of engines or the presence of vehicles you feel as if you have entered the animal kingdom by stealth and are watching their most secretive moments.

The lake changes colour as banks of cloud sail overhead; one moment the water is cobalt blue, the next it becomes a mercurial silver.

At night, moored in the shallows, you can hear the hippo come onto the banks to feed, their massive shapes dark and heavy under the star-filled night.

Painting on the lake

Against the wide panorama of this liquid landscape the shapes of trees and animals stand out starkly. Compositions come readymade as the twisted verticals of the trees make a perfect counterbalance to the horizontals of the lake. The rotund shapes of the larger mammals add the third dimension to this land of contrasting lines and shapes.

Being in a boat, low on the water, lowers the eye level, giving the wildlife greater dominance in the landscape. The mammoth size of a full-grown elephant and the nostrils of a hippo will appear to be much larger from the well of a boat than from the seat of a vehicle.

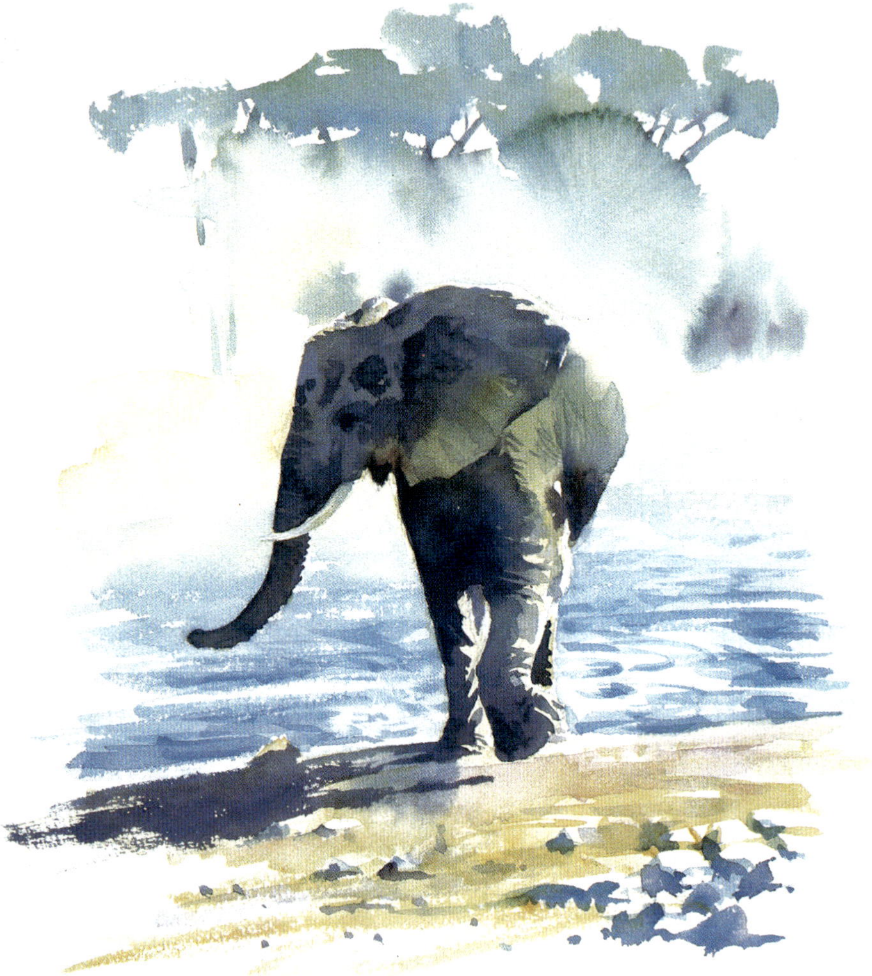

▲ LIFE-GIVING WATER
23 x 21 cm (9 x 8 in)
The proportion and shape of an elephant are utterly unique.

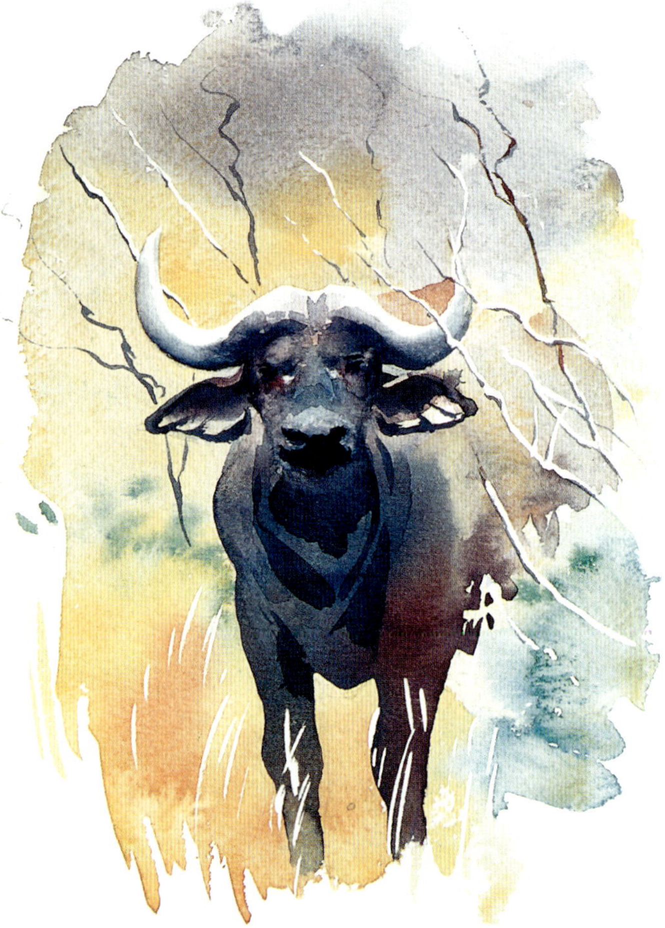

Relative proportions

A convincing shape needs few details. Look at the proportion of the head to the body, the length of the neck, the bulk of the torso and the shape and length of the legs, and the spaces between them. Compare the sizes of the various elements. Is the head, for example, as wide as the neck is long?

Be careful to place the eyes correctly, for the viewer is immediately drawn to them.

◀ BORN TO BE WILD
18 x 13 cm (7 x 5 in)
The buffalo's ears always seem too low down, but there they are!

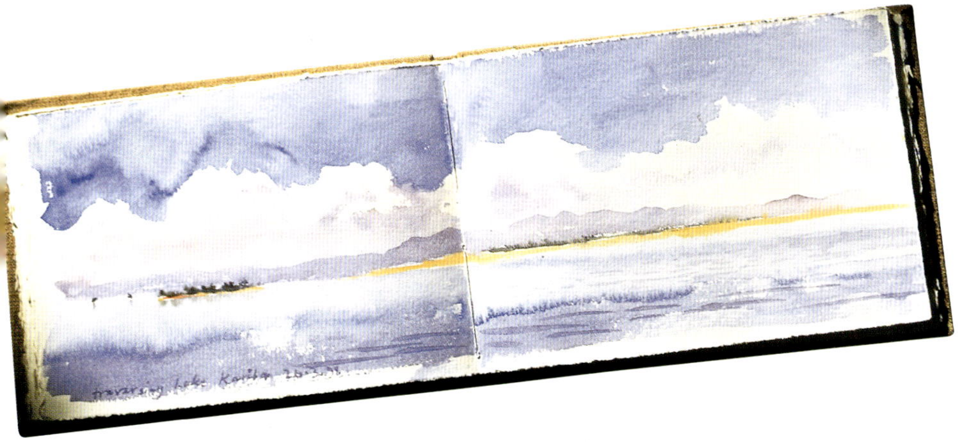

Looking at shape

Shape is defined from the outside in and determined by the inside out. Choose the shape and proportion of your painting to suit the subject matter. A wide landscape view may need to be narrow in height and a tall subject, such as a lone giraffe, will favour a vertical composition.

Watercolour pictures do not need flush borders to be finished paintings. Irregular margins of white paper around an image are not only attractive, but practical, giving you complete freedom of composition.

▲ LAKE KARIBA
20 x 56 cm (8 x 22 in)
The wide panorama of the lake is conveyed by painting across the spine of the sketchbook.

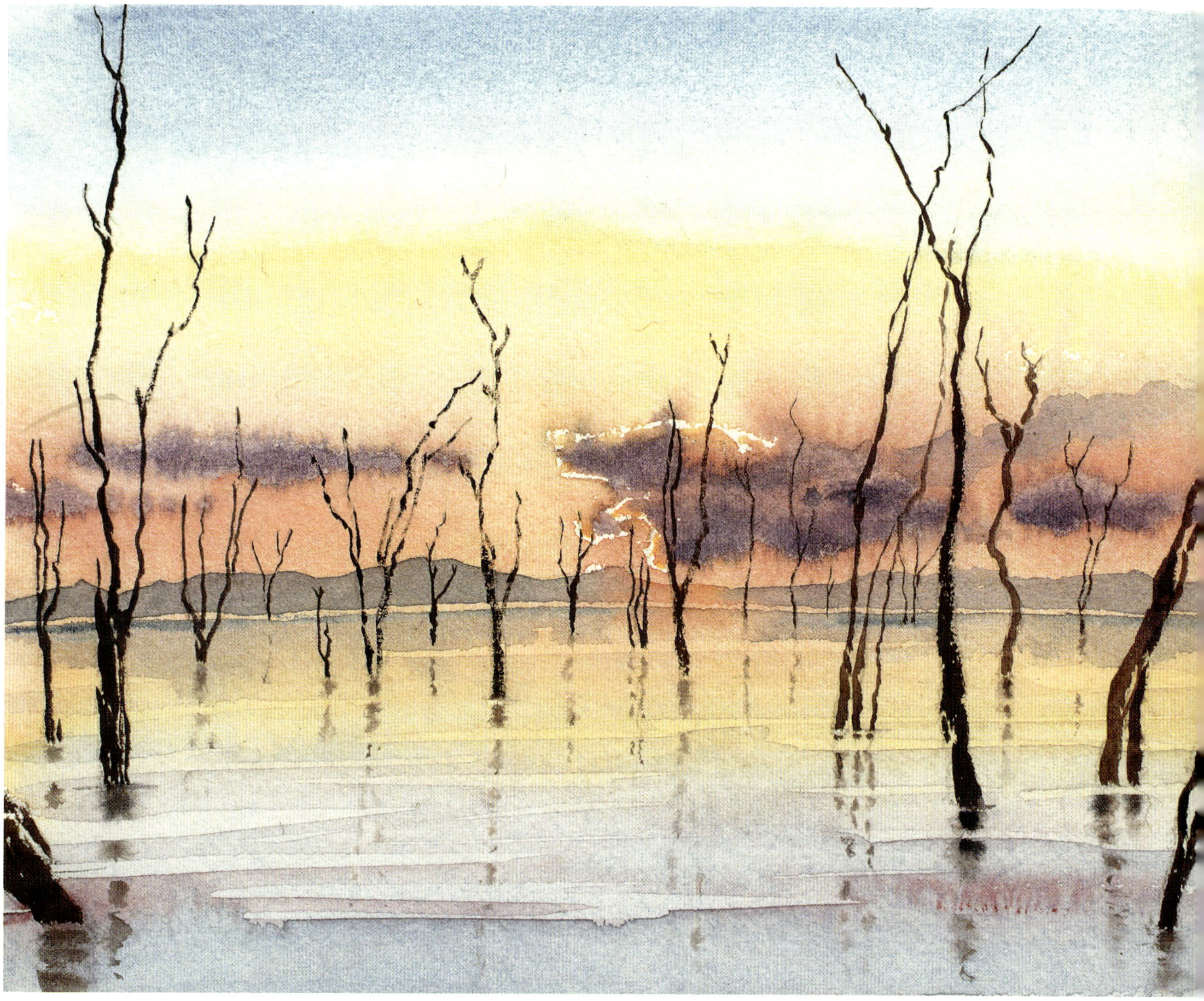

► KARIBA SUNSET
18 x 25 cm (7 x 10 in)
The shapes made between the tree branches are as relevant to the sketch as the lines of the branches themselves.

Exploring shape and line

Watercolour paintings are made up of lots of different sized washes, each with its own shape. If the shapes are interesting they will arrest the eye. These shapes include both the obvious shapes of objects themselves and the no less vital shapes of the spaces between those objects.

Shapes come in all widths and lengths. Loading them with meaning, freshness and energy will make your paintings sing.

Shapely lines

Painted lines, however thin, are narrow shapes. To find the direction of a line look at its angle to the verticals and horizontals in the view. Hold a pencil in an outstretched hand to help assess this angle.

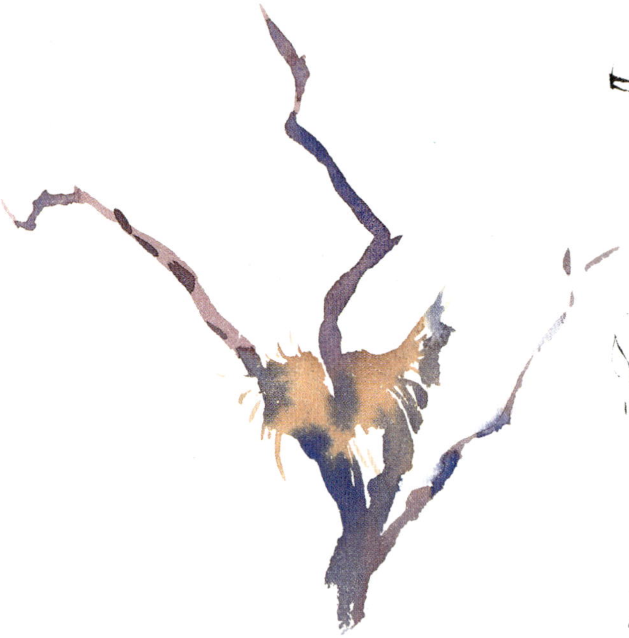

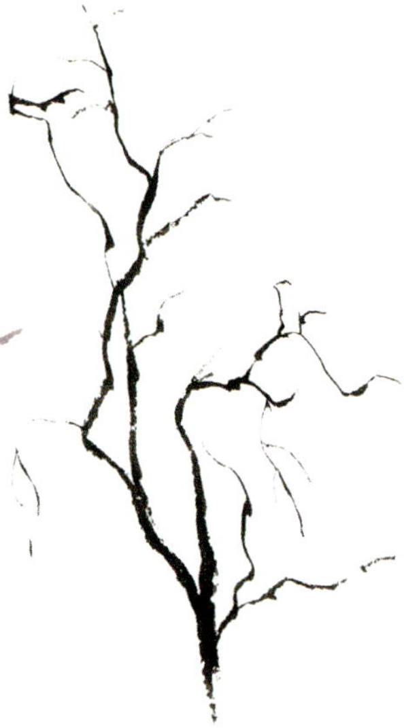

▲ *The versatile tip of a sable brush imbues a line with character. For a really fine line a rigger is useful. The long hairs and narrow shape paint fine, even lines that are ideal for tree branches, whiskers, grasses, stamens and rigging.*

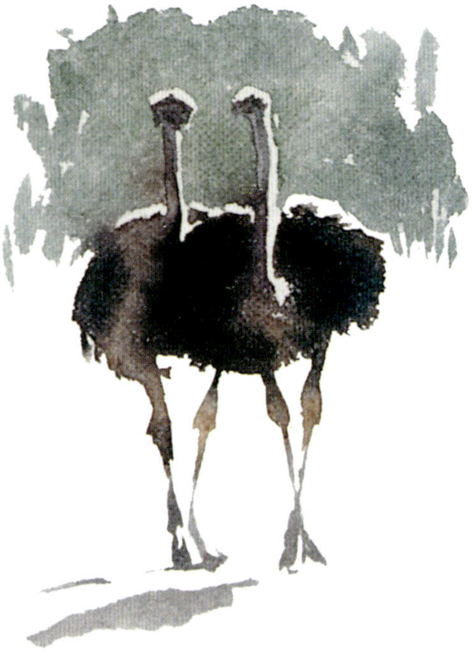

▲ *The shapely thighs, knees and calves of the ostriches' legs are all painted in one brushstroke with the tip and body of a size 7 sable brush.*

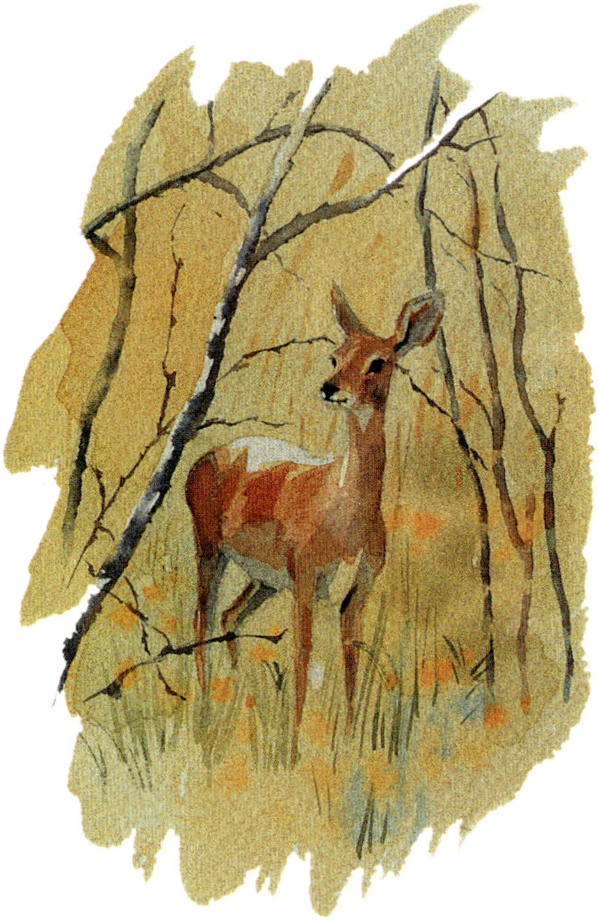

◄ *The brush is a very versatile tool. Down the length of a line you can alter its width with the slightest pressure. In this sketch the branches and grasses all are made with the same sable brush, a size 5.*

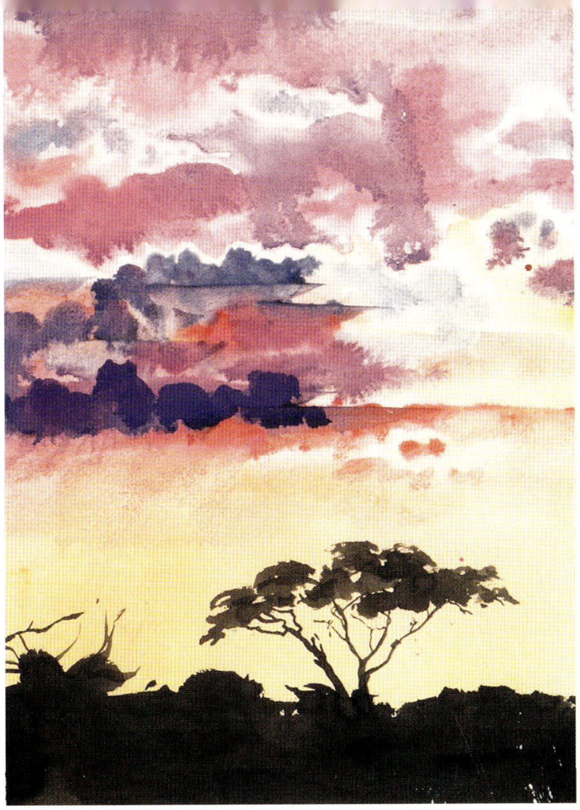

► A LANDSCAPE OF CLOUDS
56 x 38 cm (22 x 15 in)
There are no more than twenty brushstrokes in this painting. The clouds are built up with a series of flat, colourful, overlapping shapes, the silhouetted landscape is one wash and the tree is a construction of small shapes and lines.

Broad shapes

Watercolour's greatest asset is the beauty of its translucent washes. Paintings are made up of successive shapes of flat or modelled colours that overlap to form a convincing image on the page. Each wash will count towards the whole; therefore the shape of each wash matters.

Brushmarks may look spontaneous and carefree, but they are not careless. The tip and body of a sable brush will provide you with any shape you require.

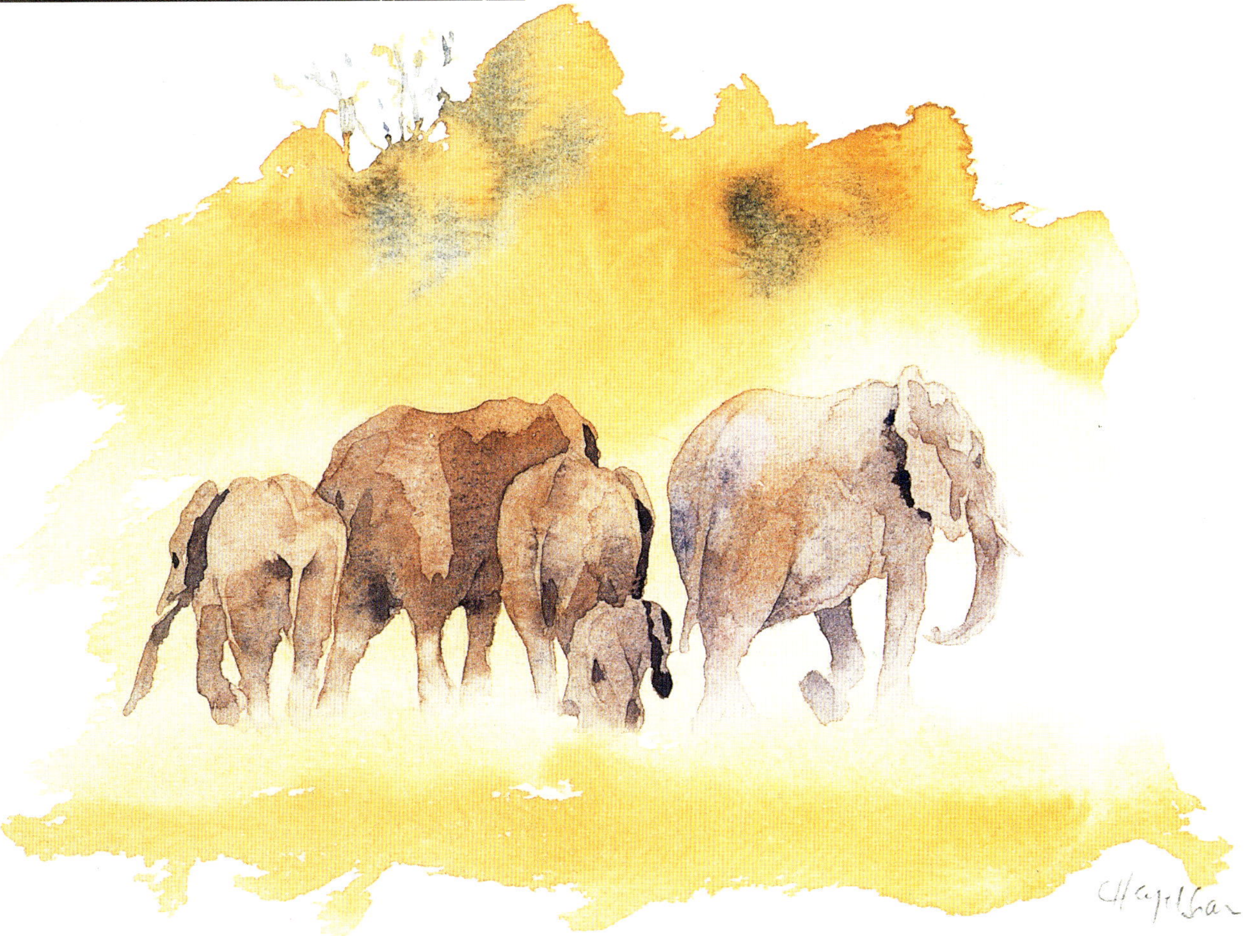

► *The elephants started as a pale silhouette. They were then distinguished one from another with a little modelling of their forms. Each wet-on-dry wash has its own shape that suggests the bulk of the bodies, the ears and tails.*

Positive and negative shapes

A painting is made up of positive and negative shapes. The positive shapes are the concrete, outline shapes in the painting and the negative shapes are the space-shapes around and between them.

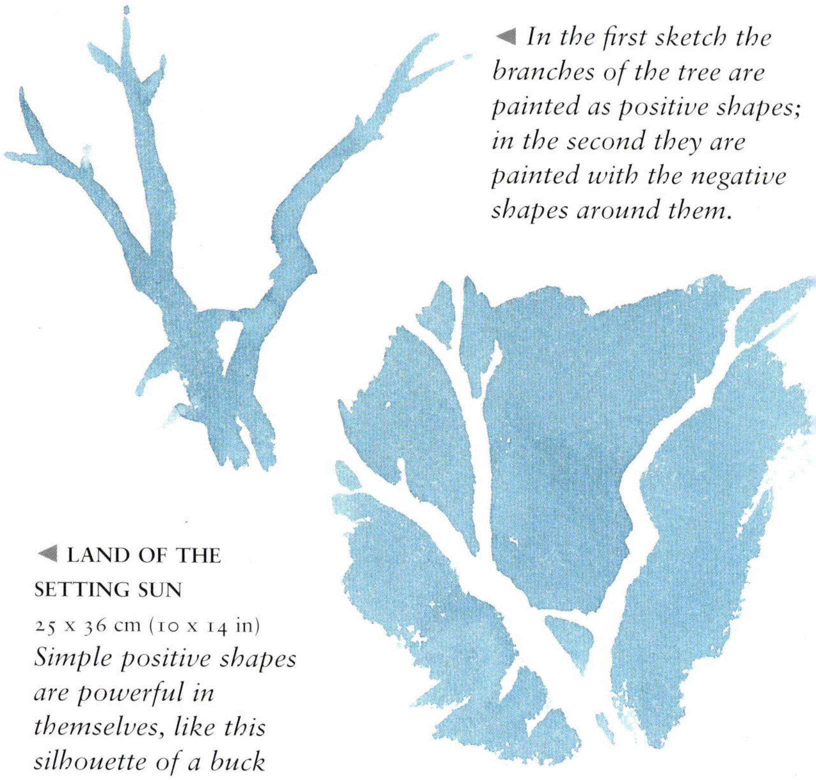

◄ *In the first sketch the branches of the tree are painted as positive shapes; in the second they are painted with the negative shapes around them.*

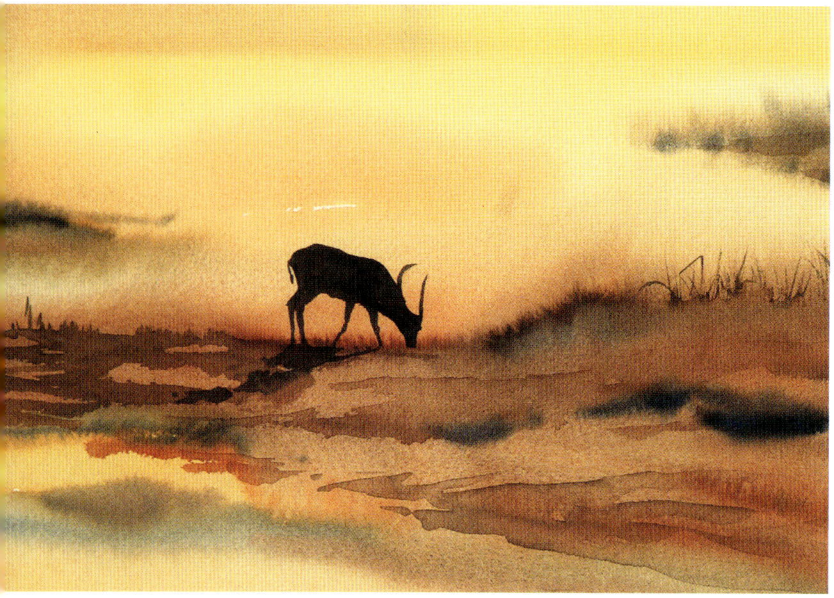

◄ LAND OF THE SETTING SUN

25 x 36 cm (10 x 14 in)

Simple positive shapes are powerful in themselves, like this silhouette of a buck against the background of the lake at sunset.

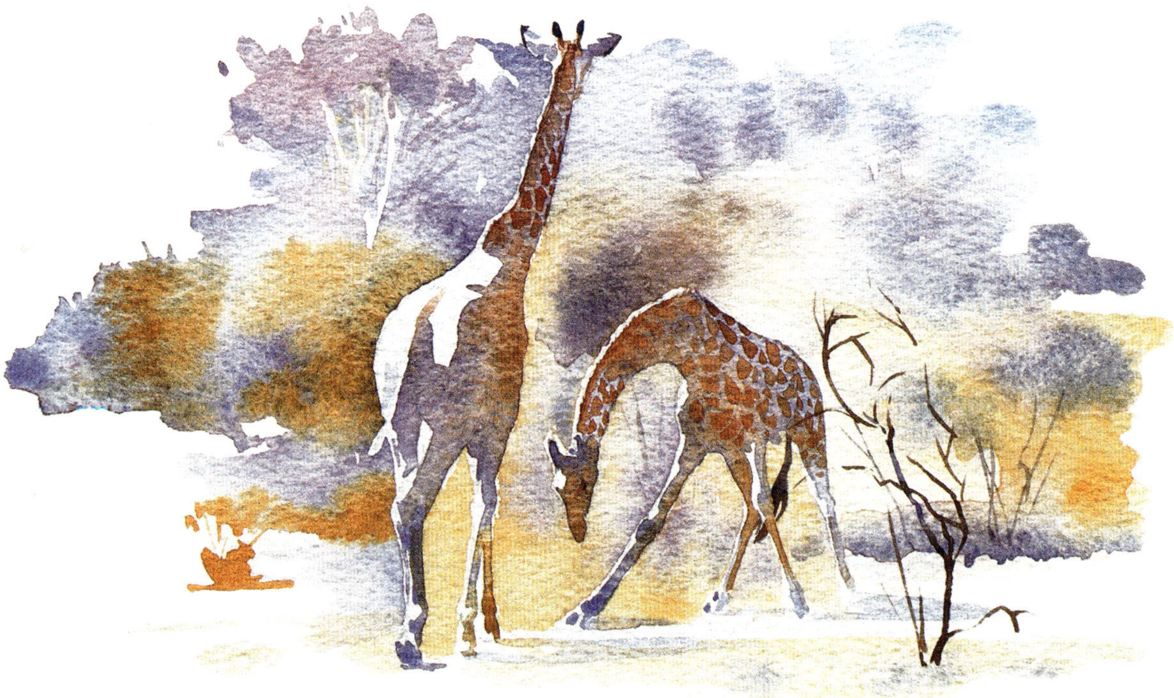

◄ LONG-NECKS

18 x 25 cm (7 x 10 in)

In this painting shape is paramount. The positive shapes of the giraffe and the shape of untouched white paper for the highlight on the back, the negative shapes between the legs, below the bending neck and the space between the two animals all come together to make a graceful painting.

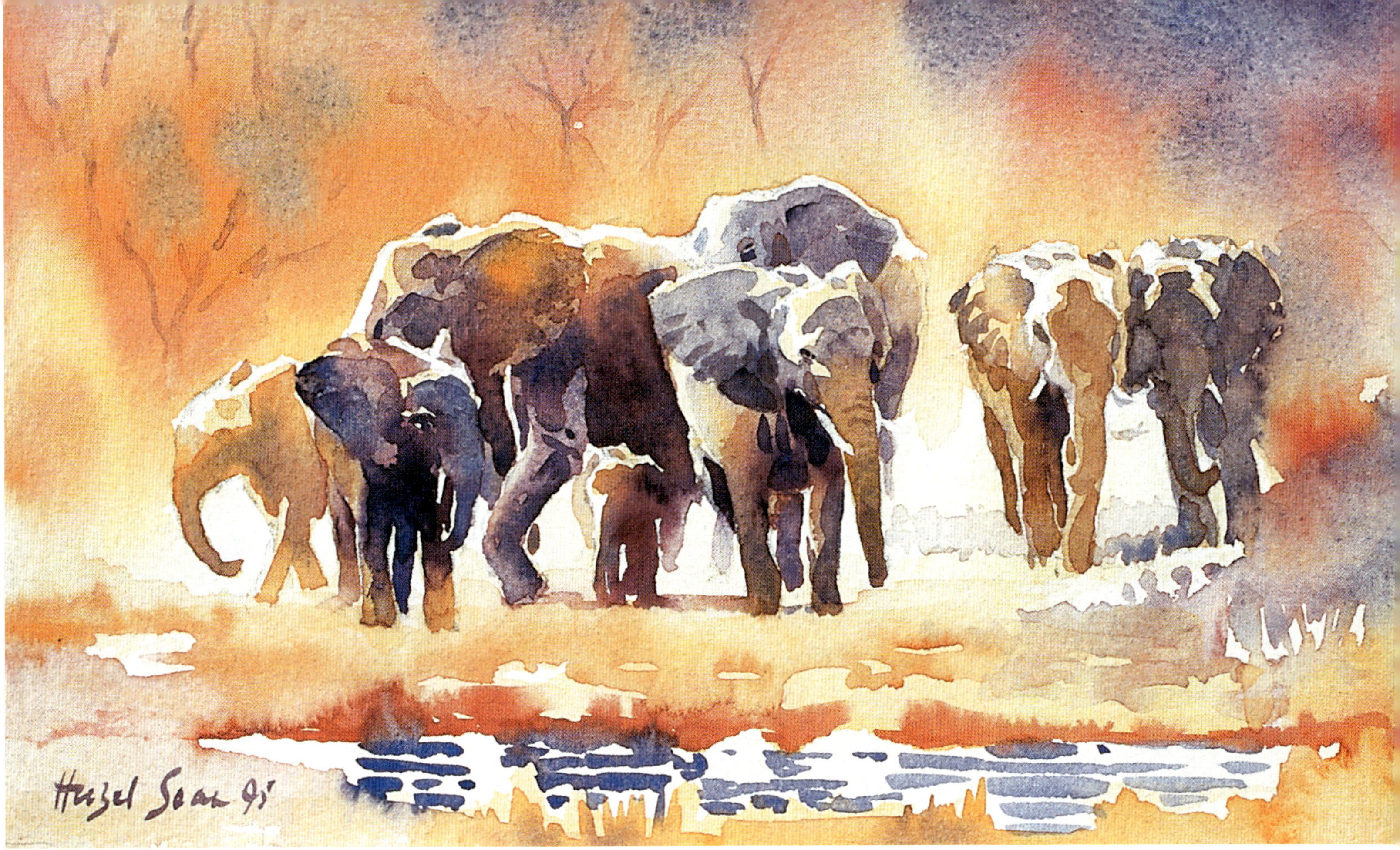

▲ AFRICAN HARMONY
20 x 28 cm (8 x 11 in)
Any number of colours can be blended in a wash, but to ensure unity in the painting use a limited palette.

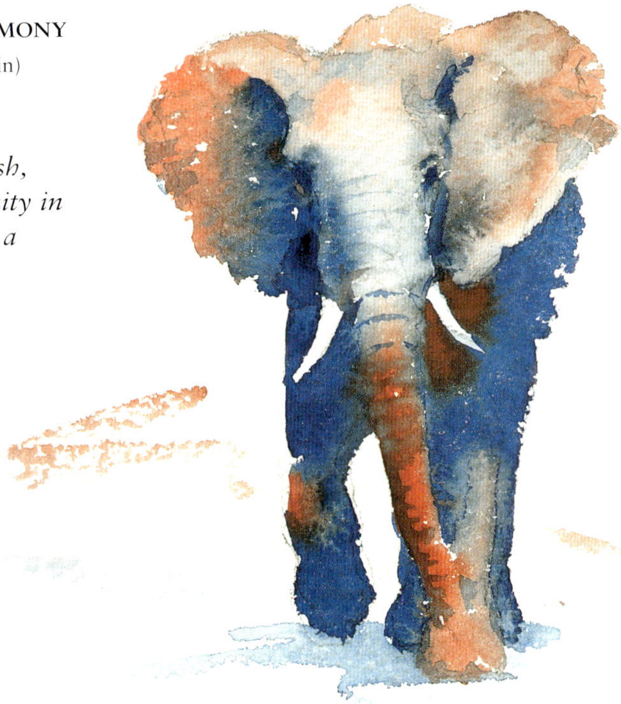

◄ *Strong wet-in-wet colour is touched down at the point where it needs to be most intense, and spreads out into the shape of the elephant.*

Blending colours in a shape

An exciting property of watercolour is the ability to blend colours within a single wash or shape. Delicious blends occur almost by default. Resist the urge to 'improve' the drying wash.

Backruns can create exciting and unpredictable textures; sometimes these look lovely, but at other times they may destroy the elegance of a wash. Watch your painting as it dries and lift out excess water with the corner of a tissue or tip of a brush.

Safari sketchbook

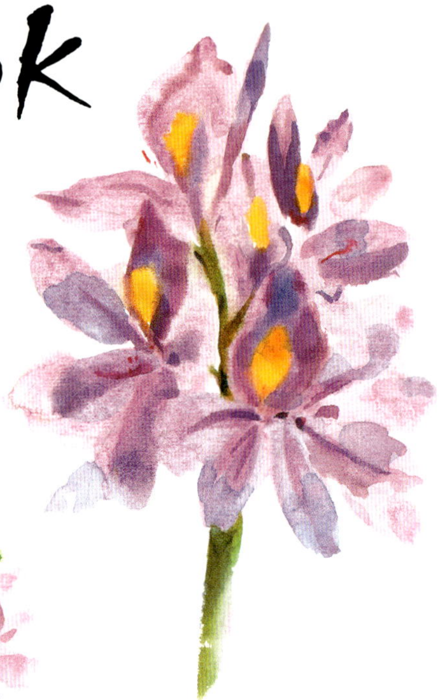

Hippos and hyacinths

In summer the shorelines of Lake Kariba are overtaken with the attractive, but invasive, water hyacinth. For the painter these beds of floating flowers make pleasing lilac borders to the green of the grassy banks. The animals, however, have to wade through the choking gardens to reach the sustaining lake. Within the dense blue-green foliage hippo lie camouflaged. Overhead the eagle soars freely, searching the waters for unsuspecting prey.

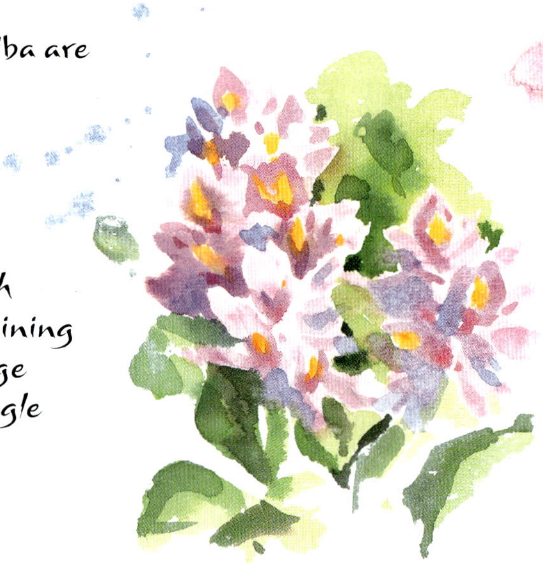

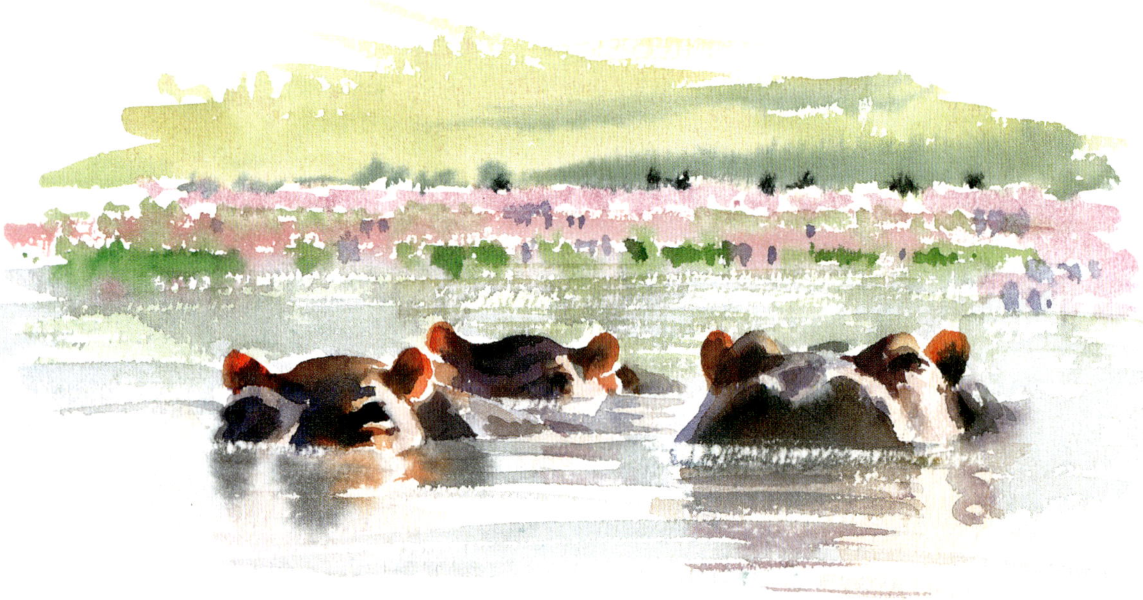

Of all the wild animals in the African bush the benign-looking hippo is renowned for taking the most human lives.

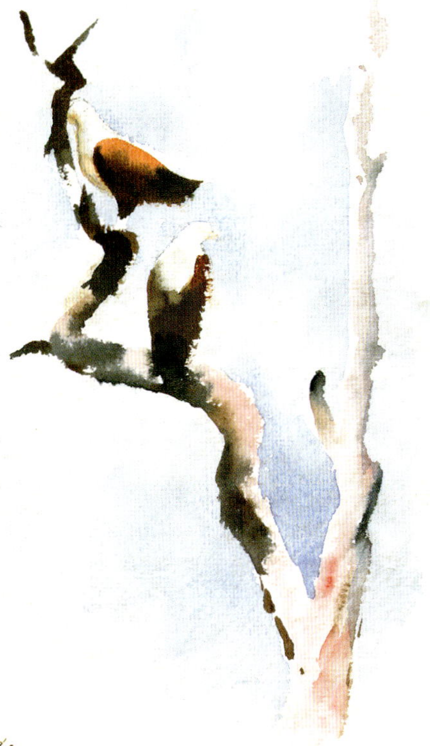

Dead trees provide excellent vantage points.

Campfire tale

Hidden hippos

While painting a herd of elephant from a small boat on the lake, we were suddenly jolted by a hippo escaping from the water-hyacinth beds beneath us. She settled herself a short way off and began calling. We realized her child must be camouflaged in the shallows and trapped on the other side of our boat.

Hippo do not like to be separated from their young and have been known to torpedo boats from under the water. Up and down she went, holding her long breaths. We switched off the engine, our hearts pumping, unable to breathe. The dilemma? — whether we waited as still as possible in the hope of allaying her fears, or whether we started the engine and tried to get out of there as fast as possible. After an interminable time we decided to risk escape. We started the engine and the hyacinths burst into life beside us as the baby hippo made a dash for freedom. With great relief we did the same.

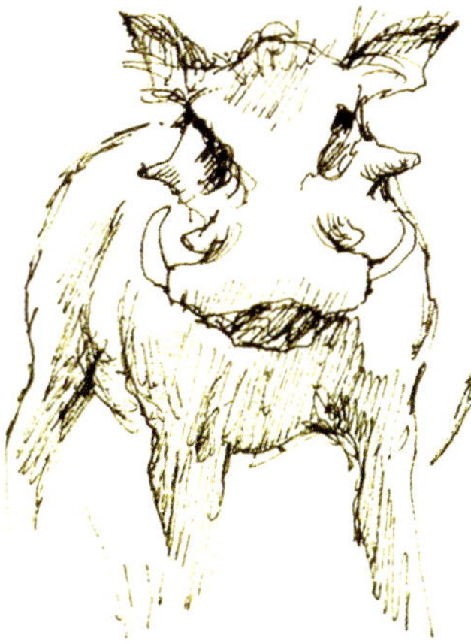

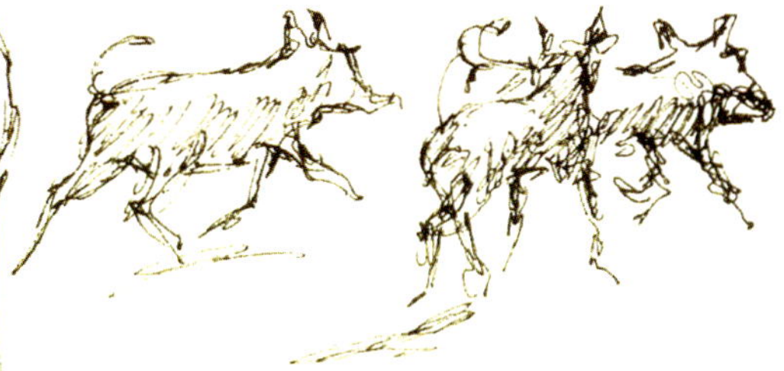

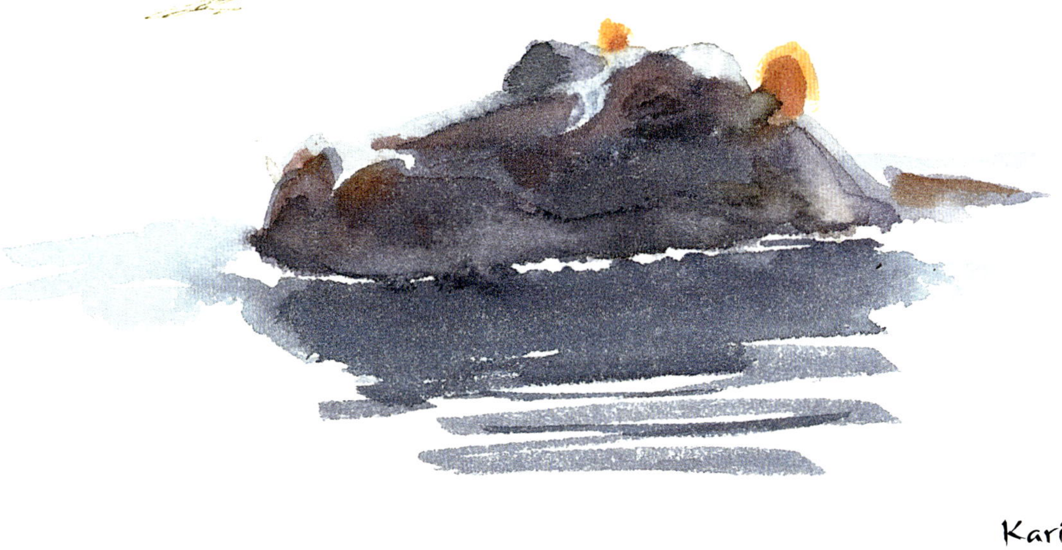

Kingdom of the Cats:

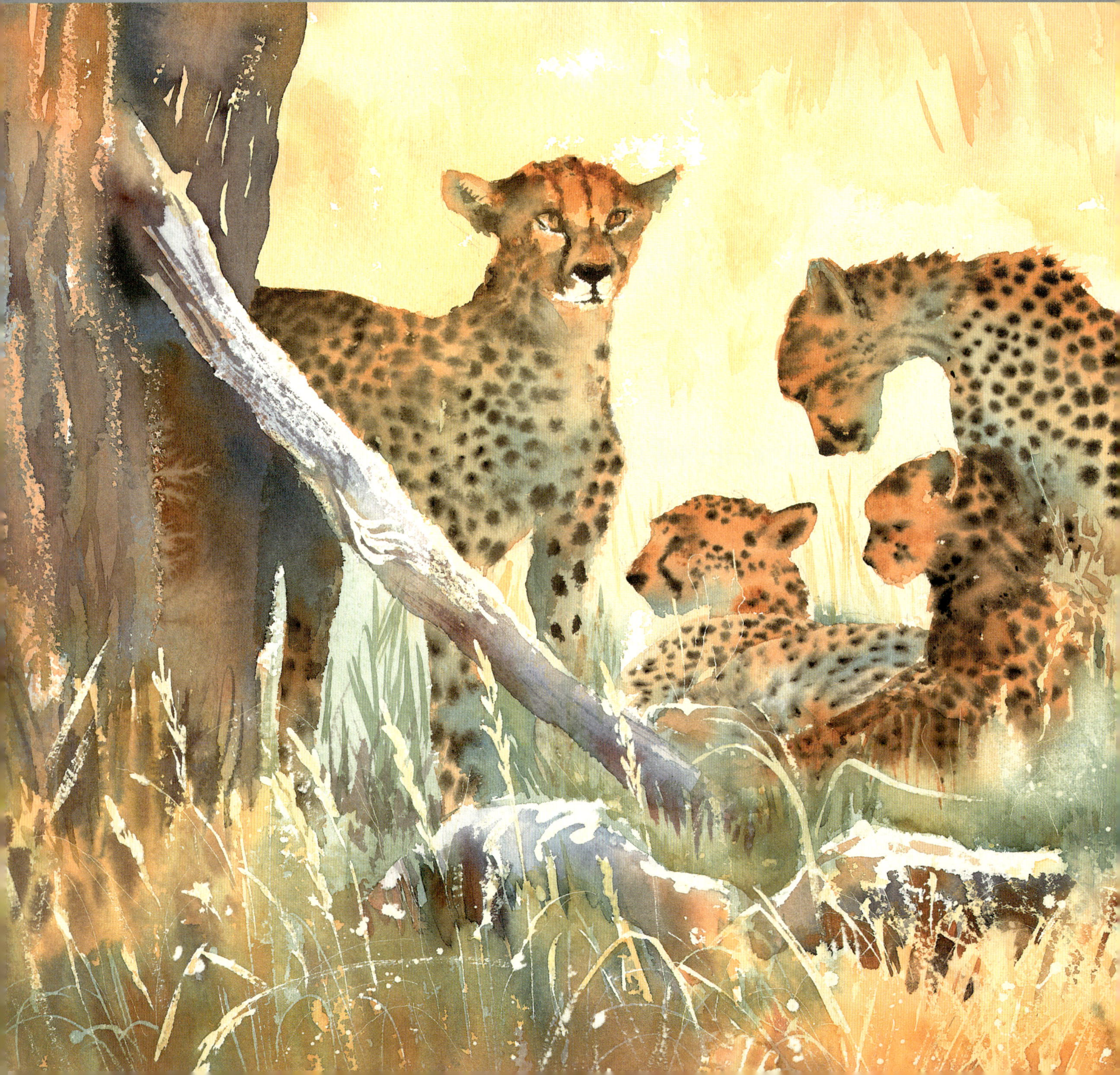

The Kalahari Desert

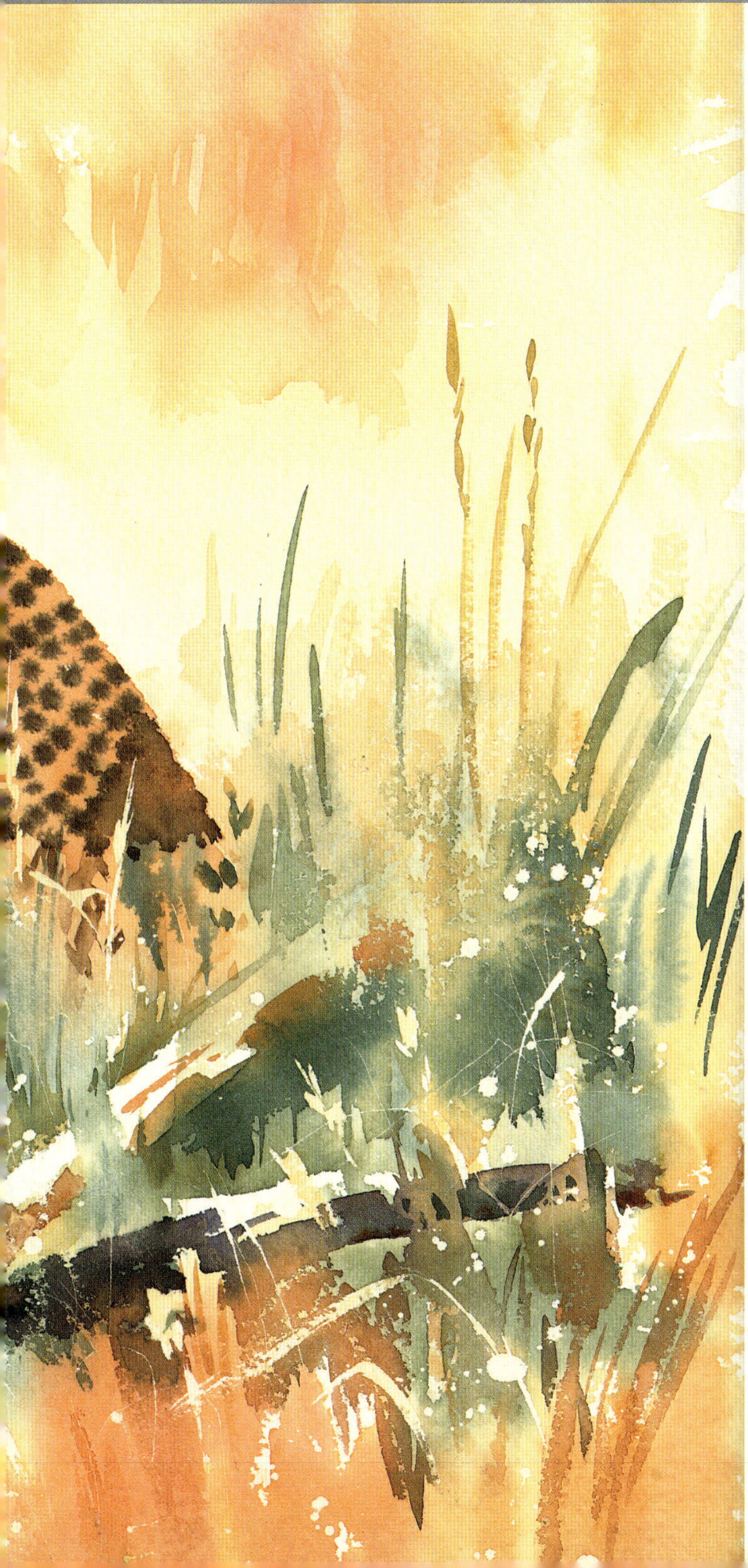

Sharpening the perception

Amber eyes keep closing
in the laziness of heat.
Docile, she lies drowsing,
in simulated sleep.
Then the shrouded rustle,
the amber eyes alert,
the softened limbs are stiffened
and the spoor imprints the dirt.

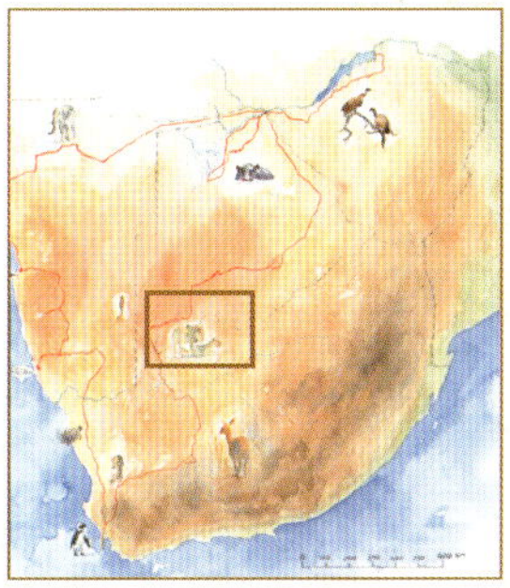

◄ CAMOUFLAGE
41 x 56 cm (16 x 22 in)

Life in a thirsty land

The safari returns south, crossing the Kalahari Desert on the border of Botswana and South Africa. Gone are the lush greens of the Zambezi Valley and the Chobe's verdant banks; in the Kalahari the riverbeds flow, on average, just once in a decade.

In this vast thirstland the lack of rain has created dusty plains and rolling dunes decorated sparsely with long grasses and scrubby trees. Yet this scorched kingdom supports a remarkable variety of animals. Herds of gemsbok, wildebeest and springbok survive in surprisingly large numbers. Hartebeest roam the dry riverbeds and warthog wander nose-down, tail-high among the tall grass.

Feline paradise

The antelope provide food for the predators. The large cats – lion, cheetah, leopard and the African wild cat – find prey around the precious waterholes, which are fed by the ample underground water.

The lions live for days at a time beside a waterhole, waiting, mating, feeding and sleeping. Cheetah are more camouflaged, accompanied by their young among the blonde grasses. The elusive leopard is harder to spot, its lovely markings perfectly matching the dappled light beneath the taller trees.

The dusty roads run close to the waterholes, making perfect painting territory for the artist.

▼ THE TIDE OF THE DESERT
28 x 38 cm (11 x 15 in)
From the top of the undulating dunes the wildebeest can be seen raising the dust in their stride.

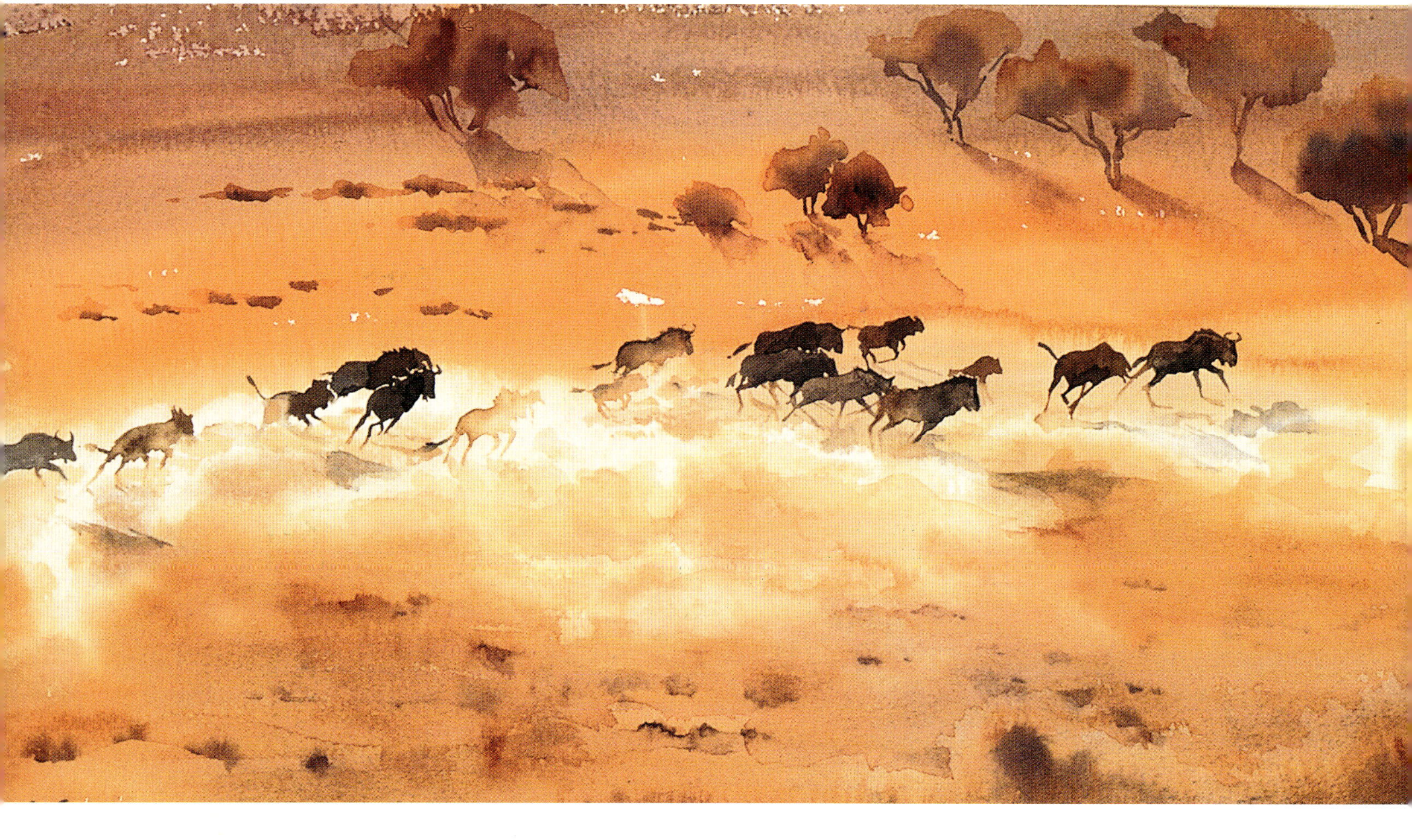

► DRY RIVER VALLEY
20 x 20 cm (8 x 8 in)
The birds gather straw from the veld and build thermally insulated homes in the camelthorn trees.

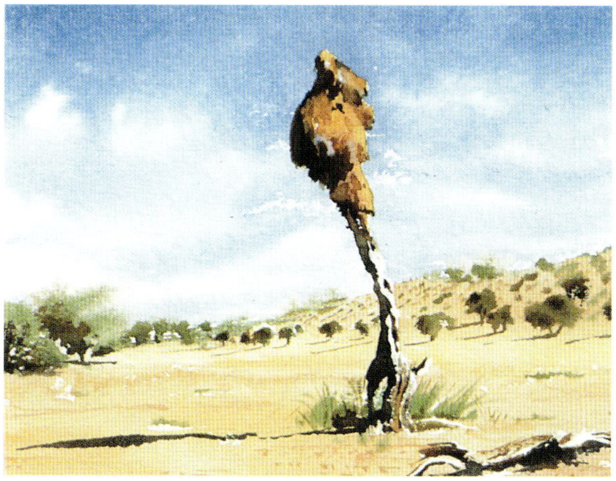

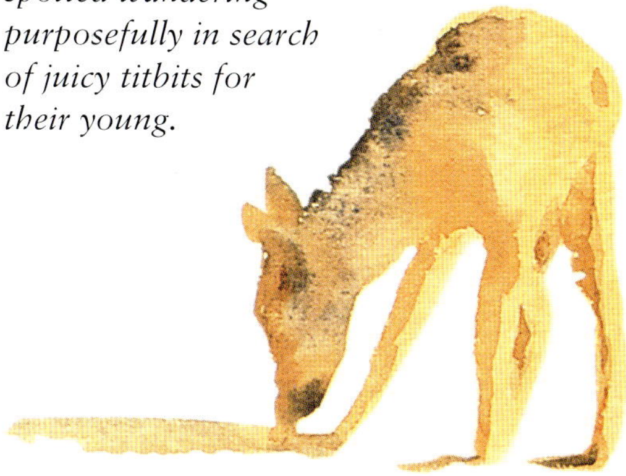

► *Jackals are often spotted wandering purposefully in search of juicy titbits for their young.*

Scavengers and foragers

After the cats have had their fill along come the scavengers to clear up the carcasses. Nothing is wasted in Africa. Eager hyenas, jackals and vultures bravely approach the kill even while the cats are still eating. The desert supports many small mammals as well, such as the meerkat and the ground squirrel, which forage for food in the dusty earth. Birdlife is also abundant here; among the more familiar sights are the huge communal nests of the sociable weaverbird, heavy, bizarre-shaped thatches which festoon and burden the camelthorn trees.

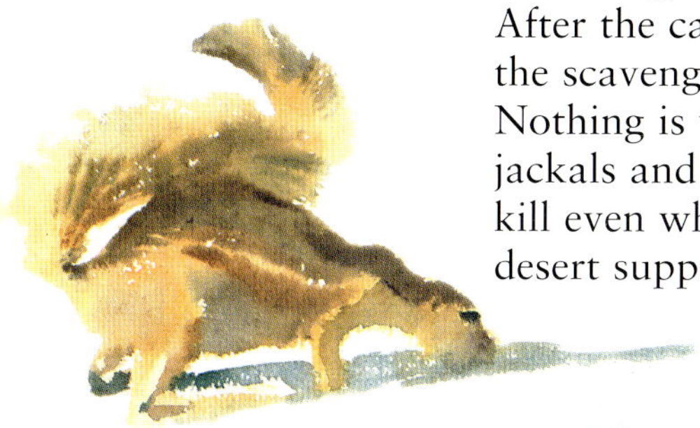

▲ *The bushy tail of the ground squirrel acts as a parasol.*

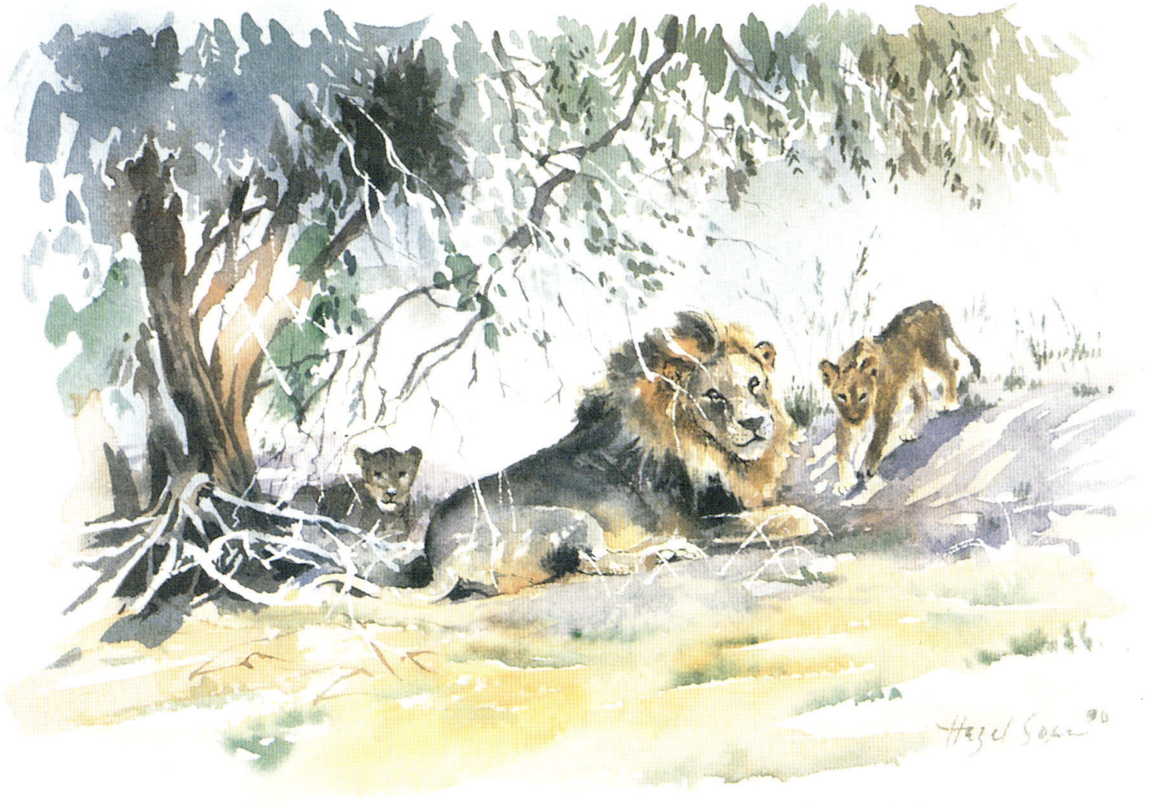

► THE LION'S DEN
20 x 28 cm (8 x 11 in)
The Kalahari lion is known for his magnificent black mane. In the lion kingdom the day is given over to rest and play away from the searing heat.

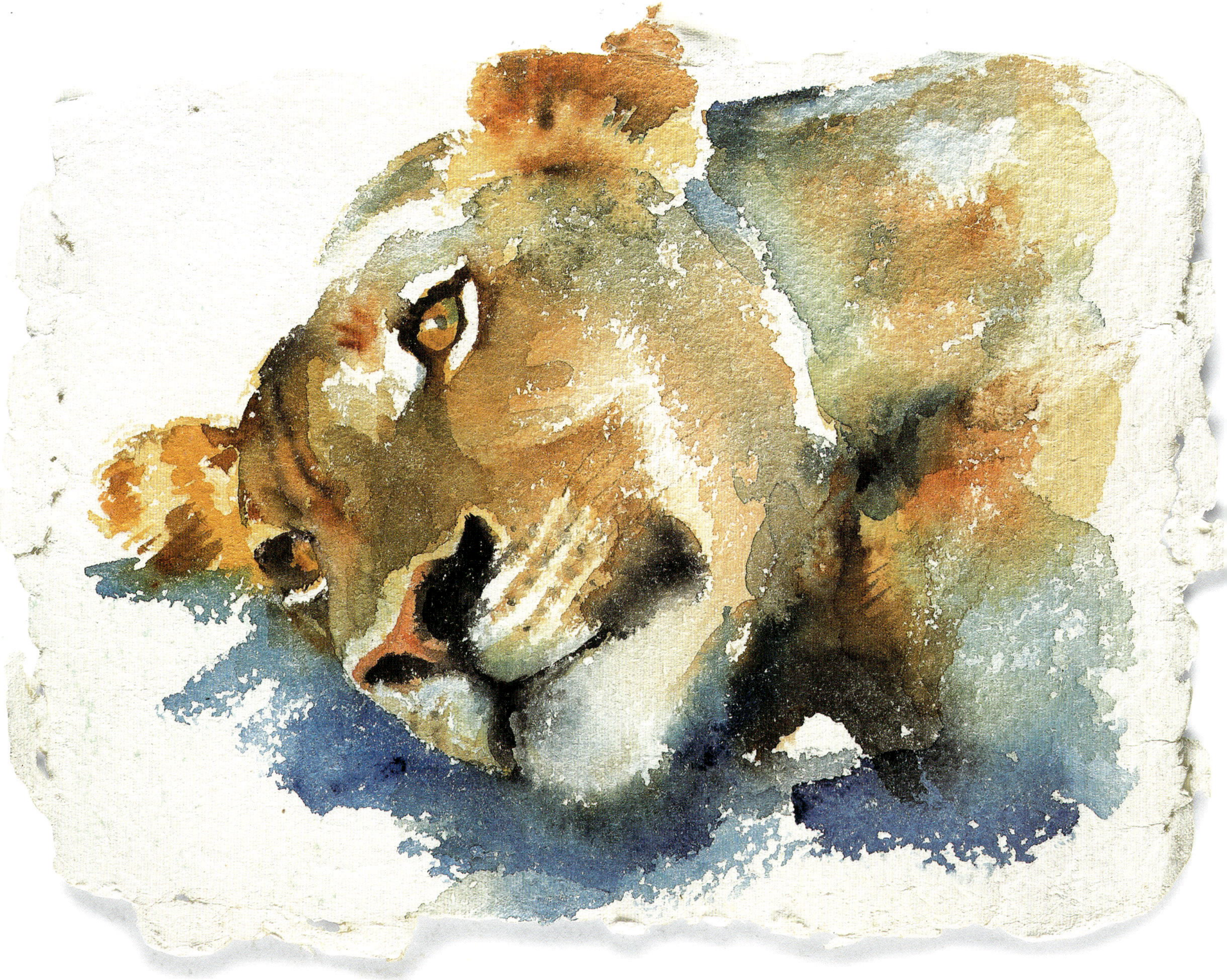

Observation and sketching

In this land of discreet camouflage observation is essential. The sedentary lives of the large cats allow time to make sketches and paintings on the spot (from the vehicle, of course!) and to take photographs to use as reference when you are back in the studio.

Sketching enables you to more fully observe and understand what you are seeing and to find out what interests you. A light pencil sketch under a watercolour will give you confidence to lay bolder brushstrokes. The sketches act as both a source of reference for finished paintings and as a wonderful memory.

▲ AFTER THE KILL
20 x 28 cm (8 x 11 in)
Wet-in-wet techniques and thin veils of wet-on-dry washes on a rough paper are ideal for the soft hair of the large cats.

The ease of a limited palette

Most of the animals in this location can be painted with a small colour range, varying from the Yellow Ochre of the lion, through the Burnt Sienna of the springbok, to the Sepia of the wildebeest. This is very satisfying as it means you can go out with few colours and concentrate on the shapes of the animals and the patterns of their hides and fur.

Lack of moisture in the air means paint dries fast. Mixing the right amount of pigment with the right amount of water is essential. The spots, whorls and stripes of animal markings can be touched in with nearly neat paint while the washes are wet.

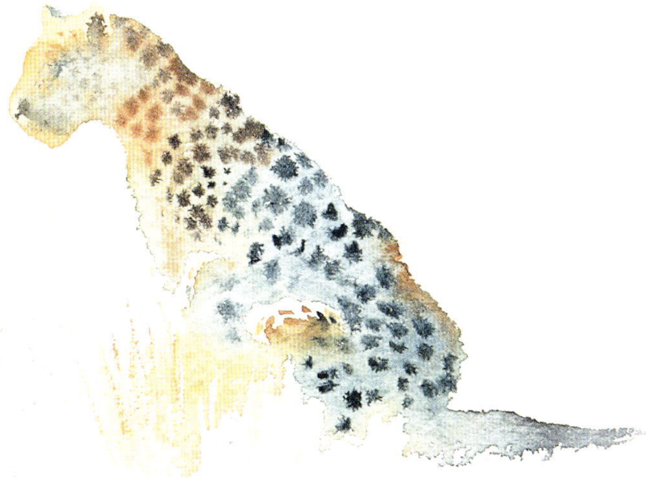

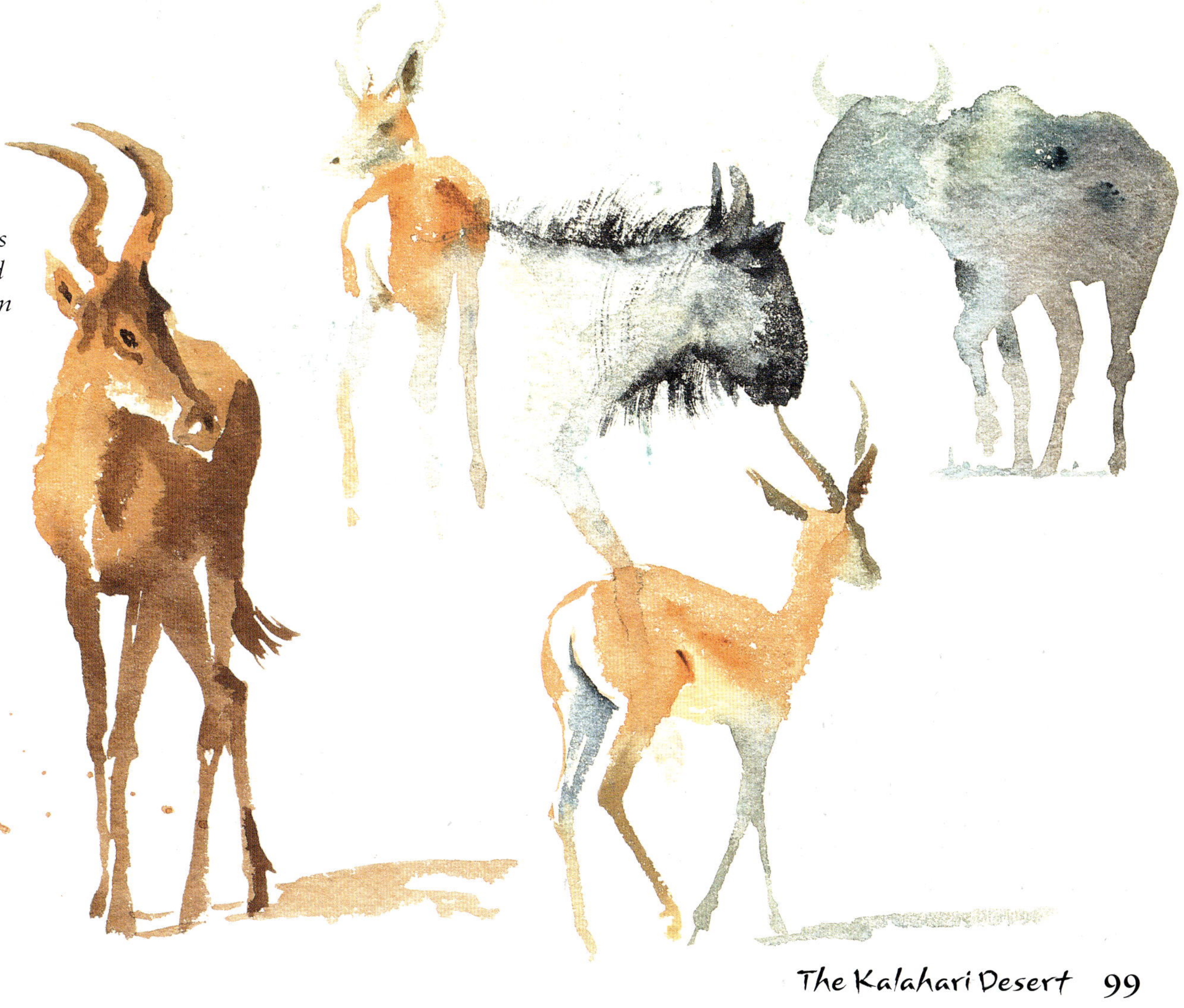

► *The different hides and coats are painted with five colours from the palette: Burnt Sienna, Alizarin Crimson, Prussian Blue, Indigo and Yellow Ochre.*

Sharpening the perception

Seeing is the prerequisite of painting. How you respond to your subject will affect how you choose to paint it. There is nothing to be gained from a formulaic approach to painting, treating every subject in the same way and in the same style. Watercolour will grow more naturally out of genuine observation and the desire to paint, than by trying to impose a style upon it. Once you start sketching you will find it difficult to stop.

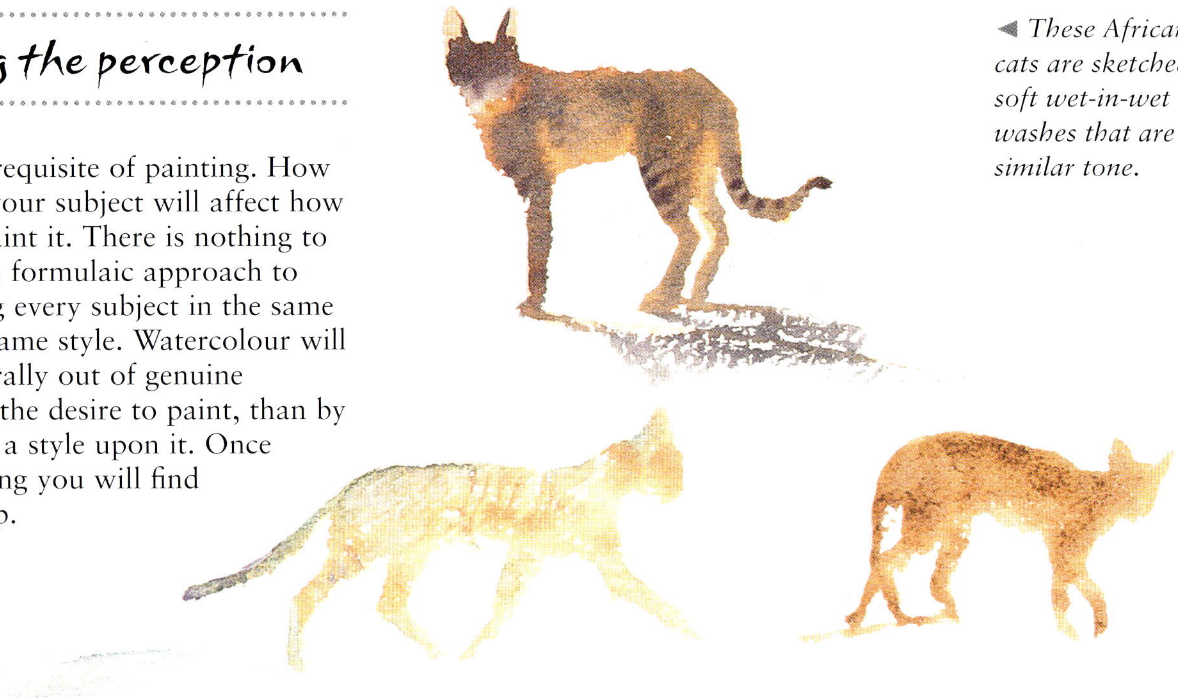

◀ *These African wild cats are sketched with soft wet-in-wet washes that are of a similar tone.*

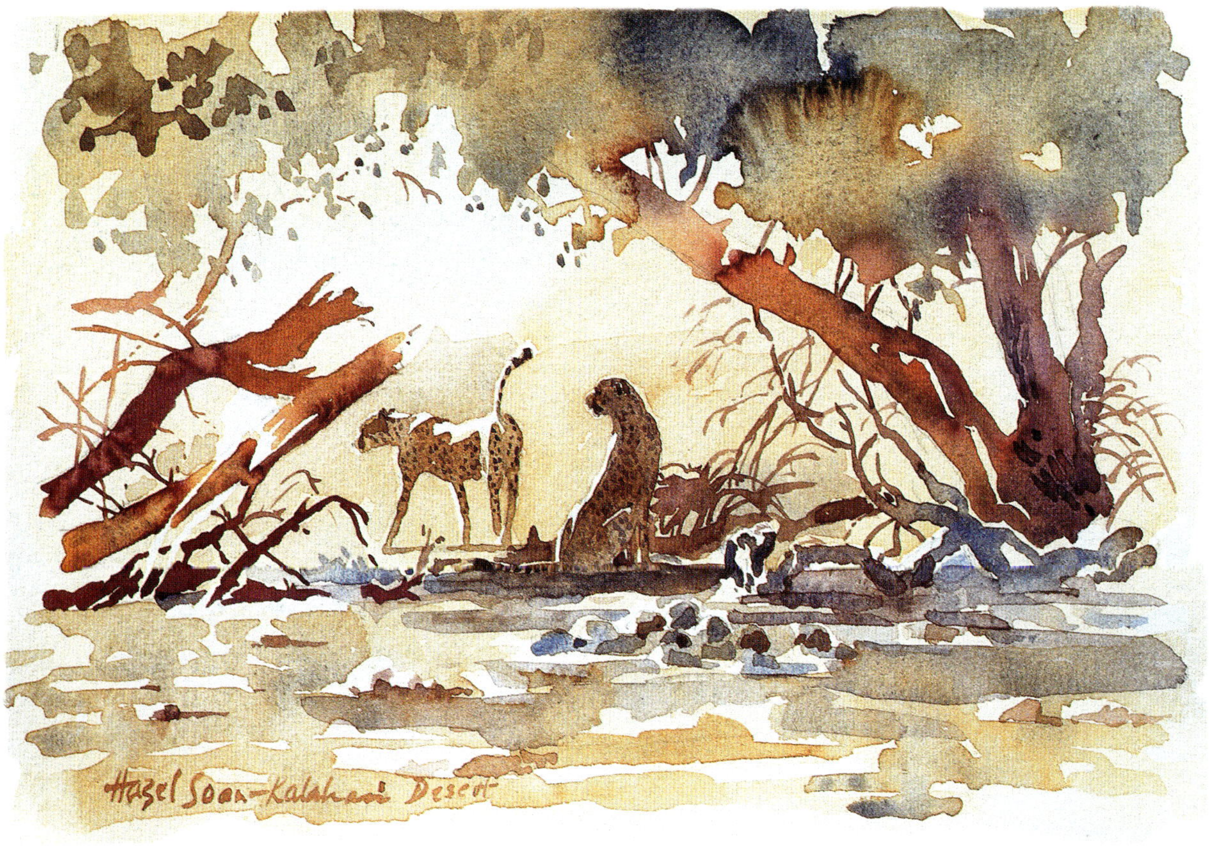

◀ DANGER IN THE SHADOWS
20 x 28 cm (8 x 11 in)
The cheetah under the tree, sheltering from the harsh light, are painted with crisp washes and strong tonal contrast.

Catching the character

The characteristics of animals are found in the poses they make and the shapes they cut in the air. The need to find the right line or shape will sharpen your observation and make your brushstrokes keen.

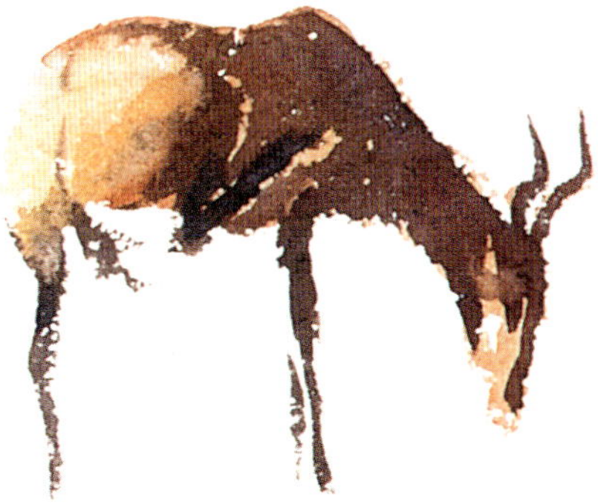

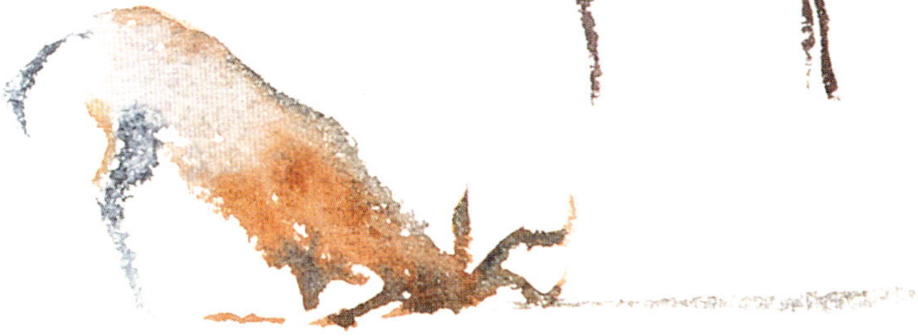

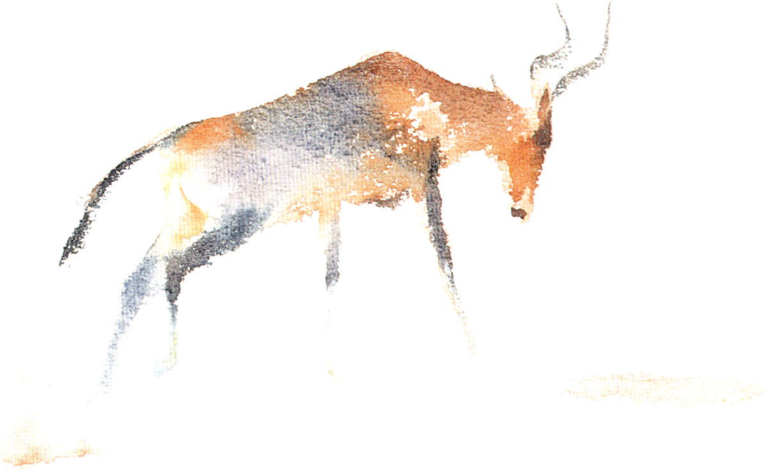

► *By making several different sketches of this red hartebeest its cheerful character becomes known. Compare these sketches with those of the more serious leopard below.*

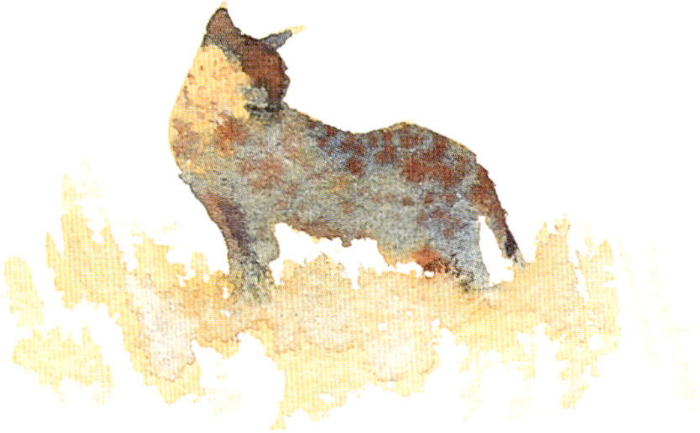

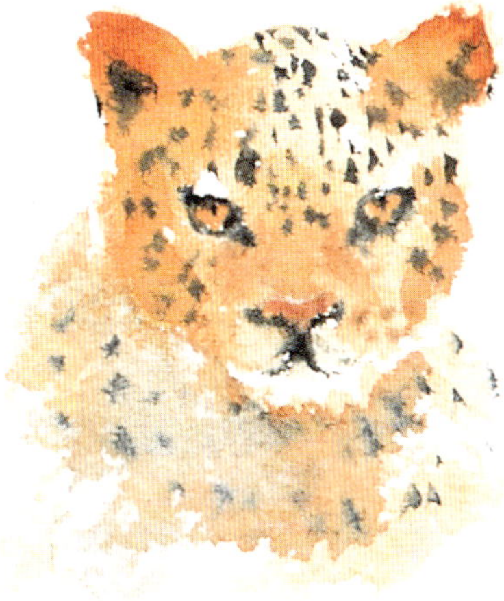

▲ *The leopard's ponderous stance and serious gaze is carried through into the pose and is reflected in the sketches.*

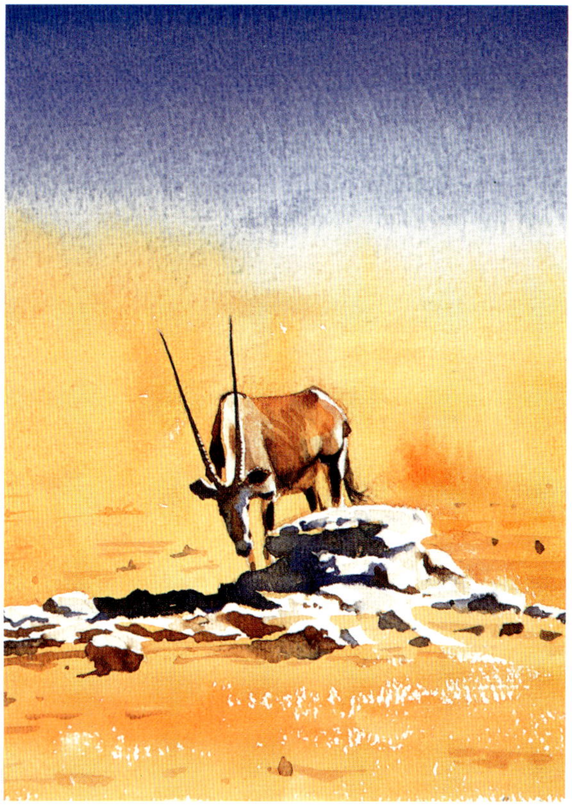

► LONELINESS OF THE LONG DISTANCE RUNNER
28 x 18 cm (11 x 7 in)
The vulnerability of the lone oryx is held in the stooping pose.

Speed of execution

Watercolours benefit from being painted quite swiftly. In a lively watercolour picture there is much less time spent with the brush on the paper than time spent looking, mixing, or waiting patiently for paint to dry. The first wash is often the freshest. Overpainting can completely destroy the texture of the brushstrokes.

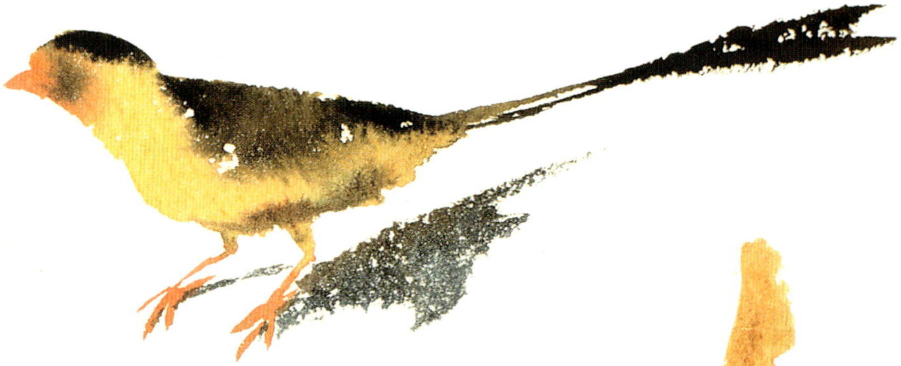

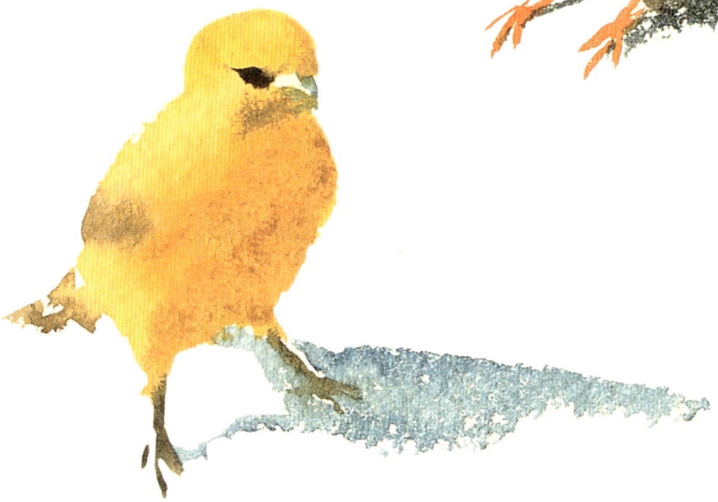

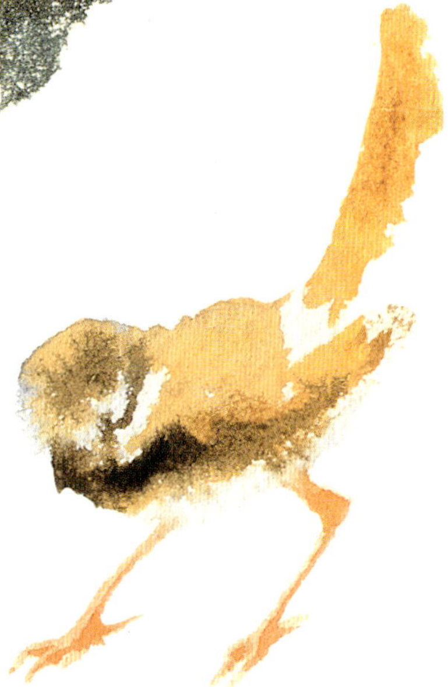

► *No kingdom of cats would be complete without birds! These colourful characters look more charming for the swiftness of the brushstrokes and washes that make up their forms. Success in wet-in-wet washes comes from judging the right moment to add the colours.*

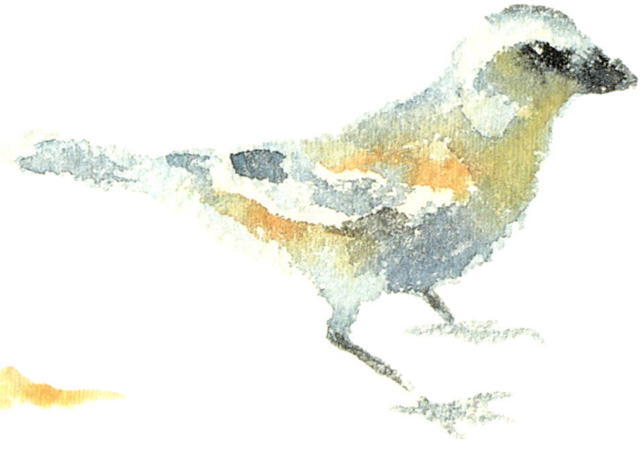

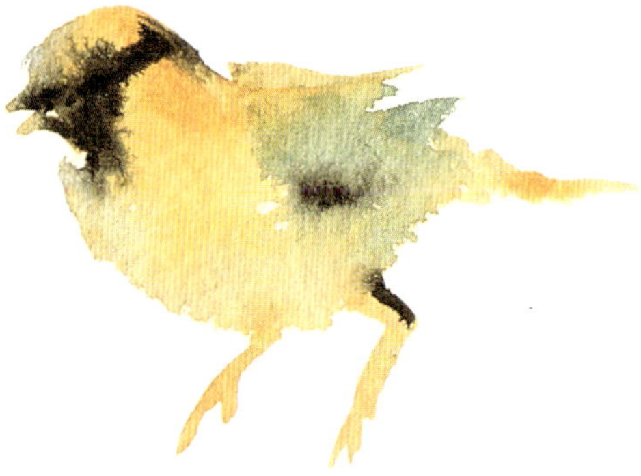

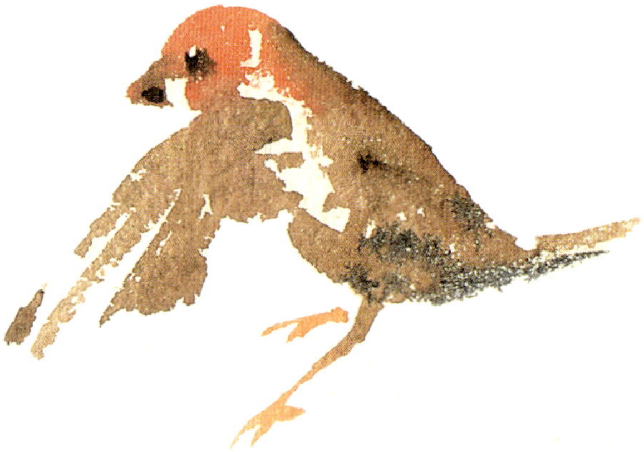

The right moment

Just as timing is crucial in the predator's kingdom so in watercolour the right colour added in the right place and at the right time does not in itself take very long – but the preparation for that moment takes much longer. Wait and think before you touch the paper with the brush. More paintings are ruined by impatience than anything else. Left alone watercolour will do lovely things; all you have to do is lay it and leave it, and resist the urge to fiddle.

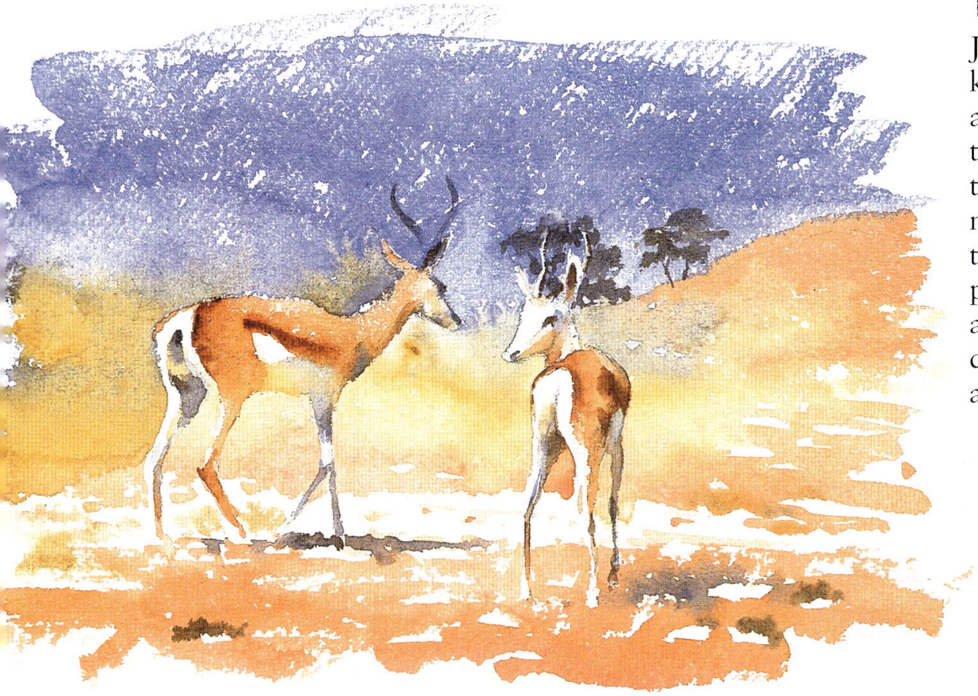

▲ *Freshness is found by laying the paint crisply and cleanly with hardly any overpainting.*

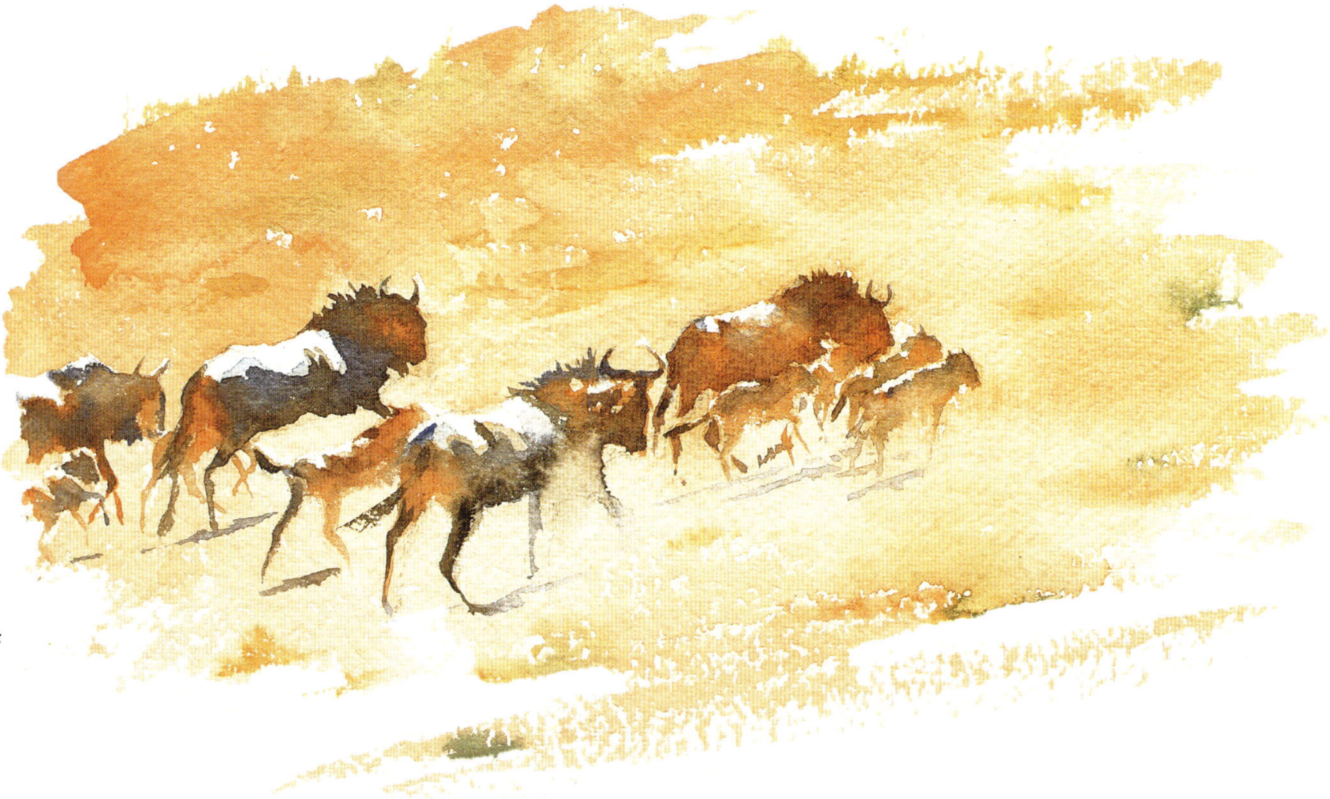

► *This watercolour is not overworked by needless attention to detail or accuracy. Each brushstroke is significant.*

Safari sketchbook

In the lion's den

The Kalahari lion is the largest of the desert predators. The prides in this region have large territories because the density of prey is so low. Lions have no natural enemies. They live in groups, often hunting as a team, but their life is precarious in the desert terrain.

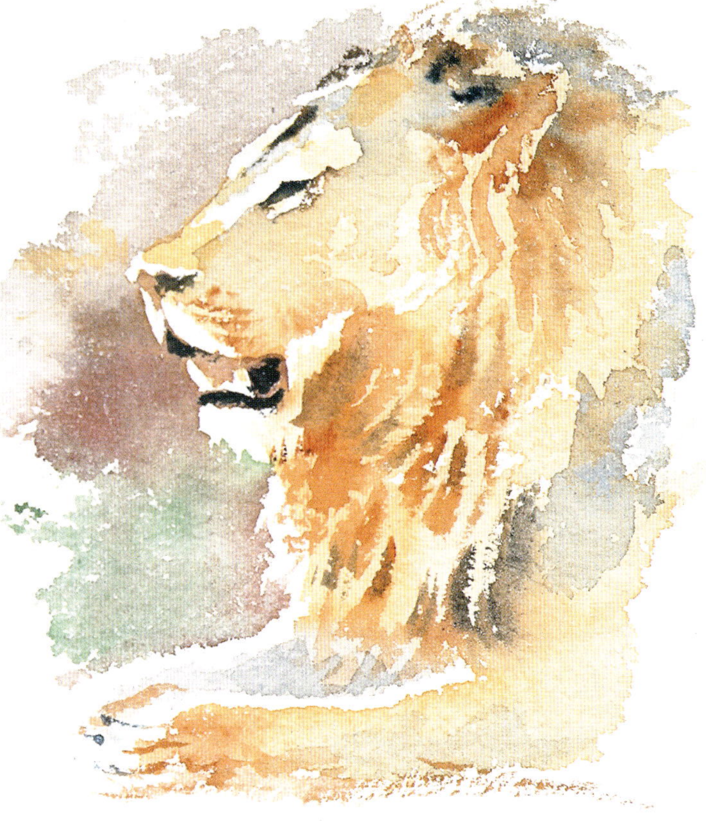

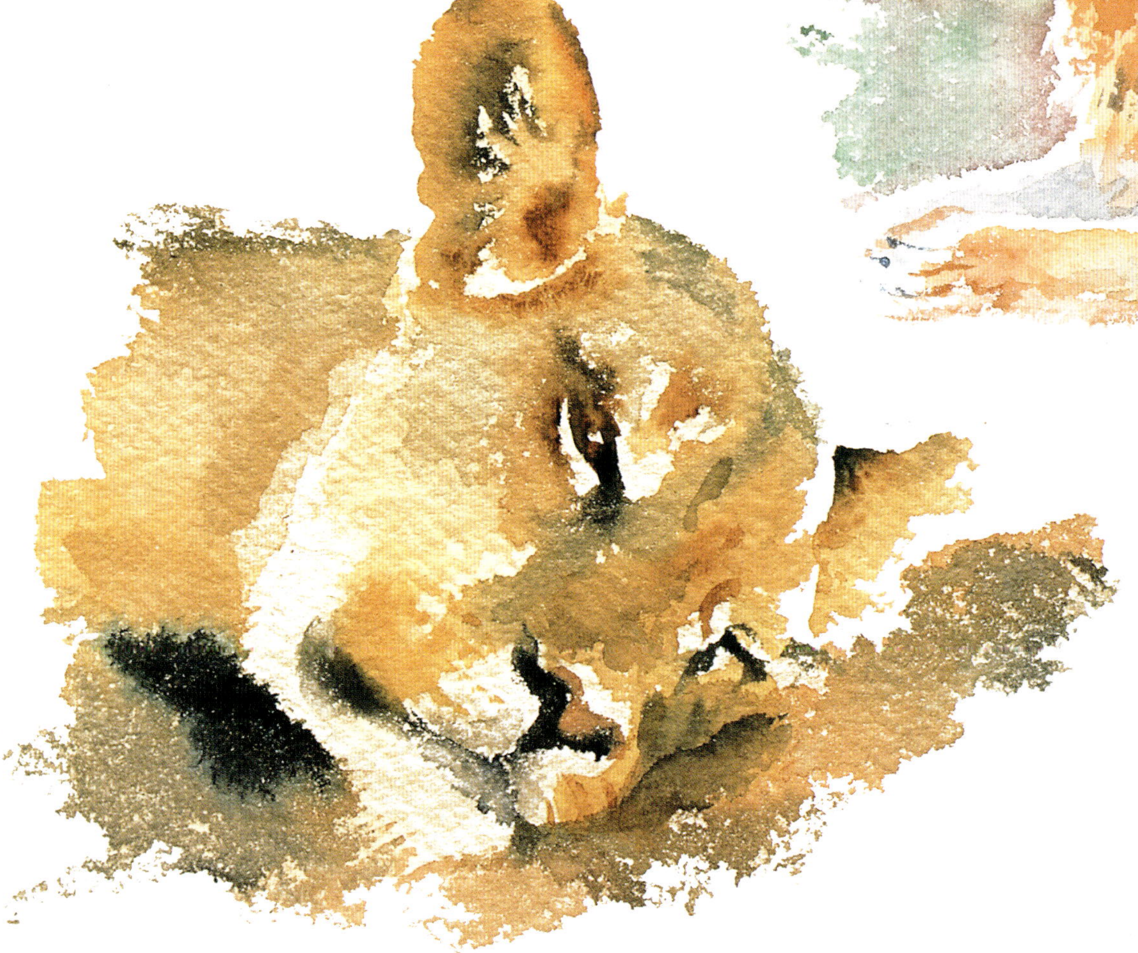

The pride may consist of more than one dominant male, with several lionesses and lots of cubs.

The lion's spoor.

Campfire tale

Stuck in a rut

Getting stuck is always a risk on safari; especially beside a set of fresh lion prints! We had followed the spoor across a belt of sandy dunes. The paw size was enormous and etched perfectly in the soft sand. We stopped to look, but when we tried to drive on we could not budge. The wheels spun, the engine whirred and the tyres just dug in deeper. John looked warily around and got out to let the air out of the tyres in an effort to free the wheels. He cleared the sand from behind the tyres and placed large stones to help them grip. But in vain — there was nothing for it but to winch ourselves out.

Fortunately there was a large tree not too far away. He looped the winch cable around the trunk while I kept a good look out. The cable reeled in interminably slowly. The adrenalin was pumping, and my eyes were everywhere, remembering a previous occasion when a lion had chased towards us with snarling jaws and piercing yellow eyes.

This time, however, all was well, at last the vehicle freed itself from its dusty bonds and we were able to drive on. We found the lion and his mate later, under a tree, fat-bellied and sleepy from a recent kill.

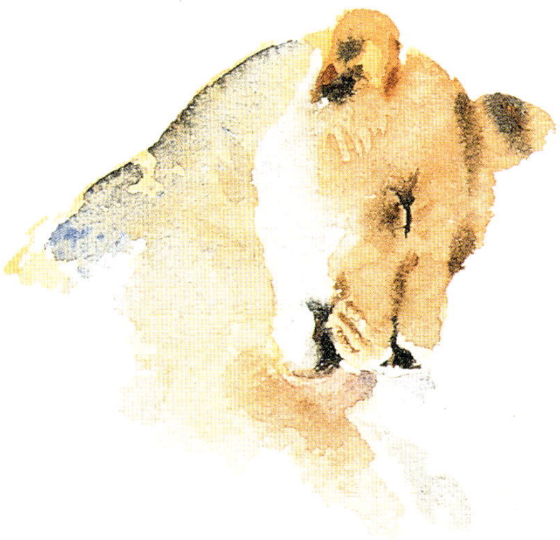

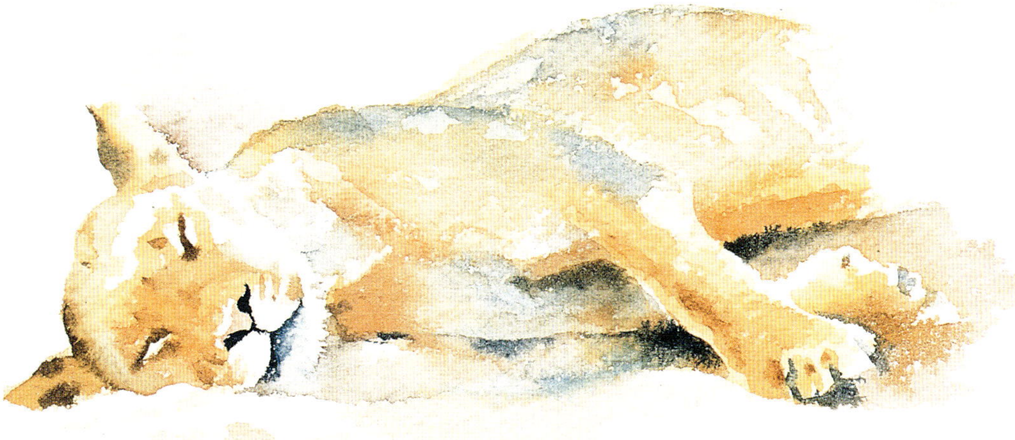

The Riches of Emptiness:

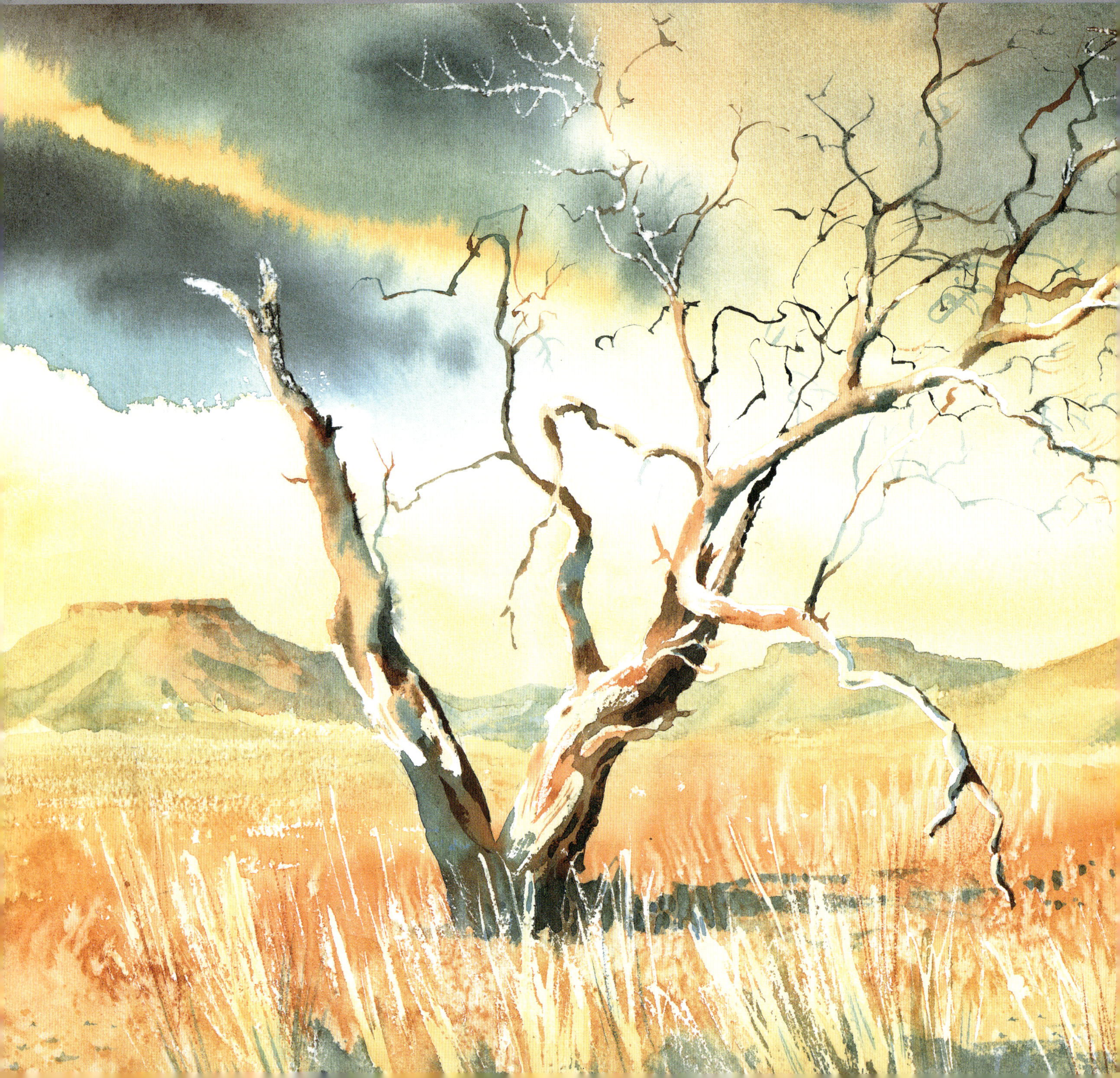

The Karoo

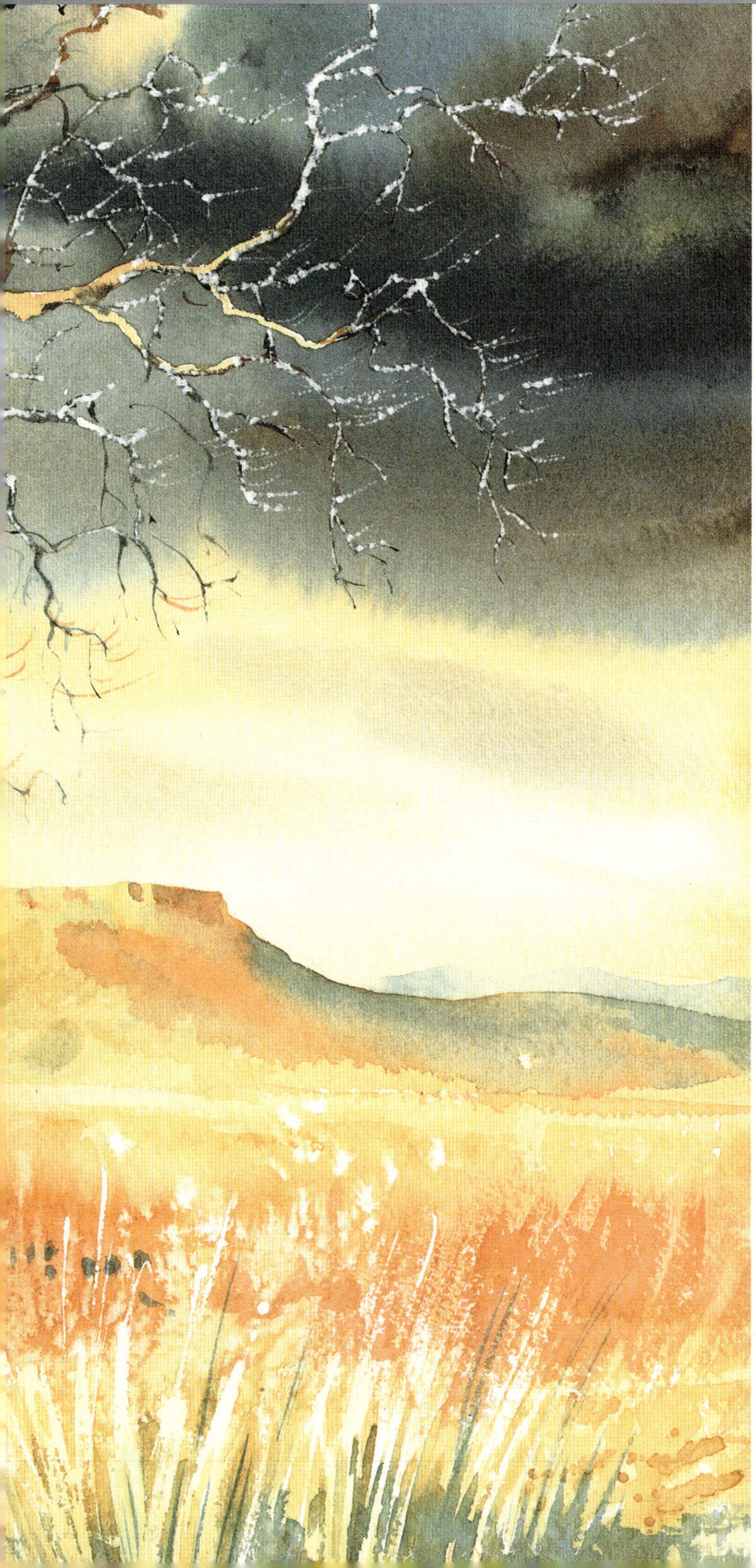

Tapestries of texture

Mirage, mirage on the road,
is this the fiercest heat of all?
Where does the distant ribbon race?
Where the rise and where the fall?
Simmering cauldron,
shimmering pools
that cannot quench the thirst,
you test the tired traveller's pace
'til he concedes you're lying first.

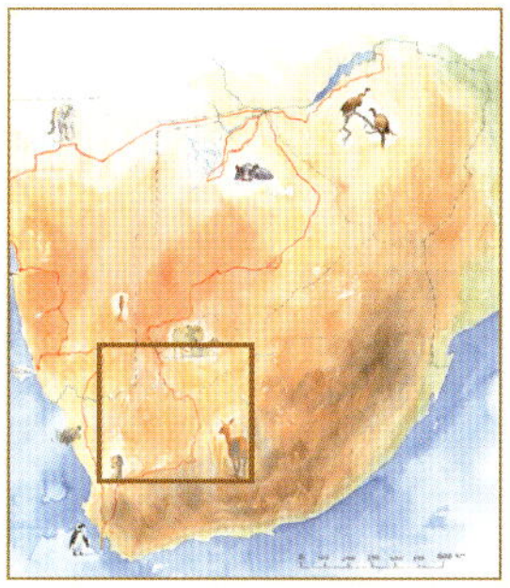

◄ INTRUDER
40 x 56 cm (16 x 22 in)

A remote place

The return to Cape Town traverses the great Karoo, a screed landscape of minimal rain and scanty soil interrupted by outcrops of rock and flat-topped hills. It is a remote and melancholy place by day, but at dawn and dusk it is transformed by the clarity and brilliance of the sun's golden light.

At first light the oblique rays and crystal-clear air model the rocky surfaces with fascinating shadows. When evening comes the hills are tinged with purple and rose, and the sky begins to glow. The defiant sun becomes less aggressive in its larger, lower form and artfully smears the horizon with blended strips of red, yellow and green beneath the dark cerulean sky. As the earth turns away the sun departs in fiery red, returning the landscape to darkness. Then, little by little, the stars prick holes in the blanket of the night and the heavens are sparkling in a dazzling panoply of light.

Remnant of the past

The African word 'karoo' means 'thirstland', an arid place that is not true desert. This area is the remnant of a high-lying shallow basin that now forms the central plateau of SouthAfrica. Buried in its ancient sediments are many fossils of plants and animals, the past inhabitants of the dessicated swamps.

▼ KOPPIES

20 x 28 cm (8 x 11 in)

Where the soft rock has eroded away, outcrops of small irregular hills topped with vertical-edged crusts form the distinctive flat-topped 'koppies' of the South African landscape.

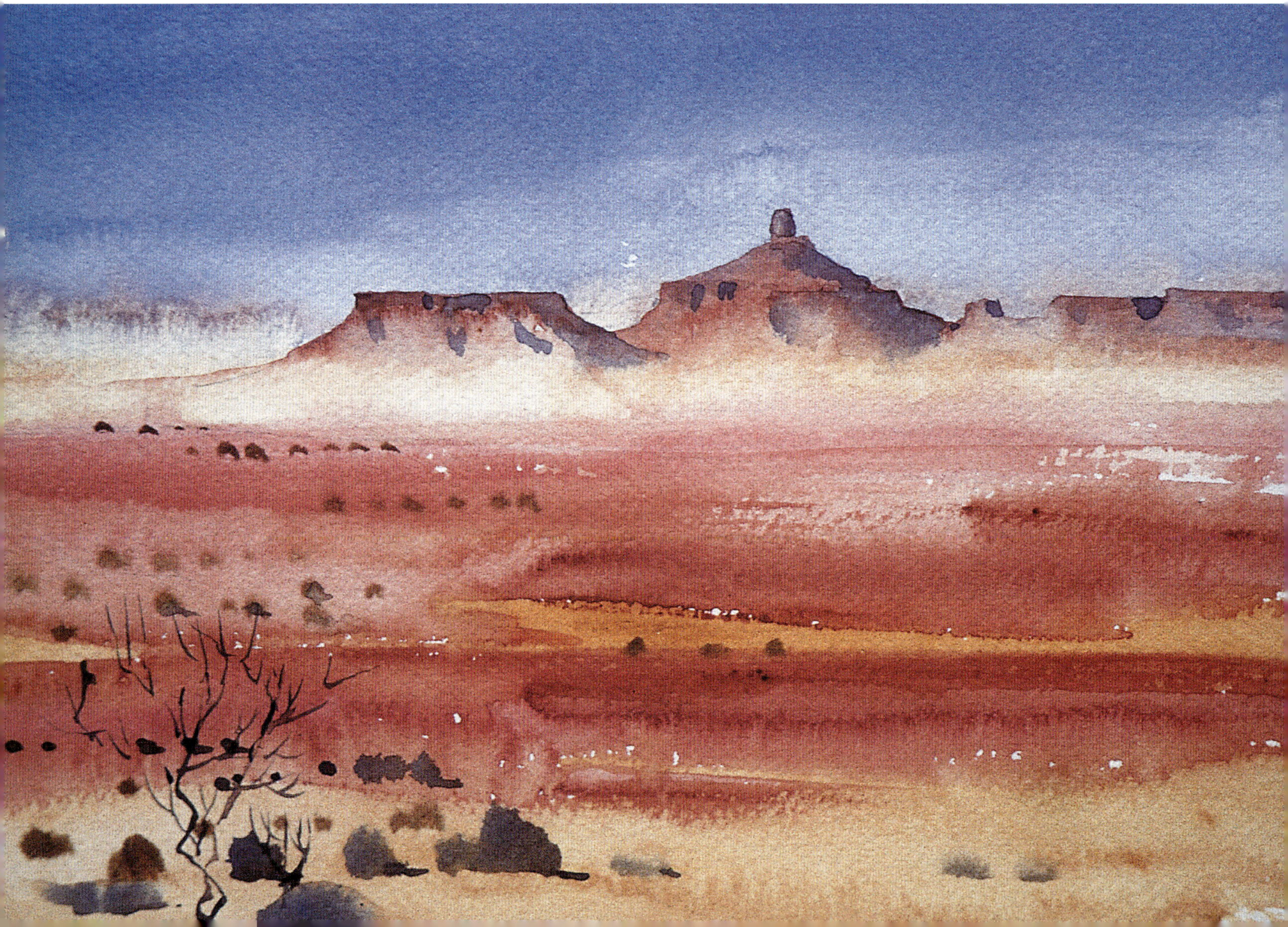

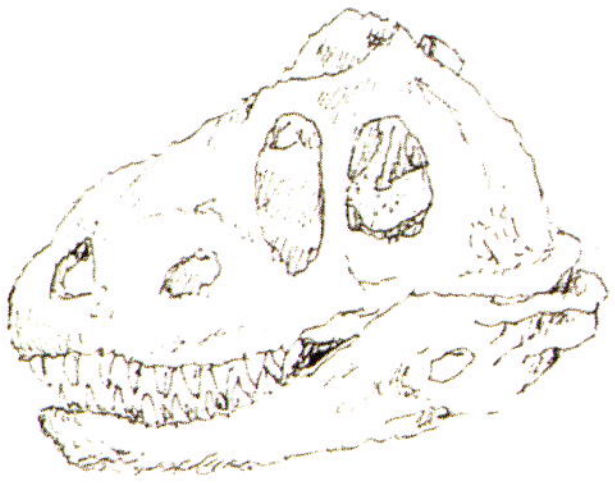

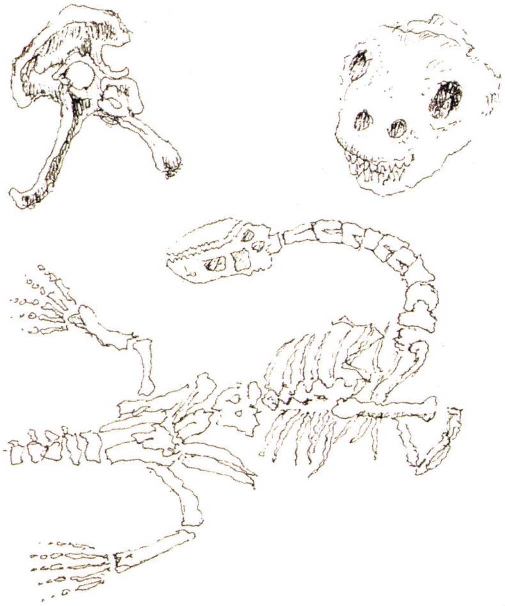

► *At the Karoo National Park you can walk among uncovered fossils.*

The Cederberg

To reach the Cape the traveller crosses the mighty rock wilderness of the Cederberg. Here the sandstone landscape bucks and folds, throwing up unusual rock shapes, cutting ravines and digging caves. Old cedar trees grow on the mountains, giving the area its name. Translucent pools shimmer like gems in the heart of the range or spill their contents as tinkling waterfalls over the fiery red rock. The novel rock formations take the form of arches, bridges and crosses, making eerie totems against the clear blue sky. Among the maze of caves sporadic paintings decorate the rocks with naive animals and figures.

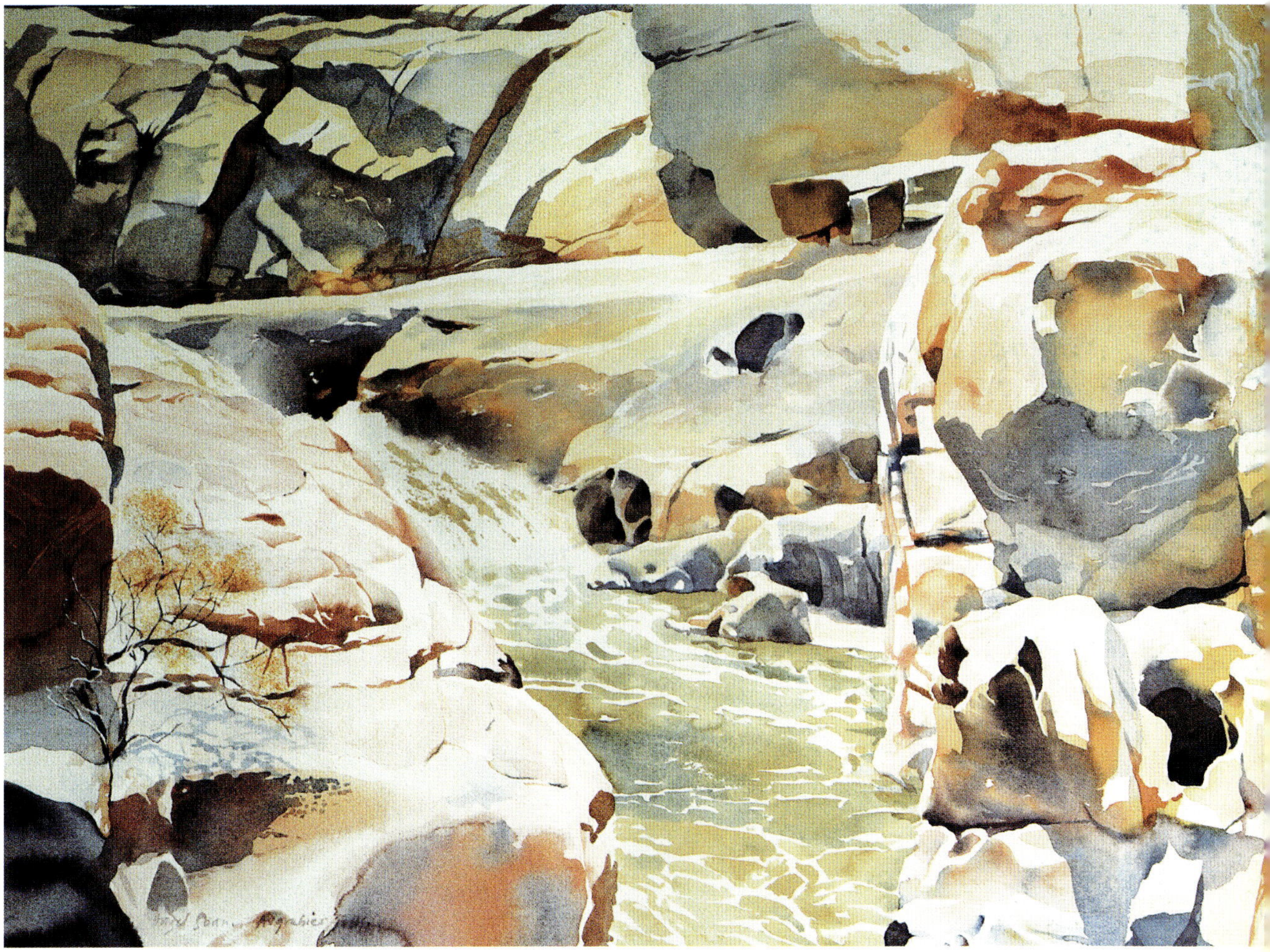

► THE TUMBLING STREAM
56 x 76 cm (22 x 30 in)
The clear light turns the rocky waterfalls into mosaics of light and dark shapes. A combination of wet-in-wet and wet-on-dry techniques is used for the smooth texture of the water-worn rocks.

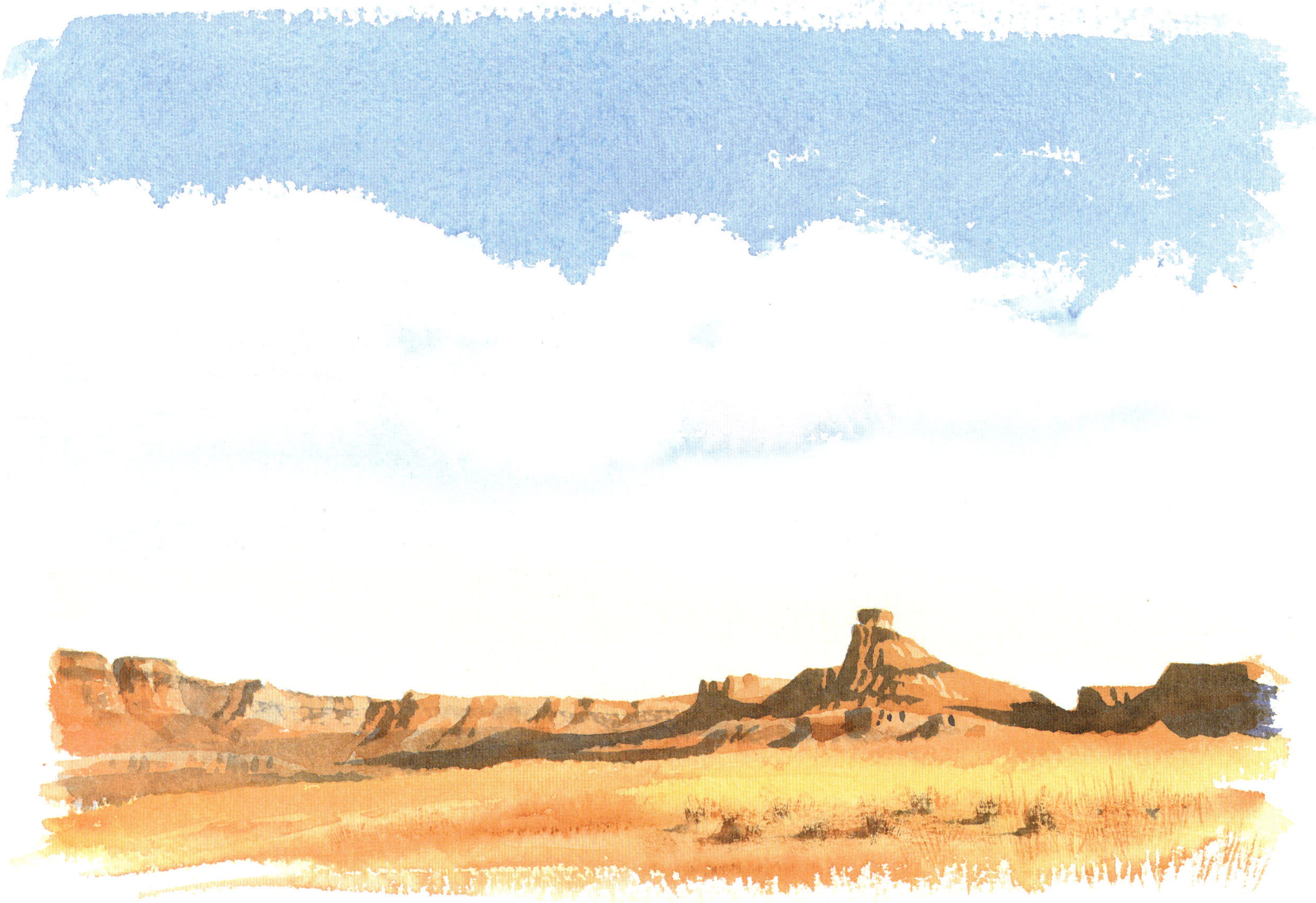

Painting wide open spaces

The endless expanse of emptiness may seem uninteresting at first, but the simple scheme of a large sky coming down to meet a skyline trimmed with mountains and a foreground of rich dry grass is music to a painter's eyes.

There is something intensely pleasurable about laying an unadulterated, gently graded watercolour wash for a sky. Clouds can be created with drier washes: where the paint breaks up across the paper surface irregular broken patches of white paper are left gleaming in the blue of the sky. Puffy cumulus clouds can even be lifted out with a tissue. Keep the tops of the white clouds crisp and blend the darker bases of the clouds into the sky wash below with a wet-in-wet wash.

Arid terrain

Dry brushwork lends itself perfectly to the scrubby landscape interspersed with stones and coarse grasses. The tufts of long grass

▲ **THE RICHES OF EMPTINESS**
20 x 30 cm (8 x 12 in)
The wide open spaces offer vast skies and landscapes of clouds. Here the paper is wetted under the cloud bank and the soft undersides of the clouds are brushed in wet-in-wet.

▶ OPPOSING FORCES
23 x 15 cm (9 x 6 in)
In stony landscapes the grasses grow between the rocks, throwing fine lines up against a shaded backdrop. These light lines can be preserved from the washes with masking fluid, creating attractive lights against darks.

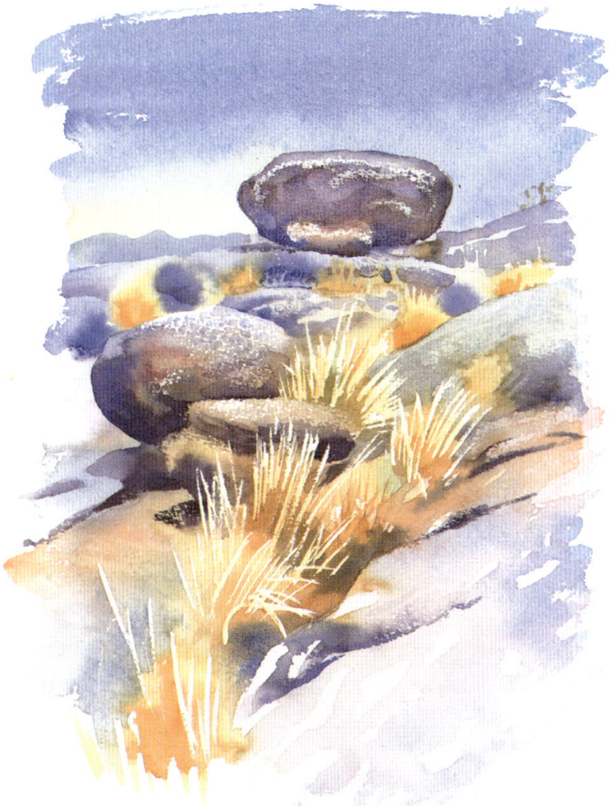

can be rendered with a splayed brush or dry brushstroke and individual blades can be painted with the fine lines of the rigger.

Keep your eye on the overall form the landscape takes before you get carried away with the details. Grasses can be scratched out of a dark wash with a blade or painted in with opaque colours such as Lemon Yellow, Cadmium Yellow or white. Grasses, seed pods or dead branches rising up above the horizon will add interest or a focal point to an empty landscape. A few blades in the right position are all you need to suggest many. Use the direction of the brushstroke to show the fan-like growth or to hint at a breeze in the scorched air.

During the day the harsh light flattens the landscape so painting is more exciting in the early morning or the late afternoon when the slanting light illuminates the unusual forms.

▼ KAROO AT DAWN
25 x 51 cm (10 x 20 in)
Dry brushstrokes from a flat brush mimic the regular pattern of the tufted grasses that carpet the arid landscape.

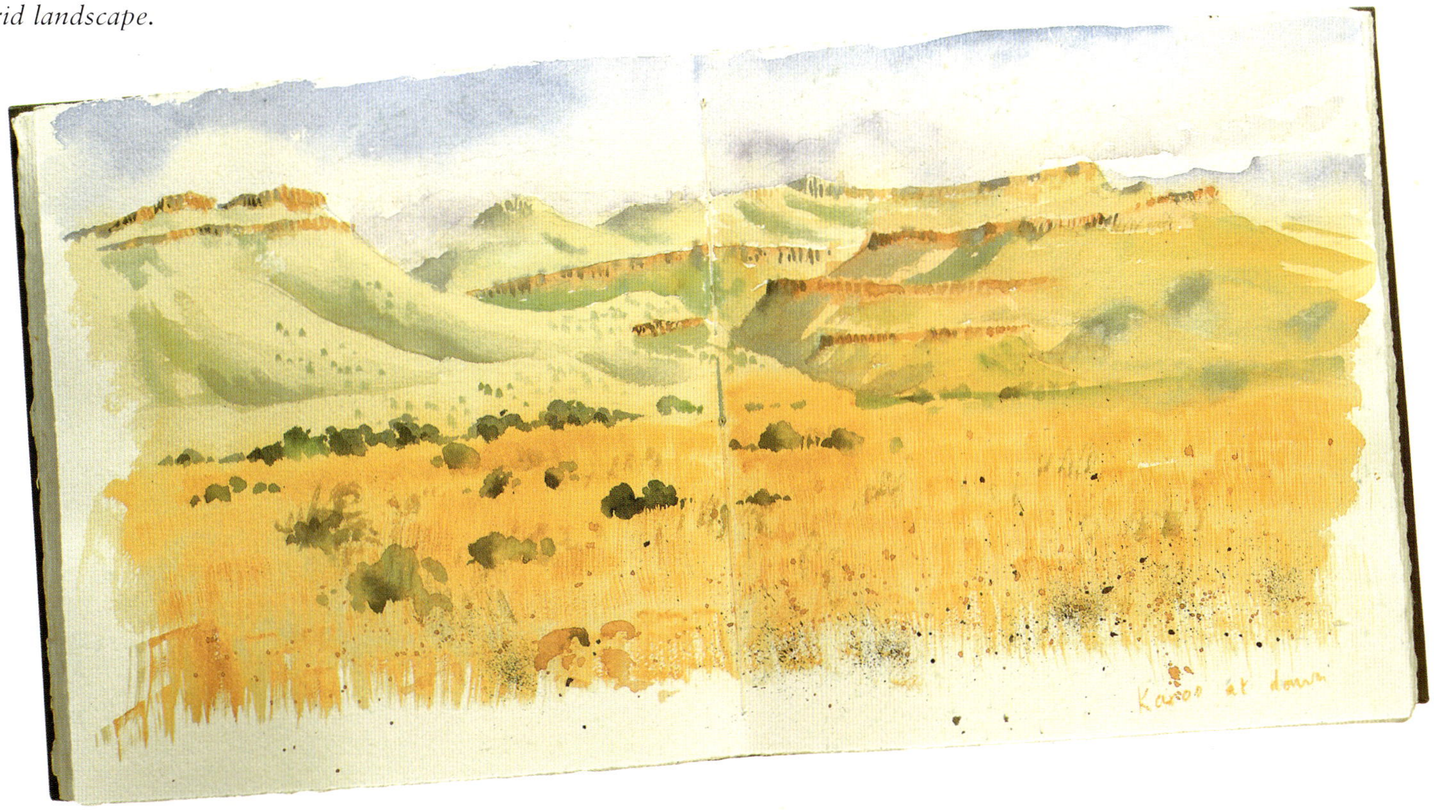

Tapestries of texture

The surface of dry and rocky landscapes are full of texture. In watercolour there are many ways of portraying the impression of texture without actually painting any detail. These techniques are not only fun to do, but also create confidence in painting with watercolour.

Ground textures

The flecked textures of scattered stones, coarse soil, exposed strata or gravel roads can be portrayed by using dry brush, flicking or spattering.

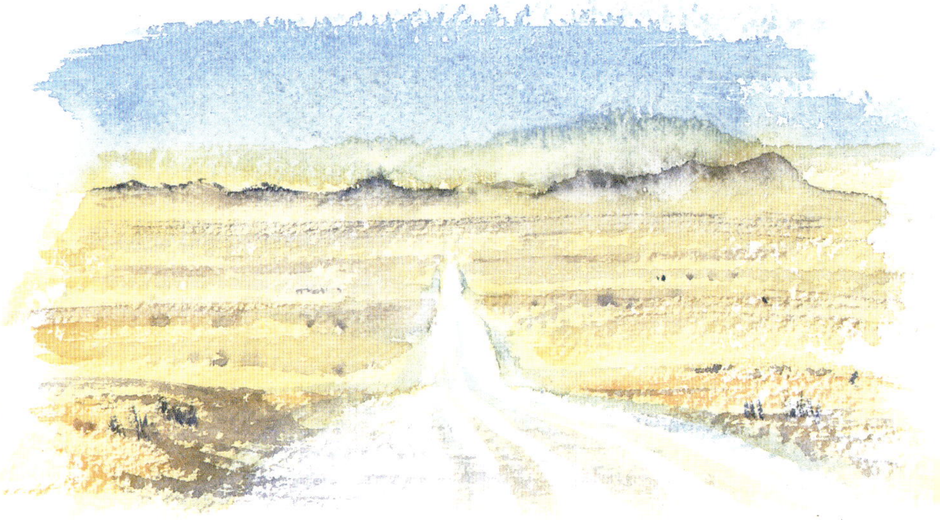

▲ *The dry brush creates a rough texture that can be enhanced by using rough paper. The horizontal nature of the ground is emphasized with the brushstroke.*

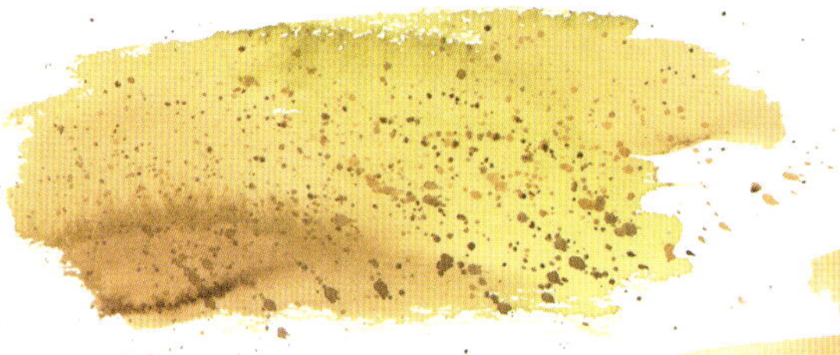

▲ *Indicate random stones by flicking a loaded brush across the paper.*

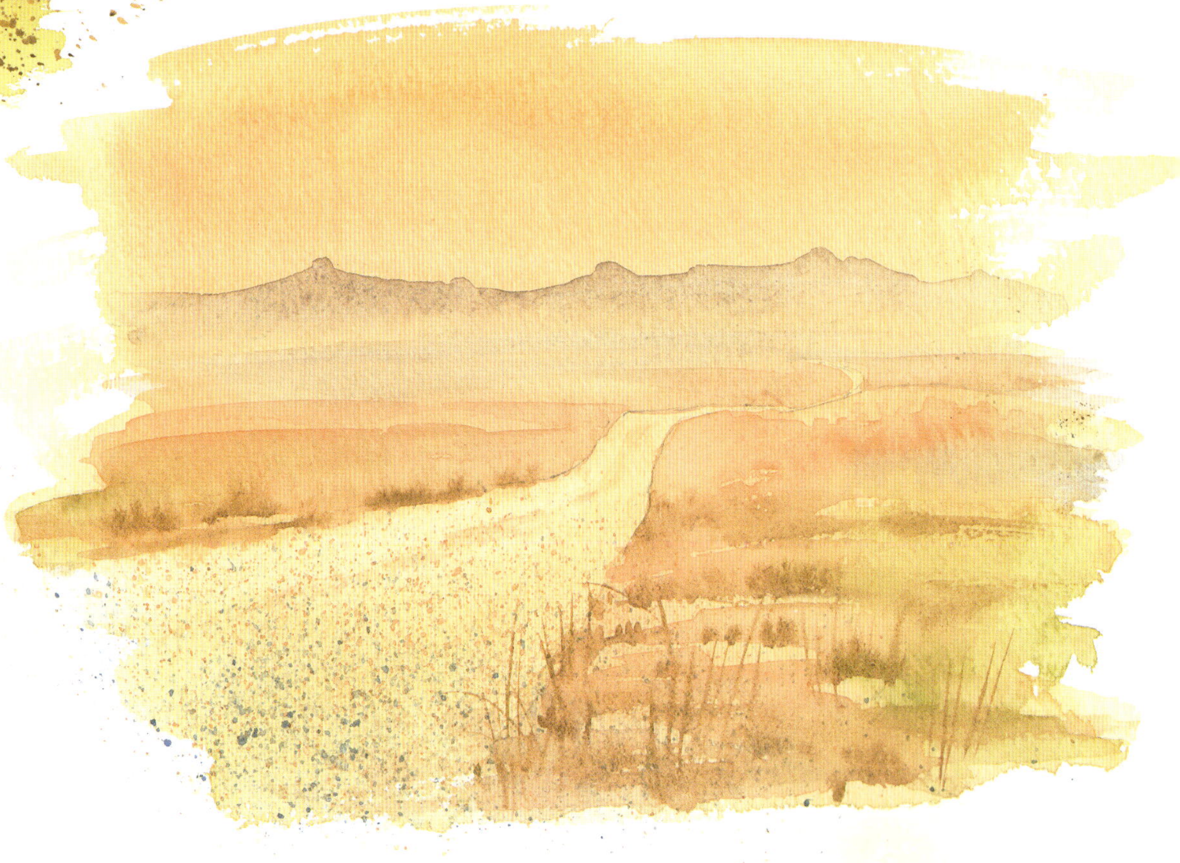

► *The gravelly texture of fine stones can be suggested with the spattering of paint from a toothbrush. Cover the areas you want to protect as spattering and flicking tend to be random!*

Rough ground

The uneven texture of rough ground is patterned with multiple lights and shades as sunlight catches the crests of bumps, which form shadows in the troughs. Using a wax resist, scratching off or scattering salt crystals into a wet wash are ideal methods for retaining or reintroducing the highlights in a painting.

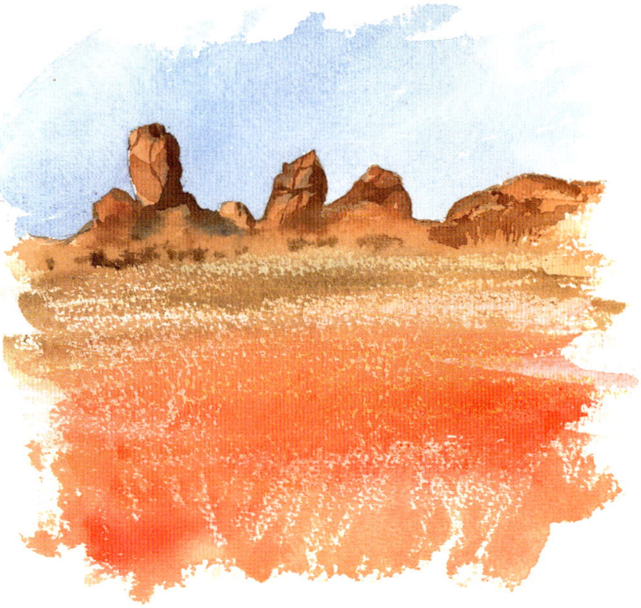

► *Wax rubbed on paper resists the watercolour, leaving a broken patina to the subsequent wash.*

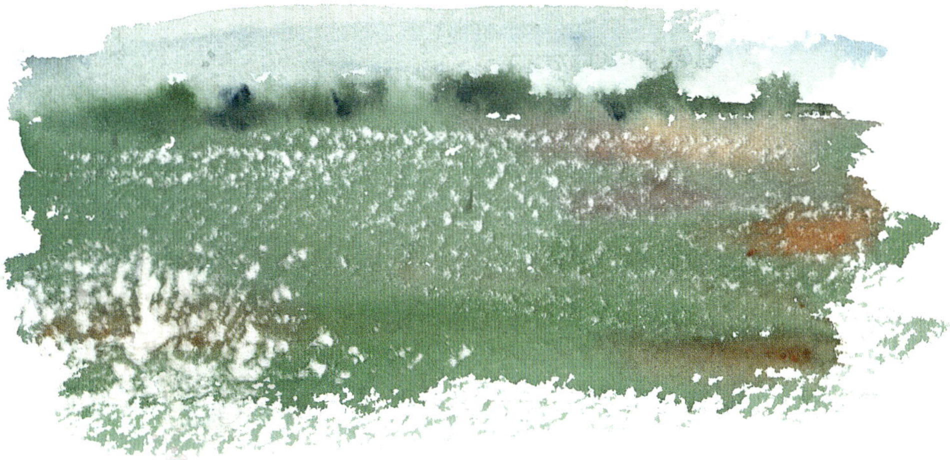

◄ *Scratching off some of the surface pigment with the side of a blade will reveal flecks of white paper underneath.*

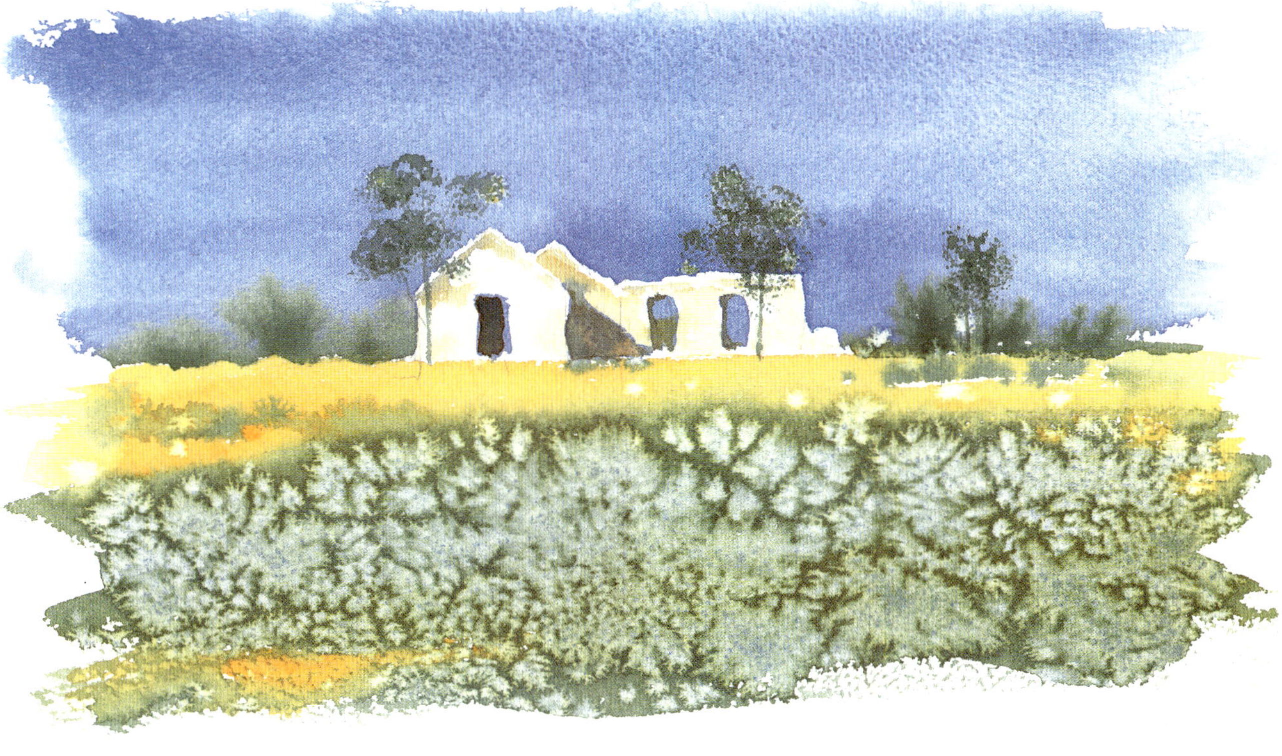

► **ABANDONED**
15 x 25 cm (6 x 10 in)
The massed texture of the white flowers is created by dropping crystals of table salt into a wet green wash. They take a long time to dry, so you have to be patient before brushing the salt off.

The grain of rocks and stones

The surfaces of features within a landscape often have prominent textures. The same textural techniques used for the ground textures can be used to paint the patina of rocks and the roughness of bark, but there are also other techniques. These include sponging, painting shadows and overlaying layers of wax resist with several washes.

The painted textures of the surfaces of rocks and stones hint at their ancient origins and give them character.

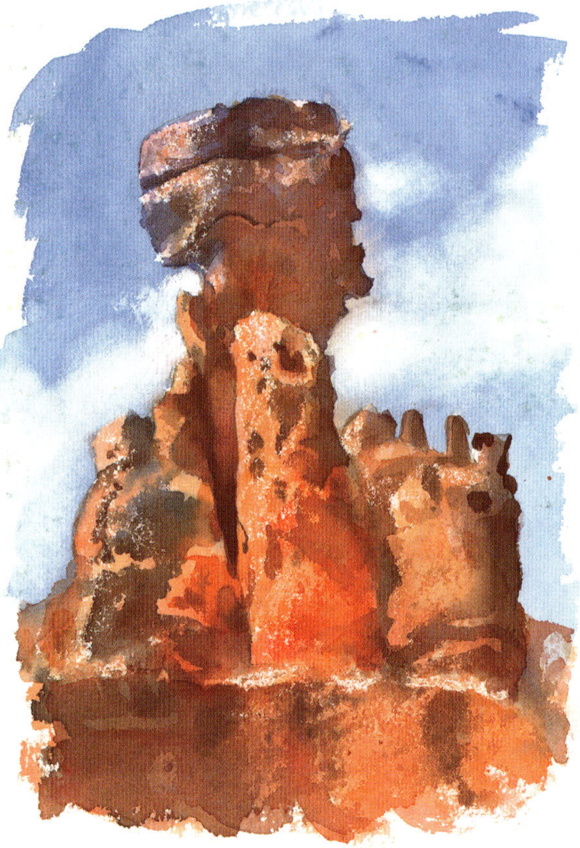

◄ *The scoured textures of the sandstone rocks and their rugged form are constructed with several layers of wax resist overlaid with watercolour washes.*

▲ *A scattering of stones can be described with patches of cast shadow that stretch out from the shady side.*

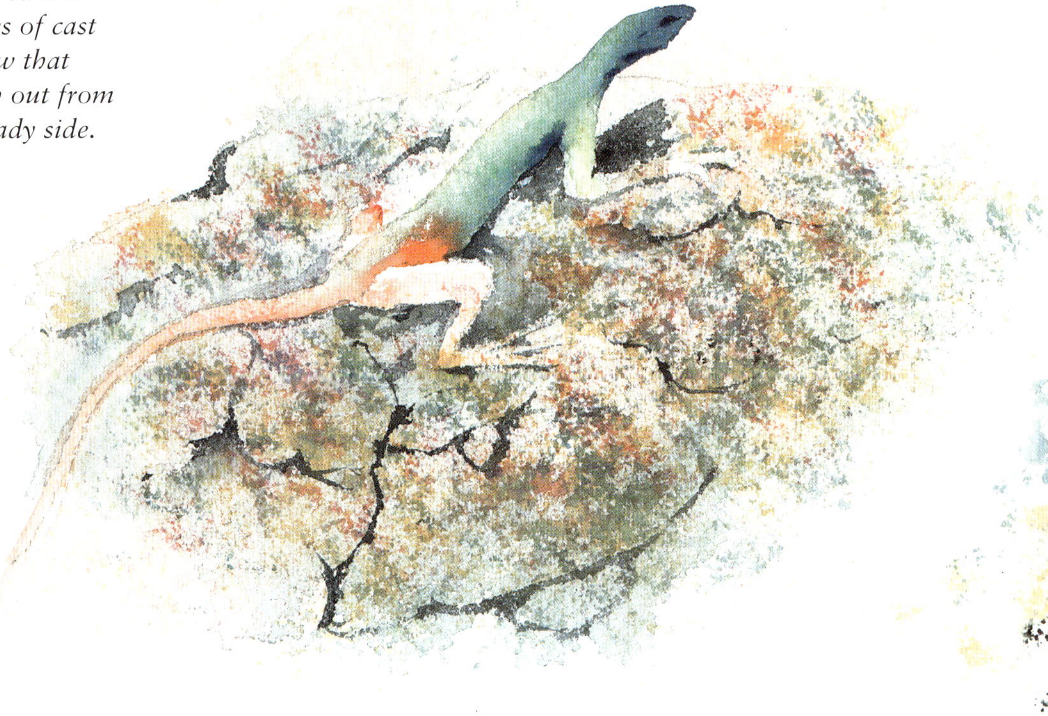

◄ *The speckly patina of granite rocks is created with a natural sponge. Successive layers of watercolour are patted onto the paper to build up the required texture.*

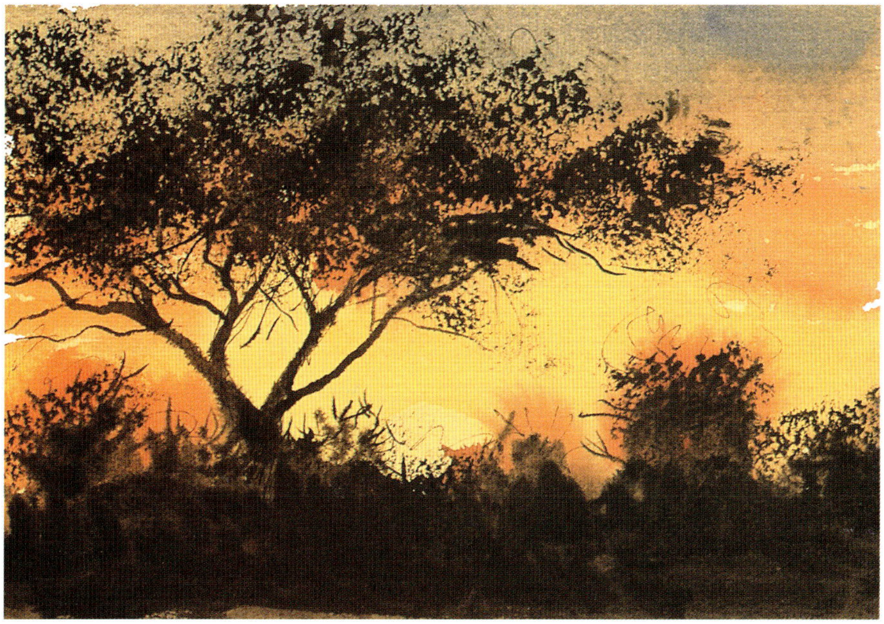

Textures for grass and trees

The structure of grass is essentially found in linear brushstrokes. The fabric of foliage, however, is established through form. Masses of leaves can be ably portrayed with the body of the brush or with a natural sponge.

► *Dry brush painted on rough Khadi paper creates the texture of scrubby trees.*

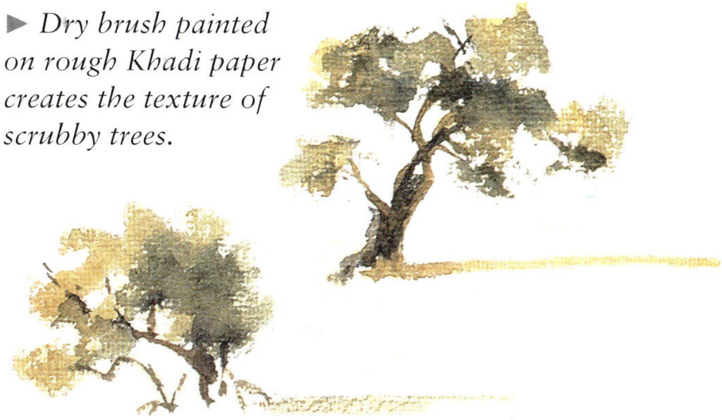

▲ AFRICAN NIGHT
13 x 18 cm (5 x 7 in)
The random patina of a natural sponge is perfect for depicting trees with light-textured foliage.

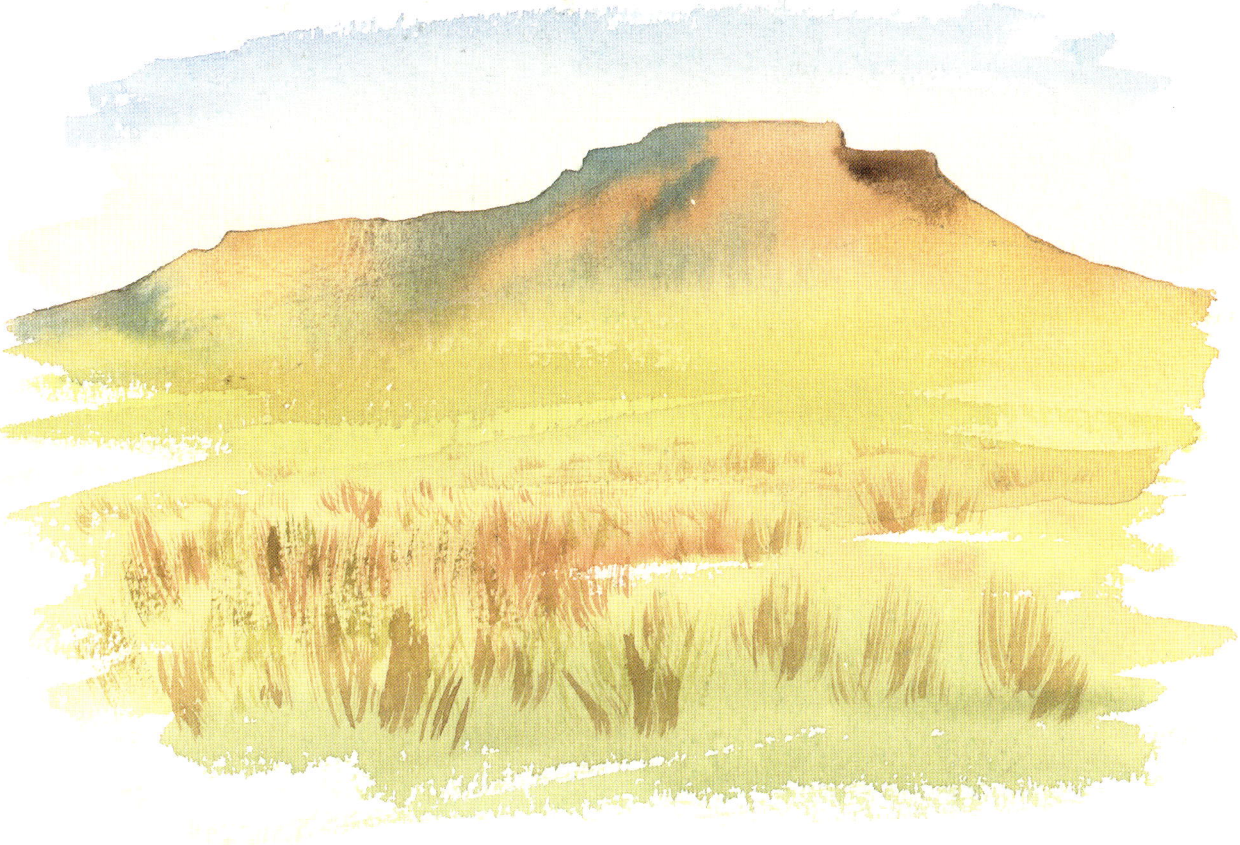

► *The textural effect of both wet and dry brushstrokes is enhanced by splaying the hairs of the brush.*

Heartbeat of Africa:

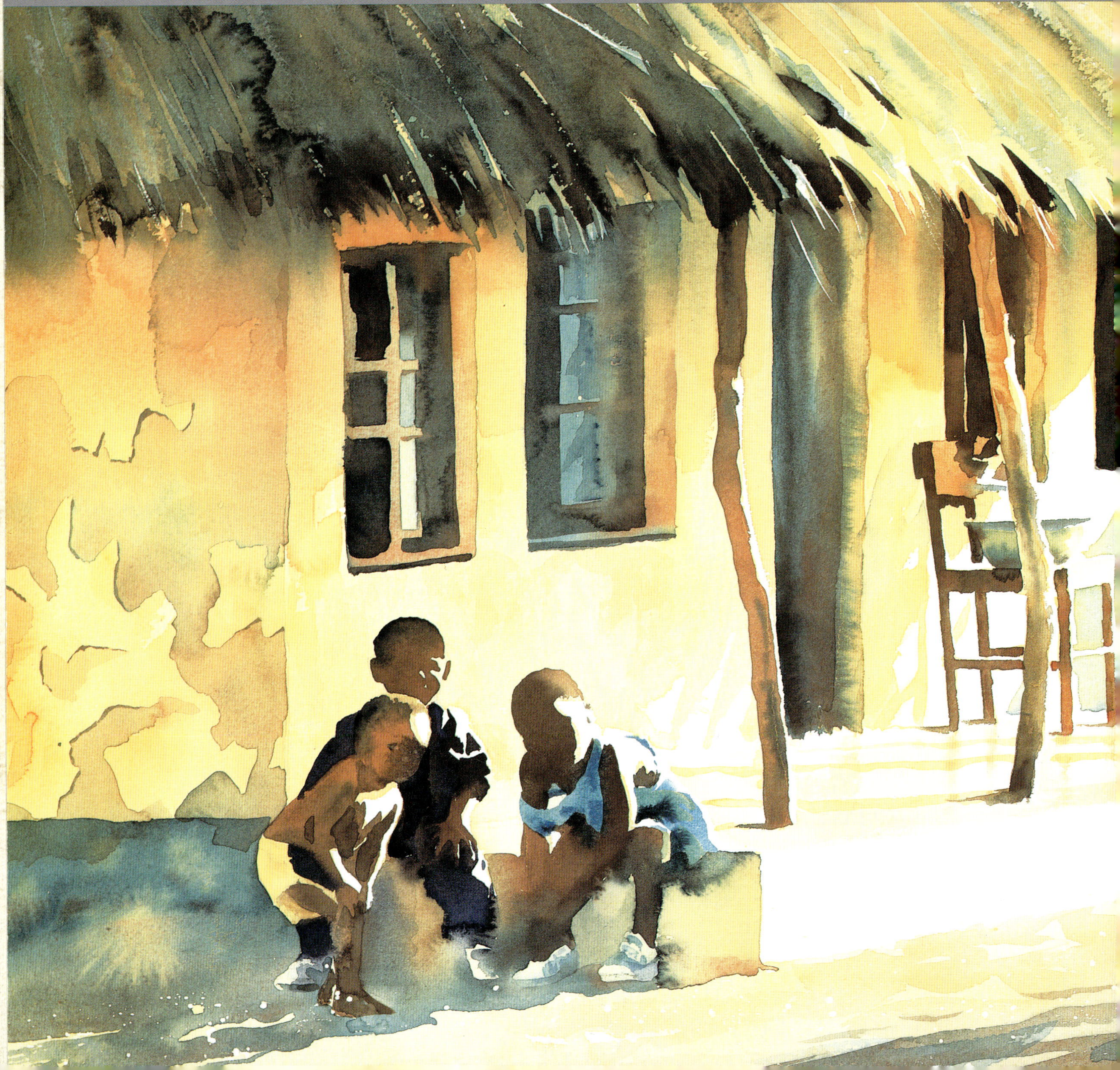

The People of the South

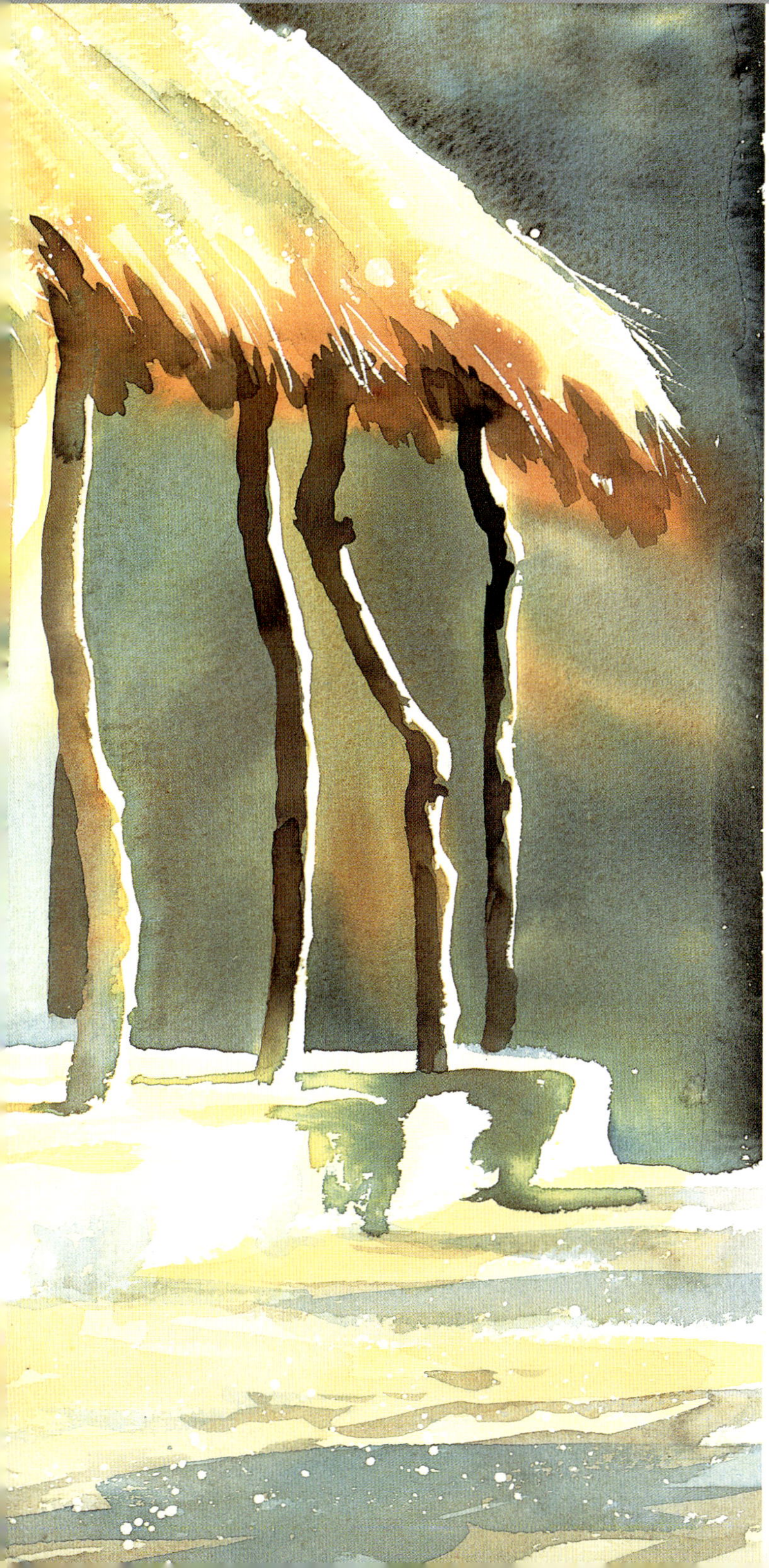

Breathing life into paintings

Voices in the morning light
Calling,
Mother Africa upon their lips.
Falling
In and out of line, day after day.
Hopeful
For a future that is coming, but
Stalling.

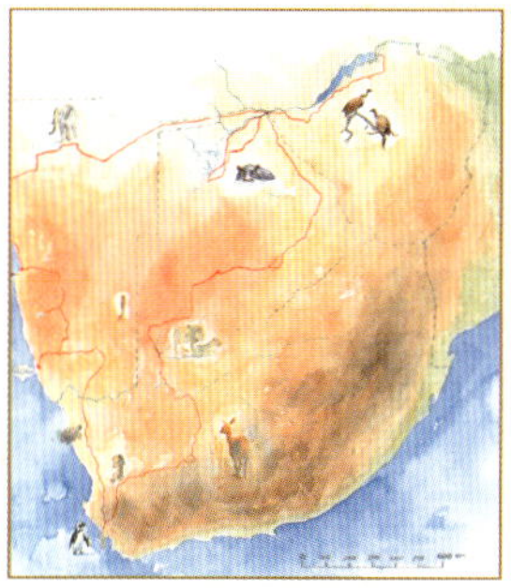

◄ CHILDREN OF THE DUST
43 x 56 cm (17 x 22 in)

A warm welcome

No journey would be complete without memories of the people met along the way. The people of Southern Africa are friendly and hospitable, quick to laugh and eager to offer hospitality. Even those with very little will honour the traveller with an invitation to their home.

The residents of warm countries live outdoors a lot more than those of colder climes. In Africa, in any village or town, people can be seen sitting around under trees, resting by the roadside, chatting, sleeping, marketing their wares. In rural areas life remains simple, but even in a sophisticated city like Cape Town there are still fishermen to be seen on the beaches at dawn, drawing in the nets in biblical manner much as the disciples might have done two thousand years ago. The catch is often meagre and it is hard to see how these men earn a living.

Life is not easy for the poor and families in remote rural areas are often separated while the breadwinners venture away to the cities for work.

▼ MARKET DAY
56 x 76 cm (22 x 30 in)
Markets are excellent places to enjoy the colourful patterns and fabrics for which Africa is renowned.

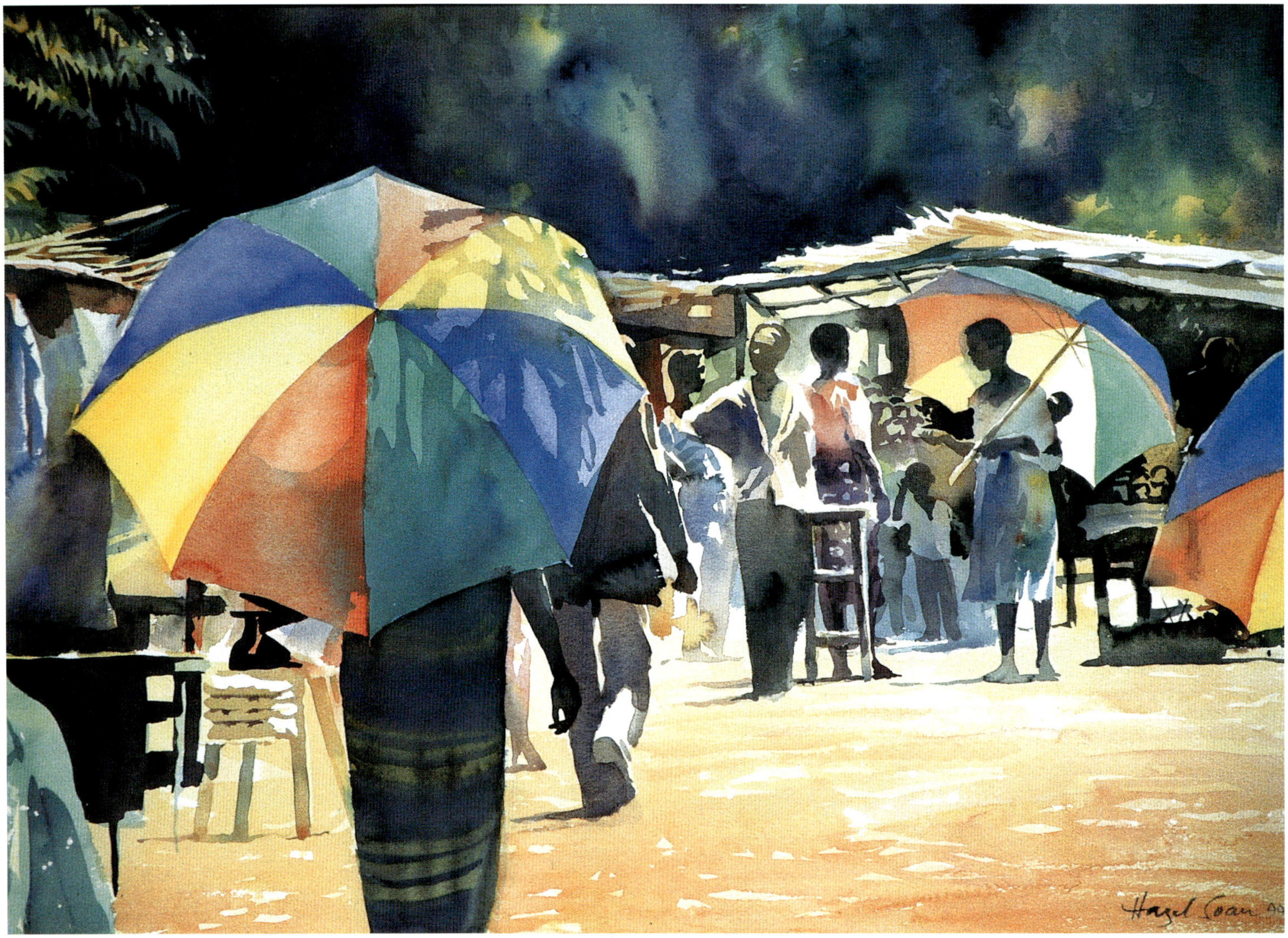

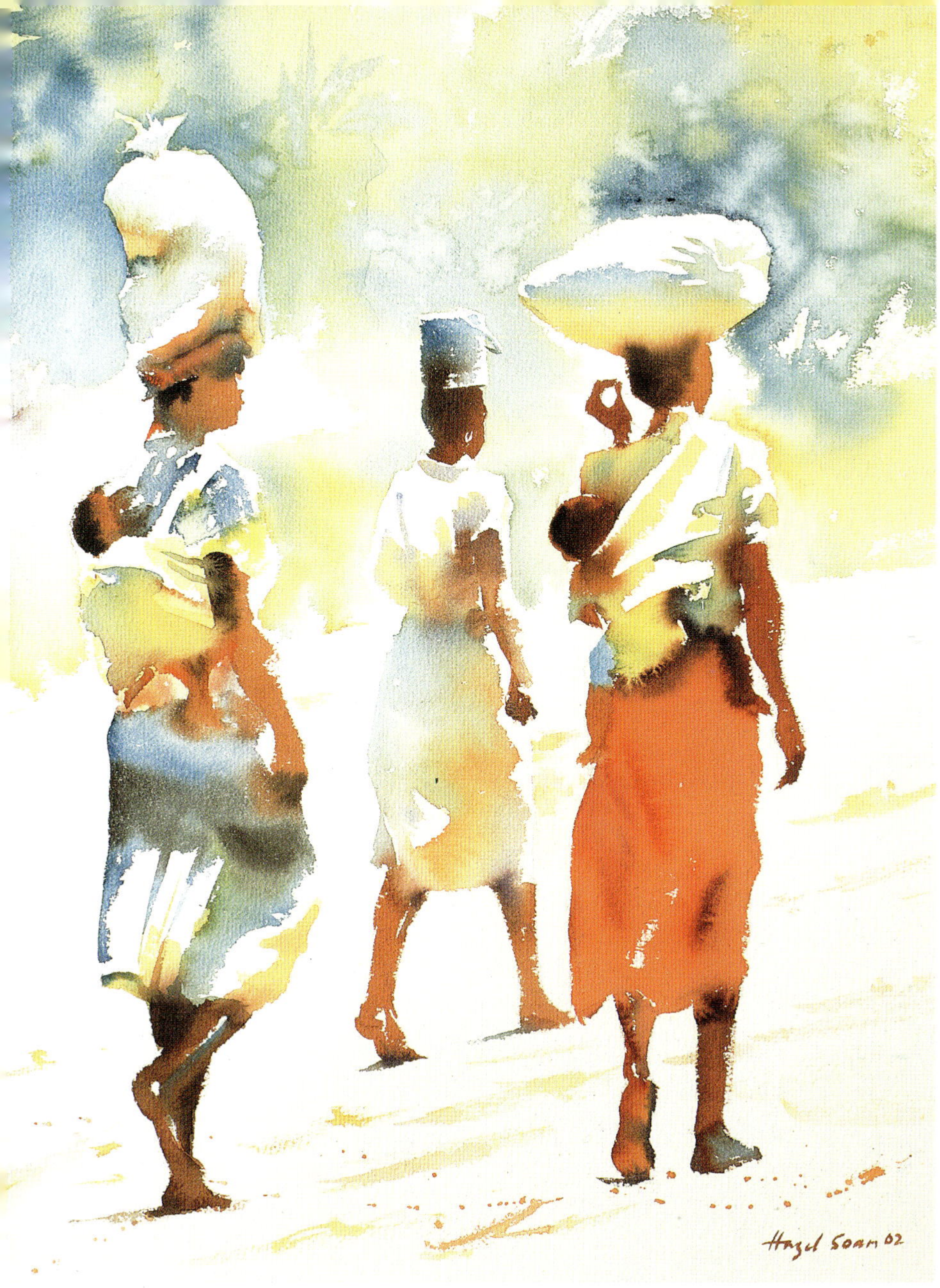

Painting people

Painting people is physically no different from painting any other subject, but somehow seems more vital. The innate power of painting often conveys emotions more succinctly than the written word.

As with any subject, appreciating the overall shape is important. Tone suggests form, colourful clothes bring vibrancy and movement adds life.

The proportion of the figure is paramount, and primarily the size of the head in relation to the body. Generally the size of an adult's head will go into the body seven times. Elongation will make figures appear more elegant.

Avoid being too literal; wet-in-wet washes will both reveal and obscure imagined details within the figure's pose. Concentrate on the suggestion of weight and balance and the connections between people.

Smiling children

In the villages of Southern Africa there are always plenty of children playing, making toys out of discarded crates, worn tyres and wire coat hangers. The children are smiling, wide eyed and inquisitive and the novelty of having an artist to watch for a few hours provides great entertainment. The children crowd around, exclaiming in awe as they watch their friends materialize upon the painted page.

▲ ROAD TO THE VILLAGE
76 x 56 cm (30 x 22 in)
Women are often seen carrying mealie bags, pails of water and huge bundles of firewood on their heads, their babies strapped to their backs with a blanket.

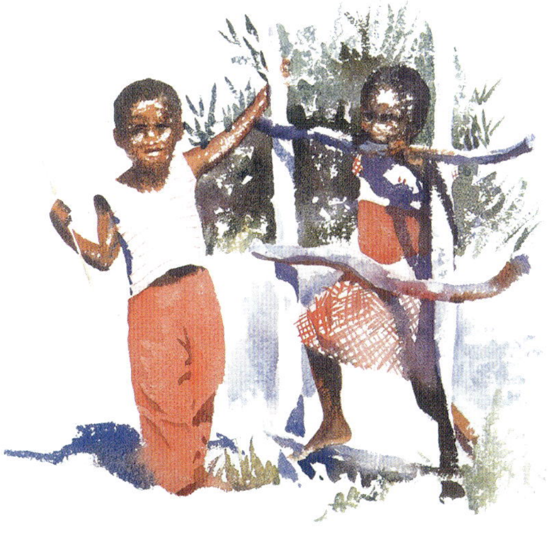

◀ CHILDREN IN RED
41 x 51 cm (16 x 20 in)
The proportion of a child's head is large in relation to the body compared with an adult's frame. The younger the child the larger the proportion of the head.

Breathing life into paintings

Watercolour is an evocative medium, benefiting from the ambiguity of wet-in-wet blends. You only have to look at clouds in the sky and notice how readily they take on known shapes to realize how little actually needs to be painted for an image to be convincing. It does not matter if the interpretation of the viewer does not match the original intention of the artist; that will not lessen the success of the painting. The art of watercolour is to say the most with the minimum of means.

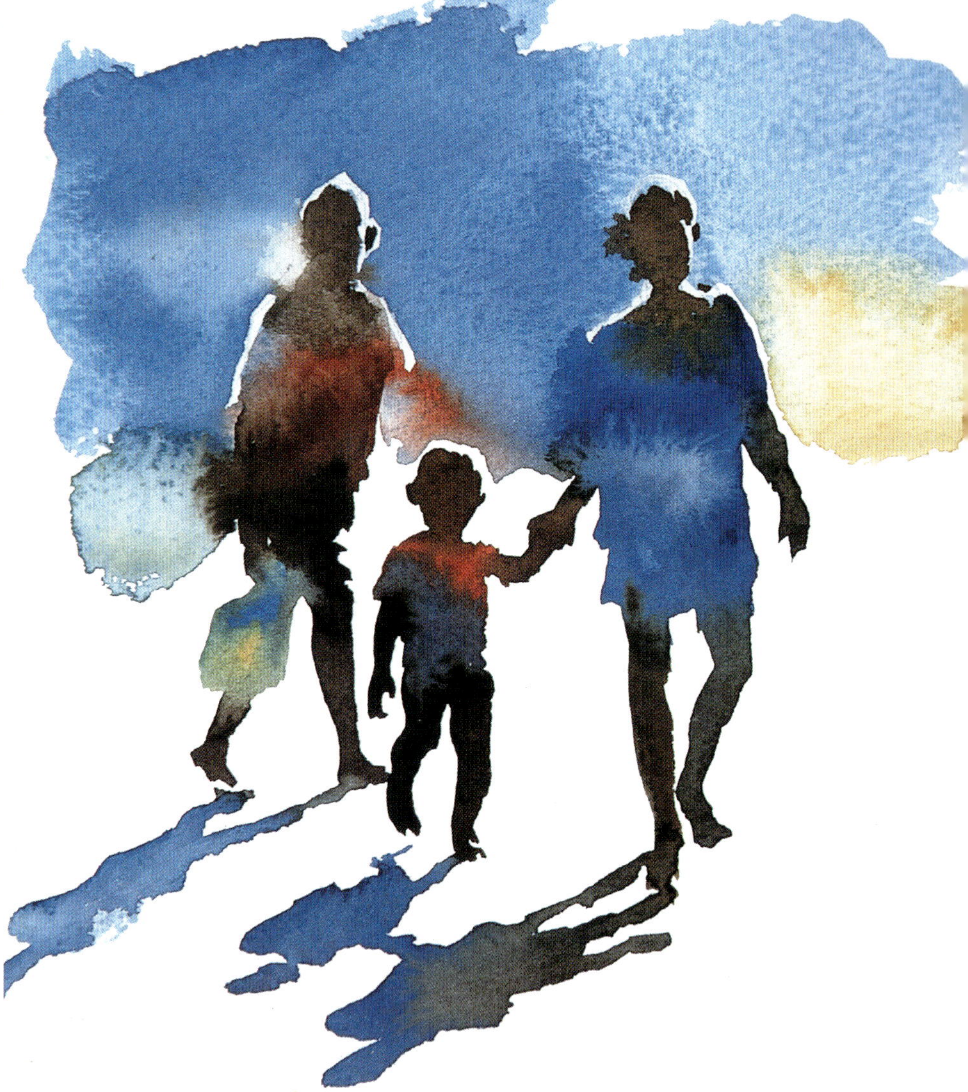

▲ TOWNSHIP BOYS

15 x 10 cm (6 x 4 in)

In this simple painting of two teenagers and a child there is no detail, all the clothes are blended wet-in-wet, and even the carrier bag merges with the body. The beauty is in the delicious colour runs and gentle ambiguity within the figure shapes.

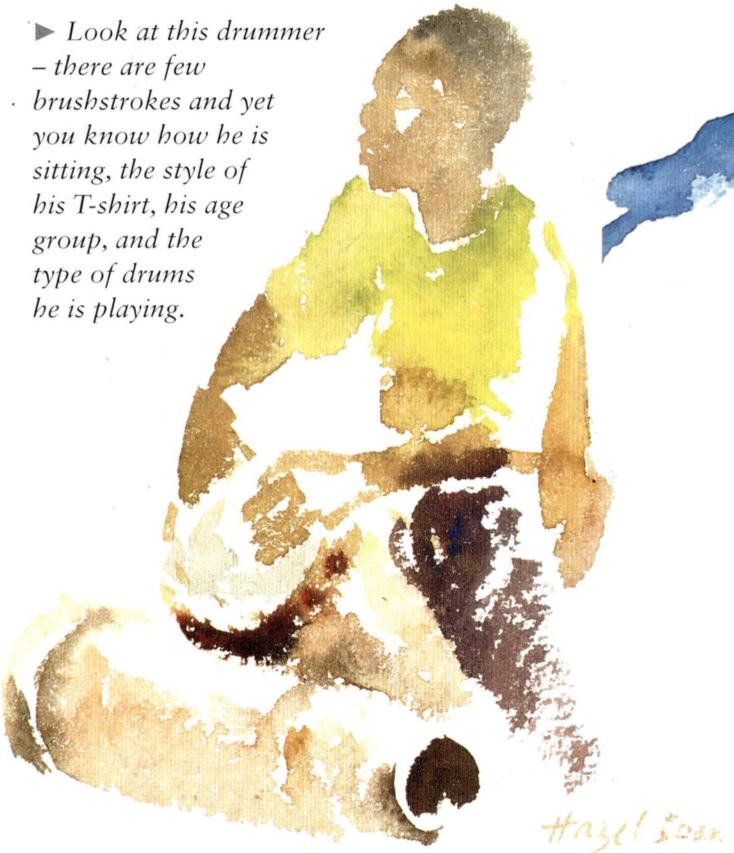

► *Look at this drummer – there are few brushstrokes and yet you know how he is sitting, the style of his T-shirt, his age group, and the type of drums he is playing.*

► COMBI
56 x 76 cm (22 x 30 in)
Crowd a picture with life. Painting many characters distracts the eye from errors.

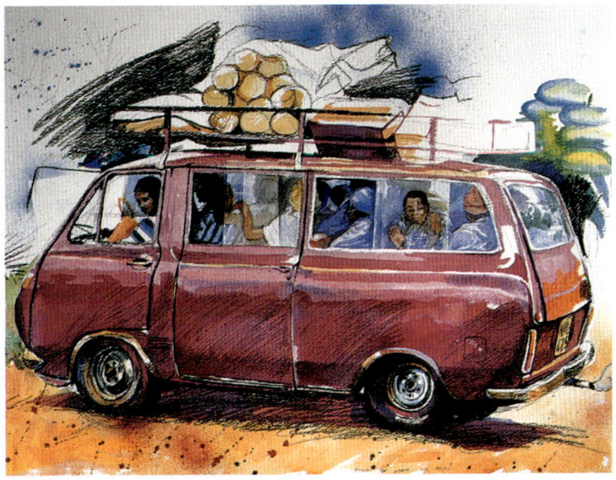

Vitality of movement

If you give the figures in your painting a moving pose rather than a static stance they will look more lively and less wooden, even if they are painted inaccurately. Once again it is the shape that counts in creating a believable pose. You can indicate that a person is walking towards you just by showing one foot higher than the other. Figures in motion can be painted in much the same way as the wildlife – dry brushstrokes, unfinished feet!

► SOCCER AT LOW TIDE
41 x 51 cm (16 x 20 in)
When a figure is leaning, the ankle that is carrying the weight will line up with the nape of the neck. Look at the two left-hand children in this painting and draw an imaginary line from the neck to the ankle bearing the load.

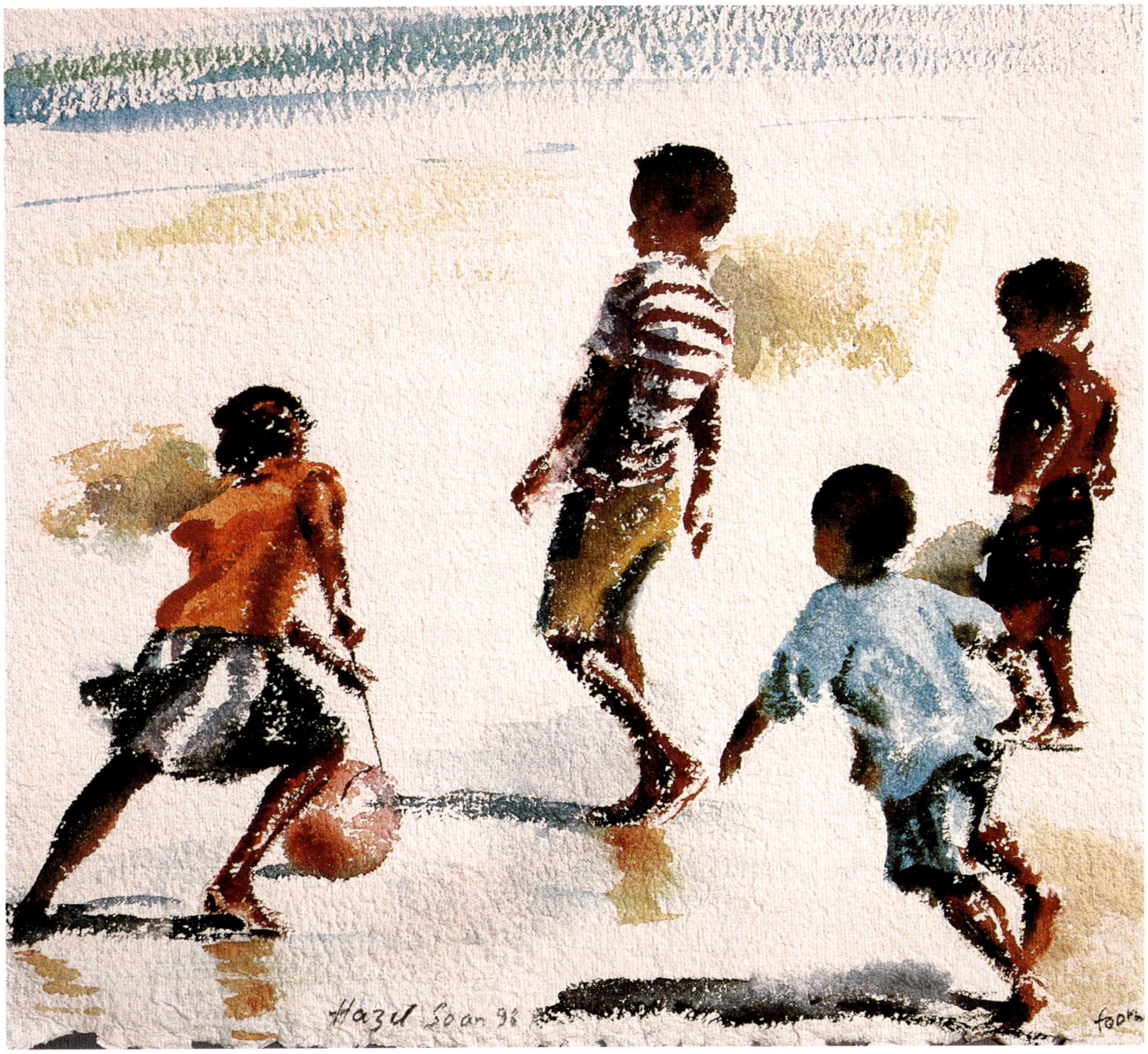

Making an impact

Paintings have a unique power. They may be small and completely flat, but they are able to invite the viewer to step inside and wander visually around. What is this power that breathes life into paintings and makes them appear real? It cannot just be technique. It must be something to do with the concentration, enjoyment and involvement of the painter and the very nature of creation.

Emotional input

To maximize this impact choose subjects to paint that move you emotionally, or are dear to you. If you love what you are painting that emotion will enter the picture.

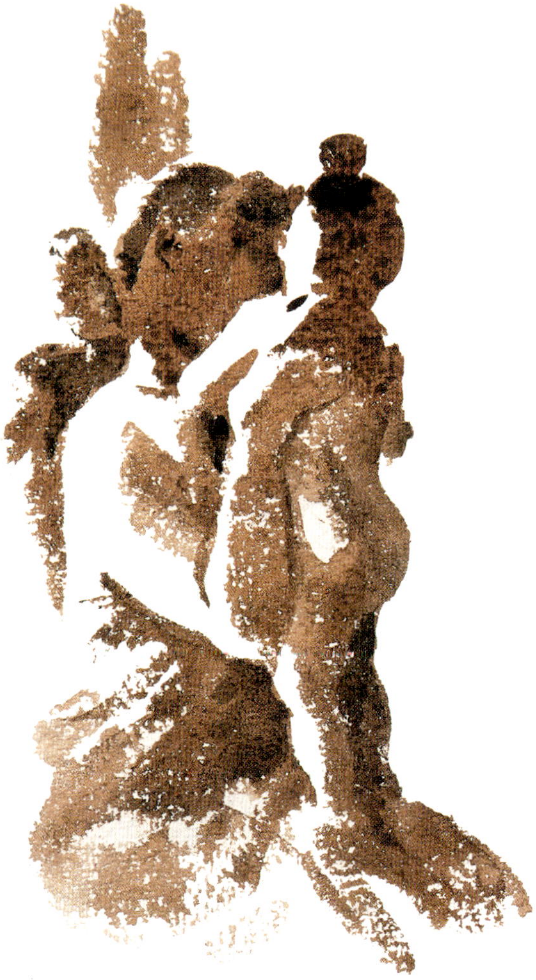

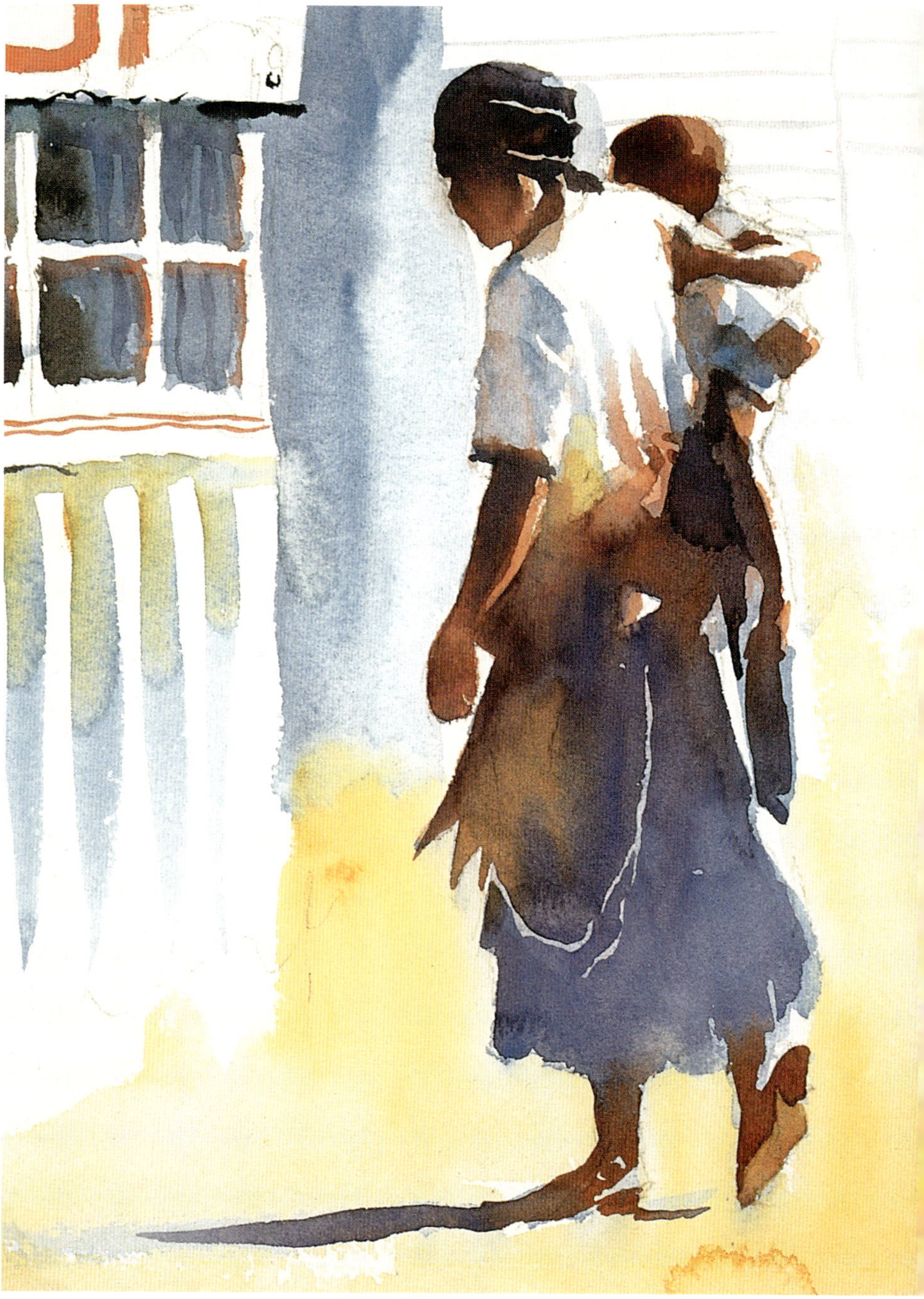

◄ *In this Sepia sketch only the shadows are painted, yet it is charged with the bond of love between a mother and her child.*

▲ A HARD LIFE
30 x 20 cm (12 x 8 in)
Here the leaning gait hints at the onerous burden poverty puts upon a mother.

▶ LEONARD, MY GUIDE
28 x 28 cm (11 x 11 in)
Look carefully at the different skin tones, especially in the limbs.

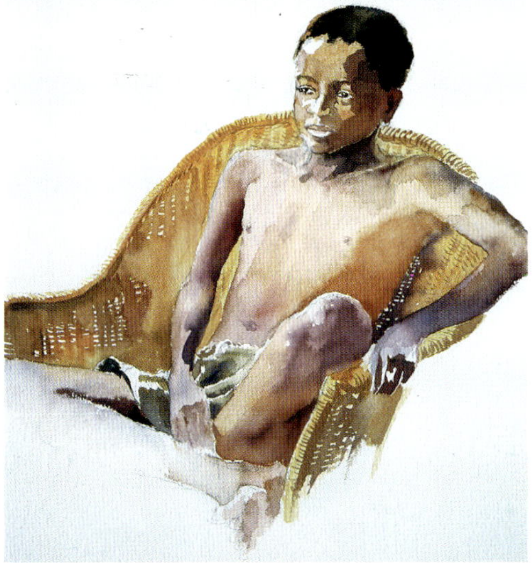

The power of the portrait

Painting portraits of people willing to pose is one of the most fulfilling ways to spend painting time. The chance to study someone's face close up, to follow every curve and wrinkle and catch the twinkle in the eyes, to have unrushed time to study the folds of clothes and the rhythm of hair is an artistic luxury. Happily, in Africa life is often less hectic and people are glad to pose for the passing painter.

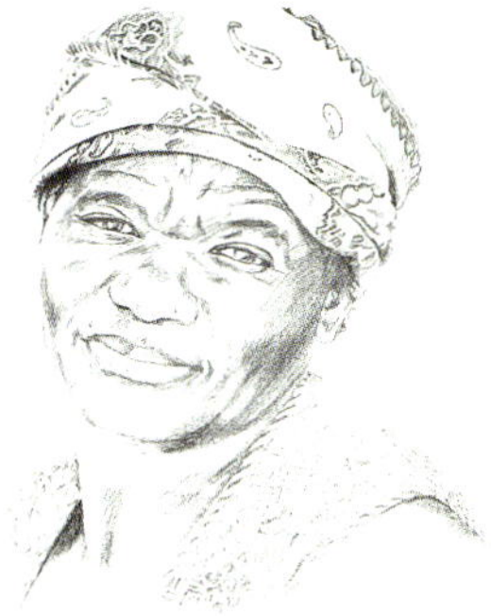

▲ DEAREST ELSIE
56 x 51 cm (22 x 20 in)
To find the relative positions of the eyes, nose and mouth draw imaginary vertical lines between them. The spaces between the features are just as important to the likeness of the subject.

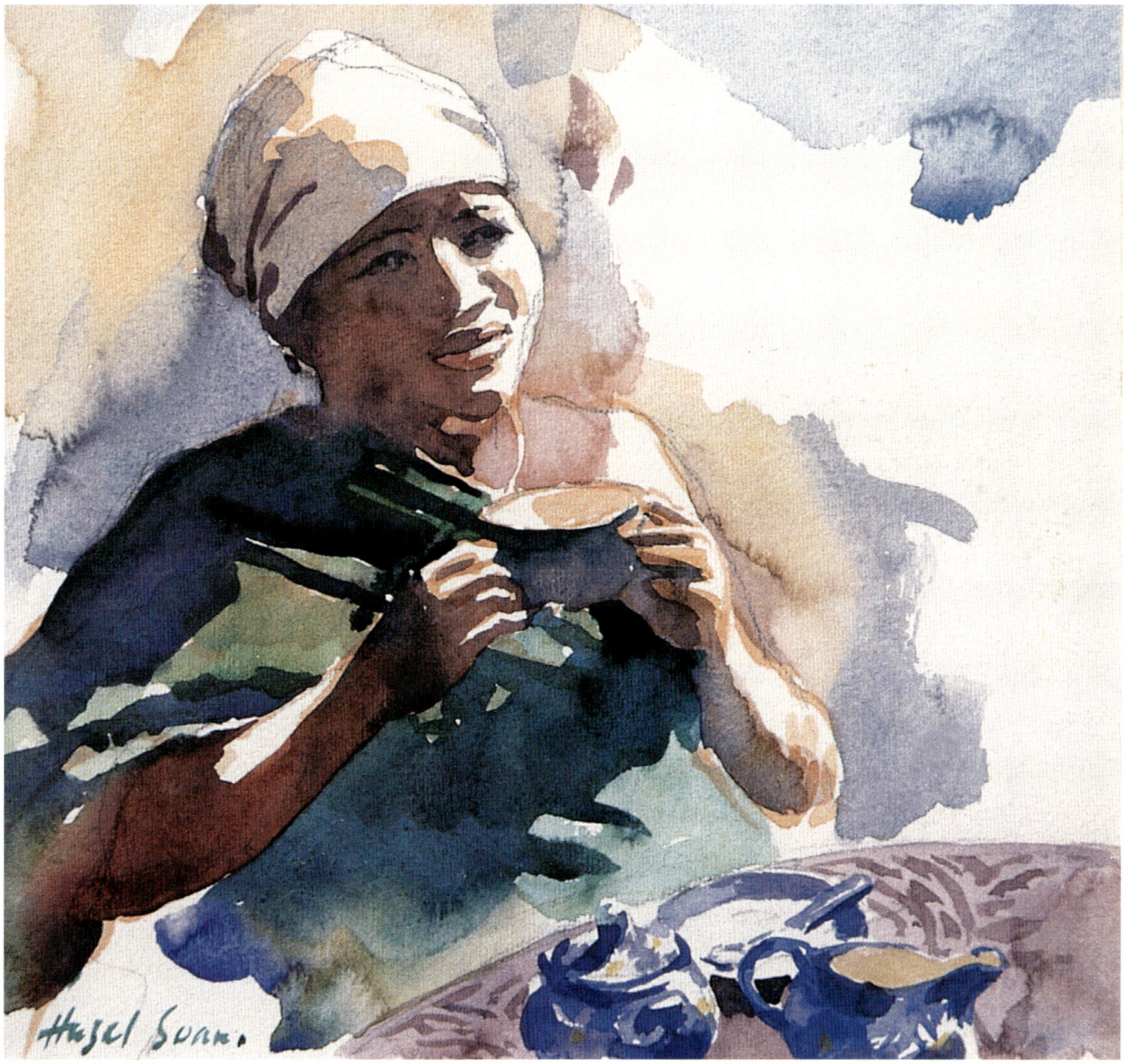

▶ FLORRIE TAKING TEA
20 x 20 cm (8 x 8 in)
Grasp any opportunity offered! Both artist and model were supposed to be taking a tea break, but this pose was too tempting to let pass!

Safari sketchbook

A place in the sun

The variety of homes in Southern Africa is as fascinating as the people themselves. The nomadic San still construct temporary shelters with materials from their natural environment, using branches, bark, grasses and animal skins.

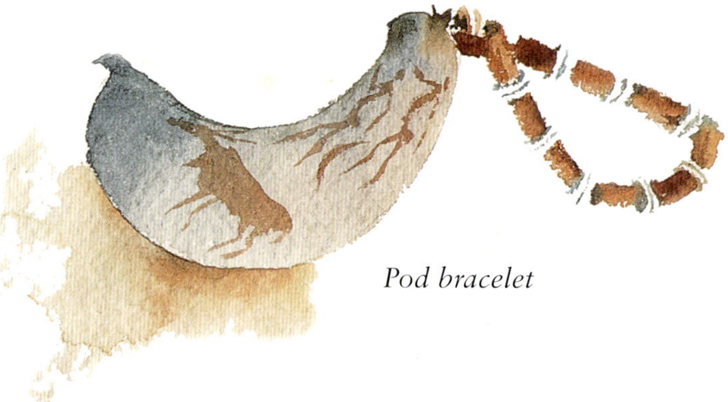

Pod bracelet

In remote rural areas villagers build homes from mud and thatch. Several 'rondavels' make up one home and are often decorated with striking designs. Discarded fizzy-drink cans are incorporated as patterns in the mudwork or strung together to make colourful doors and screens.

Apparently the thatched rondavels were built round to protect against rhino attack. The short-sighted rhino could not get a focus on the curved surface, I have heard!

The town and city dwellings are bordered by township shacks. Many people are hampered by poverty, but some of the shacks are ingeniously embellished with multiple-wrapper 'wallpaper' in Andy Warhol style.

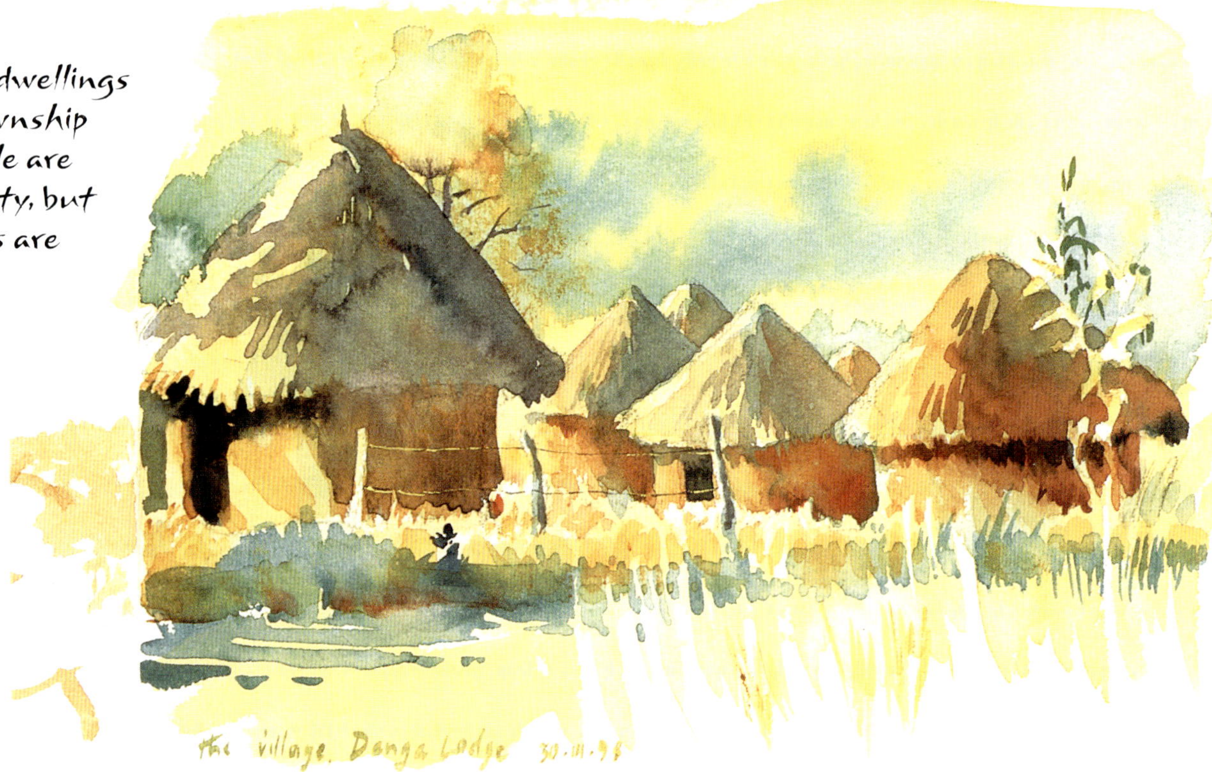

TALE END

Epilogue

At art college one of my tutors remarked how surprised he was that artists did not travel more, given that they had one of the most flexible livelihoods on earth and could use their freedom to travel.

To my great benefit I noted his remark and have travelled extensively, painting wherever I go. An artist does not need to go far for inspiration, but travel definitely acts as a catalyst to new ideas. Travel feeds the eyes and the act of painting enhances the sights encountered on the journey. Later the experiences are recalled through the paintings, and the sketches and photographs provide an enormous bank of reference for rainy days back home.

I am a great believer in taking risks. New places, new subject matter, new colours, new techniques, will all stretch the creative muscles. Risks in painting are not usually life threatening!

I hope this book encourages you to take your paints on a journey; both a physical adventure and an artistic one. I have fallen in love with Africa; perhaps you will, too.

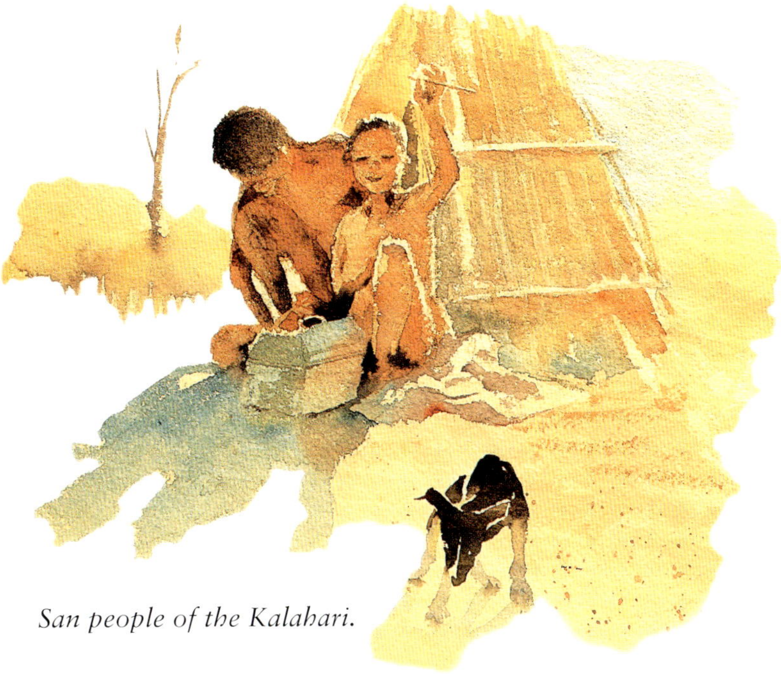

San people of the Kalahari.

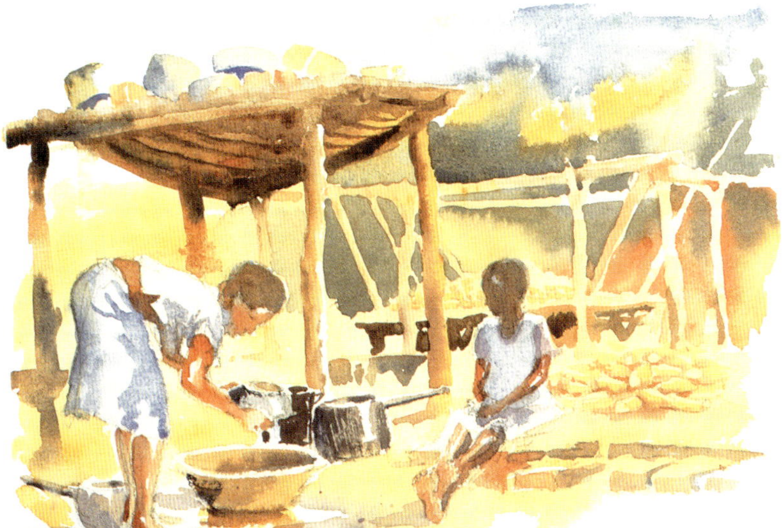

Maize is the staple diet in most regions.

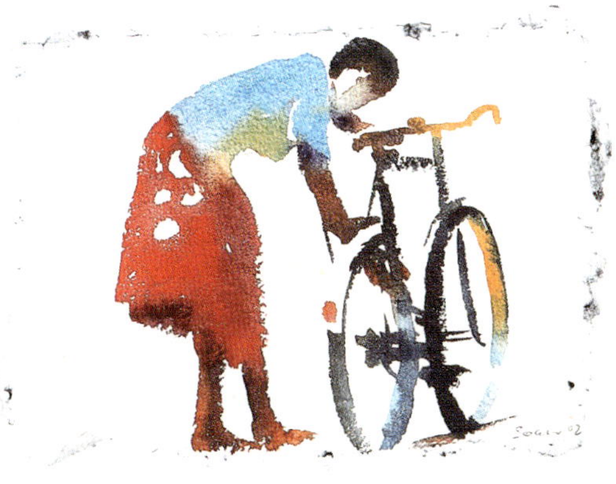

Index

Page numbers in *italic* refer to captions